New Immigrants in New York

Completely Revised and Updated Edition

New Immigrants in New York

Completely Revised and Updated Edition

Edited by Nancy Foner

COLUMBIA UNIVERSITY PRESS

New York

Columbia University Press
Publishers Since 1893
New York   Chichester, West Sussex

Library of Congress Cataloging-in-Publication Data

New immigrants in New York / edited by Nancy Foner—
   Completely revised and updated edition.
      p.   cm.
   Rev. ed. of: New immigrants in New York. 1987.
   Includes bibliographical references and index.
   ISBN 0–231–12414–7 (cloth : acid-free paper) —
   ISBN 0–231–12415–5 (pbk).
      1. Minorities—New York (State)—New York. 2. Immigrants—
New York (State)—New York. 3. New York (N.Y.)—Social conditions.
4. New York (N.Y.)—Emigration and immigration. 5. New York
(N.Y.)—Economic conditions. I. Foner, Nancy, 1945– II. New
immigrants in New York.

F128.9.A1   N48   2001
304.8'7471—dc21   2001017469

Contents

Preface

Originally, this volume was meant to provide some fairly basic revisions to *New Immigrants in New York,* which, after more than a decade of heavy immigration, had become badly out of date. As it turned out, an entirely new book emerged. The book's format is the same as in the first edition and so is the overarching theme: how New York City has been transformed by the recent immigration and how the immigrants themselves have been changed by the move to New York. Yet most of the authors are new: Pyong Gap Min, Robert Smith, Paul Stoller, Milton Vickerman, Richard Wright and Mark Ellis, and Min Zhou. Those who had chapters in *New Immigrants in New York* (Patricia Pessar, Ellen Kraly, and Annelise Orleck) ended up writing completely different ones; now, in two cases, there are also coauthors (Pamela Graham and Ines Miyares). Given the new chapters as well as the many changes since the late 1980s among New York's immigrants, in New York City itself, and in the field of immigration studies, the introductory chapter has been totally revamped.

Since 1987—the year that *New Immigrants in New York* was published—a growing number of researchers have been studying the city's newcomers. Groups that were tiny in the late 1980s, like Mexicans and West Africans, have become a much more significant presence. Groups that were already large fifteen years ago have not only grown in number and spread out to new locations, but also are different in many other ways. And the field of immigration studies has also developed and changed, leading researchers to ask new questions, to use new analytic concepts and theoretical frameworks, and to highlight social and cultural processes, such as transnational practices, that received scant attention earlier. These changes are all reflected in the chapters that follow.

A few words of thanks to those who helped in putting the book together. John Michel at Columbia University Press was a wonderful editor. Not only did he suggest that I update *New Immigrants in New York* in the first place, but in addition, once the project was under way, he served as a valuable sounding board and source of advice. Thanks, too, to Barbara Storey, assistant editor, for helping with details in the publication process.

Finally, I am grateful to the two anonymous reviewers for Columbia University Press for providing useful suggestions that have, I believe, made this a better book. And, of course, my appreciation to all of the authors in the volume for their responsiveness and commitment to the project and for the quality of their contributions.

chapter one

Introduction: New Immigrants in a New New York

Nancy Foner

2.5 Mill

1/3

A t the dawn of a new millennium, New York is again an immigrant city. In the last four decades, more than two and a half million immigrants have settled in New York City. They come, in the main, from Latin America, the Caribbean, and Asia, although sometimes it seems as if every country in the world is represented. In 1970, 18 percent of New York City's residents were foreign-born, the lowest percentage of the century. By 1998, immigrants constituted over a third of the city's population, fast approaching levels at the turn of the twentieth century. How have the new immigrants affected New York City? And, conversely, how has the move to New York influenced their lives?

This collection of original essays addresses these two main questions. The volume's approach to the new immigration is two-pronged: it combines "micro" and "macro" levels of analysis. Case studies explore the move to New York from the immigrants' viewpoint, analyzing the way New York has influenced their social and cultural worlds and the consequent emergence among them of new meanings and new patterns of behavior. The essays also demonstrate that the city itself

1

has been deeply affected by the new immigrants. Their very presence in such large numbers has had a dramatic impact on the city's economy; its neighborhoods; and a host of social, economic, and cultural institutions. In fact, a dialectical relationship or interplay exists between the two kinds of changes. As immigrants change when they move to New York City, they affect the life of the city in particular ways. And, as immigrants play a role in transforming New York City, this "new" New York in turn influences them.

The seven chapters on particular groups deal with the experiences of a broad range of populations: Chinese, Dominicans, Jamaicans, Koreans, Mexicans, Soviet Jews, and West Africans. The groups were chosen to give a sense of the diversity of the new immigrant populations in New York City; with the exception of West Africans, these are among the most numerous new immigrant groups in the city. All of the case studies are based on in-depth research and long-term familiarity with the group in question.[1]

Setting the stage for the case studies, a demographic chapter by Ellen Kraly and Ines Miyares shows how U.S. immigration policy has influenced the number and types of immigrants coming to New York and, in turn, how these immigrants have affected the city's demographic structure. The chapter by Richard Wright and Mark Ellis examines the ways that the newcomers are fitting into, and at the same time are changing, New York City's labor market.

In this introductory chapter, I provide general background on the new immigration. As I sketch out the factors shaping the experiences of the newest New Yorkers—and the ways in which they are transforming the city—I point to common themes as well as differences among new immigrant populations and raise some questions about patterns in the future.

The New Immigration: Background

New immigrants are usually considered those who have arrived since 1965, but it is not just the date of entry that differentiates them from immigrants who came to New York City in record numbers in the last great wave, at the turn of the twentieth century (see Foner 2000a for a full comparison of New York's two great waves of immigration). Today's arrivals come from a much wider array of nations and cultures. Whereas immigrant arrivals a century ago were overwhelmingly European, today they are mainly from Asia, the Caribbean, and Latin America. More men than women came in the immigrant stream in the last great wave; in the 1980s and 1990s, female immigrants outnumbered males (Lobo, Salvo, and Virgin 1996). And while many arrive now, as in the past, with little education and few skills, a much higher proportion of contemporary newcomers have college degrees and professional backgrounds.

The reasons for the current massive influx are complex and multifaceted. A crucial factor, as Ellen Kraly and Ines Miyares's chapter shows, was the change in U.S. immigration law in 1965 that abandoned the national origins quota system favoring northern and western Europeans (see also Reimers 1992; Zolberg 1999). Since then, immigration policy has emphasized family reunification and, to a lesser extent, skills within the context of annual immigration ceilings that, after a series of legislative changes, stood at 675,000 in the mid-1990s.[2] The big winners were Asians, who had been severely restricted from immigration, and natives of the English-speaking Caribbean, who had been subject to small quotas for dependencies. United States policies with regard to refugees also allowed the large-scale admission of particular groups, Soviet Jews and Cubans being especially prominent in the New York area.

Economic factors, of course, have also underpinned the large-scale immigration to New York in recent years. Neither the resource base nor the levels of economic development in immigrants' home countries are adequate to meet the needs and expectations of their expanding populations. The United States holds out the promise of steady employment, higher wages, and improved living standards. In their chapter, Patricia Pessar and Pamela Graham describe conditions in the Dominican Republic in the 1980s that propelled thousands to emigrate: escalating oil prices, a sharp decline in exports, and massive foreign debt as well as structural adjustment measures dictated by the International Monetary Fund, which led to a "general pauperization of the population" and a "shrinking of the middle class." Per capita income declined—and unemployment rose. In 1987, the minimum monthly salary for full-time work in the United States was six times higher than that in the Dominican Republic; by 1991, it was thirteen times higher.

Political factors in sending countries have also played a role. Unstable or oppressive conditions have driven some people out of their homelands. Moreover, changing exit policies in some sending countries have enabled large numbers to emigrate in recent years. In the Dominican Republic, restrictive emigration policies during the Trujillo era (1930–1960) made it extremely difficult for Dominicans to move to the United States; only after the dictator's death in 1961 did Dominican migration to this country become significant. Indeed, initially, the migration flow included many who were fearful of the new political regime and popular unrest (Pessar and Graham, this volume). In China, as Min Zhou explains in her chapter, emigration was highly restricted between 1949 and 1976 (the end of the Great Cultural Revolution), a period when communication with overseas relatives was seen as antirevolutionary and subversive. In the late 1970s, when China opened its doors, it also relaxed emigration restrictions. In pursuing scholarly and technological exchanges with the United States, the Chinese government has, unintentionally, stimulated emigration because many students and scholars who come to the United States for advanced education and training end up staying. Another group described in this book, Soviet Jews, were allowed to emigrate in significant numbers only after 1971, although in the early 1980s, Soviet authorities again slammed shut the doors. By the late 1980s, in the context of political changes in the Soviet Union, the policy toward Jewish emigration was again liberalized, a situation that leads Annelise Orleck to speak of a Fourth Wave of emigrés in the post-1987 period (see Orleck, this volume).

Once begun, migration has a kind of snowball effect. Immigration movements become self-perpetuating so that migration can be thought of as a process of progressive network building. Network connections lower the costs, raise the benefits, and reduce the risks of international migration. Douglas Massey has elaborated a theory of cumulative causation, arguing that "once the number of network connections in an origin area reaches a critical threshold, migration tends to become self-perpetuating because each act of migration creates the social structure needed to sustain it. Every new migrant reduces the costs and risks of subsequent migration for a set of friends and relatives, and some of these people are thereby induced to migrate, thus further expanding the set of people with ties abroad and, in turn, reducing the costs for a new set of people, some of whom are now more likely to decide to migrate, and so on" (Massey 1999:45). By allocating most immigrant visas along family lines, U.S. immigration law reinforces and formalizes the operation of migrant networks. Moreover, as Robert Smith argues in his chapter, the amnesty program of the 1986 Immigration Reform and Control Act stimulated migration from Mexico to New York by giving formerly undocumented immigrants the legal right to reunite their families in the United States.

"We opened the road" is how one Mexican migrant, Don Pedro, described the beginnings of migration from the town of Ticuani in the 1940s. Unable to get a bracero contract, Don Pedro and his brother hitched a ride to New York, thereby initiating a migration from the Mixteca region that accounts for approximately two-thirds of New York's Mexican population. By now, says Robert Smith, most people in many Mixteca towns who want to leave have done so. But if migration from the Mixteca region is decreasing, new migration chains from other Mexican areas have begun so that more and more Mexican New Yorkers hail from Mexico City and elsewhere. Among Soviet Jews, Orleck argues, family ties are now the most important reason for migration: "It is a chain migration that seems likely to continue until there are few Jews left in the lands that once made up the USSR."

As in the past, New York City continues to be one of the major receiving centers for new immigrants in this country. (Los Angeles is the other leading new immigrant city, with large numbers also settling in Miami, San Francisco, Chicago, Washington, D.C., and Houston.) The city has a particular attraction for certain groups, the Caribbean connection being especially strong. Of those immigrants legally admitted to the United States between 1990 and 1998, over half of the Dominicans, 40 percent of the Jamaicans, and 26 percent of the Haitians intended to live in the New York metropolitan area. Over a quarter of the Soviets and nearly one-quarter of the Pakistanis and mainland Chinese were also heading for New York. Alternatively, less than 1 percent of the Mexicans— the largest immigrant group in the nation—planned to live in the New York area, as well as less than 5 percent of the Vietnamese, Salvadorans, and Iranians (Kraly and Miyares, this volume).

Some groups, like West Indians, have a long history of settlement in New York and initially gravitated there in the post-1965 years because of the presence of a long-established immigrant community (see Foner 2001). In general, the presence of large numbers of friends and relatives continues to attract immigrants to the city and the surrounding region. Once an immigrant community develops, it tends to expand as compatriots are on hand to offer newcomers a sense of security and the prospect of assistance. "Moving to New York," as one Jamaican woman told me, "became the thing to do. Most of my friends were here" (Foner 1987). New York is also appealing because newcomers do not stand out; the city has a tradition of immigration with many different immigrant and racial groups.

The city itself has an image that draws certain groups. With large numbers of Caribbean people in New York, the city has become, in the words of Bryce-Laporte (1979:216), the special object of their "dream[s], curiosity, sense of achievement, and desire for adventure." The city is salient in Caribbean immigrants' mental map as a center of North American influence and power and as a logical entry point into the country. New York is beginning to become significant for other populations, too. Migration from Neza, the nickname for a slum outside of Mexico City from which many recent migrants have come, has become so common that migrants now say they live in "Neza York" (Smith, this volume).

New York City's Impact on the New Immigrants

"Our deity La Ciguapa, arrived in New York City," goes a poem by a New York–based Dominican. "The subway steps changed her nature" (quoted in Torres-Saillant 1999:44). The move to New York City has a profound effect on new immigrants, and their lives change in innumerable ways when they settle there. New York, as a major U.S. city, offers newcomers the economic opportunities of an advanced industrial society and exposes them to key values and institutions of American culture. But New York is special in many respects. That immigrants have settled there rather than, say, Los Angeles or Miami influences them in particular ways. It is thus necessary to appreciate the role of New York as a specific urban context. At the same time, immigrants' experiences in New York are mediated by the cultural beliefs, social practices, and human capital they bring with them, as well as by other sociodemographic features of their particular immigrant group. Moreover, even as they settle in New York, immigrants often continue to maintain ties with their homelands—and these transnational connections also have consequences for their lives in the city.

The City as Context

In a symposium on "The City as Context" (*Urban Anthropology* 1975), several anthropologists stressed the importance of the unique features of particular cities in urban research. With regard to immigration, Jack Rollwagen (1975) criticized studies that implicitly assumed that the life of an immigrant group would be exactly the same regardless of the city in which the group lived—what he called "the city as constant" argument. Rather, he suggested, there will be noticeable contrasts between immigrant groups from the same cultural background who settle in different American cities, if only because the size of the immigrant group and available opportunities in various cities diverge. In a recent article, Caroline Brettell (2000) points to other features that need to be considered: the city's history of dealing with immigrants and the number of immigrants from different sending societies, the presence or absence of residentially segregated immigrant receiving areas, the structure of the city's labor market, and the particular urban ethos (or dominant set of values) that shapes economic and institutional life. Also important, I would argue, are the city's racial/ethnic structure, political system, and civic institutions.

Ideally, to best understand the importance of the particular urban context for the immigrant experience, we should compare similar immigrant populations in two or more cities.[3] Elsewhere, I have attempted such comparisons for West Indians, arguing that the size of New York's West Indian community, its long history, and the presence of large numbers from many different nations have provided a base for a much broader range of West Indian neighborhoods and organizations and a launching pad for a greater number of successful political candidates than is the case in other U.S. cities where they settle. That West Indian New Yorkers live in a city with a large native black population—and where no one immigrant group dominates—also gives their experiences a particular shape (see Foner 1985, 1998, 2001). The characteristics of the West Indian immigrants who come to New York—especially the range of human capital they bring with them—also helps account for the particular trajectory of incorporation there, something that also comes out in a comparison of Chinese communities in New York City, with its heavily working-class Chinese immigrant population, and Los Angeles, with a larger proportion of middle- and upper-class Chinese immigrants (Waldinger and Tseng 1992; see Zhou, this volume).

Yet even if we look at immigrant groups in only one city, as the chapters in the present volume do, the "city as context" framework points to the way specific social and economic features of New York City affect the lives of new immigrants. A number of these features are, themselves, a product of the recent mass immigration.

New York stands out as America's quintessential immigrant city. It served as the historic port of entry for European immigrants in the late nineteenth and early twentieth centuries and still attracts a significant share of the nation's new arrivals. The census figures presented in Ellen Kraly and Ines Miyares's chapter tell much of the story. Since 1900, 10 percent or more of the nation's foreign-born population has lived in New York City. For much of the twentieth century, a fifth or more of New York City residents were foreign-born, the figure reaching 41 percent in 1910 and, by 1999, almost as high at 35 percent.

What is striking about New York City's immigrant population is not just the numbers but its extreme heterogeneity. In Los Angeles, the nation's other premier immigrant capital, the foreign-born population is overwhelmingly Mexican, Salvadoran, and Guatemalan, with relatively few Europeans and only tiny proportions of Caribbeans (Waldinger 1996a). New York City has attracted sizable numbers of nearly all European as well as most Asian, West Indian, and Latin American nationalities. Indeed, as Kraly and Miyares note, between 1990 and 1996 alone, as many as twenty countries each sent more than 5,000 immigrants to the city. There is, moreover, a huge native minority population: African Americans and Puerto Ricans. The product of a massive migration from the South between World War I and the 1960s and from Puerto Rico after World War II, U.S.-born blacks and Hispanics of native stock (native born to native parents) made up about a quarter of the city's population in the late 1990s.[4]

As a result, ethnic diversity is the expectation in New York—a fact of life, as it were. This is welcoming for many immigrants, although for some it can be confusing. Soviet Jewish teenagers whom Annelise Orleck studied in the 1980s were confounded when they entered high school, wanting to know where the Americans were: "It is . . . hard to know what we are supposed to be becoming. Everybody here is from someplace else" (Orleck 1987:295).

The large numbers of immigrants in so many groups, coupled with settlement patterns in the city, mean that New York's neighborhoods provide a familiar environment for many new arrivals. Immigrant settlements draw newcomers to the city in the first place, and they offer comfort and security once they arrive—a kind of home away from home. Ethnic neighborhoods provide a basis for communal life. Formal associations are found in many immigrant neighborhoods—and shops, restaurants, and street corners are informal meeting places. Ethnic neighborhoods also provide economic opportunities in the form of clientele and, in some cases, workers for immigrant enterprises. Large immigrant concentrations have spawned small businesses that serve the needs of new arrivals, ranging from Russian restaurants and groceries along Brighton Beach Avenue to Dominican bodegas and travel agencies in Washington Heights and Korean stores, with Korean-language signs, in downtown Flushing. New York's Chinatown is not just a place of residence but also a place of work—a classic case of an ethnic enclave economy. In addition to the several hundred factories and about 800 restaurants that are owned and staffed by Chinese, other businesses include grocery stores, import/export companies, barbershops and beauty salons, banks, law firms, and real estate agencies. Even if they don't work in a Chinese neighborhood in Manhattan, Queens, or Brooklyn, immigrants can find information there about jobs in other places and transportation to get to jobs elsewhere (Zhou, this volume).

In general, the immigrant employment sector in New York City, consisting of enterprises organized and controlled by immigrants, has generated jobs for substantial numbers in certain groups. A large proportion of Chinese immigrants work in businesses owned by coethnics—garment factories alone, according to Zhou, employ three out of five immigrant Chinese women in Chinatown; Chinatown restaurants employ at least 15,000 Chinese workers. Koreans have particularly high rates of self-employment—higher than any other new immigrant group in the city. Their businesses may well involve, as either owners or employees, more than three-quarters of employed Koreans in New York City (Min, this volume). As Paul Stoller describes in his chapter, many of the new West African arrivals set up as street vendors, a good number operating out of the Harlem market at 116th Street and Lenox Avenue that is owned and run by the Masjid Malcolm mosque.

These comments raise the larger question of how New York City's economy shapes the employment possibilities available to new immigrants. The recent influx has occurred at a time of economic restructuring, as New York City has witnessed a shift from goods production to services (see Sassen 1988, 1991; Waldinger 1996a). In their chapter, Wright and Ellis note that manufacturing has been in almost continuous employment contraction for the last thirty years. Meanwhile, an increasing share of the city's new employment is in "high-end" jobs in business services, law, investment banking, advertising, and consulting, as well as "low-end" service jobs—in domestic service, hotels and restaurants, and personal services. Even though the city has experienced what Wright and Ellis call a period of "anemic employment growth" in the last three decades, immigrants have found plenty of job opportunities, partly because the native white population has shrunk dramatically, leaving gaps for other groups to fill. In the 1970s and 1980s, half a million native whites left the New York City workforce; more than 250,000 native whites also left the city's workforce between 1990 and 1997 (Wright and Ellis, this volume).

If the economic context is crucial in shaping immigrants' experiences, so other specific features of New York City should be noted also. As immigrants seek shelter, they enter what is in all likelihood the tightest housing market in the nation, where median rents are also among the highest nationally. According to a 1996 study, half of immigrant renter households paid more than 30 percent of their income for rent; almost a third paid more than 50 percent (Schill, Friedman, and Rosenbaum 1998). On the positive side, the City University of New York (CUNY) is the largest urban public university system in the nation—in 1995, it had more than 213,000 students in ten senior colleges, six community colleges, a technical college, a graduate school, a law school, a medical school, and an affiliated school of medicine. In 1998, 48 percent of CUNY's first-time freshmen were foreign-born (Crook et al. 2000). New York City also operates an extensive municipal health care system that focuses on serving the city's poor, with eleven acute-care hospitals, five neighborhood family care centers, forty outreach clinics, and a city emergency medical service (Opdycke 1995). City agencies and nonprofit organizations offer a wide array of services to the latest arrivals. These include several hundred community-based organizations in the nonprofit immigrant service-delivery system, ranging from the large Federation Employment Guidance Services, which mainly serves Jewish immigrants, to the much smaller Accion Latina. Among the services the different organizations provide are benefits and business counseling, citizenship services, crime victim services, employment and training services, and general legal services (Cordero-Guzman and Navarro 2000).

New York City's political system also affects newcomers. The city, as Roger Waldinger observes, "presents newcomer groups with a segmented political system, organized for mobilization along ethnic group lines, and a political culture that sanctions, indeed encourages, newcomers to engage in ethnic politics" (1996b:104). A large number of political prizes are up for grabs—many within reach of the newest groups. The New York City Council has fifty-one members; the city sends fifty-nine representatives to New York's State Assembly and twenty-four to the State Senate. New York also has fifty-nine community boards (with fifty members each) and thirty-five community school boards (with fifteen members each) whose elections are open to noncitizens (Waldinger 1996b:104; Mollenkopf 1999).

In seeking office and in pressing their political demands, politicians based in new immigrant communities often appeal for support along ethnic lines, as the chapter on Dominicans by Pessar and Graham makes clear. After redistricting occurred in the early 1990s, the Washington Heights Dominican community was key in electing Guillermo Linares (who had been a school board president) to the city council; when an upper Manhattan assembly district was reconfigured to increase the odds of election of Latino candidates, a Dominican won (see also Min, this volume, on the election of Koreans to community school boards). West Indians, as Philip Kasinitz (1992) describes in *Caribbean New York,* have used the ethnic card to gain city- and statewide elected offices from constituencies in Brooklyn (see also Vickerman, this volume). But ethnic politics is not simply a matter of one group being pitted against another. New York's great diversity puts a premium on building ethnic coalitions for citywide office, most notably, in mayoral races (cf. Waldinger 1996b). The city's political system, John Mollenkopf (1999:423) notes, "encourages, indeed requires, groups to make deals with each other, and elected officials from all racial and ethnic groups have an incentive to seek support from immigrants."

Transnational Connections

Immigrants may be deeply affected by and involved in life in New York, but at the same time they often maintain close ongoing ties with their home communities. This dual orientation is what social scientists have in mind when they speak of transnational practices, which refer to the multistranded social relations, along family, economic, and political lines, that link together migrants' societies of origin and settlement. In this way, migrants are said to build "transnational social fields" that cross geographic, cultural, and political borders (Basch 2001).[5]

Immigrant New Yorkers often send money to relatives back home. Low-cost phone calls enable them to keep in touch with those they left behind; inexpensive air travel facilitates actual visits. With videotapes, people in Brooklyn or Queens can participate vicariously in weddings and village festivals in India or the Andes. Some manage businesses "there" as well as "here"—and political involvements also often span borders. A good many immigrant New Yorkers continue to participate in the politics of their home society. Given new dual-citizenship provisions in a number of countries, some can vote in home-country elections even after they become U.S. citizens.[6]

In this volume, Paul Stoller describes traders who send money to wives and children in West Africa; retain a strong allegiance to West African–based trading cartels; and, in a number of cases, travel back and forth between Africa and the United States as part of their businesses. Dominican New Yorkers, Pessar and Graham argue, are simultaneously incorporated into the political systems of New York *and* their country of origin—these engagements, they stress, are not mutually exclusive strategies. Dominicans in Washington Heights who cast their ballots in New York City elections may also attend public forums and rallies to support presidential candidates in the Dominican Republic. Recent electoral reforms in the Dominican Republic permitted voting in presidential elections from outside the country, although implementation has been stalled by debates over the logistics of managing voting from abroad. In the late 1990s a legislative candidate for the Dominican city of Santiago was actually a member of the political party's New York section.

The consequences of involvement in home-country politics are complex—and often contradictory. Although such involvement does not inevitably draw energies and interests away from political engagement on behalf of the immigrant community in New York, this can happen (see Jones-Correa 1998). Alternatively, concerns about the country of origin can provide a catalyst for involvement in U.S. politics (Wong 2001), and flourishing home country–based organizations can strengthen migrants' ability to mobilize a base of support for political issues and elections in New York (see Basch 1987). In this regard, Robert Smith (this volume) observes that Mexican organizations in New York, directly sponsored by the Mexican government partly to bolster support for the dominant political party in Mexico, could well contribute to "the potential political capacity" of Mexicans in the city.

Within immigrant groups, the frequency, depth, and range of transnational ties are likely to vary by class, age, gender, and documented status, to name just four factors. Some groups, moreover, are characterized by more intense, regular, and dense transnational connections than others, although this is a topic that is just beginning to be explored (see Levitt 2000). If Dominicans and Mexicans are often touted as highly transnational, then the Soviet Jews described by Orleck in her chapter clearly are not. She reports that most don't even care to visit their old home, feeling there is nothing left of the world they knew and nothing to go back to. "Everyone I know is here," one person told her. When asked whether she continued to follow news from home, a Brighton businesswoman replied impatiently: "America is my country, not Russia. I have no one left there to worry about. My family is all here or in Israel."

Features of New Immigrant Groups and New Patterns in New York

That new immigrants are deeply influenced by New York's particular urban context does not mean that they become homogenized in a so-called "melting pot" in the city. The old and new blend in many ways in response to circumstances in their new home—a kind of New Yorkization process (cf. Foner 1999). As Glazer and Moynihan wrote some forty years ago, in New York, immigrants become "something they had not been, but still something distinct and identifiable" (1963:14). The particular blend of meanings, perceptions, and patterns of behavior that emerges is shaped, to a large degree, by the culture, social practices, and skills and education newcomers bring with them when they arrive—as well as by a variety of sociodemographic features of their particular immigrant group.

Premigration Cultural and Social Patterns

New immigrants come to New York carrying with them a "memory of things past" that operates as a filter through which they view and experience life in the city. Some of their former beliefs and social institutions may persist intact, although usually they undergo change, if only subtly, in form and function in response to circumstances in New York. What needs stressing is that premigration values, attitudes, and customs do not simply fade away; rather, they shape, often in a complex fashion, the way individuals in each group adjust to and develop new cultural patterns in New York.

Take something as basic as cooking and cuisine. Newcomers may add hamburgers, pizza, and fried chicken to their diets in New York and concoct new dishes that use ingredients available there, but they still also eat such traditional foods as plantain and curried goat (Jamaicans) or pickled herring and *shashlyk* (Soviet Jews). Immigrant languages are alive and well in New York—indeed, lack of proficiency in English may limit patterns of association as well as the ability to obtain jobs in the mainstream economy.

Premigration family and religious patterns also have an impact. Of course, they may fill new needs and acquire new meanings in New York or be transformed in significant ways. In a contemporary version of West African polygynous marriage practices, a West African street trader described in Paul Stoller's chapter maintained two families—one in New York and another in West Africa. South Asian families in New York still often arrange their children's marriages or, in a modified "semiarranged" pattern, introduce suitable, prescreened young men and women who are then allowed a courtship period during which they are to decide whether they like each other well enough to marry (see Dasgupta and Dasgupta 1998; Foner 1999; Lessinger 1995). In her chapter, Orleck mentions that many Central Asian "Bukharan" Jews also continue to arrange their children's marriages in New York; when the children resist, serious conflicts, sometimes resulting in physical violence, may result. Although Dominican households often become less patriarchal and more egalitarian in New York, premigration attitudes toward gender roles do not disappear altogether. In tune with patterns on the island, wives in better-off Dominican immigrant families often withdraw from the workforce under pressure from their husbands as a way to symbolize their household's respectability and elevated economic status (Pessar 1987, 1999). Jamaican women—who, unlike Dominicans, come from a society with a strong tradition of female employment—would, in my experience, not dream of doing this (Foner 2000b).

Religious beliefs and practices from the old country are what draws many to places of worship in New York, from Pentecostal churches among West Indians to Hindu temples among South Asians; they also explain the continuation of customs like Haitian voodoo ceremonies (see Abusharaf 1998; Brown 1991; Lessinger 1995; McAlister 1998). West African traders, Stoller tells us, are almost all practicing Muslims; if able, they pray five times a day, follow Muslim dietary restrictions, and attend services at the Masjid Malcolm Shabazz in Harlem.

Human Capital and Modes of Economic Incorporation

The human capital concept refers to the knowledge or skills that individual immigrants bring with them, but it can be applied to groups as well. Every group, of course, has highly skilled people as well as those who are unlettered and have little training. Yet clearly some groups have human capital advantages that others do not share.

The best-educated groups are from Asia, Africa, Western Europe, and the Middle East; the most poorly educated are from Latin America and the Hispanic Caribbean. West Indians fall somewhere in the middle. An analysis of 1990 census data shows that among post-1965 working-age immigrants, about a third of Soviets and Koreans were college graduates; for Mexicans and Dominicans, it was less than 6 percent. An astounding 43 percent of Mexicans had less than a ninth-grade education. Dominicans (31 percent) and Chinese (24 percent) were not far behind. (About a fifth of the Chinese, however, were college graduates.) Nine percent of Jamaicans had less than a ninth-grade education; 13 percent were college graduates (Cordero-Guzman and Grosfoguel 1998; Foner 2000a).

Not surprisingly, groups with high proportions of college graduates do relatively well in New York's economy—though factors other than education and skills also determine occupational success. Lack of U.S. job experience and English, for example, often prevents immigrants who held professional or highly regarded jobs in their home countries from getting work of comparable status here. Indeed, well-educated immigrants who cannot find jobs congruent with their occupational backgrounds frequently turn to entrepreneurial pursuits as a better alternative than low-level service or factory jobs—one reason for the proliferation of small businesses in the Korean community.

Once a group becomes concentrated in certain sectors of the economy, this, in itself, affects how its members fare. Much has been written about ethnic enclaves, in the sense that Alejandro Portes and his colleagues have developed the term, consisting of spatially clustered networks of businesses owned and staffed by members of the same minority group (for a useful overview of the development of the concept, see Light and Gold 2000:11–15). Manhattan's Chinatown is a well-known example, where Chinese factory owners often get credit from Chinese financial institutions, rent space from Chinese landlords, buy equipment and materials from Chinese vendors, and employ largely Chinese workers, who in turn consume products from local Chinese merchants (Kasinitz 2001; see Zhou 1992, this volume). On the down side, wages in ethnic enclaves are often lower and working conditions worse than in the mainstream economy; in Chinatown, many end up trapped in poorly paid jobs (see Kwong 1997; Zhou, this volume). Yet enclaves promote self-employment and may serve as a buffer between the community and the ups and downs of the larger economy; a potential springboard for upward mobility for the most successful (and their children); and a safety net for the less fortunate, who cannot find work in the general labor market. Indeed, much the same can be said of what Light and Gold call "ethnic ownership economies," where an immigrant or ethnic group maintains a private economic sector in which it has a controlling ownership stake (2000:9).

There are, of course, other kinds of occupational concentrations that do not involve self-employment. Ethnic niches are simply places in the labor market where members of particular ethnic groups are overrepresented—and they, too, can bring advantages. When a group becomes concentrated in an industry or occupation, this facilitates the entry of additional coethnics through job referrals and training so that ethnic niches become, as Waldinger puts it, self-reproducing (see Waldinger 1996a; Model 1993). In his chapter, Robert Smith argues, in fact, that Mexicans' lack of concentration in many niches in New York's economy is a problem because it means that many lack on-the-job ethnic ties to provide positions for fellow immigrants and for their children.

Much depends on the kinds of niches a group establishes. Koreans have benefited from their concentration in small businesses—and from their dense web of trade associations, ethnic media and organizations, and churches in what Min calls an "institutionally complete community" that reinforces, supports, and further encourages entrepreneurial activity. Dominicans, however, have suffered from their early concentration in manufacturing, an industry marked by deteriorating wages and massive job loss over the past few decades (Pessar, this volume; see also Grasmuck and Grosfoguel 1997). Philip Kasinitz points out that Jamaican niches in health care and public employment do not provide anything like the opportunity to employ coethnics or to accumulate capital or establish credit that small-business ownership does. In fact, educational credentials and bureaucratic requirements limit the scope of network hiring in white-collar and especially in public-sector employment (Kasinitz 2001; Kasinitz and Vickerman 2001).

Demographic Factors

The demographic composition of an immigrant group can also have an impact on patterns that develop in New York. The group's sheer size, as well as spatial concentration, influences, among other things, whether it can support a sizable number of ethnic businesses and provide enough votes to elect its own candidates. Dominicans' concentration in northern Manhattan, as Pessar and Graham show, has been an asset at the ballot box in putting Dominicans into office; residential segregation among West Indians, while clearly disadvantageous in many respects, has helped them gain seats in the City Council and State Assembly. Conversely, as Smith argues, Mexican immigrants' geographical dispersion makes political mobilization among them problematic.

Sex and age ratios in each group affect marriage and family patterns. For example, a markedly unbalanced sex ratio will encourage marriage outside the group or consign many to singlehood or the search for spouses in the home country. Most of the traders Paul Stoller studied had left wives behind in West Africa; some had occasional interludes with American (usually African American) women, and a few married African Americans, occasionally as their second wives. A sizable proportion of old people in an immigrant group's population may, as occurs among Russian Jews in Brighton Beach, ease the child-care burden of working women (Orleck 1987). Korean families often bring elderly relatives to New York for this reason. Pyong Gap Min has described how his own mother-in-law came to this country in 1981 "at the age of 58 as a temporary visitor to help with childcare and housework as my wife and I were struggling with three children, a small business, and my Ph.D. program. The next year my wife, a naturalized citizen, filed petitions for her parents' permanent residence" (1998:87). The presence of an elderly mother or mother-in-law in Korean immigrant households has other implications—it puts less pressure on husbands to help out—and thus may end up reinforcing patriarchal practices.

Race

Immigrants' race has crucial consequences for their experiences and reactions to New York life. Whereas whiteness is an asset for newcomers of European ancestry, dark skin brings disadvantages. Because of their skin color—and because American society's generalized negative view of blacks is so different from racial conceptions in their home countries—black immigrants develop new attitudes and new perceptions of themselves in New York. As Milton Vickerman's chapter shows, Jamaicans have trouble coming to terms with the degree of interpersonal racism they encounter in their daily lives in New York (see Waters 1999). Apart from everyday slights and insults, racial discrimination influences where Jamaicans, and other black immigrants, live; the opportunities they find on the job; and the kinds of associations and political organizations they join (see Foner 1987, 2000a, 2001; Vickerman 1999; Waters 1999). Other immigrants of color confront racial discrimination too, but this tends to be less problematic than for immigrants of African ancestry who are defined as black. Indeed, dark-skinned Hispanic immigrants face barriers and discrimination that their light-skinned coethnics do not experience (see Foner 2000a, chapter 5).

The Impact of New Immigrants on New York City

If the newest New Yorkers have undergone transformations as they adjust and adapt to life in their new home, then also they have brought innumerable changes to the city. The particular way each immigrant population affects New York varies, of course, depending on such factors as its size and residential concentration, occupational makeup, and race and cultural background. The very cultural and social patterns that emerge among each group in response to circumstances in the city are also involved. However, there are some broad spheres and institutions where virtually all new immigrant groups have had an impact.

New York's Population Structure

The new immigration has brought about a dramatic demographic transformation in New York City. Immigration to the city, according to Immigration and Naturalization Service (INS) figures, averaged 112,600 for the years 1990 to 1994, up from 85,600 for the 1980s and 78,300 in the 1970s (Lobo, Salvo, and Virgin 1996). By 1999, New York was home to a record 2.7 million foreign-born residents, 35 percent of the city total. How many of the immigrants were unauthorized, or undocumented, is difficult to say. A widely accepted estimate by the INS put the number of undocumented immigrants in New York State at 540,000 in 1996, the vast majority of these living in New York City.

In the late 1990s, Dominicans were the city's largest foreign-born group. The next largest was former Soviets, followed by Chinese, Jamaicans, and Mexicans. After that, in descending order, were immigrants from Guyana, Ecuador, Haiti, Trinidad and Tobago, and Italy (Kraly and Miyares, this volume).

The newcomers are spread throughout the city, but, as Kraly and Miyares show, there are particular patterns of settlement for each group. In the late 1990s, seven out of ten of the city's Soviet immigrants lived in Brooklyn and 90 percent of Koreans in Queens. Queens, in fact, was home to 55 percent of the city's Asian immigrants and 60 percent of South Americans. Haitians, Trinidadians, and Barbadians were concentrated in Brooklyn while Jamaicans were divided among Brooklyn, Queens, and the Bronx. About 40 percent of the city's Dominicans lived in Manhattan, with another 29 percent in the Bronx and 20 percent in Queens; the Chinese were in Brooklyn, Queens, and Manhattan.

Local Neighborhoods and Communities

The new immigration has altered the landscape of the city. New York now boasts three Chinatowns, a little Odessa-by-the-Sea, Caribbean Brooklyn, and a Dominican colony in Washington Heights. With continuing immigration, new ethnic neighborhoods and ethnic conglomerations have cropped up in every borough.

Certain sections of the city have taken on a new cultural character. In Crown Heights and East Flatbush in Brooklyn, for example, West Indian beauty parlors, restaurants, record stores, groceries, and bakeries dot the landscape, and Haitian Creole and West Indian accents fill the air. "[When I walk] along . . . Nostrand Avenue," the novelist Paule Marshall notes, "I have to remind myself that I'm in Brooklyn and not in the middle of a teeming outdoor market in St. George's, Grenada or Kingston, Jamaica." Several neighborhoods in the northeast Bronx (Williamsbridge and Wakefield) and southeastern Queens (Springfield Gardens and Cambria Heights) also now have a definite West Indian flavor.

In their chapters, Min Zhou and Annelise Orleck describe how the number of Soviet Jewish and Chinese settlements has multiplied in response to growing immigration. Although Brooklyn's Brighton Beach, or "Little Odessa," continues to serve as an emotional and cultural home base for Soviet Jews across the New York area, they have spread out to nearby Bay Ridge, Bensonhurst, and Borough Park as well as to the Co-op City apartment complex in the Bronx. A community of Central Asian Jews flourishes in Forest Hills, where 108th Street is now known as "Bukharan Broadway." Manhattan's expanding Chinatown has spilled over into adjacent districts, including the City Hall area, Little Italy, and the East Village, and two new satellite Chinatowns have developed in Flushing and Sunset Park; visible Chinese clusters can also be found in Woodside and Elmhurst in Queens and Bay Ridge, Borough Park, and Sheepshead Bay in Brooklyn (see also Kwong 1987; Lin 1998; Zhou 1992). Dominicans have branched out from their ethnic enclave in upper Manhattan's Washington Heights to Inwood to the north, and Hamilton Heights to the south, as well as to neighborhoods in Bronx, Brooklyn, and Queens (see Kraly and Miyeras, this volume).

The new immigration has created not only large and dense ethnic settlements but also polyethnic neighborhoods that are amalgams of newcomers from all parts of the world. Elmhurst is one of New York's most diverse immigrant areas, with large numbers of Chinese, Colombians, Koreans, Filipinos, Asian Indians, Dominicans, and Ecuadorians. Between 1991 and 1995, according to INS figures, the area constituting Elmhurst's zip code, 11373, received more people from more countries than any other zip code in the United States. Although Flushing is often referred to as a new Chinatown in the making, it is in fact home to a growing number of Central and South American as well as Chinese, Indian, and Korean immigrants who join a native-born white population that remains substantial. Astoria, known for its large Greek presence in the 1980s, welcomed large numbers of Asians and Latin Americans from different countries in the early 1990s—thereby becoming another ethnic stew.

As the chapters on the different groups in this volume demonstrate, clusters of new immigrants have given rise to new ethnic businesses and affected the composition of schools and churches in communities all over the city. Several schools in Washington Heights, Patricia Pessar tells us, have even been named after Dominican heroes. Neighborhood-based immigrant institutions and organizations like community centers, voluntary associations, and political groups have emerged, as have new churches and temples (see Sanjek 1998 for the impact of immigrants on community life in Elmhurst-Corona).

Immigrants have played a key role in revitalizing many neighborhoods that had fallen on hard times. In Brighton Beach, Soviet Jews breathed fresh life into a fading community. When they began to arrive in the mid-1970s, Brighton was in decline; apartments stood empty as elderly Jewish residents died or moved to Florida, and the main commercial avenue was a dying strip of old stores. Soviet Jews have filled apartments and turned the avenue into a thriving commercial center, with nightclubs, restaurants, state-of-the-art electronics stores, and clothing boutiques selling European designer clothing (Orleck, this volume). Another Brooklyn neighborhood, Sunset Park, was in the "throes of a long twilight" that began in the 1950s when the area was devastated by, among other things, a drastic cutback in jobs on its waterfront and in industry and the exodus of tens of thousands of white residents for the suburbs. Louis Winnick argues that in Sunset Park, as in many other city neighborhoods "outside the yuppie strongholds of Manhattan and other favored areas of Brooklyn and Queens," immigrants have been the leading factor in neighborhood revitalization: "Owing to their high employment rates and multiple wage earners, the new foreigners have injected large doses of new purchasing power into the rehabilitation of an aging housing stock and the resurrection of inert retail streets" (Winnick 1990:62). One of the latest neighborhoods to benefit from the influx of new immigrants, according to a *New York Times* report, is south Harlem, where West Africans and their businesses are helping to revive the area's economy (Rozhon 2000).

Influences on Cuisine and Popular Culture

Within as well as beyond their own neighborhoods, recent immigrants have added their sounds and spices to the city's cultural and culinary life.

Restaurants and groceries run by newcomers have exposed New Yorkers, native and immigrant alike, to new cuisines and foods. Some twenty years ago, Bernard Wong (1982) wrote about Chinese immigrants broadening New Yorkers' tastes beyond Cantonese cooking to regional dishes from Shanghai, Hunan, and Szechuan. Since then, Thai, Vietnamese, Korean, Jamaican, and Indian restaurants—to name but a few—have become common on the city's restaurant scene. In the wake of the new wave of Mexican immigration, New York, a *New York Times* reporter writes, is finally shedding its reputation as a city with terrible Mexican food (Asimov 2000).[7]

Musically, too, new immigrants have had an influence. Jamaican reggae and dance hall as well as Dominican merengue have become staples of the city's popular music scene (see Austerlitz 1997:125–35 on merengue in the diaspora). "Today," writes Philip Kasinitz, "African American young people dance to Jamaican dance hall music and imitate Jamaican patois. . . . Puerto Ricans dance to merengue" (1999:29). There are new ethnic theaters and new ethnic parades and festivals representing practically every immigrant group in the city. West Indian Carnival, for example, which has been celebrated every Labor Day on Brooklyn's Eastern Parkway since 1969, draws crowds of one to two million people (Kasinitz 1992); the Dominican Day Parade in August, now given a Fifth Avenue route, attracts thousands of participants and onlookers (Pessar, this volume); and the Colombian Independence Day celebration in Flushing Meadows–Corona Park was, by the 1990s, the park's largest event (Sanjek 1998:216). The ethnic media are flourishing. By one count, in 1997 the city boasted 143 foreign-language newspapers and magazines, twenty-two television stations and twelve radio stations, in more than thirty languages (Dugger 1997). And a spate of novels emerging out of the new immigrant experience has enriched the city's literary tradition, among them *How the Garcia Girls Lost Their Accents* by Julia Alvarez (1992) and *Drown* by Junot Diaz (1996) featuring Dominicans; *Typical American* by Gish Jen (1992) and *Eating Chinese Food Naked* by Mei Ng (1998) featuring Chinese; *Breath, Eyes, Memory* by Edwidge Danticat (1995) featuring Haitians; and *Native Speaker* by Chang-Rae Lee (1995) featuring Koreans.

Race and Ethnicity

Clearly, a major impact of the new immigration is the way it has changed, and is changing, the racial and ethnic dynamics of the city. More and more, in political and street-level discourse New Yorkers think of a four-race framework of white, black, Hispanic, and Asian (Sanjek 1994). The proportion of Asians and Hispanics is growing; the proportion of whites is on the decline. In 1998, according to census estimates, 35 percent of New Yorkers were white; 8 percent were Asian; 26 percent, black; and 31 percent, Hispanic. Gone are the days when Hispanic meant Puerto Rican; Puerto Ricans now account for less than half of the city's Hispanic population, outnumbered by a combination of Dominicans, Mexicans, Ecuadorians, and Colombians. Asian no longer means Chinese but also Koreans, Indians, and Filipinos (to name the largest groups). The black population is being Caribbeanized—and a small but growing number of Africans are also adding new diversity. Altogether, by 1998 almost a third of the non-Hispanic black population was foreign-born.

This new racial and ethnic amalgam is changing perceptions of race and ethnicity (see Foner 2000a) as well as creating new alliances, relationships, and divisions. In *The Future of Us All,* Roger Sanjek (1998) provides a detailed ethnography of interethnic relations in the extraordinarily diverse community of Elmhurst-Corona, emphasizing what brings the residents of different backgrounds together. All over the city, countless examples exist of amicable relations developing among immigrants from different countries, as well as between immigrants and the native-born, in work, school, and neighborhood contexts (on these relations among workers in a New York nursing home, see Foner 1994). Sometimes, close friendships develop; occasionally, romantic involvements, even marriages, result. In his chapter, Paul Stoller mentions a three-year relationship between a West African trader and an African American social worker; another trader married an African American schoolteacher, partly as a way to obtain immigration papers but also because he had fallen in love. According to one account, an increasing number of marriages are taking place between Dominicans and Puerto Ricans (Itzigsohn and Dore-Cabral 2000:241); West Indian–African American unions are not unusual, especially among second-generation West Indians. And census figures show high rates of intermarriages between Asian Americans and non-Hispanic whites (Liang and Ito 1999).

Less happily, conflict is also part of the story. In this volume, Pyong Gap Min discusses the black boycotts of Korean stores as well as friction between Korean merchants and white suppliers (see also Min 1996); Paul Stoller mentions "a low-grade fever of resentment" between West African traders and African American customers; and Min Zhou writes of tensions between immigrant Chinese and longtime residents in multiethnic neighborhoods like Flushing. Dominican and Puerto Rican political leaders have sometimes been at odds, with Dominican leaders complaining of a Latino leadership that pursues a narrow Puerto Rican agenda (Pessar and Graham, this volume; see also Smith, this volume, on Mexicans and Puerto Ricans).

In his chapter, Milton Vickerman gives a nuanced picture of relations between Jamaicans and African Americans, which are characterized by both distancing and identification; Jamaicans seek to assert their ethnic identity and show they are different from African Americans at the same time that they feel a shared bond with African Americans as blacks and victims of racial discrimination (see also Foner 1987, 2001; Vickerman 1999; Waters 1999). Other groups, too, engage in distancing strategies to avoid being lumped with, and facing the same kind of discrimination and prejudice as, African Americans and Puerto Ricans. According to Smith (this volume), Mexicans see themselves as "not black" and "not Puerto Rican." Maxine Margolis notes that Brazilians believe they receive better treatment from whites when they make clear they are not Hispanic, something they try to do by emphasizing their cultural and linguistic distinctiveness (they speak Portuguese). Not only do they wish to escape the color connotations of the Hispanic label (most Brazilians are phenotypically white), but class is also involved. Brazilians, most of whom are from the middle strata of Brazilian society and well educated, consider it an insult to be confused with the city's Latino population, who typically come from poorer backgrounds and have less education (Margolis 1994, 1998).

Ethnic Division of Labor

The structure of New York City's workforce has undergone significant changes as a result of immigration—what Wright and Ellis call the remaking of the racial-ethnic division of labor. In their chapter, they update earlier analyses to tell what happened in the 1990s. Among the foreign-born: whites increasingly moved into the manufacturing, retailing, and financial/real estate sectors; blacks (mainly West Indian) made advances in high- and low-end jobs in personal services, professional services, and public employment; Hispanics continued to hold a significant share of the city's manufacturing jobs and increasingly to enter re-tailing; and Asians registered gains in manufacturing, retail trade, and profes-sional services.

As the case studies show, distinct ethnic occupational specializations continue to be a feature of the New York scene. If you hail a taxi, your driver is likely to be South Asian; if you are a patient in a hospital, it's a good bet that the nursing aide taking your temperature will be West Indian. The greengrocer on the corner is Korean, the vendor at the newsstand Indian. Immigrant occupational niches take hold for a variety of reasons. They reflect a combination of the skills, human capital, and cultural preferences in each group; the opportunities available to the group within the city's economy; and the operation of ethnic networks through which employment and referrals flow (on the making of ethnic niches in New York see Foner 2000a; Kasinitz and Vickerman 2001; Model 1993; Waldinger 1996a).

As immigrants concentrate in particular lines of work, they often put their own stamp on them, as several chapters in this volume demonstrate. Koreans have turned the traditional produce store "into an art form" and reinvented the corner grocery, adding salad bars, deli counters, and bouquets of flowers. They have also pioneered businesses, such as the now-ubiquitous nail salons, by taking what were once more exclusive products or services and making them cheaper (Lee 1999). By 1991, Koreans owned about 1,800, or 60 percent, of the New York metro-politan area's produce stores and more than 1,100 groceries and some 1,500 nail salons (Min 1996). West Indians have brought the concept of a privatized network of passenger vans to New York City, as their jitneys ply the streets of Queens and Brooklyn, offering lower prices and more frequent service than city buses (Vick-erman, this volume). West African merchants have altered the city's street-vending business, bringing high-end items, like "Rolex" watches and "Prada" bags, to the street corner.

Dominant Formal Institutions

Recent immigrants have had an impact on a wide range of dominant formal institutions in the city outside the world of work. Briefly consider three: schools, churches, and hospitals.

The surge of immigration has led to major increases in public school enrollment, which is now over the one million mark. With so many students and a limited budget, the public schools are squeezed for space. Although many immigrant students are doing remarkably well in the schools, there is no denying they bring with them a host of special needs. Many have to overcome poor educational preparation in their home countries or, at the very least, unfamiliarity with subjects taught here and with the teaching methods (and discipline) used (see Foner 2000a, chapter 7). In addition to adjusting to new norms and customs in America, many have a language problem to contend with. In one Queens elementary school, nearly 80 percent of the incoming students arrived speaking no English; among them, the children in the school spoke thirty-six different languages (Hedges 2000). In 1997–1998, close to 80,000 students were enrolled in bilingual programs in the New York City public schools. The largest number (85 percent) were of Spanish-speaking background, followed by, in descending order, Chinese, Haitian Creole, Russian, Korean, Bengali, Polish, Arabic, French, Urdu, and Punjabi (Board of Education of the City of New York 1999). In response to the immigrant influx, the city has opened several new schools designed specifically for recent immigrant children with limited English proficiency (see Foner 2000a).

The city's Roman Catholic schools have also experienced an influx of new immigrant children. And although immigrants form their own churches—witness the Koreans, with their more than 500 churches in the New York–New Jersey metropolitan area (Min, this volume)—large numbers are drawn to the Catholic church and to established Protestant congregations. New York's Catholic church has a growing Latino presence, and an increasing number of Catholic churches conduct masses in Spanish as well as other languages (see Sanjek 1998:67–68, 335–41). In the mid-1990s, fourteen churches in Brooklyn and Queens celebrated masses in French or Creole, and the thriving Haitian congregation at Saint Jerome's in Brooklyn drew an estimated 1,400 parishioners each Sunday (McAlister 1998:144–45). Catholic churches in Washington Heights have emerged as Dominican congregations, holding mass in Spanish and inviting religious officials from the island to participate in church activities. One Washington Heights church has even been named Our Lady of Altagracia (Pessar 1995:28; see Smith, this volume, on Mexican New Yorkers and the Catholic church).

The composition of the staff and patients in New York City's hospitals has changed as well. The nurses, aides, and orderlies are often West Indian or Filipino; patients, especially at municipal hospitals, are frequently non-English-speaking immigrants who bring with them their own set of cultural values regarding health and medical treatment. Some New York City hospitals have begun to establish programs to address the need for better interpreter services, although what is available, in terms of language services and responsiveness to cross-cultural health care, is often woefully inadequate (Michael 1996).[8] On a positive note, Orleck, in her chapter, notes that the emergency room staff at Coney Island Hospital, the major health facility in southern Brooklyn, keeps a Russian-language herbal remedy book on hand to figure out what herbs patients may have taken.

Conclusion: Looking Ahead

New immigrants, it is clear, not only are shaped by social, economic, and political forces in New York City, but they also act as agents of change in their new environment. The newest New Yorkers have radically transformed the city—and more changes are in store. Predicting the future is a risky business, yet it is worth reflecting on some ways that the influx of newcomers will leave its stamp on the city and on the lives of immigrants themselves in the years ahead.

The signs are that high levels of immigration will continue, at least in the near future. Even if there is some move toward restrictionism, the United States is likely to remain an immigration country for many years to come, allowing some five or six hundred thousand persons to enter a year; New York can expect to receive a disproportionate share, if only because of the networks that link newcomers to settlers (cf. Waldinger 1996c). If, as predicted, many native-born New Yorkers continue to exit for greener pastures in the suburbs and elsewhere, the foreign-born proportion of the city's population will increase.

The continued inflows will enrich and replenish the city's ethnic communities. With fresh memories and connections to the homeland, new arrivals will help to keep alive old-country traditions and orientations as well as actual transnational ties. A number of trends already evident in New York's racial-ethnic dynamics are also likely to persist—indeed, they may well accelerate.[9] Puerto Ricans' share of the city's Latino population will continue to shrink; the proportion of Dominicans, Mexicans, Ecuadorians, and Colombians will rise. In his chapter, Robert Smith points to the tremendous potential growth in New York's Mexican population given the Mexican economy's inability to meet the growing demand for jobs, the development of new migration chains from what he calls "nontraditional sending regions," and the increasing tendency for migrants to settle down in the United States. Moreover, Mexicans—and indeed, Latino immigrants generally—have very high fertility rates, which will add to their numbers. Between 1990 and 1996, there were nearly 29,000 births to Mexican-born mothers in New York, or over 3 percent of all births in the city. (Dominicans were in first place among the foreign-born, with nearly 78,000 births; Jamaicans second, with about 31,000) (New York City Department of City Planning 1999).

The Caribbeanization of the city's black population will no doubt persist—and its Africanization will become more prominent. African countries, according to a recent study, are becoming major players in New York's immigration tableau; although the numbers are still relatively small, legal immigration from Ghana increased 380 percent over the early 1990s, and from Nigeria by 220 percent.[10] Given the network-driven nature of immigration, the dominant role of family preferences in the allocation of immigrant visas, and push factors in West African sending countries, the African influx to the city is sure to accelerate. The proportion of Asians in the city—which went from less than 2 percent in 1970 to 8 percent in 1998—will also grow. Here, too, new players will be increasingly important, most notably, Bangladeshis, who were the sixth-largest source of immigrants to New York City in 1995–1996, up from fourteenth place in the early 1990s (New York City Department of City Planning 1999). As the chain migration from the former Soviet Union continues, as Annelise Orleck (this volume) predicts it will, what she calls the "Russification of Jewish New York" will also proceed apace.

It is hard to tell how different groups will fare in New York's economy of the future because so much depends on unpredictable economic conditions, yet Wright and Ellis's analysis provides some clues as to what lies ahead. Because foreign-born Hispanics are concentrated in declining sectors like manufacturing, they are more vulnerable than immigrant whites, blacks, and Asians to future job loss in traditional industries. All groups will be affected by changes in the demography of the native-born white population. Up until now, replacement labor demand has provided jobs for many new immigrants, but Wright and Ellis suggest that the loss of native-born workers through retirement and outmigration will, at some point in the not-too-distant future, slow to the extent that replacement demand will be insufficient to absorb the latest arrivals. In this context, factors such as "worker skills and education, employer preferences, discrimination, racism, union exclusion of minorities, and job networks will become much stronger determinants of ethnic group employment fortunes than they have been to date." In a worsening employment picture, Wright and Ellis think that foreign-born Hispanics (along with African Americans and native Hispanics) are especially likely to suffer.

In terms of politics, the growing number of newcomers—and naturalized citizens—will make immigrants (and especially their children) more important in New York's political arena. Dominicans and West Indians, with their large numbers, geographic concentration, and rising naturalization rates, are likely to build on their history, in the 1990s, of electing coethnics to city and state positions. The well-organized Korean community, described by Min in his chapter, is also poised to make political gains, and so are the Chinese, another large population.

Of course, immigrants' political influence is limited by the fact that noncitizens cannot vote—and continued large influxes will swell this population. So far, only a minority of the eligible foreign-born have become naturalized citizens, and this may continue to be a problem. It is most likely, as John Mollenkopf (1999:419) predicts, that "the full political incorporation of the Caribbean, Dominican, and Chinese populations must await the political maturing of the second generation, just as the full impact of the turn-of-the-century immigration was not felt until their children voted for the New Deal."

What about alliances among groups? The chapters in this volume point to several possibilities: between West Indians and African Americans around shared interests and experiences as blacks, between Dominicans and Puerto Ricans as Latinos from the Caribbean, among Latinos generally, and among various Asian groups. Broader coalitions are also likely to emerge under certain circumstances. As John Mollenkopf notes, white liberals, native-born blacks, Caribbean blacks, Puerto Ricans, and Dominicans may come together to support mayoral candidates as a way to gain influence (1999:431). By the same token, as Mollenkopf also observes, many barriers separate these groups, which have different social positions and potentially conflicting interests. Indeed, the chapters by Pessar and Graham, Smith, and Vickerman mention some of these divisions. New York West Indians' political behavior, Vickerman notes, may diverge from African Americans' because West Indians often support their own candidates, because they are more conservative on family and law-and-order issues, and because they are more concerned with legislation affecting immigrants. Smith suggests a potential division in the Latino community between those from the Caribbean (Puerto Ricans and Dominicans) and those from meso-America and Andean countries based on cultural and racial differences as well as Dominicans' and Puerto Ricans' earlier access to elected office and political clout. To further complicate matters, Pessar and Graham make clear that Dominicans and Puerto Ricans themselves are often competitors—not allies—in political contests (Pessar and Graham, this volume). Certainly, putting multiethnic coalitions together will be fraught with challenges.

These are just some intriguing questions about the shape of immigrant New York in the years to come. If the United States is the permanently unfinished country, as Nathan Glazer has written in another context, to an even greater degree the same can be said of New York City (1988:54). As we start a new century, fresh immigrant recruits keep entering New York City; newcomers who arrived in the 1970s and 1980s are by now old-timers; and a large second generation is growing up and beginning to enter the job market.[11] The chapters that follow provide a view of immigrant New York after more than thirty-five years of a massive inflow. They offer insights and raise questions that will enrich our understanding of the newcomers in America's ever-changing and quintessential immigrant city and, in the end, also broaden our perspective on immigration generally.

Notes

1. A number of full-length ethnographic accounts of immigrant groups in New York City have been published in the last ten years. See, for example, Margolis 1994,

1998 on Brazilians; Park 1997, Min 1996, 1998 on Koreans; Lessinger 1995 on Asian Indians; Chen 1992, Guo 2000, Lin 1998, Zhou 1992 on Chinese; Kasinitz 1992, Vickerman 1999, and Waters 1999 on West Indians; Grasmuck and Pessar 1991, Pessar 1995 on Dominicans; Jones-Correa 1998 on Latinos in Queens; Markowitz 1993 on Russian Jews. See also Mahler 1995a, 1995b on Salvadorans on Long Island.

2. This flexible cap of 675,000 visas does not include refugees. Immediate relatives of adult U.S. citizens can still enter without numerical restrictions. Chapter 3 of *The Newest New Yorkers, 1990–1994* (Lobo, Salvo, and Virgin 1996) discusses the implications of the 1990 act for New York City.

3. There have been surprisingly few systematic comparisons of this sort. See Baily 1999 on Italians in Buenos Aires and New York; Foner 1998 on Haitians in New York and Miami; Brettell 1981 on Portuguese in Toronto and Paris; Waldinger and Tseng 1992 and Zhou and Kim 1999 on Chinese in Los Angeles and New York.

4. If one includes U.S.-born children of foreign-born blacks and Hispanics, U.S.-born blacks and Hispanics were just over a third of the city's population (March 1998 Current Population Survey data calculated by John Mollenkopf, Urban Research Center, CUNY Graduate Center).

5. A large literature has developed on transnational practices and social fields. See, for example, Basch, Glick Schiller and Szanton Blanc 1994; Cordero-Guzman, Smith, and Grosfoguel 2001; Glick Schiller 1999; Portes, Guarnizo, and Landolt 1999; Smith and Guarnizo 1998. See Foner 2000a (chapter 6) for a comparison of transnationalism among immigrant New Yorkers today and a century ago.

6. According to one report, nearly all of the top twenty immigrant source countries to New York City in 1996 allowed some form of dual citizenship, although only a minority permitted absentee voting or voting from abroad for dual citizens (Cheng 2000; see also Renshon 2000).

7. For a historical analysis of the way immigrant cuisines have, over the centuries, added to and diversified American eating habits, see Gabaccia 1998.

8. On the problems elderly Chinese immigrants in New York face in dealing with the U.S. healthcare system, see Guo 2000. Immigrants may also bring with them particular diseases and health risks such as tuberculosis and malaria, although, at the same time, a recent study shows foreign-born women in New York City having superior birth outcomes as compared to the native-born (Joyce 2000; Michael 1996).

9. See Foner (2000a, chapter 8) on the way the growing immigration has the potential to change how current racial and ethnic categories are seen and evaluated—and perhaps the very categories themselves. On how West Indians may "tweak" the monolith of blackness, see Vickerman 2001.

10. An annual average of 430 Nigerian immigrants and 339 Ghanaians entered New York in the 1990–1994 period; in 1995–1996 the figure for Nigerians was 1,374; for Ghanaians, 1,633 (Department of City Planning 1999).

11. A series of publications will soon be forthcoming based on a large-scale study of second-generation young adults (aged eighteen to thirty-two) in the New York City area that has recently been concluded by Philip Kasinitz, John Mollenkopf, and Mary Waters.

References

Abusharaf, Rogaia. 1998. "Structural Adaptations in an Immigrant Muslim Congregation in New York." In R. Stephen Warner and Judith G. Wittner, eds., *Gatherings in Diaspora*. Philadelphia: Temple University Press.

Alvarez, Julia. 1992 [1991]. *How the Garcia Girls Lost Their Accents*. New York: Penguin.

Asimov, Eric. 2000. "Now in New York: True Mexican." *New York Times,* January 26.

Austerlitz, Paul. 1997. *Merengue: Dominican Music and Dominican Identity*. Philadelphia: Temple University Press.

Baily, Samuel L. 1999. *Immigrants in the Land of Promise: Italians in Buenos Aires and New York City, 1870–1914*. Ithaca: Cornell University Press.

Basch, Linda. 1987. "The Vincentians and Grenadians: The Role of Voluntary Associations in Immigrant Adaptation to New York City." In Nancy Foner, ed., *New Immigrants in New York*. New York: Columbia University Press.

———. 2001. "Transnational Social Relations and the Politics of National Identity: An Eastern Caribbean Case Study." In Nancy Foner, ed., *Islands in the City: West Indian Migration to New York*. Berkeley: University of California Press.

Basch, Linda, Nina Glick Schiller, and Cristina Szanton Blanc. 1994. *Nations Unbound: Transnational Projects, Postcolonial Predicaments, and Deterritorialized Nation-States*. Langhorne, Pa.: Gordon and Breach.

Board of Education of the City of New York. 1999. *Facts and Figures: Answers to Frequently Asked Questions About Limited English Proficient Students and Bilingual/ESL Programs, 1997–1998*. Office of Bilingual Education.

Brettell, Caroline. 1981. "Is the Ethnic Community Inevitable? A Comparison of the Settlement Patterns of Portuguese Immigrants in Toronto and Paris." *Journal of Ethnic Studies* 9:1–8.

———. 2000. "Urban History, Urban Anthropology, and the Study of Migrants in Cities." *City and Society* 12:129–38.

Brown, Karen McCarthy. 1991. *Mama Lola: A Vodon Priestess in Brooklyn*. Berkeley: University of California Press.

Bryce-Laporte, Roy S. 1979. "New York City and the New Caribbean Immigrant: A Contextual Statement." *International Migration Review* 13:214–34.

Chen, Hsiang-Shui. 1992. *Chinatown No More: Taiwan Immigrants in Contemporary New York*. Ithaca: Cornell University Press.

Cheng, Mae. 2000. "Citizens of the World: New Americans Are Increasingly Keeping Dual Allegiances." *Newsday,* August 7.

Cordero-Guzman, Hector, and Ramon Grosfoguel. 1998. "The Demographic and Socio-Economic Characteristics of Post–1965 Immigrants to New York City: A Comparative Analysis by National Origin." Paper presented at the Paul Lazarsfeld Center for Social Sciences, Columbia University.

Cordero-Guzman, Hector, and Jose G. Navarro. 2000. "Managing Cuts in the 'Safety Net': What Do Immigrant Groups, Organizations, and Service Providers Say About the Impacts of Recent Changes in Immigration and Welfare Laws?" Unpublished paper.

Cordero-Guzman, Hector, Robert Smith, and Ramon Grosfoguel, eds. 2001. *Migration, Transnationalism, and the Political Economy of New York*. Philadelphia: Temple University Press.

Crook, David, Claude Cheek, Mark Casazza, and J. D. Howell. 2000. *CUNY Student Data Book, Fall 1998.* Vol. 1. New York: City University of New York.

Danticat, Edwidge. 1995 [1994]. *Breath, Eyes, Memory.* New York: Vintage.

Dasgupta, Sayantani, and Shamita Das Dasgupta. 1998. "Sex, Lies, and Women's Lives." In Shamita Das Dasgupta, ed., *A Patchwork Shawl: Chronicles of South Asian Women in America.* New Brunswick: Rutgers University Press.

Diaz, Junot. 1996. *Drown.* New York: Riverhead Books.

Dugger, Celia. 1997. "A Tower of Babel, in Wood Pulp." *The New York Times,* January 19.

Foner, Nancy. 1985. "Race and Color: Jamaican Migrants in London and New York." *International Migration Review* 19:708–27.

——. 1987. "The Jamaicans: Race and Ethnicity among Migrants in New York City." In Nancy Foner, ed., *New Immigrants in New York.* New York: Columbia University Press.

——. 1994. *The Caregiving Dilemma: Work in an American Nursing Home.* Berkeley: University of California Press.

——. 1998. "Towards a Comparative Perspective on Caribbean Migration." In Mary Chamberlain, ed., *Caribbean Migration: Globalised Identities.* London: Routledge.

——. 1999. "The Immigrant Family: Cultural Legacies and Cultural Changes." In Charles Hirschman, Philip Kasinitz, and Josh DeWind, eds., *The Handbook of International Migration.* New York: Russell Sage Foundation.

——. 2000a. *From Ellis Island to JFK: New York's Two Great Waves of Immigration.* New Haven and New York: Yale University Press and Russell Sage Foundation.

——. 2000b. "Beyond the Melting Pot Three Decades Later: Recent Immigrants and New York's New Ethnic Mixture." *International Migration Review* 34:255–62.

——. 2001. "West Indian Migration to New York: An Overview." In Nancy Foner, ed., *Islands in the City: West Indian Migration to New York.* Berkeley: University of California Press.

Gabaccia, Donna. 1998. *You Are What You Eat.* Cambridge: Harvard University Press.

Glazer, Nathan. 1988. "The New New Yorkers." In Peter Salins, ed., *New York Unbound.* New York: Basil Blackwell.

Glazer, Nathan, and Daniel Patrick Moynihan. 1963. *Beyond the Melting Pot.* Cambridge: MIT Press.

Glick Schiller, Nina. 1999. "Transmigrants and Nation-States: Something Old and Something New in the U.S. Immigrant Experience." In Charles Hirschman, Philip Kasinitz, and Josh DeWind, eds., *The Handbook of International Migration.* New York: Russell Sage Foundation.

Grasmuck, Sherri, and Ramon Grosfoguel. 1997. "Geopolitics, Economic Niches, and Gendered Social Capital Among Recent Caribbean Immigrants in New York City." *Sociological Perspectives* 40:339–64.

Grasmuck, Sherri, and Patricia Pessar. 1991. *Between Two Islands.* Berkeley: University of California Press.

Guo, Zibin. 2000. *Ginseng and Aspirin: Health Care Alternatives for Aging Chinese in New York.* Ithaca: Cornell University Press.

Hedges, Chris. 2000. "Translating America for Parents and Family." *The New York Times,* June 19.

Itzigsohn, Jose, and Carlos Dore-Cabral. 2000. "Competing Identities? Race, Ethnicity and Panethnicity among Dominicans in the United States." *Sociological Forum* 15:225–47.

Jen, Gish. 1992 [1991]. *Typical American.* New York: Penguin.

Jones-Correa, Michael. 1998. *Between Two Nations: The Political Predicament of Latinos in New York.* Ithaca: Cornell University Press.

Joyce, Ted. 2000. "The Prenatal Health and Health Care Utilization of Foreign-Born Women in New York City, 1988–1998." Paper presented at the New School University.

Kasinitz, Philip. 1992. *Caribbean New York: Black Immigrants and the Politics of Race.* Ithaca: Cornell University Press.

——. 1999. "A Third Way to America." *Culturefront* 8:23–29.

——. 2001. "Invisible No More?: West Indian Americans in the Social Scientific Imagination." In Nancy Foner, ed., *Islands in the City: West Indian Migration to New York.* Berkeley: University of California Press.

Kasinitz, Philip, and Milton Vickerman. 2001. "Ethnic Niches and Racial Traps: Jamaicans in the New York Regional Economy." In Hector Cordero-Guzman, Ramon Grosfoguel, and Robert Smith, eds., *Migration, Transnationalism, and the Political Economy of New York.* Philadelphia: Temple University Press.

Kwong, Peter. 1987. *The New Chinatown.* New York: Hill and Wang.

——. 1997. *Forbidden Workers: Illegal Chinese Immigrants and American Labor.* New York: New Press.

Lee, Chang-Rae. 1995. *Native Speaker.* New York: Riverhead Books.

Lee, Jennifer. 1999. "Retail Niche Domination Among African American, Jewish, and Korean Entrepreneurs: Competition, Coethnic Advantage, and Coethnic Disadvantage." *American Behavioral Scientist* 42:1398–1416.

Lessinger, Johanna. 1995. *From the Ganges to the Hudson: Indian Immigrants in New York City.* Boston: Allyn and Bacon.

Levitt, Peggy. 2000. "Migrants Participate Across Borders: Towards an Understanding of Forms and Consequences." In Nancy Foner, Rubén Rumbaut, and Steven Gold, eds., *Immigration Research for a New Century: Multidisciplinary Perspectives.* New York: Russell Sage Foundation.

Liang, Zai, and Naomi Ito. 1999. "Intermarriage of Asian Americans in the New York City Region: Contemporary Patterns and Future Prospects." *International Migration Review* 33:876–900.

Light, Ivan, and Steven J. Gold. 2000. *Ethnic Economies.* San Diego: Academic Press.

Lin, Jan. 1998. *Reconstructing Chinatown: Ethnic Enclave, Global Change.* Minneapolis: University of Minnesota Press.

Lobo, Arun Peter, Joseph Salvo, and Vicky Virgin. 1996. *The Newest New Yorkers, 1990–1994.* New York: Department of City Planning.

Mahler, Sarah. 1995a. *American Dreaming: Immigrant Life on the Margins.* Princeton: Princeton University Press.

——. 1995b. *Salvadorans in Suburbia.* Boston: Allyn and Bacon.

Margolis, Maxine. 1994. *Little Brazil: An Ethnography of Brazilian Immigrants in New York.* Princeton: Princeton University Press.

——. 1998. *An Invisible Minority: Brazilians in New York City.* Boston: Allyn and Bacon.

Markowitz, Fran. 1993. *A Community in Spite of Itself: Soviet Jewish Emigres in New York.* Washington, D.C.: Smithsonian Institution Press.

Massey, Douglas. 1999. "Why Does Immigration Occur? A Theoretical Synthesis." In Charles Hirschman, Philip Kasinitz, and Josh DeWind, eds., *The Handbook of International Migration.* New York: Russell Sage Foundation.

McAlister, Elizabeth. 1998. "The Madonna of 115th Street Revisited: Vodou and Haitian Catholicism in the Age of Transnationalism." In R. Stephen Warner and Judith G. Wittner, eds., *Gatherings in Diaspora.* Philadelphia: Temple University Press.

Michael, Suzanne. 1996. "Immigrant Health in New York City: An Overview of Available Data and Current Issues." The Immigrant New York Series. Working Paper no. 2. New York: New School for Social Research.

Min, Pyong Gap. 1996. *Caught in the Middle: Korean Communities in New York and Los Angeles.* Berkeley: University of California Press.

———. 1998. *Changes and Conflicts: Korean Immigrant Families in New York.* Boston: Allyn and Bacon.

Model, Suzanne. 1993. "The Ethnic Niche and the Structure of Opportunity: Immigrants and Minorities in New York City." In Michael Katz, ed., *The "Underclass" Debate.* Princeton: Princeton University Press.

Mollenkopf, John. 1999. "Urban Political Conflicts and Alliances." In Charles Hirschman, Philip Kasinitz, and Josh DeWind, eds., *The Handbook of International Migration.* New York: Russell Sage Foundation.

New York City Department of City Planning. 1999. *The Newest New Yorkers, 1995–1996.* New York: Department of City Planning.

Ng, Mei. 1998. *Eating Chinese Food Naked.* New York: Washington Square Press.

Opdycke, Sandra. 1995. "New York City Health and Hospitals Corporation." In Kenneth Jackson, ed., *The Encyclopedia of New York City.* New Haven: Yale University Press.

Orleck, Annelise. 1987. "The Soviet Jews: Life in Brighton Beach, Brooklyn." In Nancy Foner, ed., *New Immigrants in New York.* New York: Columbia University Press.

Park, Kyeyoung. 1997. *The Korean American Dream.* Ithaca: Cornell University Press.

Pessar, Patricia. 1987. "The Dominicans: Women in the Household and the Garment Industry." In Nancy Foner, ed., *New Immigrants in New York.* New York: Columbia University Press.

———. 1995. *A Visa for a Dream.* Boston: Allyn and Bacon.

———. 1999. "The Role of Gender, Households and Social Networks in the Migration Process: A Review and Reappraisal." In Charles Hirschman, Philip Kasinitz, and Josh DeWind, eds., *The Handbook of International Migration.* New York: Russell Sage Foundation.

Portes, Alejandro, Luis Guarnizo, and Patricia Landolt. 1999. "Introduction: Pitfalls and Promises of an Emergent Research Field." *Ethnic and Racial Studies* 22:217–37.

Reimers, David. 1992. *Still the Golden Door.* 2d ed. New York: Columbia University Press.

Renshon, Stanley. 2000. "Dual Citizens in America." *Center for Immigration Studies Backgrounder* (July).

Rollwagen, Jack. 1975. "Introduction: The City as Context, A Symposium." *Urban Anthropology* 4:1–4.

Rozhon, Tracie. 2000. "Grit and Glory in South Harlem." *The New York Times,* March 16.

Sanjek, Roger. 1994. "Intermarriage and the Future of Races in the United States." In Steven Gregory and Roger Sanjek, eds., *Race.* New Brunswick: Rutgers University Press.

——. 1998. *The Future of Us All: Race and Neighborhood Politics in New York City.* Ithaca: Cornell University Press.

Sassen, Saskia. 1988. *The Mobility of Labor and Capital.* New York: Cambridge University Press.

——. 1991. *The Global City: New York, London, Tokyo.* Princeton: Princeton University Press.

Schill, Michael H., Samantha Friedman, and Emily Rosenbaum. 1998. "The Housing Conditions of Immigrants in New York City." Working Paper 98–2. New York: New York University School of Law, Center for Real Estate and Urban Policy.

Smith, Michael Peter, and Luis Eduardo Guarnizo, eds. 1998. *Transnationalism from Below.* New Brunswick, N.J.: Transaction.

Torres-Saillant, Silvio. 1999. "Nothing to Celebrate." *Culturefront* 8:41–48.

Urban Anthropology. 1975. "The City as Context: A Symposium" (special issue). 4:1–72.

Vickerman, Milton. 1999. *Crosscurrents: West Indians and Race in America.* New York: Oxford University Press.

——. 2001. "Tweaking a Monolith: The West Indian Encounter with 'Blackness.'" In Nancy Foner, ed., *Islands in the City: West Indian Migration to New York.* Berkeley: University of California Press.

Waldinger, Roger. 1996a. *Still the Promised City? African-Americans and New Immigrants in Postindustrial New York.* Cambridge: Harvard University Press.

——. 1996b. "From Ellis Island to LAX: Immigrant Prospects in the American City." *International Migration Review* 30:1078–86.

——. 1996c. "Ethnicity and Opportunity in the Plural City." In Roger Waldinger and Mehdi Bozorgmehr, eds., *Ethnic Los Angeles.* New York: Russell Sage Foundation.

Waldinger, Roger, and Yenfen Tseng. 1992. "Divergent Diaspora: The Chinese Communities of New York and Los Angeles Compared." *Revue Européene des Migrations Internationales* 8:91–111.

Waters, Mary. 1999. *Black Identities: West Indian Immigrant Dreams and American Realities.* Cambridge: Harvard University Press.

Winnick, Louis. 1990. *New People in Old Neighborhoods.* New York: Russell Sage Foundation.

Wong, Bernard. 1982. *Chinatown: Economic Adaptation and Ethnic Identity of the Chinese.* New York: Holt, Rinehart and Winston.

Wong, Janelle. "Political Participation in the U.S. Among Chinese and Mexican Immigrants: Transnational and Domestic Institutional Contexts." Paper presented at the Social Science Research Council Fellows' Conference, American Identities and Transnational Lives, San Diego, California.

Zhou, Min. 1992. *Chinatown: The Socioeconomic Potential of an Urban Enclave.* Philadelphia: Temple University Press.

Zhou, Min, and Rebecca Kim. 1999. "A Tale of Two Metropolises: Immigrant Chinese Communities in New York and Los Angeles." Paper presented at the conference, Los Angeles and New York in the New Millenium, University of California at Los Angeles.

Zolberg, Aristide. 1999. "Matters of State: Theorizing Immigration Policy." In Charles Hirschman, Philip Kasinitz, and Josh DeWind, eds., *The Handbook of International Migration*. New York: Russell Sage Foundation.

chapter two

Immigration to New York: Policy, Population, and Patterns

Ellen Percy Kraly and Ines Miyares

Introduction[1]

The influx of millions of immigrants into New York City in the last four decades has brought about a dramatic demographic transformation. By 1999, about one third of New York City's population was foreign-born. This level was almost as high as the proportion at the beginning of the twentieth century, and about three times the level in the U.S. population as a whole. New York City also continues to be a major destination for the immigrants who come to the United States. One in ten of the nation's foreign-born lived in New York City in 1999, and figures from the U.S. Immigration and Naturalization Service for the 1990s show the New York metropolitan area as the intended place of residence for the largest number of admitted immigrants.

This chapter describes the levels and trends in immigration that have played a critical role in the social demography of New York City and the larger metropolitan area. Our goal is to provide a social demographic backdrop to the more focused studies of particular immigrant groups that follow in the volume, as well as to assess relevant analytic tools by which patterns of immigration to New York might be considered. In the process, we provide population data that can serve as a reference for general discussions of immigration to and the immigrant populations of New York. We frame this demography of immigration to New York within the context of U.S. immigration and refugee policy, paying close attention to the shifting policy apparatus through which international migration to New York has flowed in recent decades. Even descriptive demographics analysis, however, is challenged by available data sources. Along the way we will call attention to the statistical hazards of U.S. immigration analysis.

We begin by outlining current U.S. immigration and refugee policies as well as the administrative programs that result in the many types of authorized residence among international migrants in the United States. The particular status under the Immigration and Nationality Act is a significant and essential element of day-to-day immigrant life in this country, and accordingly a critical dimension of social research concerning the immigrant experience (Miyares et al. 2000). Next, we present an overview of historical trends in immigration to the United States, by region and major country of origin, as well of the role of international migration in New York population dynamics. A closer look at recent data on the national origins of New York populations reveals differences in ethnic composition at the metropolitan, city, and county levels. We also examine the distribution of immigrant groups across places within the metropolitan area to provide a metropolitan perspective on settlement patterns of groups. Finally, we consider the settlement patterns of each of the immigrant populations discussed in the chapters of this volume.

Providing a Context: U.S. Immigration and Refugee Policies

The causes of historical and contemporary patterns of immigration to New York can be addressed on a variety of levels. At the macroscopic level, for example, economic, social, and political forces result in the structured movement of labor and the displacement of populations. This level of analysis, well represented in works such as Castles and Miller (1998), Sassen (1996) and Zolberg et al. (1986), draws attention to the increasingly transnational nature of the world's population and the subsequent changing character of migration and refugee resettlement to the United States. At the other end of the analytical spectrum is the unique combination of factors that motivate particular individuals to move to New York City—and these individuals' perceptions of their reasons for migrating.

Whether the analysis of the causes of international migration to New York and the United States focuses on the international or the individual level, immigration law and administration—the gatekeeping factors—must be considered. The immigration policy of the United States plays a significant role in determining the size and composition of legal as well as illegal migration streams. Moreover, a meaningful aspect of the immigration process to the immigrants themselves is their interaction with U.S. legal and bureaucratic arrangements. Aliens migrating to the United States are required to appreciate the intricacies of federal immigration law and administration, if only to complete the correct application forms. The New York District Office of the U.S. Immigration and Naturalization Service, located at Federal Plaza in lower Manhattan, may well be considered a landmark that contrasts sharply to Miss Liberty, standing just across the channel.

A few definitions of relevant legal concepts are in order before we elaborate on U.S. immigration policy. *Immigrants* are aliens who are legally admitted with an immigrant visa to the United States for permanent resident status. These persons obtain a "green card" and are accorded those civil rights consistent with status as a resident of the United States. Permanent resident aliens have the opportunity to obtain U.S. citizenship through the process of *naturalization,* usually after approximately five years of residence in the United States. *Admission* as an immigrant is also a legal term referring to the date immigrant status is conferred, not necessarily the date of entry to the country.

Nonimmigrants are aliens admitted on temporary visas for specific purposes for a defined period. Tourists and businesspersons, the largest groups of nonimmigrants, are usually authorized to remain in the United States for six months before an extension of stay is required. Students and employees of foreign governments and international organizations are nonimmigrants who may be authorized to reside in the United States for a much longer period. Several categories of temporary workers are identified in legislation, including temporary workers with specialty occupations (H1-B visas), workers in occupations (both agricultural and nonagricultural) for which U.S. workers cannot be found (H2 visas), and persons with exceptional talents in the arts and sciences (O and P visas). The policies governing the admission of temporary migrants to the United States are rarely included in discussions of national immigration policy. By far, nonimmigrants constitute the majority of foreign travelers and the majority of aliens entering the United States. These travelers vary in their impact on national social institutions and economic sectors as well as on particular localities. In the case of New York, for example, there are large numbers of foreign government officials, students, international representatives, intracompany transferees, and, certainly, tourists. For certain of these groups, length of stay in New York may be significant, often several years (see Kraly and Warren 1991, 1992).

Refugee status was narrowly defined under the 1965 immigration amendments as persons fleeing a Communist-dominated state or areas in the Middle East. The Refugee Act of 1980 broadened the definition to be consistent with the concept endorsed by the United Nations. Hence a refugee is

any person who is outside his or her country of nationality who is unable or unwilling to return to that country because of persecution or a well-founded fear of persecution. Persecution or the fear thereof may be based on the alien's race, religion, nationality, membership in a particular social group, or political opinion. (U.S. Department of Justice 1999, A.3–9-10)

However, as we will discuss later, refugee status is still conferred primarily in cold-war terms. Refugee applications are processed in either countries of origin or countries of first asylum[2] by federal or international agencies and then are admitted for permanent resettlement in the United States. Refugees are eligible to adjust to permanent resident status after one year's residence in the United States and may apply for naturalization after five year's residence. *Asylees* are aliens who enter the United States either on temporary visas or as undocumented entrants and who request and receive political asylum after arrival. A growing group of entrants are those under *temporary protected status;* these are awaiting evaluation of their request for asylum.

Policies Regarding Permanent Residence

Contemporary U.S. immigration policy has been evolving in punctuated steps over the past fifty years. The basic statute, the Immigration and Nationality Act, was codified in 1952. That act, also known as the McCarran-Walter Act after its principal authors, embodied the system of national origins quotas that had been set in place in the 1920s. The national origins quota system, as it stood in 1952, applied to Eastern Hemisphere nations. Visas for permanent residence were distributed on the basis of nativity and, in the case of Asians, race, within an annual limit for the Eastern Hemisphere of approximately 156,000. Annual quotas were figured on the basis of the ethnic composition of the U.S. population according to the 1920 census and, as with the quota laws of the 1920s,[3] favored what has been termed the "old-stock" northern and western Europeans. Spouses and children of U.S. citizens, however, were exempt from quota restrictions. There were no numerical limits on immigration from the Western Hemisphere (South, Central, and North America and the Caribbean). The "good neighbor" policy, instituted by the Roosevelt administration in the 1930s, was maintained, allowing unrestricted immigration from independent Western Hemisphere countries, although individuals could be denied entry on the basis of statutory grounds for inadmissibility.

Although the Immigration and Nationality Act of 1952 perpetuated a highly discriminatory system for granting immigrant visas, it did initiate certain important shifts in policy. The law created a preference system for quota visa distribution that reflected the evolving immigration policy goals concerning family reunification and occupational skills. Top priority was given to those with skills needed in the United States, then to close relatives of U.S. citizens and permanent residents. Moreover, the act continued the piecemeal, though very minor, modifications of the laws barring Asian immigration. These bars, introduced in 1882 to exclude Chinese laborers,[4] had been extended to virtually all Asians in the first decades of the 1900s. Japanese immigration was restricted by the "gentleman's agreement" of 1907, according to which the Japanese government agreed to no longer issue passports to persons seeking employment in the United States. This restriction was extended to Korea in 1910 after Japan annexed that country. Congress established the Asiatic Barred Zone in 1917 to prevent immigration from the remaining areas of Asia.[5] A significant exception was the status of Filipinos. The Philippines had become a U.S. territory as a result of the Spanish-American War of 1898. Filipinos were able to migrate to and from the United States freely until the 1930s, when annual quotas of only fifty visas were imposed.

A shift in immigration policy came with World War II and evolving diplomatic relations in Asia. The Chinese exclusion laws were repealed in 1943 because China was an ally during the war, and an annual quota for Chinese nationals, though only for 105 visas, was authorized. In 1946, a small number of immigrants from India were authorized to enter. The War Brides Act of 1945 allowed Asian women who had married American soldiers stationed in the Pacific Theater to enter the United States. The volume of total Asian immigration, however, remained severely restricted. The 1952 act gave a quota of 100 visas per year to each independent Asian country that had previously been denied a quota, but a limit of 2,000 persons annually was applied to an "Asia-Pacific triangle." Furthermore, visas for Asians were awarded on the basis of race and ethnicity rather than country of birth as for other groups. A person of Chinese ancestry, for example, came under the quota restriction for China even if he or she had been born in another part of the world.

The McCarran-Walter Act and the injustices it legitimized served as stimuli for immigration reform. During the 1950s public commissions and private groups called for comprehensive change in immigration policy. Although few changes were made in the immigration statute in that decade, interests were articulated and evidence was amassed supporting policy revisions. The discriminatory structure of the law raised difficult issues in foreign relations. Perhaps more important, the law was inconsistent with the nature of the demand for immigration to the United States. Between 1956 and 1965, only 35 percent of all immigrants admitted were quota immigrants, the rest being immediate relatives of U.S. citizens or emigrants from countries in the Western Hemisphere. Another 300,000 people were admitted as refugees during this period but were outside the bounds of the immigrant provisions of the Immigration and Nationality Act.

The 1965 amendments to the Immigration and Nationality Act represented a dramatic shift in policy. The principle of national origins as a basis for selecting immigrants was explicitly rejected. Instead, immigrant visas were to be issued on a first-come, first-served basis according to the visa preference system. The 1965 amendments applied this system to countries in the Eastern Hemisphere within an annual ceiling of 170,000 (preference) visas with a per-country limit of 20,000 each year. Also, for the first time a numerical limitation on immigration from the Western Hemisphere was set in place. The 120,000 annual ceiling was not distributed according to the preference system, however; nor was the 20,000-per-country limit imposed on Western Hemisphere nations.

In 1976, the Immigration and Nationality Act was again amended to apply the preference system and per-country limit to the 120,000 ceiling for countries of the Western Hemisphere. The logical next step occurred in 1978, when specific hemispheric limits were abolished and an annual worldwide ceiling of 290,000 immigrant visas was introduced. The Refugee Act of 1980 reduced this level to 270,000 (separate allocations for refugees were made available at that time; see the section "Refugee Policies and Programs"). Thus, for the most part, the last statutory vestige of discrimination on the basis of nationality was eliminated.

The emphasis on family reunification in current immigration policy is clear. First, the law does not restrict the annual immigration of immediate relatives (spouses and unmarried minor children) of U.S. citizens; moreover, this category was expanded from the 1952 law to include parents of adult U.S. citizens. Similarly, the preference system was modified in 1965 to emphasize even further the goal of bringing together immigrant families. Since those amendments, however, the preference system has been restructured to also grant visas on the basis of occupational skill and job creation. The current system is shown in table 2.1, which embodies the changes introduced in the Immigration Act of 1990. This legislation created a flexible annual level of immigration that was targeted at 675,000 immigrants each year, composed of 480,000 immigrants admitted as im-

Table 2.1 Visa Preference System

Preference	Description	Limit
Family-sponsored preferences		**226,000**
First	Unmarried sons and daughters of U.S. citizens and their children	23,400[a]
Second	Spouses, children, and unmarried sons and daughters of permanent resident aliens	114,200[b]
Third	Married sons and daughters of U.S. citizens and their spouses and children	23,400[b]
Fourth	Brothers and sisters of U.S. citizens (at least 21 years of age) and their spouses and children	65,000[b]
Employment-based preferences		**140,000**
First	Priority workers and their spouses and children	40,040[c]
Second	Professionals with advanced degrees or aliens of exceptional ability and their spouses and children	40,040[b]
Third	Skilled workers, professional (without advanced degrees), needed unskilled workers, and their spouses and children	40,040[b]
Fourth	Special immigrants and their spouses and children. The number of certain religious workers is limited to 5,000.	9,940
Fifth	Employment creation ("Investors") and their spouses and children	9,940
Diversity immigrants		**55,000**

Notes: [a]Plus unused family fourth preference visas. [b]Visas not used in higher preferences may be used in these categories. [c]Plus unused employment fourth and fifth preference visas.

mediate relatives or under family-based preferences, 140,000 immigrants admitted under employment-based preferences, and 55,000 "diversity" immigrants. Three of the four family-based preferences facilitate the immigration of relatives of U.S. citizens (adult children of U.S. citizens, and adult siblings); the second preference, by far the largest in visa allocation, is for spouses, minor children, and unmarried adult children of permanent resident aliens.

The employment-based preferences generally require authorization through the U.S. Department of Labor that employment sought in the United States by the alien applicant will not displace domestic workers or depress working conditions. This is the general process of labor certification. There are five employment-based preferences. The first defines priority workers as "(1) persons of extraordinary ability, (2) outstanding professors and researchers, and (3) certain multinational executives and managers" (U.S. Department of Justice 1999:A.2–3). The second preference refers to professionals and the third preference to skilled and needed unskilled workers. Special immigrants (ministers of religion, former employees of the U.S. government and Armed Forces, certain retirees of international organizations, etc.) had been exempt from numerical restriction before the 1990 law and are now admitted under the fourth preference. The fifth, or employment creation, preference grants admission to persons who are able to generate jobs for ten or more U.S. workers and also to bring sufficient capital for investment; since its inception, this preference category has been largely undersubscribed.

Finally, the current preference system includes 55,000 diversity visas. Codified in the Immigration Act of 1990, the U.S. Diversity Immigrant Visa Lottery Program annually makes 55,000 permanent resident visas available by lottery to aliens from countries with low immigration rates, commonly because of the shift in the 1965 amendments to family reunification as a visa priority. Eligible countries change from year to year based on how preference visas are awarded.[6]

To a certain degree, the structure of the preference system set up in 1965 frustrated immigration from Western Europe by emphasizing family relationships, which benefited more recent immigrants. But probably more important has been the decline in the demand for permanent migration to the United States from Western industrialized nations. In the case of Spanish-speaking countries of the Caribbean and Latin America, recent U.S. immigration policy has hardly stimulated immigration since it actually imposed numerical limits on these nations for the first time. Rather, economic conditions and political turmoil have been the major stimuli for the dramatic increase in migration to the United States from these areas since 1964. Finally, recent U.S. policy toward refugees has permitted large movements of refugees from Cuba, Southeast Asia, and the former Soviet Union.

The elimination of unrestricted immigration from Western Hemisphere countries by the 1965 amendments, along with the termination of special labor programs such as the Bracero Program[7] and an increasing demand for visas, resulted in a growth of undocumented immigration to the United States. The issue of the appropriate policy response to the undocumented alien population in the United States has dominated recent debate on immigration reform. The empirical foundation for policy analysis in this area is porous, in spite of the pervasive images of both the size and growth of the illegal population and the consequences of the phenomenon for U.S. economy and society. The official policy concerning undocumented immigration is to prevent entry into the United States by identification during the process of inspection at ports of entry, apprehension as soon as possible of persons entering surreptitiously between ports, and the identification of aliens violating the terms of their visas. Immigration policy initiatives enacted during the past two decades have included provisions to both regularize the status of the undocumented who have lived in the United States for a relatively extended period, and reduce illegal entry and visa overstay through better enforcement and identification.[8]

After more than a decade of various reform packages, Congress passed the Immigration Reform and Control Act (IRCA) in October 1986. Its most important provision was to authorize legalization for aliens who could prove they had resided in the United States continually, although without appropriate visas, since January 1, 1982. Additionally, it created employer sanctions for being actively involved in the employment of aliens not authorized to work. Before this time, undocumented aliens and those on temporary visas with employment restrictions were sanctioned, deported, or both for working without proper authorization, but there were no sanctions on employers for hiring or recruiting aliens unauthorized to work. IRCA also increased the number of visas under the preference system awarded to dependencies from 600 to 5,000 and allocated 5,000 nonpreference visas for each of the fiscal years 1987 and 1988 for countries adversely affected by the 1965 act, thus anticipating the diversity program implemented in the Immigration Act of 1990.

Refugee Policies and Programs

As with general immigration policy, the past few decades have witnessed dramatic changes in the national stance concerning the admission and settlement of refugees. Immigration laws and their subsequent emendations have been responses to changing attitudes toward immigration in general and selected source regions in particular. Refugee laws have differed in that they have tended to be ad hoc responses to post–World War II cold-war population movements. Thus, despite the use of the United Nations definition of a refugee, entry into the United States with that status has been principally limited to those fleeing Communist states. Even so, the United States has accepted for permanent resettlement more refugees since World War II than has any other country.

The roots of current refugee policy are found in various responses by the federal government to persons and populations displaced by World War II. Nearly

600,000 European refugees displaced by the war were admitted between 1945 and 1957 through presidential directive and by a series of federal statutes (Kraly 1990). The next wave of refugees followed the 1956 Hungarian uprising. A new mechanism—the parole authority of the attorney general—facilitated the admission of approximately 80,000 refugees from Hungary, and subsequently from the Cuban and Nicaraguan revolutions. Between 1959 and 1980, nearly 800,000 Cubans entered the United States for resettlement (Boswell and Curtis 1984), many as parolees.

The majority of the Cuban refugees who arrived in the first few years after the revolution settled in Miami and were from the upper and middle classes of Cuban society and thus educated professionals. Despite high levels of human capital, the Cubans needed assistance with initial resettlement needs such as housing, food, clothes, and jobs. Because they anticipated that the revolution would be short-lived, the majority of the refugees remained in the Miami area, overloading both the pre-existing Cuban community and social service agencies. In response, the Kennedy administration initiated the Cuban Refugee Program in 1961, later codified as the Refugee Resettlement Act of 1962, which attempted to relocate Cuban families to states other than Florida through incentives such as job placements, temporary financial assistance, and various welfare benefits. Approximately 300,000 Cubans participated in the refugee program, although many ultimately migrated back to Miami.

The Cuban Refugee Program laid the framework for subsequent refugee resettlement legislation. The 1965 amendments to the Immigration and Nationality Act sought to incorporate the admission of refugees within general immigration policy. A seventh preference was applied to conditional entrants, narrowly defined as persons fleeing a Communist state or the Middle East, and 6 percent of preference visas were allotted to this category. Adjustment to permanent resident status could occur after a two-year stay in the United States. Only a small number of visas for refugees were available under these provisions, and until 1976 those visas were allocated only to Eastern Hemisphere countries. This did not give the Immigration and Naturalization Service (INS) the ability to respond to refugee crises such as the continued exodus from Cuba (including the Mariel boatlift) and refugee waves following the 1979 Nicaraguan revolution. As before, the attorney general's authority was used, and again, subsequent congressional action has been required to provide a legal basis for resettlement.

The withdrawal of U.S. troops from Vietnam and the fall of South Vietnamese, Cambodian, and Lao governments to Communist regimes resulted in massive waves of refugees escaping new governments that sought retribution for wartime allegiances to the United States since 1975. The initial response was the Immigration and Refugee Assistance Act of 1975, through which the federal government subcontracted numerous volunteer agencies, referred to as volags, to assist in providing initial counseling and placing refugee families with individuals, families, and organizations willing to be sponsors. Sponsors then provided for the basic needs of refugee families assigned to them, including food, clothing, housing, and job placement for the first thirty days of residence in the United States (Zaharlick and Brainard 1987). The initial wave of approximately 130,400 Southeast Asian refugees, composed primarily of urban, educated, and often English-speaking Vietnamese, began arriving in 1975 after the fall of Saigon.

The second major wave, commencing in 1979, was larger in number, more diverse (including Vietnamese, Cambodian, Lao, Hmong, and numerous other Lao ethnic minorities). and had much greater immediate and long-term needs than the first wave. As many of these immigrants were poor farmers and fishermen, they were commonly illiterate or had received very little education and possessed few marketable skills. In response, Congress passed the Refugee Act of 1980, raising the ceiling on numbers of refugees admitted and establishing the Office of Refugee Resettlement (ORR). The ORR subcontracted the provision of resettlement services such as employment counseling, job training, English-language instruction, and physical and mental health care to numerous public and private nonprofit agencies. Additionally, refugees were automatically eligible to receive public assistance in the form of both cash payments and Medicaid for the first eighteen months after arrival (Miyares 1998a:12; Zaharlick and Brainard 1987:333).

Since the end of the Vietnam war, nearly one million refugees from the region have been resettled in the United States, although only a relatively small proportion came to reside in New York City. The contemporary refugee movement that has impacted New York City more than any other has been that from the former Soviet Union. Between 1975 and 1994, the United States resettled nearly 412,300 refugees from the various states of the former Soviet Union. This was the third-largest refugee group to enter the United States since World War II. In fact, since 1988, refugees from the former Soviet Union have been the largest country-of-origin group, surpassing the Vietnamese in numbers of annual entrants (Office of Refugee Resettlement, 1994). More than a quarter of the former Soviets entering the United States during this period settled in New York City. Between 1990 and 1994, the number of entrants from the former Soviet Union settling in New York City ranked second behind immigrants from the Dominican Republic, and by 1995–1996, Russians comprised the largest number of entrants (Miyares 1998b; New York City Department of City Planning 1996). Former Soviets arrived with substantial human capital—they were older and better educated than most recent immigrants (Chiswick 1993; Gold 1988, 1992; Miyares 1998b; New York City Department of City Planning, 1996). However, many were skilled in areas rooted in Russian culture that were not marketable in the American mainstream economy (e.g., musicians, artists, journalists, poets, athletes in sports not played in the United States). As with Cubans and Southeast Asians, they have initially relied on the assistance of sponsors and refugee programs before applying for permanent residence.

Political Asylum and Temporary Protected Status

A growing number of immigrants from countries in turmoil enter the United States without documentation and request political asylum on arrival. Some political asylees are from the same origin countries as refugees, such as Cuba and the republics of the former Soviet Union. However, most are from countries experiencing current or recent civil wars or are individuals targeted for oppression for reasons listed in the United Nations (UN) Protocol on Refugees. Because these persons request protection *after* entering the United States, they do not qualify for refugee assistance. If they would otherwise qualify for refugee status, they are either paroled or expeditiously granted asylum. If not, they can apply for *temporary protected status* while awaiting the adjudication of their asylum application.

Temporary protected status (TPS) was originally granted to Salvadorans in 1990 in response to the growing numbers of entrants from then war-torn El Salvador seeking political asylum in the United States. Although most met the requirements of the UN Protocol on Refugees, Salvadorans were not leaving a Communist state, making their requests for asylum difficult to adjudicate. TPS has since been extended to entrants in similar situations—those who meet the UN criteria for refugee status but not the U.S. criterion of "victim of Communism." Those on TPS receive a Social Security number and apply for renewable one-year work permits to be legally employable while awaiting a decision on their asylum case. If granted asylum, they become eligible to apply for permanent residence. If denied asylum, they can petition to have their deportation order suspended by meeting criteria defined by the 1996 Illegal Immigration Reform and Immigrant Responsibility Act, or IIRIRA.[9] While awaiting deportation hearings, these "temporary" immigrants can remain legally employable by applying annually for one-year work permits while the IRS considers their cases. The structure of TPS and the process of suspension of deportation allow qualified entrants to remain in the United States in a quasi-documented state for extended periods of time.[10]

Issues in Social Demographic Research on International Migration to the United States

The problems of U.S. statistics on international migration have been well documented (see Kraly 1987:49–52). In several important ways U.S. immigration statistical resources have improved in the past two decades, although specific conceptual and analytic issues continue to plague research on temporal and spatial dimensions of international migration to and from the United States.

A critical discourse has developed within the scientific community on the need to improve national statistics on international migration (Hutchinson 1958; Tomasi and Keely 1975; Kraly 1979, 1998; Levine, Hill, and Warren 1985; Woodrow-Lafield 1998; Van Hook and Bean 1998a, b). Ten years after the recommendations of the National Academy of Sciences Panel on Immigration Statistics, another critical assessment of national immigration data was conducted by the National Research Council, Committee on National Statistics (Edmonston 1996), which identified the importance of collecting reliable data on national origins, immigrant status, immigrant experiences over time in the United States, and the social context of immigration. Specifically, the report recommended (1) the addition of questions concerning immigration to both decennial census and the Current Population Survey, (2) coordinated research on migration between the United States and Mexico, (3) initiation of a longitudinal survey of immigrants in the United States, and (4) improvement of INS data for policy research.[11]

The U.S. INS continues to be the primary source of data on the number and characteristics of persons entering the United States from other countries. Statistics on persons admitted to the United States as immigrants and nonimmigrants (as well as other legal and administrative categories under the Immigration and Nationality Act) are published and available from INS in varying degrees of detail in annual and monthly reports.[12] Also available to researchers are public-use microdata files for annual cohorts of immigrant admissions.

INS statistics on immigration, that is, admission of permanent resident aliens, are most often used to measure the flow of international migration to the United States. Several major problems persist in the use of these data for population analysis. First, in any year, the number of immigrant admissions includes persons already in the United States who are adjusting status to that of permanent residence and thus should not be counted as adding to the population in that year. From 1995 to 1998, between 46 and 54 percent of immigrant admissions were composed of persons adjusting status (U.S. Department of Justice 1999, table 1). In recent annual reports, INS statistical tabulations on immigrants have increasingly differentiated new arrivals from adjustments, and this information is also available in microdata records. Another problem is that statistics on immigrants do not include the number of nonimmigrants (and undocumented migrants) who remain in the United States for a significant length of time. For example, the UN Statistical Commission recommends that persons remaining in (or intending to remain in) the country of destination for one year or more be classified as long-term immigrants. Kraly and Warren (1992) have shown that the number of non-immigrants whose length of stay in the United States is at least one year is likely to exceed 100,000 annually.[13]

The lack of reliable INS statistics on immigrants' destinations has also been a problem for research on the regional and local impacts of immigration to the United States. Without a longitudinal database on immigrants, researchers using INS data must rely on the place of intended residence as reported by aliens on their visa applications or the current residence for aliens who are already in the country and are adjusting to permanent resident status. Thus, these data reflect two different concepts, and their reliability is not well known. Published tabulations provide detail on the state of intended residence as well as selected metropolitan areas.

For purposes of research on immigration to New York City and the greater metropolitan area, perhaps the most significant improvement in INS statistical resources has been the priority given to the analysis of these data by the Department of City Planning of the City of New York. In the past decade, demographers and statisticians within the City Planning Department's Population Division, in coordination with the INS Statistics Branch, have developed an impeccable program of research on immigration in the New York City and metropolitan region using INS statistical and information systems. The report, *The NEWEST New Yorkers, 1990–1994,* provides extensively detailed analysis of the flow, characteristics, and settlement patterns among immigrants to New York City (New York City Department of City Planning 1996).[14] The analysis of immigration to New York offered in the following paragraphs builds on the strengths of that study.

U.S. census data pertaining to international migration have also been improved in the past decade, notably by the inclusion on the control card of the Current Population Survey (CPS) of questions on place of birth (and thus country of birth), and parents' place of birth.. This monthly survey now provides reliable estimates of the size and characteristics of the foreign population at the national level and for selected states, metropolitan statistical areas (MSAs), and cities. Of course, census concepts relevant for immigration research, specificity, nativity, and the identification of the foreign-born population are not the same as statistical concepts measured in INS data collection systems. But undoubtedly, the recurring collection of data on the foreign-born population in the CPS exists as a major contribution to national and regional research on the composition and distribution of immigrant populations in the United States.[15]

Three final research issues should be noted. First, tracing demographic change in the New York metropolitan area is complicated because the boundaries of metropolitan areas change from one decennial census to the next. In 1980, the New York standard metropolitan statistical area (SMSA) was composed of the five New York City counties (which comprised the central city of the SMSA) and the suburban "ring," composed of the two Long Island counties (Nassau and Suffolk), three New York counties north of the city (Westchester, Putnam, and Rockland), and Bergen County, just over the Hudson River in New Jersey. In 1990 census tabulations, however, the New York metropolitan area became one component of the larger New York–New Jersey–Connecticut–Pennsylvania consolidated metropolitan statistical area (CMSA),[16] with a population of over 18.1 million, and by 1999 an estimated 20.5 million (U.S. Bureau of the Census, 1993; Urban Institute 2000). The NY-NJ-CT-PA CMSA is composed of fifteen primary metropolitan statistical areas (PMSAs),[17] of which the New York PMSA is one. The New York PMSA is composed of the five counties of New York City plus Westchester, Rockland, and Putnam counties. Nassau and Suffolk counties, which in 1980 were part of the New York SMSA, were identified as a PMSA in 1990; similarly, Bergen County was grouped in the Bergen-Passaic, New Jersey, PMSA in 1990.

The second research issue has to do with the processes of emigration, return migration, and circulation among New York's immigrant populations. Because demographic information on out-migration from the United States remains elusive (Warren and Kraly 1985; Kraly 1998; Dashefsky 2000), we are unable to provide a quantitative portrait of the degree to which immigrants return to their countries of origin, move on to new locations, or circulate between their communities of origin and New York. Finally, there are difficulties in determining the role of unauthorized immigration in the social demography of New York (see Van Hook and Bean 1998a, b; Woodrow-Lafield 1998). INS statisticians have produced recent national estimates of the unauthorized immigrant population, building on methodology developed to "incorporate new data on the foreign-born population collected by the Census Bureau, improvements in the methodology recommended by the General Accounting Office (GAO), suggestions provided by outside reviewers, and further analyses of INS's data sources and estimation procedures" (U.S. Immigration and Naturalization Service 2000a). Using this approach, the unauthorized immigrant population resident in the United States in 1996 was estimated at about 5.0 million, and within a range of about 4.6 to 5.4 million. INS statisticians also estimated an increase in the undocumented population by about 275,000 persons each year, which is lower than previous estimates of annual change. It is estimated that Mexicans comprise over half this population, followed by persons from El Salvador and Guatemala, although it is acknowledged that estimates for these countries are likely to include persons in temporary protected status who are authorized to remain in the United States. Using this methodology the resident unauthorized immigrant population in New York State was an estimated 540,000 persons in 1996 (U.S. Immigration and Naturalization Service 2000a). Also derived from the estimation procedure were measures of the legal permanent resident alien population for 1996 for each of the fifty states. The estimate for New York State was 1,498,000, of whom 669,000 were eligible to apply for U.S. citizenship (U.S. Immigration and Naturalization Service 2000b).

Information on the size and characteristics of New York's undocumented migrant population also came as a by-product of the implementation of IRCA. Under this legalization program, 125,700 persons in New York City regularized their status, 92,200 as legalized aliens and 35,500 within the Seasonal Agricultural Workers (SAWS) program. The leading source countries and levels for legalizing aliens residing in New York City were as follows: Dominican Republic, 11,900; Mexico, 9,300; Haiti, 8,600; Colombia, 8,600; and Pakistan, 7,100 (New York City Department of City Planning 1996:xiii).

Immigration to the United States and to New York

The first and last decades of the twentieth century were characterized by high levels of immigration to the United States. These levels are shown in table 2.2 for decades between 1891 and 1998. The first decade of the twentieth century witnessed the largest number of immigrants admitted to the United States (8.8 million), the vast majority (92 percent) originating in Europe. Declining levels of immigration between 1911 and 1941 reflect increasingly restrictive immigration policies as well as warfare and turmoil in Europe and the Great Depression. During these decades, growing proportions of immigrants came from Canada and Mexico. Since World War II, levels of immigration have increased in each decade, going from 2.5 million to 7.3 million between the decades of 1951–1960 and 1981–1990. With the end of the national origins quota system in 1965, the national origin composition of immigrant streams shifted to include larger proportions of Asians. During 1961–1970, 13 percent of immigrant admissions originated from countries in Asia. In the next decade this proportion increased to 35 percent and has remained at about that level in subsequent decades.

In the last decade of the twentieth century, U.S. immigration kept up at a steady pace: between 1991 and 1998, 7.6 million immigrants were admitted as permanent resident aliens. In the ten-year period from 1989 to 1998, 10.2 million immigrants were admitted. Though this might be considered a century record, recall that "admission" is a legal-administrative concept; nearly 2.7 million, or 26 percent, of these immigrants were persons in the process of legalization under IRCA and thus had resided in the United States since before 1982. The national origin profile of IRCA immigrants is strikingly different from that of other immigrant admissions. Three-quarters of those persons in the process of legalization under IRCA between 1989 and 1998 reported their country of last residence as Mexico, and about 13 percent reported prior residence in Caribbean and Central American countries. Among non-IRCA immigrants admitted during these years, Mexico was also the leading single country of last residence but constituted only 13 percent of total admissions.

What about New York City? As shown in figure 2.1, between the early 1980s and mid 1990s, the annual level of immigration to New York increased from about 60,000 to 120,000, also reflecting the spike in levels during the years of IRCA admissions. Overall, the proportion of U.S. immigrants reporting intended residence in New York City has varied, remaining close to 20 percent between 1965 and 1975 and declining in the early 1990s, when the largest proportions of IRCA immigrants resided in California. The share of immigrants intending to reside in New York increased to over 15 percent in the mid-1990s but declined in the late 1990s. It is notable that except for those years of the highest levels of IRCA admissions, 1989–1992, New York has been the city of intended residence reported by the largest number of U.S. immigrants.

Immigration and Population Change in New York

International migration flows to the United States and to New York are reflected in the stock of immigrants in the population at any single point in time. As shown

Table 2.2 Immigration to the United States, by Area and Selected Country of Last Residence, 1881–1998

Area and country of last permanent residence	1881–1890	1891–1900	1901–1910	1911–1920	1921–1930	1931–1940	1941–1950	1951–1960	1961–1970	1971–1980	1981–1990	1991–1998	1989–98 Total	1989–98 IRCA[b]	1989–98 non-IRCA
						Number									
Total immigration	5,246,613	3,687,564	8,795,386	5,735,811	4,107,209	528,431	1,035,039	2,515,479	3,321,677	4,493,314	7,338,062	7,605,068	10,232,475	2,688,395	7,544,080
Europe	4,735,484	3,555,352	8,056,040	4,321,887	2,463,194	347,566	621,147	1,325,727	1,123,492	800,368	761,550	1,132,002	1,350,366	39,302	1,311,064
Germany	1,452,970	505,152	341,498	143,945	412,202	114,058	226,578	477,756	190,796	74,414	91,961	72,792	95,263	1,763	93,500
Ireland	655,482	388,416	339,065	146,181	211,234	10,973	19,789	48,362	32,966	11,490	31,969	54,865	71,588	1,288	70,300
Italy	307,309	651,893	2,045,877	1,109,524	455,315	68,028	57,661	185,491	214,111	129,368	67,254	58,346	85,681	1,138	84,543
Poland	16,978	96,720	(a)	4,813	227,734	17,026	7,571	9,985	53,539	37,234	83,252	145,487	177,130	16,036	161,094
Soviet Union	213,282	505,290	1,597,306	921,201	61,742	1,370	571	61	2,465	38,961	57,677	386,327	405,676	42	405,634
United Kingdom	807,357	271,538	525,950	341,408	339,570	31,572	139,306	202,824	213,822	137,374	159,173	128,671	164,686	7,722	156,964
Asia	69,942	74,862	323,543	247,236	112,059	16,595	37,028	153,249	427,642	1,588,178	2,738,157	2,436,751	3,055,050	120,674	2,934,376
China	61,711	14,799	20,605	21,278	29,907	4,928	16,709	9,657	34,764	124,326	346,747	289,954	334,791	4,275	330,516
India	269	68	4,713	2,082	1,886	496	1,761	1,973	27,189	164,134	250,786	295,633	353,041	17,743	335,298
Japan	2,270	25,942	129,797	83,837	33,462	1,948	1,555	46,250	39,988	49,775	47,085	55,442	67,327	1,634	65,693
North America	424,663	37,897	344,608	1,101,772	1,474,470	152,209	303,697	845,605	1,438,790	1,685,999	3,152,920	3,334,129	4,910,662	2,393,463	2,517,199
Canada	393,304	3,311	179,226	742,185	924,515	108,527	171,718	377,952	413,310	169,939	156,938	357,564	400,500	13,482	387,018
Mexico	1,913	971	49,642	219,004	459,287	22,319	60,589	299,811	453,937	640,294	1,655,843	1,931,237	3,017,083	2,011,269	1,005,814
Carribean	29,042	33,066	107,548	123,424	74,899	15,502	49,725	123,091	470,213	741,126	872,051	822,526	1,022,758	110,402	912,356
Central America	404	549	8,192	17,159	15,769	5,861	21,665	44,751	101,330	134,640	468,088	422,766	670,282	258,318	411,964
South America	2,304	1,075	17,280	41,899	42,215	7,803	21,831	91,628	257,954	295,741	461,847	443,152	589,785	92,754	497,031
Africa	857	350	7,368	8,443	6,286	1,750	7,367	14,092	28,954	80,779	176,893	280,230	335,512	37,047	298,465
Oceania	12,574	3,965	13,024	13,427	8,726	2,483	14,551	12,976	25,122	41,242	45,205	45,584	57,539	5,438	52,101
Country not specified	789	14,063	33,523	1,147	228	0	142	12,491	93	12	1,032	23,220	23,561	717	22,844

Percent

Total immigration	100.0	100.0	100.0	100.0	100.0	100.0	100.0	100.0	100.0	100.0	100.0	100.0	100.0	100.0	100.0
Europe	90.3	96.4	91.6	75.3	60.0	65.8	60.0	52.7	33.8	17.8	10.4	14.9	13.2	1.5	17.4
Germany	27.7	13.7	3.9	2.5	10.0	21.6	21.9	19.0	5.7	1.7	1.3	1.0	0.9	0.1	1.2
Ireland	12.5	10.5	3.9	2.5	5.1	2.1	1.9	1.9	1.0	0.3	0.4	0.7	0.7	0.0	0.9
Italy	5.9	17.7	23.3	19.3	11.1	12.9	5.6	7.4	6.4	2.9	0.9	0.8	0.8	0.0	1.1
Poland	0.3	2.6	(a)	0.1	5.5	3.2	0.7	0.4	1.6	0.8	1.1	1.9	1.7	0.6	2.1
Soviet Union	4.1	13.7	18.2	16.1	1.5	0.3	0.1	0.0	0.1	0.9	0.8	5.1	4.0	0.0	5.4
United Kingdom	15.4	7.4	6.0	6.0	8.3	6.0	13.5	8.1	6.4	3.1	2.2	1.7	1.6	0.3	2.1
Asia	1.3	2.0	3.7	4.3	2.7	3.1	3.6	6.1	12.9	35.3	37.3	32.0	29.9	4.5	38.9
China	1.2	0.4	0.2	0.4	0.7	0.9	1.6	0.4	1.0	2.8	4.7	3.8	3.3	0.2	4.4
India	0.0	0.0	0.1	0.0	0.0	0.1	0.2	0.1	0.8	3.7	3.4	3.9	3.5	0.7	4.4
Japan	0.0	0.7	1.5	1.5	0.8	0.4	0.2	1.8	1.2	1.1	0.6	0.7	0.7	0.1	0.9
North America	8.1	1.0	3.9	19.2	35.9	28.8	29.3	33.6	43.3	37.5	43.0	43.8	48.0	89.0	33.4
Canada	7.5	0.1	2.0	12.9	22.5	20.5	16.6	15.0	12.4	3.8	2.1	4.7	3.9	0.5	5.1
Mexico	0.0	0.0	0.6	3.8	11.2	4.2	5.9	11.9	13.7	14.2	22.6	25.4	29.5	74.8	13.3
Carribean	0.6	0.9	1.2	2.2	1.8	2.9	4.8	4.9	14.2	16.5	11.9	10.8	10.0	4.1	12.1
Central America	0.0	0.0	0.1	0.3	0.4	1.1	2.1	1.8	3.1	3.0	6.4	5.6	6.6	9.6	5.5
South America	0.0	0.0	0.2	0.7	1.0	1.5	2.1	3.6	7.8	6.6	6.3	5.8	5.8	3.5	6.6
Africa	0.0	0.0	0.1	0.1	0.2	0.3	0.7	0.6	0.9	1.8	2.4	3.7	3.3	1.4	4.0
Oceania	0.2	0.1	0.1	0.2	0.2	0.5	1.4	0.5	0.8	0.9	0.6	0.6	0.6	0.2	0.7
Country not specified	0.0	0.4	0.4	0.0	0.0	0.0	0.0	0.5	0.0	0.0	0.0	0.3	0.2	0.0	0.3

Source: U.S. Department of Justice 1999; U.S. Immigration and Naturalization Service 2000c.
Notes: aPoland was recorded as a separate country between 1820–1898 and since 1920. From 1899–1919 Poland was included with Austria–Hungary, Germany, and USSR. bTotals may not add to 100% due to rounding. cIRCA refers to persons who were legalized their immigrant status under the provisions of the Immigration Reform and Control Act of 1986.

Figure 2.1 Immigrants Intending Residence in New York City or Metropolitan area,[a] 1965–1998[b]

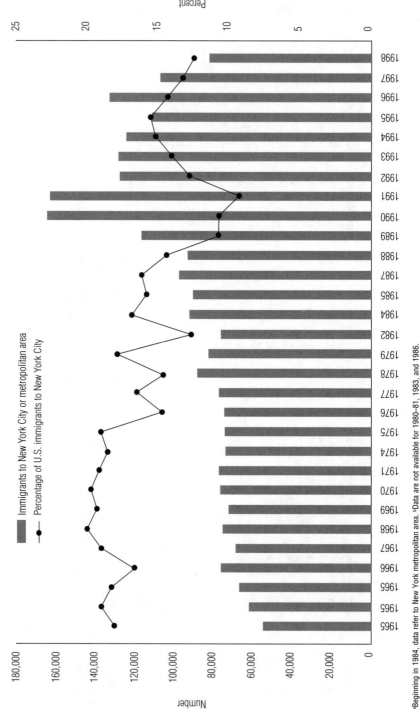

Immigrants to New York City or metropolitan area

Percentage of U.S. immigrants to New York City

[a]Beginning in 1984, data refer to New York metropolitan area. [b]Data are not available for 1980–81, 1983, and 1986.
Source: U.S. Department of Justice, 1966–99; U.S. Immigration and Naturalization Service, 2000c.

Figure 2.2 Percentage Foreign-Born, United States and New York City, and Percentage of U.S. foreign-born in New York City, 1900–1999

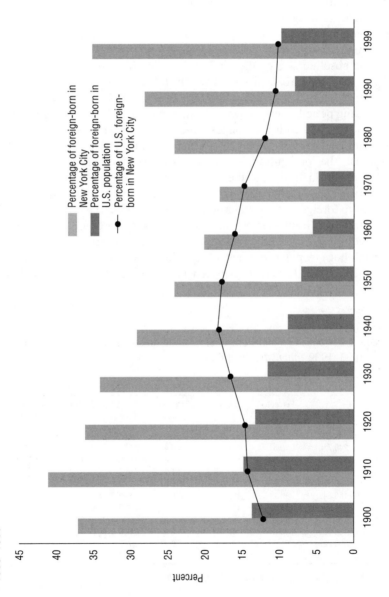

in figure 2.2, the proportion of the total U.S. foreign-born population that resided in the five boroughs of New York increased from about 12 percent in 1900 to about 18 percent midcentury (note the trend line). The vertical bars displayed in figure 2.2 also reveal the significance of immigration in the population composition of New York City. In 1910, according to census data, over two-fifths of the New York population was foreign-born. This proportion declined until the 1970s, but since then it has since steadily increased. Using estimates from the Current Population Survey (CPS) for 1999, it appears that 35 percent of New York City's population is foreign-born, a proportion that mirrors the level at the beginning of the twentieth century.

The absolute size of the total and foreign-born populations in the United States and New York City is shown in table 2.3 for each census year in the twentieth century, and, using CPS estimates, for 1999. Relative change over the preceding period is also shown. The national population has increased throughout the century, with the smallest amount of change registered during the Depression and the largest percentage increases during the postwar baby boom. In contrast, the foreign-born population increased from 10.4 million in 1900 to 14.3 million in 1930, and then declined to 9.6 million in 1970; between 1940 and 1950, the foreign-born population decreased by nearly one-fifth, that is, deaths to foreign-born persons outnumbered annual levels of immigration to the country. Significant increases in levels of immigration following the 1965 immigration reforms were reflected in the dramatic growth in the size of the foreign-born population after 1970, which increased by 46 percent between 1970 and 1980, 40 percent between 1980 and 1990, and over one-third in the nine years since the 1990 census.

Table 2.3 Population and Population Change for the United States and New York City, 1990–1999 *(population in 1,000s)*

	United States				New York City			
Year	Total	Percent change	Foreign-born	Percent change	Total	Percent change	Foreign-born	Percent change
1999	271,736	9.3	26,448	33.8	7,644	4.4	2,651	27.3
1990	248,710	9.8	19,767	40.4	7,323	3.5	2,083	24.7
1980	226,546	11.5	14,080	46.4	7,072	−10.4	1,670	16.2
1970	203,210	13.3	9,619	−1.2	7,895	1.4	1,437	−7.8
1960	179,326	18.9	9,738	−6.6	7,783	−1.4	1,559	−16.2
1950	150,845	14.1	10,431	−10.5	7,892	5.9	1,861	−13.0
1940	132,165	7.3	11,657	−18.4	7,455	7.6	2,139	−9.3
1930	123,203	16.2	14,283	1.9	6,930	23.3	2,359	16.3
1920	106,022	15.0	14,020	2.9	5,620	17.9	2,028	4.3
1910	92,229	21.0	13,630	30.5	4,767	38.7	1,944	53.1
1900	76,212		10,445		3,437		1,270	

Source: Kraly 1987; U.S. Bureau of the Census 1993; Urban Institute 2000.

Patterns of population change for New York City stand in marked contrast to those for the nation as a whole. The nation's total population increased throughout the twentieth century; population growth in New York City was generally lower than in the nation as a whole, and in two decades it was negative. The city's foreign-born population declined in absolute terms, from 2.3 million in 1930 to a low of 1.4 million in 1970. Since then, the city's foreign-born population has steadily grown: 16 percent between 1970 and 1980, 25 percent between 1980 and 1990, and 27 percent between 1990 and 1999. In 1999 the total foreign-born population of New York City was approximately 2.7 million, the largest ever.

A closer look at the population change in New York—for the state, the New York metropolitan area, and the suburban counties—shows that in 1999, just under one-fifth of New York State, and just over one-fifth (22 percent) of the NY-NJ-CT-PA CMSA was foreign-born (table 2.4). About one-third of both the

Table 2.4 Population and Population Change, for United States, New York Metropolitan Area, and New York City, by Nativity: 1980–1999 *(population in thousands)*

Geographic Area	Population			Change during period (%)	
	1980	1990	1999	1980–1990	1990–1999
United States					
Total	226,546	248,710	271,736	9.8	9.3
Foreign-born	14,080	19,767	26,448	40.4	33.8
% Foreign-born	*6.2*	*7.9*	*9.7*		
New York State					
Total	15,169	17,990	18,317	18.6	1.8
Foreign-born	2,389	2,852	3,501	19.4	22.8
% Foreign-born	*13.6*	*15.9*	*19.1*		
NY-NJ-CT-PA CMSA (1990)					
Total		18,087	20,520		13.5
Foreign-born		3,554	4,603		29.5
% Foreign-born		*19.6*	*22.4*		
New York PMSA					
Total	8,275	8,547	8,793	3.3	2.9
Foreign-born	1,833	2,286	2,904	24.7	27.0
% Foreign-born	*22.1*	*26.7*	*33.0*		
Remainder of CMSA					
Total		9,540	11,727		22.9
Foreign-born		1,268	1,699		34.0
% Foreign-born		*13.3*	*14.5*		
New York City					
Total	7,072	7,323	7,644	3.5	4.4
Foreign-born	1,670	2,083	2,651	24.7	27.3
% Foreign-born	*23.6*	*28.4*	*34.7*		

Source: Kraly, 1987; U.S. Bureau of the Census, 1993; Urban Institute, 2000; Gibson and Lennon, 1999.

New York primary MSA and New York City was foreign-born in 1999, compared to 15 percent of the remainder of the CMSA. Nearly universally, as shown in the final columns of table 2.4, population change in the foreign-born population has outpaced the total population in New York populations (the exception being New York State between 1980 and 1990, when both the total and foreign-born populations increased by about 20 percent). Interestingly, for both the total and foreign-born populations, the largest percentage increase between 1990 and 1999 (note the shift in the number of years) was observed for those counties outside of the New York PMSA—23 percent for the total population and 34 percent for the foreign-born population.

Figure 2.3 Percentage Foreign-Born of New York City Boroughs, Late 1990s

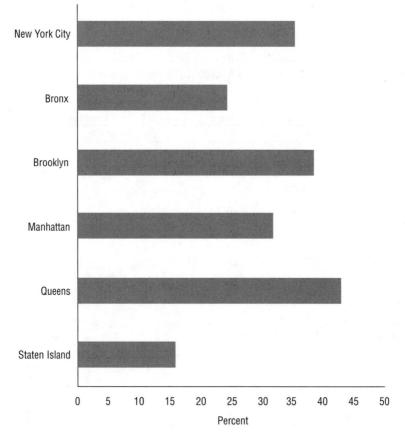

Composition of the Foreign-Born Population of New York

New York City's foreign-born population has reached unprecedented numbers, but, as figure 2.3 indicates, immigrants do not distribute themselves evenly across the five boroughs. In the late 1990s[18] Queens County had the largest proportion of immigrant stock, 43 percent, followed by Brooklyn, 39 percent, and Manhattan, 32 percent. One-quarter of the population of Bronx and 16 percent of the population of Staten Island was foreign-born. Embedded within these aggregate measures for New York boroughs are diverse mosaics of ethnic groups, representing accumulated histories of immigrant settlement patterns. Each geographic scale of analysis—CMSA, PMSA, New York City, and boroughs—provides a different image of ethnic composition, with increasing diversity among places as the geographic scale becomes more fine-grained. Table 2.5 represents a census-based representation of ethnic composition by showing the country of birth of the immigrant populations for places within the New York metropolitan region.

While the national origins composition of the three highest geographic levels, CMSA, NY MSA, and New York City, is quite similar, on the county level there are striking differences (see table 2.5). In terms of the regional composition of the foreign-born population of New York boroughs, The Bronx, Manhattan, and Queens had lower proportions of Europeans than Brooklyn and Staten Island (and than the New York metropolitan region and primary metropolitan area as well). Former Soviets comprise the largest share of European immigrants in Brooklyn— 18 percent of the county's foreign-born population overall. Although Staten Island has the smallest foreign-born population, both proportionately and absolutely, among New York City counties, the largest European group residing there was also the former Soviets.

Nearly one-third of Queens's foreign-born population is Asian, with relatively large proportions from China and Taiwan, and Korea. Over a quarter of Staten Island's foreign-born population is of Asian birth, with a large proportion, about 13 percent, born in the Philippines. In both relative and absolute terms, The Bronx's Asian population is quite small, under 5 percent. The foreign-born population of The Bronx is mainly (60 percent) from countries in the Caribbean; about 37 percent were born in the Dominican Republic and about 16 percent in Jamaica. Over one-third of Manhattan's foreign-born population is from the Dominican Republic. Queens is also home to large numbers of Dominicans, but they make up only about 8 percent of the borough's very large foreign-born population. In fact, only about one-fifth, 18 percent, of the foreign-born population of Queens are from the Caribbean, compared to much higher proportions in The Bronx and about one-third in Manhattan and Brooklyn. Brooklyn, however, has a relatively small proportion of Dominicans among its foreign-born population. Persons born in Haiti and in Trinidad and Tobago comprise about 10 percent of the immigrant stock in Brooklyn. A large proportion, about one-fifth, of the foreign-born popu-

Table 2.5 Composition of the Foreign-Born Population, by Region and Country of Birth, for New York, for MSAs, and Counties Within the NY-NJ-CT-PA CMSA, Late 1990s

Region and County of Birth	NY-NJ-CT-PA CMSA	NY PMSA	New York City	Boroughs					Remainder NY PMSA	Remainder CMSA
				Bronx	Brooklyn	Manhattan	Queens	Staten Island		
Total foreign-born (population in 1000s)	100	100	100	100	100	100	100	100	100	100
	4,510	2,875	2,639	297	829	479	989	44	236	1,635
Europe	23	22	21	12	30	14	18	44	29	27
Germany	1	1	1	0	1	2	1	3	1	2
Greece	1	1	1	1	0	0	2	0	1	1
Ireland/Eire	1	1	1	4	0	1	1	0	2	1
Italy	4	4	3	3	3	2	4	8	9	6
Poland	3	3	3	0	6	1	1	0	2	4
Portugal	1	0	0	0	0	0	0	2	3	3
Great Britain	2	1	1	1	1	2	1	5	5	3
Former USSR	6	8	8	1	18	1	5	18	1	3
Other Europe	4	3	3	2	1	6	4	8	5	4
Asia	21	20	20	4	13	22	30	26	15	22
Bangladesh	1	1	1	1	0	0	2	1	0	1
China, Taiwan, H.K.	6	7	8	0	9	11	8	3	3	4
India	3	2	2	1	0	1	5	0	4	5
Japan	1	1	1	0	0	4	0	0	2	2
Korea/South Korea	2	2	3	1	0	0	7	1	0	1
Philippines	2	1	2	0	0	1	3	13	0	4
Other Asia	5	4	4	1	3	4	6	7	7	5

North America	36	40	42	70	46	52	27	11	27	30
Canada	1	0	0	0	0	1	0	0	2	2
Mexico	4	5	5	3	3	12	5	4	6	3
Central America	6	5	5	7	4	4	5	0	8	8
El Salvador	2	1	1	0	0	1	2	0	3	3
Guatemala	1	1	1	1	0	1	1	0	3	2
Honduras	1	1	1	3	1	1	1	0	1	1
Other Central America	2	2	2	3	3	1	1	0	2	3
Caribbean, Total	25	29	32	60	37	35	18	7	11	17
Cuba	2	1	1	2	1	2	1	0	1	5
Dominican Republic	11	13	14	37	5	32	8	0	3	5
Haiti	4	4	4	0	10	0	2	0	4	4
Jamaica	4	5	6	16	6	1	5	2	3	2
Trinidad & Tobago	2	3	4	1	9	0	1	6	0	1
Other Caribbean	2	2	2	1	6	0	1	0	0	0
South America	15	14	13	7	9	9	21	13	18	16
Colombia	4	3	3	1	1	2	6	2	9	5
Ecuador	4	4	4	2	3	4	5	0	1	4
Guyana	3	4	4	4	4	0	6	6	0	2
Peru	2	1	1	0	1	0	2	1	5	3
Other South America	2	2	2	0	1	2	2	4	4	3
Africa, Total	3	3	2	4	2	1	2	5	10	3
Oceania, Total	0	0	0	0	0	0	0	0	0	0
Elsewhere	1	1	1	3	1	1	1	0	0	2

Source: Urban Institute 2000.

lation of Queens originates from South America, notably Colombia, Ecuador, and Guyana.

Distribution of the Foreign-Born Population Within New York

Immigrants settle in distinctive geographic patterns, but these patterns can shift over time with new immigrant streams. This is certainly the case for New York City. Table 2.6 provides an introduction to patterns of settlement of the foreign-born population within the New York metropolitan area, and also among the city's five boroughs. In the late 1990s, nearly two-thirds (64 percent) of the foreign-born population in the larger New York metropolitan area (NY-NJ-CT-PA CMSA) was living in the New York primary metropolitan area (New York City plus Westchester, Rockland, and Putnam counties), with 36 percent in the remainder of the metropolitan region. (This distribution is essentially the reverse of the residential distribution of the native-born population, 37 percent of whom live in the New York PMSA and 63 percent in the remaining metropolitan areas in the region.) Nearly three-fifths, 59 percent, of the total metropolitan foreign-born population, moreover, resided in the five counties of New York City, with just over one-fifth (22 percent) in Queens, and just under one-fifth (18 percent) in Brooklyn. Looking just at the distribution of the population within the city, 37 percent of New York City's foreign-born population resided in Queens, compared to 28 percent of the native-born; only 11 percent of the foreign-born resided in Bronx county, compared to 19 percent of the native-born.

Table 2.6 Distribution of the Population, by Nativity, Within the New York CMSA and New York City, Late 1990s

Metropolitan Residence	Metropolitan distribution			New York City distribution		
	Total population	Native-born	Foreign-born	Total population	Native-born	Foreign-born
			Percent			
New York, NY-NJ-CT-PA CMSA	100	100	100			
(population in 1000s)	*20,187*	*15,666*	*4,521*			
New York, NY PMSA	43	37	64			
New York City	37	31	59	100	100	100
(population in 1000s)				*7,482*	*4,843*	*2,639*
Bronx	6	6	7	16	19	11
Kings (Brooklyn)	11	9	18	29	28	31
New York (Manhattan)	7	6	11	20	21	18
Queens	12	9	22	31	28	37
Richmond (Staten Island)	1	2	1	4	5	2
Remainder of CMSA	57	63	36			

Source: Urban Institute 2000.

Using the same pooled CPS data, table 2.7 provides the distribution of the foreign-born population within the larger New York metropolitan area, by country of birth, in the late 1990s. About half (52 percent) of the European-born population reside New York City, with a quarter in Brooklyn (Kings County). A high proportion are immigrants from the former Soviet Union, four-fifths of whom live in the city, with 57 percent residing in Brooklyn; by comparison, 43 percent of the metropolitan area's Italian foreign-born and 31 percent of British reside in New York City. Among the Asian foreign-born, Bangladeshi, Chinese, and Koreans are heavily concentrated in New York City. Over half of Bangladeshis in the larger metropolitan area and 69 percent of Koreans live in Queens. About three-quarters of the metropolitan population of immigrants from China (which includes Taiwan) reside in New York City, with large proportions in Manhattan, Brooklyn, and Queens.

Within the CMSA, many of the foreign-born populations from North America are heavily concentrated in New York City, particularly immigrants from the Caribbean. Three-quarters of the Caribbean foreign-born live in the city, with 28 percent in Brooklyn. Nearly nine out of ten Trinidadians in the CMSA live in New York City, 70 percent of them in Brooklyn. Dominicans are also concentrated in the city—about a quarter (23 percent) live in the Bronx; about one-third (32 percent) in Manhattan; and about 16 percent in Brooklyn. Among persons born in Haiti, 60 percent in the larger metropolitan area live in New York City; nearly half (48 percent) live in Brooklyn. Central American groups are more likely to live outside of the city. Only about one-third of Guatemalan and Salvadoran immigrants in the CMSA live in New York City, with one-quarter of the Salvadoran population residing in Queens. The relatively recent settlement of Mexicans in the New York metropolitan area is primarily concentrated in New York City, with about two-thirds of Mexican foreign-born in the five city counties, about 28 percent in Manhattan, and 22 percent in Queens.

Among foreign-born populations from South America, Guyanese are most concentrated in New York City: four-fifths of those born in Guyana who reside in the CMSA live in the city proper, with about 43 percent in Queens. Almost two-thirds of Ecuadorans and about two-fifths (44 percent of Colombians reside in New York City, but just under one-third of persons born in Peru. Finally, Africans in the CMSA are spread throughout the metropolitan region; about three-fifths (57 percent) reside in the New York PMSA, but only two-fifths live in New York City.

Recent Immigration to New York City and Patterns of Settlement Among Selected Immigrant Groups

If New York City has become a truly immigrant city once again, it also stands out from other urban areas that are receiving large numbers of newcomers. A comparison with the United States's other immigrant capital, Los Angeles, is particu-

Table 2.7 Distribution of Foreign-Born Population by Residence Within the NY-NJ-CT-PA CMSA, for Regions and Countries of Birth: Late 1990s

Region and Country of Birth	NY-NJ-CT-PA CMSA	(population in 1000s)	NY PMSA	New York City	Boroughs					Remainder NY PMSA	Remainder CMSA
					Bronx	Brooklyn	Manhattan	Queens	Staten Island		
Total population	100	20,187	43	37	6	11	7	12	1	6	57
Total foreign-born	100	4,510	64	59	7	18	11	22	1	5	36
Europe, total	100	1,058	59	52	3	24	6	17	2	6	41
Germany	100	57	40	37	2	8	15	10	3	4	60
Greece	100	43	61	58	9	2	5	41	0	3	39
Ireland/Eire	100	46	63	51	27	1	7	16	0	11	37
Italy	100	199	54	43	5	14	4	19	2	11	46
Poland	100	134	56	52	0	38	4	10	0	3	44
Portugal	100	60	12	2	0	0	0	1	0	10	88
Great Britain	100	92	44	31	2	7	8	12	2	13	56
Former USSR	100	262	83	81	1	57	2	18	3	1	17
Other Europe	100	166	59	52	3	6	17	24	2	7	41
Asia	100	930	62	58	1	11	11	32	1	4	38
Bangladesh	100	45	67	67	4	6	4	52	1	0	33
China, Taiwan, H.K.	100	268	78	76	0	27	20	29	1	2	22
India	100	149	47	41	2	3	3	34	0	6	53
Japan	100	49	49	39	0	0	36	2	0	10	51
Korea/South Korea	100	94	77	76	3	1	2	69	1	1	23
Philippines	100	109	37	37	0	2	6	24	5	0	63
Other Asia	100	217	59	52	2	12	10	27	2	7	41

North America	100	*1,635*	70	68	13	23	15	16	0	4	30
Canada	100	*41*	34	23	1	7	10	6	0	11	66
Mexico	100	*201*	75	68	5	12	28	22	1	7	25
Central America	100	*272*	52	45	7	13	7	17	0	7	48
El Salvador	100	*82*	43	36	1	4	6	25	0	7	57
Guatemala	100	*49*	49	34	4	4	14	13	0	15	51
Honduras	100	*44*	68	63	20	19	8	17	0	4	32
Other Central America	100	*98*	54	49	9	23	5	13	0	5	46
Caribbean	100	*1,121*	75	75	16	28	15	16	0	2	25
Cuba	100	*106*	30	29	5	4	9	11	0	1	70
Dominican Republic	100	*477*	81	80	23	8	32	16	0	2	19
Haiti	100	*166*	65	60	0	48	0	11	0	5	35
Jamaica	100	*192*	81	77	25	27	2	24	0	4	19
Trinidad & Tobago	100	*106*	88	88	3	70	1	12	2	1	12
Other Caribbean	100	*61*	92	92	3	75	0	15	0	0	8
South America	100	*657*	60	54	3	11	7	32	1	6	40
Colombia	100	*172*	56	44	1	4	6	32	1	12	44
Ecuador	100	*163*	64	62	4	13	12	33	0	1	36
Guyana	100	*134*	81	81	9	25	2	43	2	0	19
Peru	100	*86*	43	31	1	5	1	23	1	12	57
Other South America	100	*101*	50	42	0	7	11	23	2	8	50
Africa	100	*130*	57	39	9	11	4	13	2	19	0
Oceania	100	*11*	50	44	5	0	10	29	0	5	0
Elsewhere	100	*59*	48	46	13	9	10	15	0	2	0

Source: Urban Institute 2000.

Table 2.8 Immigrants Admitted, by Top Countries of Birth, for United States, and New York and Los Angeles–Long Beach Metropolitan Areas as Intended Residence, and Percentage of U.S. Immigrants Intending Residence in New York: 1990–1998

Country of birth	United States	New York	Los Angeles– Long Beach	United States	New York	Los Angeles– Long Beach	% New York of total U.S.
	Number			*Percent*			
Total	9,141,551	1,141,780	1,186,905	100.0	100.0	100.0	12.5
Canada	129,301	4,623	5,164	1.4	0.4	0.4	3.6
China, PR	378,532	87,472	36,241	4.1	7.7	3.1	23.1
Colombia	228,350	30,399	4,863	2.5	2.7	0.4	13.3
Dominican Republic	347,734	187,866	384	3.8	16.5	0.0	54.0
El Salvador	260,383	9,961	103,517	2.8	0.9	8.7	3.8
Guatemala	118,130	6,602	49,470	1.3	0.6	4.2	5.6
Haiti	151,193	39,075	272	1.7	3.4	0.0	25.8
India	341,688	36,325	14,262	3.7	3.2	1.2	10.6
Iran	121,852	4,348	39,786	1.3	0.4	3.4	3.6
Jamaica	167,819	66,402	1,583	1.8	5.8	0.1	39.6
Korea	174,954	19,027	30,604	1.9	1.7	2.6	10.9
Mexico	2,608,940	19,339	536,659	28.5	1.7	45.2	0.7
Pakistan	106,277	24,940	4,719	1.2	2.2	0.4	23.5
Peru	103,399	15,685	8,904	1.1	1.4	0.8	15.2
Philippines	495,809	29,794	73,840	5.4	2.6	6.2	6.0
Poland	171,237	32,098	1,826	1.9	2.8	0.2	18.7
Soviet Union, former[a]	387,200	108,800	49,155	4.2	9.5	4.1	28.1
Taiwan	105,750	7,497	23,549	1.2	0.7	2.0	7.1
UK	159,114	9,515	8,244	1.7	0.8	0.7	6.0
Vietnam	392,567	4,803	32,527	4.3	0.4	2.7	1.2
Other	2,119,076	347,882	160,784	23.2	30.5	13.5	16.4

Source: U.S. Department of Justice 1991–1999; U.S. Immigration and Naturalization Service 2000c.
Notes: [a] For 1995 and subsequent years, data for countries of the former Soviet Union are classified separately in INS statistics. Data shown here for years after 1994 represent the sum of immigrant admissions from Russia and Ukraine.

larly illuminating. Table 2.8 provides data on the country of birth of immigrants admitted during 1990–1998, for total immigrants and those intending residence in the New York or the Los Angeles–Long Beach metropolitan area. In this period, over 1.1 million immigrants said that they intended to reside in the New York metropolitan area, and just about 1.2 million immigrants intended to live in Los Angeles. (Recall that these numbers will include a large proportion already in the United States who have adjusted status, including persons in the process of legalization under IRCA.)

New York has an extremely diverse immigrant population and offers an attraction for certain immigrant groups. Nearly 17 percent of immigrants intending to settle in New York were born in the Dominican Republic; very few Dominicans went to Los Angeles. Put another way, over half (54 percent) of all immigrants from the Dominican Republic intended to settle in New York. One-quarter of all immigrants from Haiti and a full 40 percent from Jamaica intended to live in New York. New York had over twice the proportion of immigrants from the People's Republic of China (nearly 8 percent) as Los Angeles, but a lower proportion of

Chinese from Taiwan. Nearly a quarter (23 percent) of immigrants from mainland China intended to reside in New York. Nearly one-quarter of immigrants from Pakistan also meant to settle New York. So did over a quarter of all immigrants from the former Soviet Union, who comprised nearly 10 percent of immigrants to New York in this period. Although New York's Mexican population is growing, it pales against the level of Mexican immigration to Los Angeles. Nearly half (45 percent) of the immigrants intending to live in Los Angeles were Mexicans, compared to about 2 percent reporting New York. Los Angeles also had a higher proportion of immigrants from El Salvador and Guatemala as well as the Philippines. A particularly telling piece of data is the much larger proportion of immigrants from countries of birth designated "other" (30 percent) for New York compared to Los Angeles. This is an indicator of the higher degree of national origins diversity among immigration streams to the New York metropolitan area compared to flows to Los Angeles, or to the country as a whole.

Figure 2.4 shows the size of immigrant streams to the five boroughs of New York City for the 1990–1996 period for the top forty countries of birth. These INS data have been provided by the New York City Planning Department and *exclude* persons in the process of adjusting their status under IRCA. The range in size of immigration streams for this period is significant, from about 2,500 immigrants from Afghanistan to nearly 150,000 from the Dominican Republic. Amazingly, over half of these forty source countries each generated more than 5,000 immigrants to New York City during this period. For the immigrant groups included in this volume, INS statistics indicate the following numbers of legal admissions to New York City for fiscal years 1990–1996:

Dominican Republic	149,313
Former USSR	106,954
China, including Taiwan	83,540
Jamaica	44,819
Korea	11,774
Mexico	4,756
West African countries	10,914

Included among West African countries are Ghana (4,962), Nigeria (4,896), Senegal (712), and a total of 344 from Mali, Gambia, and Burkina Faso (New York City Department of City Planning, unpublished tabulations).

What are the settlement patterns of these seven immigrant groups within New York City? Figure 2.5 shows the distribution of each group across the five boroughs and reveals their distinctive settlement patterns at the county level based on reported residence in New York City among all immigrants admitted between 1990 and 1996. Among Dominicans, the largest immigrant stream to New York during this period, four-fifths reported Manhattan, and over one-quarter reported the Bronx as their likely place of residence. Three-quarters of former Soviets in-

Figure 2.4 Immigrants[a] Intending Residence in New York City for Leading Countries of Origin, 1990–1996

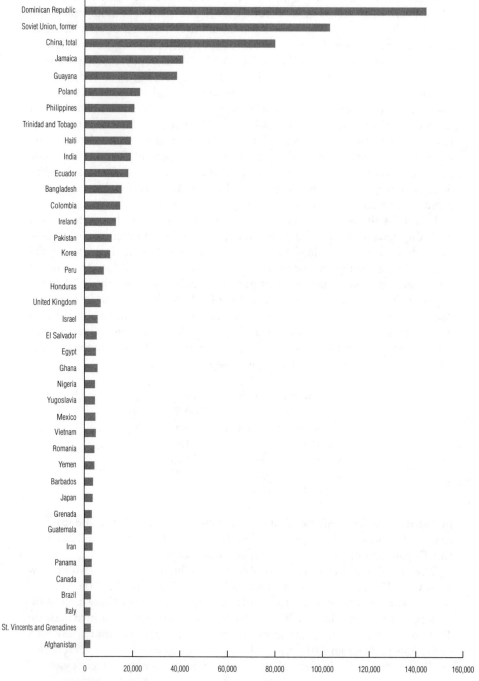

[a]Data do not include IRCA adjustments.
Source: New York City Department of City Planning 2000.

Figure 2.5 Intended New York City Borough of Residence for Selected Immigrant Groups,[a] 1990–1996

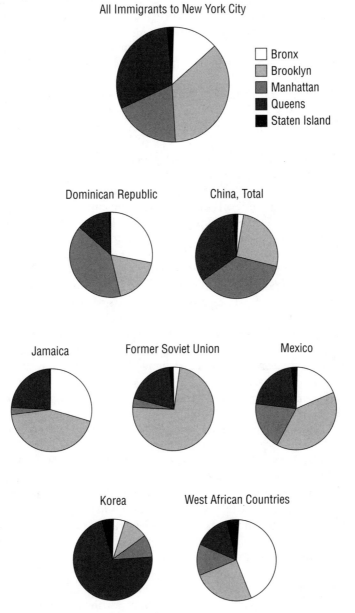

[a]Data do not include IRCA adjustments
Source: New York City Department of City Planning 2000.

dicated residence in Brooklyn and one-fifth in Queens, whereas Chinese immigrants preferred for Manhattan as well as Queens and Brooklyn. More than two-fifths of Jamaicans intended to live in Brooklyn, and another 30 percent gave The Bronx as a likely residence. Three-quarters of immigrants from Korea gave Queens as their destination. Recent immigrants from Mexico were perhaps the least concentrated in one or two boroughs among these immigrant groups: Brooklyn was the choice of about two-fifths of admitted Mexicans and The Bronx, Brooklyn, and Queens of about one-fifth each. Immigrants from the West African countries considered in Paul Stoller's fieldwork (many of whom are Ghanaians) were concentrated in The Bronx; about a quarter went to Brooklyn. A large proportion—nearly half—of immigrants from Senegal, however, reported intended residence in Manhattan.

A final collection of maps reveals at a finer geographic scale—zip codes—intended settlement for each of the eight groups of immigrants admitted between 1990 and 1996, an indicator of one aspect of the demographic impact of immigration in urban communities. These maps are complementary to those produced by the New York City Department of City Planning for the 1990–1994 period for *The NEWEST New Yorkers 1990–1994,* yet they differ from the Planning Department's maps in two ways. Two additional years of immigrant admissions have been included, bringing the data up to 1996. Also, we computed immigration rates for zip code areas rather than mapping absolute numbers of immigrant admissions. These rates compare immigrant admissions per 10,000 total population within the zip code area, as reported in the 1990 census,[19] thus measuring the level of immigrant settlement *relative* to the size of the resident population. Bear in mind that the level and range of immigration rates vary dramatically among immigrant groups given the number of immigrant admissions relative to total population size of zip codes. Thus, the settlement patterns in these maps show relative residential concentrations specific to each immigrant group. Data categories are determined through natural breaks in the distribution of rates.

Figure 2.6a displays immigration rates for total immigrant admissions to New York City between 1990 and 1996 for zip codes. Total immigration (currently residing or intended residence) for these years was 794,341 persons from all reported countries of birth. Within Manhattan, the highest immigration rates are in Hamilton and Washington Heights (in upper Manhattan) and Chinatown, Tribeca, and the Lower East Side. Within Brooklyn, Bensonhurst, Sheepshead Bay, Brighton Beach, and Greenpoint witnessed the highest rates of overall immigration in the early to mid-1990s. In Queens, Flushing and Jamaica experienced among the highest immigration rates in the city as a whole.

Figure 2.6b shows immigration rates for persons from the Dominican Republic that, given the significant role of Dominican immigration in overall immigration to New York, mirror to some degree the patterns for the total flow. Highest immigration rates per resident population are shown in upper Manhattan. Within

Figure 2.6a Total Immigrant Admissions, for New York City Zip Codes, 1990–1996

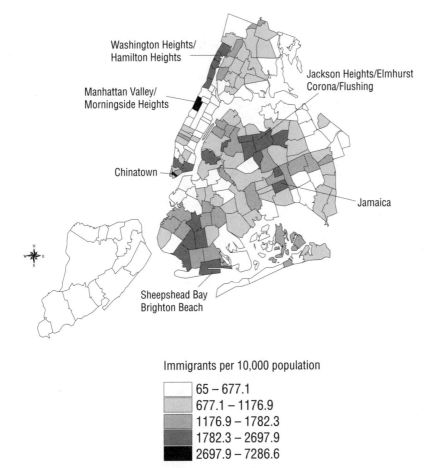

Immigrants per 10,000 population

☐	65 – 677.1
☐	677.1 – 1176.9
☐	1176.9 – 1782.3
☐	1782.3 – 2697.9
■	2697.9 – 7286.6

Source: New York City Planning Office 2000; U.S. Bureau of Census 2001.

The Bronx, Dominicans settle in large numbers, relative to the total population, in Tremont, University Heights, Highbridge, and Morris Heights. In Brooklyn, Dominican immigrants go to Williamsburg and Bushwick, and in Queens, to Corona. Figure 2.6c shows the concentration of recent immigrants from the former Soviet Union in the Bay Ridge, Bensonhurst, Gravesend, Homecrest, and Brighton Beach sections of Brooklyn; within Queens, in Flushing, Rego Park, Jamaica, Forest Hills, and Kew Gardens. Chinese, as shown in figure 2.6d, have the highest rates of immigration observed for Chinatown and Tribeca in lower Manhattan as

Figure 2.6b Immigrants from Dominican Republic

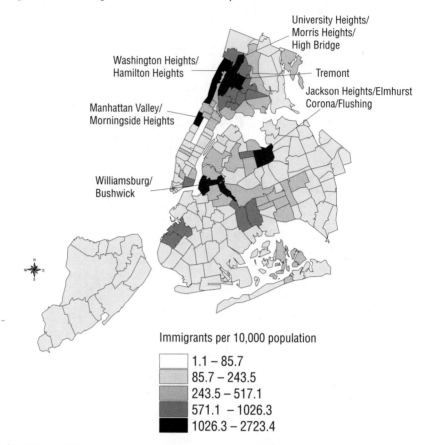

Immigrants per 10,000 population

	1.1 – 85.7
	85.7 – 243.5
	243.5 – 517.1
	571.1 – 1026.3
	1026.3 – 2723.4

Source: New York City Planning Office 2000; U.S. Bureau of Census 2001.

well as in the Cathedral section of the Upper West Side. In Brooklyn, the Sunset Park area has witnessed relatively high rates of Chinese immigration, as have the Elmhurst and Murray Hill areas of Queens.

Recent Jamaican immigrants (figure 2.6e) settled in three areas within the city during this period: in The Bronx, in the Norwood and Baychester areas; in Brooklyn, in the Flatbush, Brownsville, and Crown Heights sections; and in Queens, in Cambria Heights, St. Albans, Rosedale, and Springfield Gardens. The highest ratio of Korean immigration to resident population (figure 2.6f) occurs in the Trinity area in Manhattan's financial district. Other areas of Korean settlement include Flushing, Murray Hill, and Sunnyside in Queens. Large proportions of

Figure 2.6c Immigrants from former Soviet Union

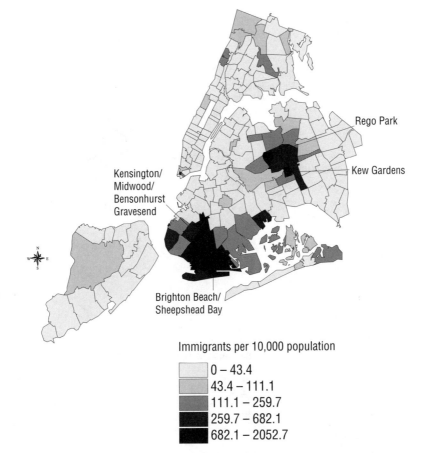

Immigrants per 10,000 population

	0 – 43.4
	43.4 – 111.1
	111.1 – 259.7
	259.7 – 682.1
	682.1 – 2052.7

Source: New York City Planning Office 2000; U.S. Bureau of Census 2001.

recent Mexican immigrants (figure 2.6g) settle on the Upper West Side of Manhattan, in the Cathedral area; the Astoria section of Queens; and, in Brooklyn, in Bushwick, Fort Greene, and Sunset Park. Finally, immigrants from selected countries in West Africa (figure 2.6h) are spread throughout New York City. The highest rate of settlement is in The Bronx, in the Highbridge section, and also Tremont, Morrisania, and Williamsburg. Relative to resident population, a large immigration rate is seen for West Africans in the Far Rockaway community of Queens. Similarly, a high rate of immigration by West Africans is observed in the Stapleton-Fox Hills area on Staten Island.

Figure 2.6d Immigrants from China

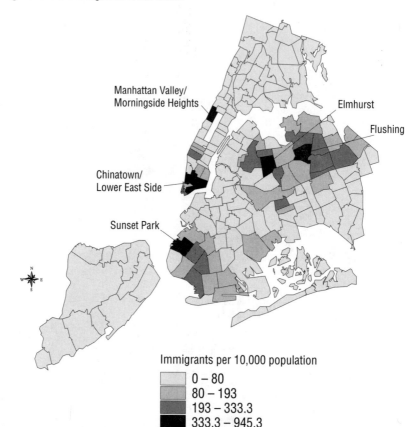

Source: New York City Planning Office 2000; U.S. Bureau of Census 2001.

Summary and Conclusions

In this chapter we have provided a broad policy and demographic perspective on trends and patterns in immigration to New York City and the New York metropolitan region. In so doing, we have sought to reveal one dimension of the social landscape of New York City, which derives its topography from a rich diversity of immigrants. The changes in U.S. immigration policy and administration that we described have implications for immigration and the experience of immigrants in New York. The discussion of analytic issues that challenge social demographic research has implications for students and scholars alike. Although federal statistical resources on immigration have improved in recent

Figure 2.6e Immigrants from Jamaica

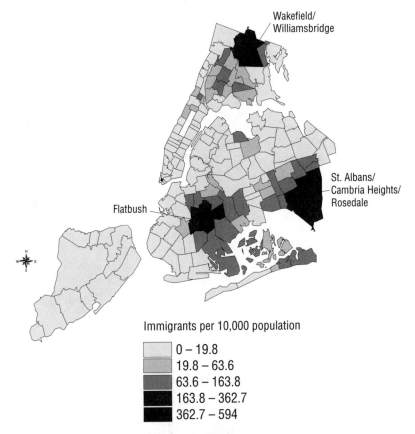

Wakefield/
Williamsbridge

St. Albans/
Cambria Heights/
Rosedale

Flatbush

Immigrants per 10,000 population

0 – 19.8
19.8 – 63.6
63.6 – 163.8
163.8 – 362.7
362.7 – 594

Source: New York City Planning Office 2000; U.S. Bureau of Census 2001.

years, problems persist in U.S. immigration data, notably, the absence of comprehensive and reliable data on emigration and circulation and on unauthorized migration. The analytic richness of the studies of specific immigrant groups that follow becomes especially important in understanding these dimensions of the process of international migration and transmigration, and the immigrant experience in New York City.

In analyzing the role of immigration in the population dynamics of New York we have shown that during recent decades and at each geographic scale, the foreign-born have increased in absolute number and in their proportion of the overall population. The New York metropolitan area continues to be the urban community in the United States that the largest number of new immigrants choose

Figure 2.6f Immigrants from Korea

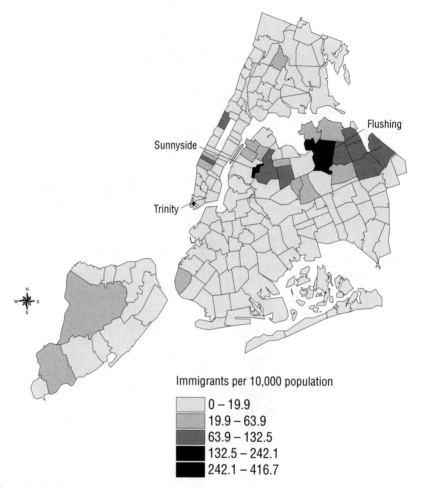

Source: New York City Planning Office 2000; U.S. Bureau of Census 2001.

as their initial residence. Over half of all immigrants from the Dominican Republic choose New York, as do two-fifths of Jamaican, one-quarter of Haitian and of Pakistani immigrants, and nearly 30 percent of immigrants from the former Soviet Union. During much of the 1990s, the Dominican Republic, the former Soviet Union, China, Jamaica, and Guyana have been the top source countries of authorized immigration to New York City.

The implications of these trends in immigration are significant for the city

Figure 2.6g Immigrants from Mexico

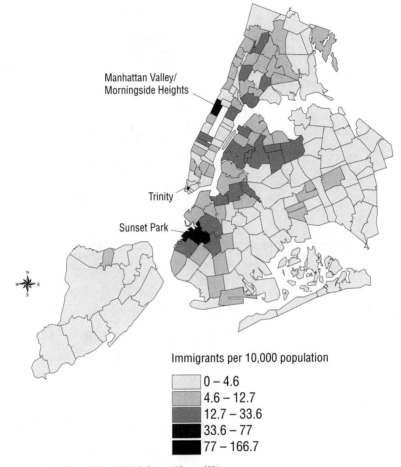

Immigrants per 10,000 population

- 0 – 4.6
- 4.6 – 12.7
- 12.7 – 33.6
- 33.6 – 77
- 77 – 166.7

Source: New York City Planning Office 2000; U.S. Bureau of Census 2001.

and its local communities. In the last years of the twentieth century, 35 percent of New York City's population was foreign-born, first-generation immigrant stock, and it is likely that this proportion will continue to rise in the first decades of the new millennium. Immigrants will, in the foreseeable future, continue to have a dramatic impact on the social demography of local communities throughout the city and the larger metropolitan area. As a result, population change in New York City and the New York metropolitan area remains, in good part, a story of immigration.

Figure 2.6h Immigrants from West African countries

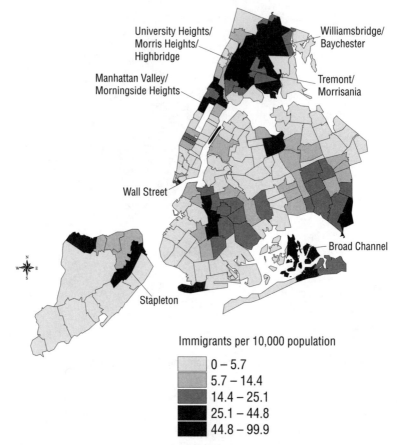

Source: New York City Planning Office 2000; U.S. Bureau of Census 2001.

Notes

1. We wish to thank Arun Peter Lobo, Population Division, New York City Department of City Planning, and Jeffrey Passel, Urban Institute, for providing both data
   and helpful comments on the chapter.
2. A country of first asylum is one that offers temporary asylum to a refugee awaiting
   either repatriation or resettlement.
3. The Quota Law of 1921 based allocation of immigrant visas on the 1910 census;
   the number of visas for a country was calculated as 3 percent of the foreign-born
   resident population of that nationality. The Immigration Act of 1924 established
   the national origins quota system in two steps; until 1929, immigrant visas were
   allocated on the basis of 2 percent of foreign-born population in the 1890 census,

which had the effect of increasing the representation of northern and western Europeans. After 1929, a fixed annual limit of 150,000 immigrant visas was established; these visas were allocated on the basis of the representation of national origin populations in the total U.S. population in the 1920 census (see U.S. Department of Justice 1999, Appendix 1).

4. The Chinese Exclusion Act barred immigration of Chinese laborers for ten years. It was made permanent in 1904, and was finally rescinded in 1943. It did not exclude the entry of teachers, diplomats, students, merchants, or tourists.

5. The 1917 Immigration Act barred immigration of laborers from the Asiatic Barred Zone, specifically listing China, India, Afghanistan, Arabia, Burma, Siam, the Malay States, Asiatic Russia, most Polynesian islands, and Indonesia.

6. Diversity visas are allotted by region and vary in relative distribution, with a 7 percent limit on any one country. In 1999, for example, 39 percent were allotted to the continent of Africa and 42 percent to Europe, excluding the United Kingdom other than Northern Ireland, and Poland. Only eight lottery visas were made available to North America, and the Bahamas was the only eligible country; and 837 were awarded to Oceania with no country restrictions. Latin America and Asia received 4.5 percent and 13 percent of the visas, respectively, but high-immigration countries such as China and the Dominican Republic were also excluded.

7. The Bracero Program was designed to bring temporary workers from Mexico to the United States to alleviate wartime labor shortages. Between 1942 and 1964, when the program came to a close, approximately 4.8 million braceros, or laborers, entered the United States. Bracero contracts were for fixed durations, but many braceros stayed in the United States as undocumented migrants after expiration of the contract.

8. A significant number of undocumented aliens are visa overstayers, that is, entrants on temporary visas who remain in the United States after the expiration of their visas.

9. Both IIRIRA and the 1997 Nicaraguan Adjustment and Central American Relief Act (NACARA) define the criteria for suspension of deportation as (1) seven years of continuous residence, (2) "good moral character" (no criminal record), (3) "extreme hardship" upon return (on May 20, 1999, Salvadorans and Guatemalans were extended a presumption of extreme hardship), and (4) evidence of a settled life in the United States.

10. In many cases, Salvadorans and Guatemalans have been on TPS or a similar program, ABC, for a decade while awaiting final adjudication of their asylum cases. ABC resulted from a out-of-court settlement of a lawsuit brought by the American Baptist Churches (*American Baptist Churches* v. *Thornburgh* (760 F. Supp. 796, N.D. Cal. 1991) in response to systematic discrimination against Salvadorans and Guatemalans requesting asylum because they did not come from Communist states.

11. Moreover, the need for coordination among sending and receiving countries for more comprehensive measurement of international population movements and migration continues to be expressed on the international level (see, e.g., Kritz, Lim, and Zlotnik 1992).

12. INS data on immigration are available on the World Wide Web as a link to "Statistics" from the INS home page *www.ins.usdoj.gov*.

13. While it is theoretically possible to generate estimates of long-term immigration to the United States using INS statistical and information systems, the institutional resources of the agency have not been mustered to do so. The generation of such estimates would be of value not only for national research on the demography of international migration, but also for international research on population flows and exchange.

14. This report was prepared by Arun Peter Lobo, Joe Salvo, and Vicky Virgin.

15. Unfortunately, the recommendation of the National Research Council (Edmonston 1996) for the inclusion of the question regarding parents' birthplace was not implemented in the 2000 decennial census. As in previous censuses, the sampled population (those persons receiving the "long form") within Census 2000 were asked questions on place (and country) of birth, citizenship status, race, and Hispanic/Latino origin or identity. Also included again on the long form are two questions that address the timing of immigration to the United States: year of entry among foreign-born persons and place of residence five years prior to the current place of residence. Analyses of 1980 and 1990 census data by Ellis and Wright (1998) have cast a remarkably critical light on both the reliability and the validity of these data. They raise significant concerns about the value of census data on year of immigration in the comparison of immigrant cohorts over time and for census-based studies of the relationships between immigrant settlement and overall geographic mobility among the U.S. population (cf. Frey 1994).

16. "The United States Office of Management and Budget (OMB) defines metropolitan areas (MAs) according to published standards that are applied to Census Bureau data. The general concept of an MA is that of a core area containing a large population nucleus, together with adjacent communities having a high degree of economic and social integration with that core. Currently defined MAs are based on application of 1990 standards (which appeared in the *Federal Register* on March 30, 1990) to 1990 decennial census data and to subsequent Census Bureau population estimates and special census data. Current MA definitions were announced by OMB effective June 30, 1999. Standard definitions of metropolitan areas were first issued in 1949 by the then Bureau of the Budget (predecessor of OMB), under the designation 'standard metropolitan area' (SMA). The term was changed to 'standard metropolitan statistical area' (SMSA) in 1959, and to 'metropolitan statistical area' (MSA) in 1983. The collective term "'metropolitan area' (MA) became effective in 1990. MAs include metropolitan statistical areas (MSAs), consolidated metropolitan statistical areas (CMSAs), and primary metropolitan statistical areas (PMSAs)" (U.S. Bureau of the Census 2000).

17. The other PMSAs in the NY-NJ-CT-PA CMSA are Bergen-Passaic, New Jersey; Bridgeport, Connecticut; Danbury, Connecticut; Dutchess County, New York; Jersey City, New Jersey; Middlesex-Somerset-Hunterdon, New Jersey; Monmouth-Ocean, New Jersey; Nassau-Suffolk, New York; New Haven-Meriden, Connecticut; Newark, New Jersey; Newburgh, New York–Pennsylvania; Stamford-Norwalk, Connecticut; Trenton, New Jersey; and Waterbury, Connecticut.

18. CPS data are pooled for the years 1996–1999.

19. Because the numerator is not actually derivative from the denominator, this measure is actually a ratio rather than a rate, and thus should be considered an approximation of an immigration rate.

References

Boswell, Tom D., and James R. Curtis. 1984. *The Cuban-American Experience.* Totowa, N.J.: Rowman and Allanheld.

Castles, Stephen, and Mark J. Miller. 1998. *The Age of Migration: International Population Movements in the Modern World,* 2d ed. New York: Guilford Press.

Chiswick, Barry R. 1993. "Soviet Jews in the United States: An Analysis of Their Linguistic and Economic Adjustment." *International Migration Review* 27(2):260–85.

Dashefsky, Arnold. 2001. "American Emigration Abroad." In James Ciment, ed., *Encyclopedia of American Immigration,* Armonk, N.Y.: M. E. Sharpe.

Edmonston, Barry, ed. 1996. *Statistics on U.S. Immigration: An Assessment of Data Needs for Future Research.* Committee on National Statistics and Committee on Population, Commission on Behavioral and Social Sciences and Education, National Research Council. Washington, D.C.: National Academy Press.

Ellis, Mark, and Richard Wright. 1998. "When Immigrants Are Not Migrants: Counting Arrivals of the Foreign-Born Using the US Census." *International Migration Review* 32:127–44.

Frey, William H. 1994. "The New White Flight." *American Demographics* 16:40–41.

Gibson, Campbell, and Emily Lennon. 1999. *Historical Census Statistics on the Foreign-Born Population of the United States: 1850–1990.* U.S. Bureau of the Census, Population Division. Population Division Working Paper no. 29. Washington, D.C. *http://www.census.gov/population/www/documentation/twps0029/twps00.html.*

Gold, Steven J. 1992. *Refugee Communities: A Comparative Field Study.* Newbury Park, Calif.: Sage.

——. 1988. "Refugees and Small Business: The Case of Soviet Jews and Vietnamese." *Ethnic and Racial Studies* 11:411–38.

Hutchinson, Edward P. 1958. "Notes on the Immigration Statistics of the United States." *Journal of the American Statistical Association* 55:963–1025.

Kraly, Ellen Percy. 1998. "Emigration: Implications for U.S. Immigration Policy Research." In Mexican Ministry of Foreign Affairs and U.S. Commission on Immigration Reform, eds., *Migration Between Mexico and the United States: Binational Study,* vol. II, *Research Reports and Background Materials,* pp. 587–618. Austin: Morgan.

——. 1990. "U.S. Refugee Policies and Refugee Migration Since World War II." In R. W. Tucker, C. B. Keely, and L. Wrigley, eds., *Immigration and U.S. Foreign Policy,* pp. 73–98. Boulder: Westview Press.

——. 1987. "U.S. Immigration Policy and the Immigrant Populations of New York." In N. Foner, ed., *New Immigrants in New York.* New York: Columbia University Press.

——. 1979. "Sources of Data for the Study of U.S. Immigration." In S. B. Couch and R. S. Bryce-Laporte, eds., *Quantitative Data and Immigration Research,* Research Institute on Immigration and Ethnic Studies, Research Notes no. 2, pp. 34–54. Washington, D.C.: Smithsonian Institute.

Kraly, Ellen Percy, and Robert Warren. 1992. "Estimates of Long-Term Immigration in the United States: Moving U.S. Statistics Toward United Nations Concepts." *Demography* 29:613–28.

——. 1991. "Long-Term Immigration to the United States: New Approaches to Measurement." *International Migration Review* 25:60–92.

Kritz, Mary, Lin Lim, and Hania Zlotnik, eds. 1992. *International Migration Systems: A Global Approach.* Oxford: Clarendon Press.

Levine, Daniel, Kenneth Hill, and Robert Warren, eds. 1985. *Immigration Statistics: A Story of Neglect.* Washington, D.C.: National Academy of Sciences.

Miyares, Ines M. 1998a. *The Hmong Refugee Experience in the United States: Crossing the River.* New York: Garland.

——. 1998b. "'Little Odessa'—Brighton Beach, Brooklyn: An Examination of the Former Soviet Refugee Economy in New York City." *Urban Geography* 19(6):518–30.

Miyares, Ines M., Alison Mountz, Richard A. Wright, and A. J. Bailey. 2000. "The State, Immigrants, and Refugee Law: Salvadoran Adaptations to Legal Limbo." Paper presented at the Annual Meeting of the Association of American Geographers. Pittsburgh.

New York City Department of City Planning. 1996. *The NEWEST New Yorkers 1990– 1994.* New York: Department of City Planning.

New York City Department of City Planning. Population Division. 2000. Unpublished tabulations of Immigration and Naturalization Service data on immigrant admissions.

Office of Refugee Resettlement, 1994. *Report to the Congress FY 1994 Refugee Resettlement Program.* Washington, D.C.: U.S. Department of Health and Human Services.

Sassen, Saskia. 1996. *Losing Control? Sovereignty in an Age of Globalization.* New York: Columbia University Press.

Tomasi, Silvano, and Charles B. Keely. 1975. *Whom Have We Welcomed?* Staten Island: Center for Migration Studies.

U.S. Bureau of the Census. 1993. *1990 Census of Population and Housing. Population and Housing Characteristics for Census Tracts and Block Numbering Areas.* New York-Northern New Jersey-Long Island, NY-NJ-CT-CMSA (Part) New York: NY PMSA. Washington, D.C.: Government Printing Office.

U.S. Census Bureau. 2001. *1990 Census Lookup. http://venus.census.gov/cdrom/ lookup/CMD = LIST/DB = C90STF3B/LEV = ZIP.*

——. 2000. *About Metropolitan Areas. http://www.census.gov/population/www/ estimatesaboutmetro.html.*

U.S. Department of Justice. 1999. *1997 Statistical Yearbook of the Immigration and Naturalization Service.* Washington, D.C.: Government Printing Office.

——. 1991–1999. *Statistical Yearbook of the Immigration and Naturalization Service.* Washington, D.C.: Government Printing Office.

U.S. Immigration and Naturalization Service. 2000a. *Illegal Alien Resident Population. http://www.ins.undoj.gov/graphics/aboutins/statistics/illegalalien/index.html.*

——. 2000b. *State Population Estimates: Legal Permanent Residents and Aliens Eligible to Apply to Naturalization. http://www.ins.usdoi/gov/graphics/aboutins/ statistics/prest.html.*

——. 2000c. Unpublished tabulations of immigration data.

Urban Institute. 2000. Unpublished tabulations of Current Population Survey data.

Van Hook, J., and Frank D. Bean. 1998a. "Estimating Unauthorized Mexican Migration to the United States: Issues and Results." In Mexican Ministry of Foreign Affairs and U.S. Commission on Immigration Reform, eds., *Migration Between*

Mexico and the United States: Binational Study, vol. II, *Research Reports and Background Materials,* pp. 511–50. Austin: Morgan.

——. 1998b. "Estimating Authorized Immigration." In Mexican Ministry of Foreign Affairs and U.S. Commission on Immigration Reform, eds., *Migration Between Mexico and the United States: Binational Study,* vol. II, *Research Reports and Background Materials,* pp. 619–682. Austin: Morgan.

Warren, Robert, and Ellen Percy Kraly. 1985. "The Elusive Exodus: Emigration from the United States." In *Population Trends and Public Policy 8.* Washington, D.C.: Population Reference Bureau.

Woodrow-Lafield, Karen. 1998. "Viewing Emigration at Century's End." In Mexican Ministry of Foreign Affairs and U.S. Commission on Immigration Reform, eds., *Migration Between Mexico and the United States: Binational Study,* vol. II, *Research Reports and Background Materials,* pp. 683–94. Austin: Morgan.

Zaharlick, Annemarie, and J. Brainard. 1987. "Demographic Characteristics, Ethnicity and the Resettlement of Southeast Asian Refugees in the United States." *Urban Anthropology* 16:327–74.

Zolberg, Aristede, Astri Suhrke, and Sergio Agua. 1986. "International Factors in the Formation of Refugee Movements." *International Migration Review* 20:151–69.

Immigrants, the Native-Born, and the Changing Division of Labor in New York City

Richard Wright and Mark Ellis

P resident Lyndon Johnson signed the Hart-Celler Immigration Act of 1965 into law on Liberty Island in New York Harbor. This legislation transformed immigration to the United States in ways unanticipated by even the bill's most fervent supporters and its cosponsors. In the last thirty-five years, the number of people migrating to the United States has grown tremendously, and immigrants to the United States arrive much more frequently from developing and transitional countries than they do from Europe. New York City serves as both a principal entry point and, more specifically, a place of residence and work for large numbers of these new immigrants.

A decade after this landmark immigration legislation, New York City endured a deep and widespread fiscal crisis. Un-

The National Science Foundation (Grant # SBR-9310647) helped make this research possible. Thanks go to Nancy Foner for her comments and Darby Green and Enru Wang for their research assistance. This essay significantly modifies and extends our previous analysis of New York City's ethnic and racial division of labor published in *Urban Geography* in 1996.

employment rose dramatically, and the city entered a period of profound readjustment as certain industrial sectors contracted rapidly, with effects ultimately ramifying throughout the whole economy. Although the depression of the mid-1970s is long past, the economy continues to experience moderate business cycles and to undergo restructuring in terms of marked job losses or gains in certain industrial sectors. Despite these swings and shifts in employment, immigrants have continued to arrive in the metropolitan area at relatively sustained rates. This chapter joins the theme of employment growth and decline and economic restructuring with the question of how immigrants and natives fit into the restless labor market of New York City. How have the two most significant changes in New York City's economy of the last forty years—its restructuring into a "world city" of globalized advanced capitalism and the transformation of its workforce by immigration—affected the employment fortunes of the city's ethnic and racial groups?

The entry of a large number of new workers into an economy like New York's is a complex process. Workers arrive from other countries with skills, literacy levels, English-language ability, and levels of education that are different from those of the native-born. Some arrive alone, whereas others arrive already knowing through friends and family what sort of work they will do and where they will live. They also come for different reasons. Some have fled civil war or political persecution. Most come seeking higher-paying work. All strive for a better life than the one they led elsewhere.

They also arrive in a place that is changing, in part due to immigration itself. Just as the number of immigrants coming to the city has altered significantly over the last thirty years, so has the city's economy. How immigrants enter into an economy such as New York's is far removed from a simple one-for-one replacement of a foreign-born worker for a native-born one. Changes in the composition of the native-born workforce through population aging and out-migration parallel the arrival of immigrants. The structure of the foreign-born workforce itself changes through continued immigration as well as emigration and migration to other parts of the United States. All this occurs against a backdrop of changes in the types of industries and occupations that make up the city's employment base as well as general cycles of growth and decline.

We begin this essay by considering how demography, race, nativity, and associated social networks operate in the labor market. We then track some aggregate trends in the city's economy since 1970. We also describe in general terms who has been migrating to and from the city, both nationally and internationally. The centerpiece of our analysis and the bulk of this essay involves developing an understanding of the shifting ethnic division of labor in the city—the distribution of group employment across industrial sectors. In particular, we show sectors in which the foreign-born now concentrate and how people came to those jobs. We pay special attention to the shifting fortunes of seven different racial/ethnic groups and by so doing address some fundamental questions of minority and native-born/foreign-born job competition. We foreground the role of social networks, population age structure, and time of arrival to characterize some of the main changes in the ethnoracial division of labor in New York City since 1970.

The Ethnic/Racial Division of Labor

The shift from a goods-producing economy to a service-based one is nowhere more apparent than in the largest cities of the United States. Analysis of the changing labor demands associated with this shift falls generally into two camps. The first centers on the emergence of a mismatch between the demands of new employment and the skills of urban residents, leaving certain groups (notably unskilled minorities) increasingly adrift from the economic mainstream (e.g., Kain 1968; Wilson 1987). The other view concentrates on expanding sectors of the economy. It acknowledges that the shift to services involves either the relative or absolute decline in manufacturing employment in many localities, but it suggests that new urban economies are also the locus of polarized employment opportunity with expansion of high- and low-wage service jobs. In this second perspective on urban economic restructuring, native-born workers fill the majority of job openings in well-paying service employment. Although a substantial number of immigrants come to the United States with skills, training, and education, most recent arrivals take the new, relatively low-paying jobs (Borjas 1999; Sassen 1996). This second perspective also speaks to the paradox of immigrants successfully finding jobs even in a reconfigured manufacturing sector (Portes and Bach 1985; Sassen 1988; Waldinger 1996).

Other perspectives exist, however. In the context of New York City, Roger Waldinger (1996) suggests that explanations such as the mismatch and polarization theses place undue emphasis on demand-side forces. These demand-side approaches fail, most importantly, to fully account for the continued economic marginality of many African American residents. In New York City, blacks historically have not been concentrated in declining sectors relative to other ethnic groups, nor have they been disproportionately excluded from expanding sectors. The most important industrial sector in decline in New York City is manufacturing. In 1970, manufacturing represented 13 percent of African American total employment in the city compared to 18 percent for foreign-born blacks, 17 percent for native whites, 25 percent for foreign-born whites, 33 percent for foreign-born Hispanics, 33 percent for native Hispanics, and 23 percent for foreign-born Asians. By 1997, the number and proportion of jobs held by African Americans in manufacturing had shrunk considerably. Since 1970, however, African Americans in general have been at a relatively low risk of displacement from sectoral contractions relative to other groups and forces at play. In New York City, immigrants have taken most new jobs, even in contracting sectors. Simply put, the distribution of African Americans in manufacturing or by industry does not sufficiently explain their worsening relative position in New York City's labor market. Fundamentally, demand-side theories beg the question of how to account for different outcomes among (similarly skilled) groups in the same regionally defined labor market.

Part of the answer lies in the city's demographics—specifically, the age and the size of the native-born white population (Bailey and Waldinger 1991; Waldinger 1996). Between 1970 and 1980, native whites lost over 400,000 jobs in New York City. Employment as a whole declined by a little over 270,000 during the same period. In the 1980s and 1990s, this trend continued. Total employment in the city grew 11 percent in the 1980s, while the representation of native-born whites dropped by 8 percent. Between 1990 and 1997, total employment growth was smaller (2 percent). At the same time, over a quarter of a million (roughly one-fifth of the 1990 total) native-born whites left the workforce. Native white New Yorkers moved to the suburbs or beyond or retired from the labor force. Some of the jobs left by this group created employment vacuums and set up a variegated chain of vacancies filled by different, and younger, other groups. African Americans filled some of these jobs, but the majority were taken by newly arrived workers from other countries. African Americans were drawn disproportionately to public-service work and the transportation sector, whereas immigrants filled niches in the private sector (in wholesaling, retailing, and certain services). The early immigrants who gained toeholds in these fields secured employment for later arrivals through tight social networks, which act as the source of information to coethnics looking for work and the backbone of ethnic capital supply to budding immigrant entrepreneurs. In consequence, immigrant networks, constructed either locally or transnationally, direct different immigrant groups toward particular types of employment (Granovetter 1974; Ellis and Wright 1999; Portes and Sensenbrenner 1993).

Immigrant networks are likely to be modified by human capital, in the form of skills, training, and years of education, and forms of social capital, such as gendered social networks. Thinking about the labor market as segregated and networked helps to explain some of the industrial and occupational specialization in almost all metropolitan labor markets in the United States. Such an approach also is especially useful in the context of New York City's economy in the last several decades because it can clarify how immigration continues at a rapid pace in the face of the metropolitan area's changing labor market, where many new jobs pay very poorly—at or about the minimum wage.

Data and Definitions

The data for this study come from several sources. Annual data on employment in New York City and the United States come from the Bureau of Labor Statistics. For the analysis of employment change in the 1970s and 1980s, we rely on employment data from the Public Use Micro Sample of the U.S. censuses of 1970,

1980, and 1990 (U.S. Bureau of the Census 1973, 1983, 1993). To perform the analysis for 1990–1997, we pooled the Annual Demographic Files of Current Population Survey (CPS) for 1996–1999 (U.S. Bureau of the Census 1996–1999).[1]

We recognize seven main subpopulations in New York City's labor market. These seven groups make up the vast majority of workers in the metropolitan area. Three are native-born groups—(non-Hispanic) whites, African Americans (we use the terms African Americans and native-born blacks interchangeably), and Hispanics. Note that native-born refers to all those born in the United States *and* its dependent territories. Thus native-born Hispanics include Puerto Ricans. The other four groups are foreign-born: Hispanics, non-Hispanic whites, non-Hispanic blacks, and Asians. These U.S. census–based categories are no doubt problematic; for example, the term "whites" groups together people of Polish, Irish, Russian, Italian, and Middle-Eastern descent; foreign-born Asians include Japanese, Korean, Indian, and Chinese; and Cubans, Dominicans, and, more recently, Mexicans comprise that foreign-born category of people self-identifying in the census as Hispanic. Nevertheless, these classifications allow us to describe with broad-brush strokes some key trends in employment in New York City by ethnicity and nativity.

Our analysis centers on change in employment by industry by race, ethnicity, and nativity. Related questions concerning occupational change and income redistribution and associated issues of income inequality and poverty occupy only a peripheral place in our study. Similarly, issues of human capital attributes such as skills and years of education arise in discussion but are not the focus of direct analysis. Our main concern is with the industries in which New York City's major ethnoracial groups are working, and how the distribution of groups across industries has changed as sectors have differentially weathered the storms of restructuring. As the economic well-being of groups stems largely from the sorts of jobs they perform, our analysis provides insight into the changing fortunes of New Yorkers by race and ethnicity.

Employment Trends in the City

To provide a broad context for our whole analysis, figure 3.1 describes the percentage of annual change in employment in New York City. The graph captures the main rhythm of employment change between 1965 and 1997. Booms tended to be relatively modest in magnitude (the highest rate of annual employment growth being 2.4 percent in 1997) compared with some periods of recession (in 1990, over 5 percent of the previous employment base was lost). This graph identifies three recessions in the study period (the early to mid-1970s, the early 1980s, and the early 1990s). These recessions were not unique to New York; they also occurred nationally. As for any local region, however, each recession in New York had unique qualities.

Figure 3.1 Annual Percentage of Change in Employment in New York City

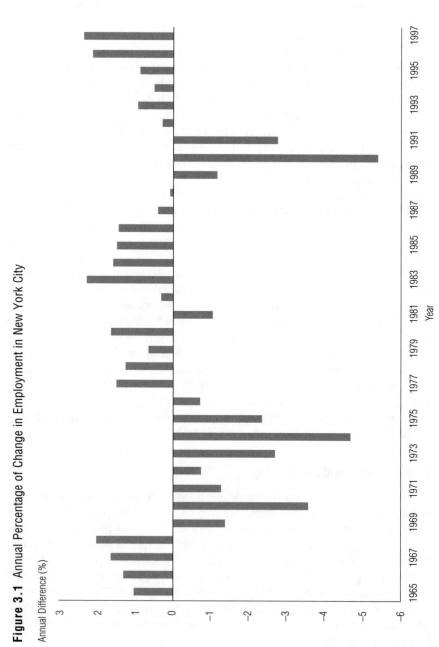

Source: Bureau of Labor Statistics.

Between 1969 and 1977, employment in the city declined 610,000, or 16.1 percent. The 1973–1975 recession the city endured is the renowned period of near fiscal collapse, but what is less well known is that by 1973 employment in the metropolitan area was already 7 percent below that of the 1969 peak. Employment losses in manufacturing accounted for almost half the total jobs lost in this recession (Brauer and Flaherty 1992). Manufacturing has never recovered; this sector has been in almost continuous employment contraction for thirty years. Starting in 1977, the city's economy began to revive, and total employment grew in most years for the subsequent decade until the stock market crash of October 1987. From 1987 until 1990 employment in the city again declined steeply, with losses concentrated mainly in construction, trade, manufacturing (again), and FIRE (finance, insurance, and real estate) (Brauer and Flaherty 1992). The 1990s was a period of overall job growth, with major employment gains concentrated in the service sectors (notably business and personal services).

The forces at work behind these trends are well known. Since 1970, employment in manufacturing in most U.S. cities and the country as a whole declined as production factors such as market access, labor access, transport links, and so on became increasingly irrelevant. Instead, production factors such as nonunionized labor in the United States and offshore, new high-technology modes of production, and new transport systems (e.g., interstate highways and containerization) dictate new geographies of production for many manufacturing activities. That said, not all manufacturing has vacated the city. Some 300,000 jobs remain in manufacturing—notably in garment and apparel production, and printing and publishing—because location in New York still matters for industries that are tied to fashion and culture and can remain competitive using local supplies of cheap labor.

Some of the same restructuring forces that decentralized much manufacturing and warehousing employment have contributed to the growth of new jobs in the city. The globalization of production that helped gut New York's traditional employment base reinforced its primacy as the world's financial center, generating many "high-end" jobs in business services, law, investment banking, advertising, and consulting. The flip side of this transformation has been growth in "low-end" jobs (those that are poor paying and frequently unstable and without benefits)—in domestic service, hotels and restaurants, and personal services—which make up an increasing share of the city's new industrial mix.

The most recent upswing in employment trends in New York mirrors that of the nation. We can begin to represent this broader context by comparing employment growth and decline in the city with that of the United States. Figure 3.2 shows that the city has rarely been in step with aggregate employment growth in the nation. The graph also shows that for the last thirty years, New York City has on only three occasions outperformed the country as a whole in terms of growth. Those three times were consecutive years during the recession of the early 1980s and reflect the ailing national economy of the time rather than New York's eco-

Figure 3.2 The Difference Between Percentage of Annual Employment Growth in New York City and in the United States

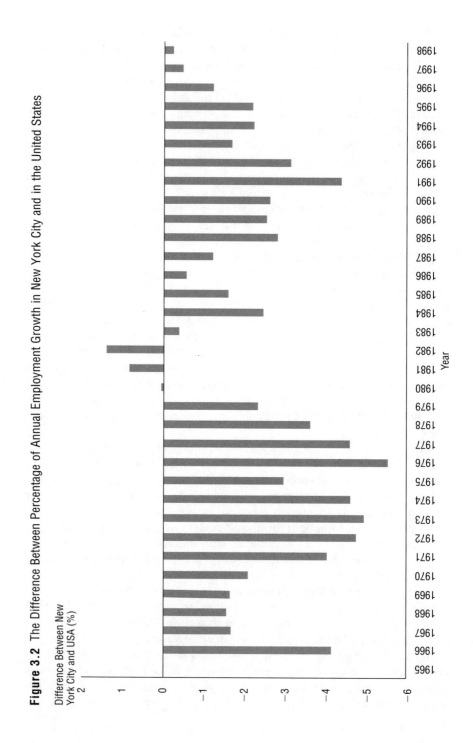

Difference Between New
York City and USA (%)

Year

nomic vitality. The main conclusion from figure 3.2 is that New York City, unlike some other important immigrant destinations (most notably Los Angeles), has not experienced higher-than-average job growth over the last thirty years. On the contrary, immigrants arriving in the city since 1965 came to a place that in terms of total job creation was being outperformed by other places in the nation.

In terms of aggregate demand for labor, then, New York's economy should not have attracted immigrants. That the opposite occurred suggests that aggregate labor demand alone cannot explain why so many immigrants have come to New York. New York's consistent appeal for immigrants stems in part from the foundation of ethnic niches developed by arrivals of the 1960s and 1970s in sectors formerly dominated by natives, mostly whites, who had either retired or departed for greener pastures outside the city (Waldinger 1996). Immigrant networks channeled later arrivals into these niches as jobs opened up through standard processes of job turnover. In this way immigration could continue, perhaps even expand, without growth in total employment.

To explore the details of this story for each ethnoracial group, we use several different methods of decomposing employment change in the city. Figure 3.3 offers a first step in this decomposition process by dividing total employment into eleven principal industrial sectors for four different years. The column heights reflect total employment and indicate that employment in the city dropped by about 8 percent from about 3.2 million jobs in 1970 to fewer than three million jobs in 1980. From that low point, the total number of jobs has increased to about 3.3 million in 1997. Perhaps the most interesting part of the figure, however, is the sectoral makeup of total employment by decade.

The shift away from goods production toward service production is clear when we contrast manufacturing with some other key sectors. In 1970, manufacturing had the largest proportion of jobs in the city (19 percent); by 1997, manufacturing jobs comprised only about 10 percent of total employment. The second-largest sector in 1970 (the public sector) grew only modestly, adding about 40,000 jobs over the twenty-seven-year period. The main engine of growth—at least in terms of sectoral change—has been the expansion of jobs in professional and business services (banking, securities, insurance, consulting, etc.)—which grew 77 percent between 1970 and 1997. Professional services is now the largest of the 11 sectors we identify and analyze. In the late 1960s, the growth of jobs in professional services, business services, and public employment spurred overall employment (Waldinger 1996:34). The former two sectors, we argue, remain the main engines of growth in the city's economy.

Given these sectoral shifts, how have different racial, ethnic, and nativity groups fared? Figure 3.4 shows that in 1997 native-born whites still dominated the New York City workforce, but their proportion of the city's labor pool has declined considerably since 1970. The six other groups, two native-born and four immigrant, increasingly contribute to the city's workforce. African American employment shrank more slowly in the city's economy in the 1970s (−4 percent for

Figure 3.3 Sectoral Change in Employment: New York City 1970, 1980, 1990, 1997

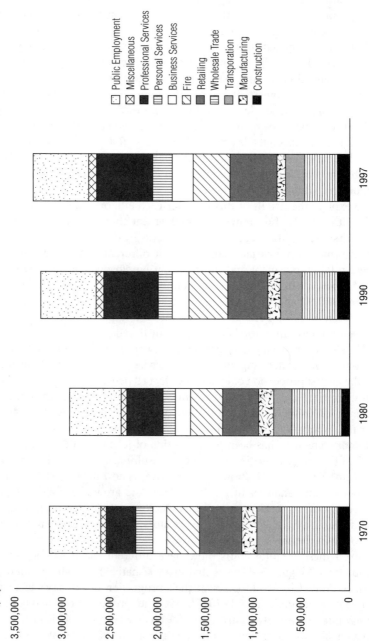

Employment

Public Employment
Miscellaneous
Professional Services
Personal Services
Business Services
Fire
Retailing
Wholesale Trade
Transporation
Manufacturing
Construction

Year

Source: U.S. Bureau of the Census 1973, 1983, 1993, 1996–1999.

Figure 3.4 Total Employment by Race/Ethnicity in New York City: 1970–1997

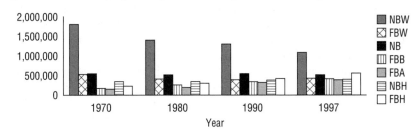

Source: U.S. Bureau of the Census 1973, 1983, 1993, 1996–1999.

native blacks versus –8 percent for the city as a whole) and grew at a slightly above average rate than the city as a whole in the 1980s (12 percent for native blacks vs. 11 percent for the city). In the first seven years of the 1990s, African Americans again lost employment as a whole, while the city's employment grew modestly (2 percent). Native-born Hispanics (mostly Puerto Ricans) were the only major "nonimmigrant" group to experience job growth in the 1970s. In the 1980s they boosted their representation in the labor force by 22 percent, more than twice the city's growth rate. This trend continued in the 1990s, albeit at a slower rate (8 percent). Foreign-born Hispanics have steadily increased their presence in the labor market over the 1970–1997 period, but in a much different fashion than the native-born. By 1990, they overtook native-born Hispanics in terms of total numbers. By 1997, spurred by arrivals from the Dominican Republic and a much larger post-1990 stream from Mexico and Central America, they became the largest aggregate minority group in the city's workforce. Figure 3.4 also highlights the recent change in the proportion of foreign-born whites (made up mostly of people from the former Soviet Union, but also the United Kingdom and Canada) in New York City's economy. In the last decade, this group changed from being a declining proportion of the workforce to one with an increasing number of jobs and an increasing share of all employment.

Remaking the Racial/Ethnic Division of Labor

Overall, then, immigrant groups from developing and transitional countries all garnered significantly greater portions of the available jobs in New York City during the 1970s, 1980s, and 1990s. How have particular ethnic groups fared as the city's employment base shifted away from manufacturing to the new service economy? Have some groups gained jobs because they were well positioned to take advantage of the shifts? Did other groups lose jobs because they were disproportionately concentrated in sectors that collapsed?

We can answer these questions by separating each group's employment growth or decline into three different sources (see Wright and Ellis 1996, 1997 for more details). The first subcomponent we define as employment change attributable to the overall economy.[2] This component measures the effect of the metropolitan economy's strength as a whole. It tests the hypothesis "Does a rising tide raise all boats?" In other words, it captures the effect of a healthy economy or a declining economy on each sector for each of the seven groups studied.

A second subcomponent of employment growth or decline measures whether a particular group gained or lost employment because of an unusual concentration in a particular sector. Extracting this subcomponent addresses a critical question for any analysis of urban labor market process, for it speaks directly to the theory of employment mismatch. Mismatch occurs if a racial or ethnic group is concentrated in declining sectors.[3] An emphasis on mismatch has broad currency in the literature—for example, William Julius Wilson's thesis on the plight of central-city African Americans leans heavily on such an approach (Wilson 1987; see also Warf 1990; Fainstein 1993).

The remaining portion of employment change is attributable to yet another source: the *group shift* effect.[4] Ettlinger and Kwon (1994) note that immigrants frequently fashion their own opportunities in the urban labor market. They utilize Porter's (1990) term "competitive advantage" to refer to the potential for actors "to create job opportunities not necessarily given by the structure of the economy and/or by ethnic identity" (Ettlinger and Kwon 1994:418). This advantage can originate in the group's competitive strength in leveraging jobs in individual sectors, an advantage that often lies in the ability of group networks to channel coethnics into job openings. This competitive advantage does not necessarily result in *better* jobs, measured in terms of either job quality or remuneration. Rather, it allows some groups to do better than others in terms of developing and expanding niches in specific economic activities (see Light and Bonacich 1988; Light and Gold 2000; Zhou and Portes 1995).[5] The expansion of a group's employment in any industry also depends on growth in the overall size of a group's workforce regardless of any inherent sector-specific group competitive advantage. Therefore, unlike the first two components that isolate demand influences on employment change, this last component measures the effect of group characteristics—thus the term we use for it, the *group shift effect*. This effect identifies disproportionate "shifts" in group employment after accounting for citywide economic conditions and sector-specific shares of jobs. Groups with positive shifts gain employment in a sector at a rate above that expected from the average for all groups for that sector. Groups with negative shifts obtain jobs under the expected sectoral rate.

We can calculate these three subcomponents for either a particular industry by racial or ethnic group or as a sum over all industries for a particular group. The figures we refer to depict the totals for these components of change. These are snapshots of each component's aggregate effect on group employment trends in each decade. We elaborate on the role of specific sectors in group employment in our discussion of these figures.

Native-Born Whites

Despite significant declines in the number of native-born whites in New York's workforce to the point where they now comprise about one-third of the total workforce, they remain by far the most numerous subgroup identified in this study. Figure 3.5 presents information on native-born white job performance by industrial sector. This group lost employment in most sectors in each of the time periods analyzed. The best decade in terms of employment growth by sector for this group was the 1980s, when native-born whites registered job growth in six of the eleven sectors. In the 1970s, however, native-born whites increased their numbers in only two sectors. In the 1990s, they experienced employment decline across the board. Between 1970 and 1997, native-born whites lost many more jobs than any other population subgroup. In the 1980s, their representation in the labor market declined by 8 percent—in the other two decades, the decline was at least 20 percent.

We decompose these employment changes and report the aggregate findings in figure 3.6. Data for individual sectors (not shown) flesh out some of our broader discussion. The group shift effect is the main force behind the overall decline of the white workforce in the city in each decade. A large factor in this effect was the aging of the white population; native-born whites were retiring and suburbanizing, and other (mostly younger foreign-born) workers entered. As such, the aggregate group shift effect signals the drying up of white labor-market entrants rather than the inability or unwillingness of whites to compete for jobs. Large negative group shift effects for the public sector, specifically in the 1970s, signal attrition (not layoffs) in the native-born white municipal workforce (Waldinger 1996). In the 1970s, whites also shifted out of manufacturing in response to sharp declines in real wages and increased employment instability. In the 1980s, the lion's share of the negative group shift effect was concentrated in professional services. Although this sector saw a 4 percent growth in native-born white employment, this expansion was completely overshadowed by the sector's overall growth rate (54 percent for the decade). In other words, many of the new professional-sector jobs went to members of other groups. Retailing and manufacturing also contributed to the negative group shift effect of native-born whites in the 1980s, a pattern that also prevailed in the 1990s.

In sharp contrast to the total losses generated by group shift, the total industry mix effect for native whites was almost neutral in every decade. Overall, then, the particular jobs native-born whites held at the beginning of each decade had relatively little to do with their relentless decline in employment share over the subsequent ten years. Native-born whites continued to occupy some high-growth industrial concentrations, most notably in professional services in the 1970s and 1980s. Without such concentrations, native-born white decline would have been much greater in the 1980s than it actually was. The gains enjoyed by native-born whites in booming sectors were offset or significantly reduced by their losses from concentration in declining sectors, most especially manufacturing. All told, the

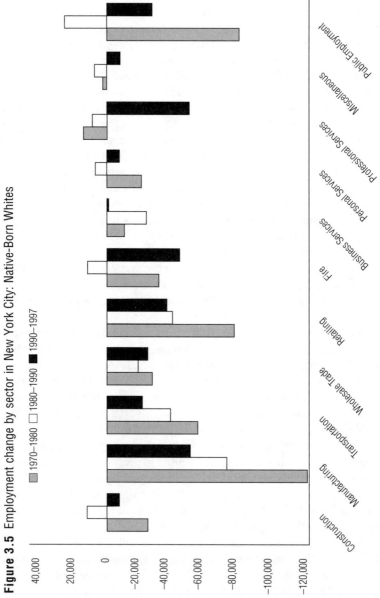

Figure 3.5 Employment change by sector in New York City: Native-Born Whites

Legend: ■ 1970–1980 □ 1980–1990 ■ 1990–1997

Categories: Construction, Manufacturing, Transportation, Wholesale Trade, Retailing, Fire, Business Services, Personal Services, Professional Services, Miscellaneous, Public Employment

Scale: 40,000; 20,000; 0; −20,000; −40,000; −60,000; −80,000; −100,000; −120,000

Figure 3.6 Components of Employment Change for Native-Born Whites in New York City

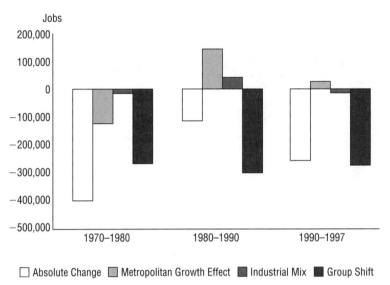

Source: U.S. Bureau of the Census 1973, 1983, 1993, 1996–1999.

story for native-born whites is one of job loss from declining industries but no large-scale movement of those who lost jobs into new growth industries in which whites hold some competitive advantage. Many of those who left declining industries departed the city's workforce entirely through either retirement or out-migration. This mass exit generated demand for replacements that came in unequal numbers from other native-born and foreign-born groups.

Foreign-Born Whites

In the 1970s and 1980s, the patterns of employment change by sector and the components of change for foreign-born whites in New York City generally resemble those for native-born whites (figure 3.7). In the 1970s, foreign-born whites suffered significant job loss in manufacturing, other losses occurring particularly in wholesale and retail trade, and gains registering in professional services and construction. The difference between whites who were immigrant and native occurs in services. In business services, foreign-born white employment was stable, while native white employment tumbled 20 percent. In professional services, native employment stagnated while immigrant white employment in the city grew over 27 percent. In the 1980s, the deep job loss of foreign-born whites was concentrated in manufacturing and wholesaling as they retired from or left declining industries, much as native whites had done. As did native whites, their foreign-born

Figure 3.7 Change in Employment by Sector in New York City: Foreign-Born Whites

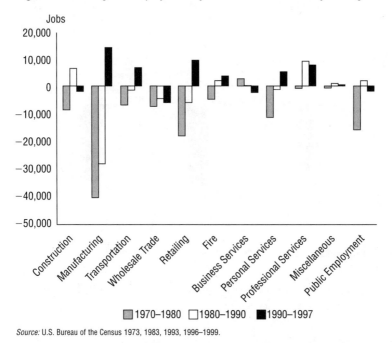

Source: U.S. Bureau of the Census 1973, 1983, 1993, 1996–1999.

Figure 3.8 Components of Employment Change for Foreign-Born Whites in New York City

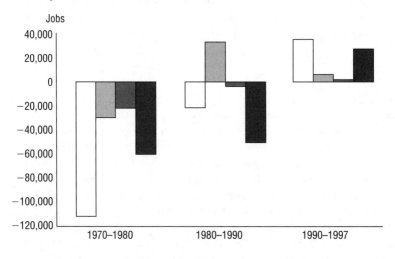

Source: U.S. Bureau of the Census 1973, 1983, 1993, 1996–1999.

counterparts experienced employment loss in almost every sector in the 1970s and 1980s largely because of shrinkage in overall group supply. The overall growth of New York's economy in the 1980s slowed this decline somewhat.

Between 1990 and 1997, however, foreign-born whites show a dramatic change: their representation in the city's labor force increased by 12 percent as immigrants and refugees arrived in large numbers from the former USSR and its satellites.[6] Figure 3.8 reflects this switch as the group shift effect becomes positive in spite of weak metropolitan growth. Immigrant whites moved into manufacturing, retailing, and finance/real estate, where they have some advantages over other groups. The contrast between figure 3.6 and figure 3.8 captures one of the main themes of our analysis. In the story of change in New York City's labor market, nativity emerges as an important axis of difference between groups. As the native white population ages, immigration is making the age structure of foreign-born whites more youthful, boosting their rates of labor force participation.

Native-Born Blacks

Total employment for African Americans changed the least of all the groups studied in this analysis. That relative stability, however, masked some significant shifts in employment distribution by sector. Figure 3.9 depicts the growth rates in employment of native-born black workers by industry. Although African Americans lost a total of 22,520 jobs (5 percent) between 1970 and 1980—with most losses in the transport sector and personal services—gains in the public sector and professional services offset a good deal of these losses. The public sector was an emerging labor market niche for African Americans in the New York economy of the 1970s, which is entirely consistent with Waldinger's account of the postindustrial transformation of the city; native blacks' "political claims gave them significant advantages" over other minority groups competing for work in public services (1992:224). In the 1980s, African American employment gains were concentrated in professional services and construction. Losses continued in manufacturing and were joined by a steep decline in public-sector employment so that despite aggregate employment growth, native blacks' relative labor market position slipped. Indeed, in the 1990s, native-born blacks lost jobs across almost all sectors.

Figure 3.10 extracts some of the forces at work in these swings. In the 1970s, native blacks experienced a relatively small employment loss from industrial mix (about 1,500 jobs). The same thing happened in the 1980s and 1990–1997. This is an important finding because it shows that native black workers were not overconcentrated in rapidly declining sectors as the employment mismatch theory suggests (Waldinger 1996). They lost or gained jobs for other reasons. In the 1970s, the aggregate poor performance of New York City's economy significantly affected blacks. Our analysis indicates that the 3.9 percent African American employment decline between 1970 and 1980 resulted from the city's overall eco-

Figure 3.9 Change in Employment by Sector in New York City: African Americans

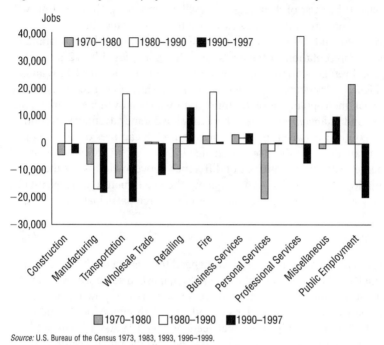

Source: U.S. Bureau of the Census 1973, 1983, 1993, 1996–1999.

Figure 3.10 Components of Employment Change for African Americans in New York City

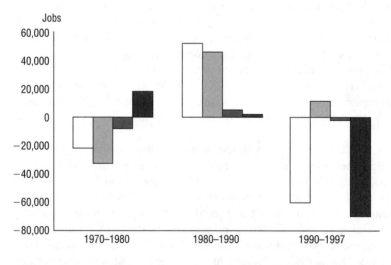

Source: U.S. Bureau of the Census 1973, 1983, 1993, 1996–1999.

nomic performance. Their fortunes ebbed and flowed in a similar pattern in the 1980s. The gain of more than 50,000 jobs is almost all accounted for by the overall rising tide of employment growth in the city. Of course, not all sectors were in step with these trends. For example, the public employment sector as a whole expanded 10 percent in the 1980s, while African American representation in it declined by about 9 percent. In the 1980s, native blacks (at least those with college degrees) also enjoyed a relatively significant comparative advantage in finance and professional services, with positive shifts into these sectors.

The 1990s, however, were disastrous, with a 12 percent decline in total native-born black employment. The modest growth of employment in the city as a whole had little effect on the fortunes of African Americans, or on their distribution by industry. Almost all of their actual employment losses are attributable to shifts out of traditional industrial concentrations, most especially the public sector. African Americans also suffered large negative group shift effects in transportation and manufacturing. These sectors shrank (about 9 percent) in the 1990s, but African American employment in them declined at a much higher rate, around 50 percent. Some of the losses are probably due to declines in aggregate African American labor supply, but their magnitude suggests that African Americans experienced a disproportionate share of job cuts and fared poorly in competition with other groups for what jobs remained. For example, in the 1990s various levels of government retrenched (Johnson 1997:36). African Americans are not only disproportionately represented in public employment, but they also have a disproportionate representation in those subareas targeted for cuts in recent years (social services and public health care) as governments subcontract out work and as welfare-to-work policies take effect (Johnson 1997).

Foreign-Born Blacks

In our analysis, foreign-born blacks in New York City are mostly from Jamaica, Guyana, Trinidad, and Haiti. Some come with undergraduate and advanced degrees; most, however, have relatively few years of formal education. Foreign-born black employment has grown rapidly since 1970. Few sectors registered decline in any of the last three decades (figure 3.11). The strongest and most sustained employment has occurred in professional services and public employment, followed by retailing. Employment in manufacturing shifted from significant gain in the 1970s to a position of loss between 1990 and 1997 (about 7,000 jobs). The increased employment in the public sector by foreign-born blacks (and Hispanics) stands in stark contrast to African American job loss. Evidently, in the 1980s and 1990s, immigrant professionals secured a large niche in the city's bureaucracy as native black employment there declined.

Decomposing these changes produces a vivid picture of growth derived overwhelmingly from group shift effects rather than any favorable concentration in growth industries (figure 3.12). The main contributors to this overall effect were,

Figure 3.11 Change in Employment by Sector in New York City: Foreign-Born Blacks

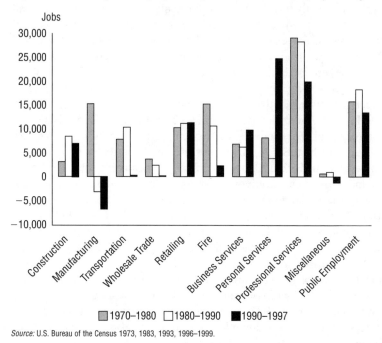

Source: U.S. Bureau of the Census 1973, 1983, 1993, 1996–1999.

Figure 3.12 Components of Employment Change for Foreign-Born Blacks in New York City

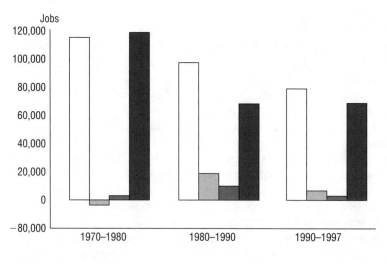

Source: U.S. Bureau of the Census 1973, 1983, 1993, 1996–1999.

in the 1970s, professional services, followed by manufacturing, the public sector, and finance–insurance–real estate. In the 1980s, foreign-born blacks leveraged employment gains in the city most notably in public employment and the transportation sector. Between 1990 and 1997, they shifted into both high-end and low-end jobs in personal services, professional services and public employment, which accounted for the majority of employment growth for this subgroup. As with whites, nativity matters in the analysis of labor market segmentation for blacks. Immigrant blacks are making advances in New York's economy as African Americans appear to experience contraction. Some of these gains are in the very sectors in which African Americans experienced large negative shifts—most notably in public employment, suggesting that nativity modified black disadvantage in New York's restructuring and downsizing labor market. That said, most immigrant black employment growth is primarily attributable to growth in group size rather than the result of positive exposure to New York's fastest-growing sectors.

Native-Born Hispanics

Until recently, native Hispanics in New York meant Puerto Ricans. In the 1990s, second-generation Americans of Mexican, Central, and South American ancestry began to take up a larger share of this population. Like African Americans and native-born whites, many Puerto Ricans left the city in the 1970s, with net migration between New York and the island favoring Puerto Rico (Jaffe et al. 1980:190). In contrast to the other two native-born groups, total employment for native Hispanics still *grew* 3 percent in the 1970s (see figures 3.13 and 3.14.) In fact, native-born Hispanics increased their representation in the city's workforce in each of the three periods under investigation. However, this total growth masks important variation by sector, most notably the deep and significant employment losses suffered by native Hispanics in manufacturing; at the same time, they realized considerable and sustained job growth in the public sector and professional services.

Analysis reveals that native Hispanic workers had positive shift effects in most sectors in each of the three periods analyzed. In the 1970s, however, the poor performance of the city's economy (negative growth effect) and a concentration in declining sectors (negative total industrial mix) substantially undermined native Hispanic labor market gains. Native Hispanics lost manufacturing jobs at a faster rate than decline in the sector as a whole. In contrast, native blacks who also lost jobs in manufacturing did so at a rate below that of total manufacturing-sector decline. This implies that in the 1970s native Hispanics were in manufacturing subsectors and occupations more vulnerable to job loss than African Americans.

In the 1980s native Hispanic workers lost 23,370 jobs in manufacturing, and these losses continued in the 1990s. In 1980, 25 percent of native Hispanics worked in manufacturing; by 1997 only 9 percent did so. This disproportionate

Figure 3.13 Change in Employment by Sector in New York City: Native-Born Hispanics

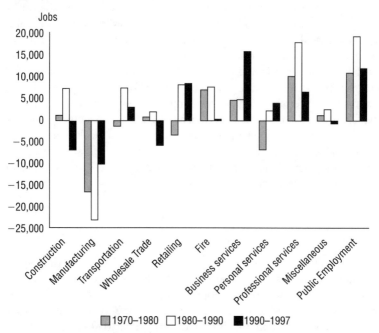

■ 1970–1980　□ 1980–1990　■ 1990–1997

Source: U.S. Bureau of the Census 1973, 1983, 1993, 1996–1999.

Figure 3.14 Components of Employment Change for Native-Born Hispanics in New York City

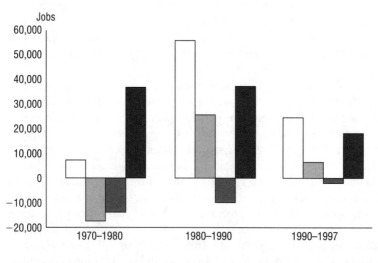

□ Absolute Change　■ Metropolitan Growth Effect　■ Industrial Mix　■ Group Shift

Source: U.S. Bureau of the Census 1973, 1983, 1993, 1996–1999.

concentration in a declining manufacturing sector is the principal reason for their negative industrial mix in the 1970s and 1980s. In each decade, however, the aggregate group shift effect has offset employment loss due to industry mix or, in the 1970s, malaise in the city economy as a whole.

Foreign-Born Hispanics

The rapid growth of immigrant Hispanics in New York's labor market is clear from both figures 3.15 and 3.16. This group experienced employment increases in almost every sector in the city in each of the three decades. Average employment growth was remarkably stable and sustained—around 55 percent in each of the three periods under investigation. These gains were largest and strongest in retailing and manufacturing. Employment growth also occurred in all the services and in the public sector. In the late 1990s, foreign-born Hispanics overtook African Americans as the second-largest group we identify in our labor market analysis.

As figure 3.16 shows, almost all of foreign-born Hispanic employment growth can be accounted by the group shift effect. The generally small, negative industrial mix effects from shift-share analysis suggest that immigrant Hispanics' specialization by industrial sector relative to the total population had relatively little influence on their overall employment growth. Despite a contraction in manufacturing employment in the 1980s, foreign-born Hispanics' share of the city's manufacturing jobs increased from 14 to 18.6 percent. Thus, in manufacturing the shift effect is positive. In both the 1980s and 1990s, however, the shift into manufacturing was dwarfed relative to that in retailing. In retail trade, immigrant Hispanic employment penetration is occurring at a much faster rate than their gains in the city as a whole, and our analysis reveals this as an emerging significant employment niche.

Foreign-Born Asians

The employment change profile of foreign-born Asians generally resembles that of foreign-born Hispanics and blacks (see figures 3.17 and 3.18). In each decade, the number of foreign-born Asians in the city's workforce increased significantly, by as much as 250 percent in the 1970s. Growth continued through the 1990s, albeit at a slower rate. In each decade, with one minor exception, employment in every sector increased, with the largest growth in manufacturing, retail trade, and professional services. As with foreign-born Hispanics, immigrant Asians registered their largest absolute job gain in the retail trade sector. Unlike every other group, foreign-born Asians actually gained jobs in manufacturing in every decade; for example, their share of manufacturing jobs went from 5 percent in 1980 to 11 percent in 1990. As with other immigrant groups, the group shift effects dominate employment change (figure 3.18), suggesting that increase in group size

Figure 3.15 Change in Employment by Sector in New York City: Foreign-Born Hispanics

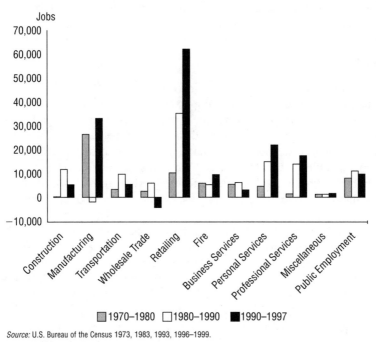

Source: U.S. Bureau of the Census 1973, 1983, 1993, 1996–1999.

Figure 3.16 Components of Employment Change for Foreign-Born Hispanics in New York City

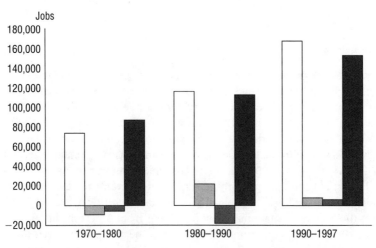

Source: U.S. Bureau of the Census 1973, 1983, 1993, 1996–1999.

Figure 3.17 Change in Employment by Sector in New York City: Foreign-Born Asians

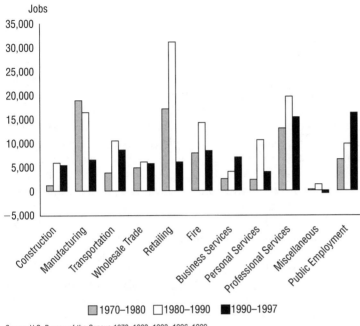

Source: U.S. Bureau of the Census 1973, 1983, 1993, 1996–1999.

Figure 3.18 Components of Employment Change for Foreign-Born Asians in New York City

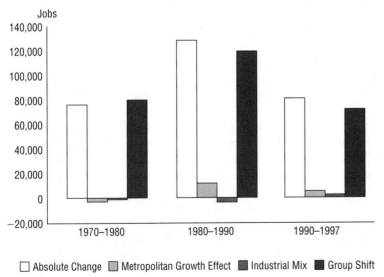

Source: U.S. Bureau of the Census 1973, 1983, 1993, 1996–1999.

rather than economic conditions in New York lay behind the expansion of Asian employment.

Discussion and Conclusions

Increased immigration in the last three decades has heightened interest in understanding the relationship between the structure of the labor force and the changing urban economies in the United States. In the main, immigrants have continued to concentrate in a few of the nation's large metropolitan areas, such as Los Angeles and New York. The number of arrivals remains high, and questions about how these newcomers fit in economically and culturally—and obtain work and secure shelter—remain as some of the most pressing issues that American society faces. In New York City, profound economic change has taken place over the last thirty years. Newcomers as well as the native-born have helped frame these changes and also have been shaped by them.

An important element of the New York story is that mass immigration has occurred despite the city's anemic employment growth of the last three decades. So why have immigrants come to New York if opportunities for employment were greater elsewhere? A main reason is the decline in size of the native-born white population. In the 1970s, 400,000 native whites left the New York City workforce. The loss slowed in the 1980s to 100,000 native whites but picked up again in the 1990s. We estimate that more than 250,000 native-born whites retired or exited the city's workforce between 1990 and 1997, even though total employment expanded slightly overall. In the 1970s, this exodus created replacement labor demand in many areas of the economy. In the 1980s, demographic succession played a reduced role in assigning ethnic groups to jobs. The absolute and relative decline in the number of native-born white workers, however, regained the 1970s pace in the 1990s, suggesting that, once again, the exit of native whites is leaving gaps for other groups to fill.

To date, these groups have largely been nonwhite minorities, but the 1990s saw some replacement labor needs met by the growth in the foreign-born white population (driven mostly by immigration from the former USSR and its successor states). White immigrants' ability to leverage new and considerable labor market advantage raises important questions about the role of race, human capital, social networks, and entrepreneurship that require careful, detailed study. The likelihood is that today's white immigrants make use of their advantages to vault past African Americans and other native-born minorities into the ranks of the city's middle class.

The 1990s also saw a large reversal of fortune for African Americans—unfortunately, for the worse. In the 1970s and especially in the 1980s, the growth effect largely explained overall native black job gains. Essentially, when the city grew, African Americans got jobs. Industrial mix has been a relatively unimportant factor. In the 1990s, however, African Americans experienced a massive deterioration in labor market comparative advantage as measured by the group shift effect. In the aggregate, the African American pattern of employment change began to resemble that of native-born whites as immigrant groups replaced them in traditional employment concentrations, such as public services.

For native Hispanics, the 1970s, in the aggregate, was a decade of minor job gain, while the 1980s saw fairly substantial job growth in all sectors except manufacturing, where employment fell by over 36 percent. Native-born Hispanics clearly differ from African Americans in terms of their sectoral employment distribution and emerging patterns of comparative advantage. Native Hispanics' higher concentration in manufacturing than in services produced negative total industrial mix effects in both the 1970s and 1980s. Unlike African Americans, they have had an unfavorable employment distribution in relation to the city's growth pattern. Also unlike African Americans, gains in services compensated the loss in manufacturing employment. For native blacks, opportunities eroded in the public sector and expanded in advanced services; for native Hispanics, labor market comparative advantage occurred only modestly in advanced services and most notably in the public sector. These distinct patterns suggest that native-born minority groups fit into New York City's present and likely future division of labor in substantially different ways. The distinctions are context specific: evidence from Los Angeles suggests that native Hispanics' sectoral employment pattern in that city is becoming more like that of native blacks (Wright and Ellis 1997).

Although African Americans lost the jobs in the 1990s that they gained in the 1980s, and although total native-born Hispanic employment grew only modestly in the metropolitan economy, foreign-born black and Hispanic employment grew very rapidly. Unlike the native groups and foreign-born whites we studied, the performance of the city's economy in general had little effect on the foreign-born populations investigated here. Growth effects were relatively minor for foreign-born blacks, Asians, and Hispanics relative to group shift effects. Overall, these immigrants continued to garner the preponderance of all jobs in the city—most notably in retail trade, but also in professional services and even the public sector.

The sectoral differences among immigrant groups point to an ethnic division of labor among the foreign-born. Most importantly, some groups are better positioned than others in terms of where they stand in the city's employment mix: immigrant blacks tend to have jobs in growth sectors whereas immigrant Hispanics do not. Essentially, immigrant blacks are more likely to work in New York's expanding service sectors than immigrant Hispanics. Immigrant blacks have enjoyed positive shifts in advanced services and private-sector basic services, but their most important emerging sector is public administration. Conversely, immigrant Hispanics' largest shift is into retail trade and personal services, and they still retain a disproportionate share of manufacturing's declining employment base. Foreign-born Asians are also overly concentrated in manufacturing but have a disproportionately high share of jobs in professional services as well. Like immigrant Hispanics, foreign-born Asians' largest positive shift is into retail trade but, unlike them, immigrant Asians also are shifting into services like FIRE. In short, immigrants are diverse and fit into New York's economy in ways that depend on their ethnicity.

That some immigrant groups are better located than others in terms of their concentration in growth sectors portends variability in their future employment fortunes. Immigrant Hispanics are more likely to suffer the consequences of ongoing job loss in sectors like manufacturing. In contrast, immigrant blacks, whites, and Asians appear to be less vulnerable to future job loss in traditional industries. Regardless, the future employment of all immigrant groups will continue to depend on the demography of the native-born population. Native-born whites, who now make up about one-third of the city's workforce, will probably continue to decline in number in the next few years. This will generate more replacement labor demand, much of it likely to be filled by immigrant groups. The 1990s saw the labor force exit of native-born workers spread to African Americans—and immigrants began filling jobs in their wake. At some time, however, and that moment may have been reached or will be shortly, the loss of native-born workers through retirement and out-migration will slow to the point that replacement labor demand will be insufficient to absorb New York's new immigrant arrivals. Unless immigration slows, or New York's employment grows to absorb new arrivals, other factors, such as worker skills and education, employer preferences, discrimination, racism, union exclusion of minorities, and job networks, will become much stronger determinants of ethnic group employment fortunes than they have been to date. It is hard to sort out the likely winners and losers in this new competition for jobs. Present trends suggest that African Americans and native- and foreign-born Hispanics will be most likely to lose out if the conditions under which New York absorbs immigrants change as anticipated.

Notes

1. To avoid double counting, we include only those people being rotated into the CPS in the pooled sample (except in 1996, when we used the outgoing rotation as well). This resulted in a total sample of 3,370 workers. We used CPS weights, adjusted to reflect the pooling strategy, to estimate numbers employed in each industry by ethnoracial group. The sample is much smaller than the decadal Public Use Micro Samples, and therefore one should not consider the estimates of 1990s employment trends as precise as those of earlier decades. That said, we have reasonable confidence in the CPS data in that they produce trends consistent with earlier decades. We attribute the estimates obtained from the pooled data to the year 1997—the year in which the midpoint of the pooled sample occurs.

2. Following Wright and Ellis (1996), we can formally express this *metropolitan growth effect* as:

$$\mathrm{MGE}_{r,i} = \mathrm{E}_{t,r,i}\,(g_m)$$

where $E_{t,r,i}$ is employment in time t of group r in sector i and g_m is the growth rate for total employment for the metropolitan area over the time period in question.

3. This is the amount of employment change attributable to the differences in the sectoral makeup of the nativity/ethnic group versus that of the metropolitan region as a whole. An *industrial mix effect* can be expressed algebraically as

$$IME_{r,i} = E_{t,r,i} (g_{im} - g_m)$$

where g_{im} is the growth rate in sector i for the metropolitan area over the time period.

4. This residual is usually called the *competitive effect* and can be formally stated as

$$CE_{r,i} = E_{t,r,i} (g_{ir} - g_{im})$$

where g_{ir} is the growth rate in sector i for the ethnic group over the time period. As this effect measures the impact of changes in group size as well as sector-specific competitive advantage we prefer to call it the *group supply effect*.

5. Each of these three components can be calculated for a given sector or summed over all sectors for a group. The complete (shift-share) identity for the analysis of intrametropolitan employment change can be formally expressed as follows:

$$E_{t+1,r,i} - E_{t,r,i} = \Sigma E_{r,i} = MGE_{r,i} + IME_{r,i} + CE_{r,i}$$

6. The native-born presence declined by 20 percent in this period.

References

Bailey, Thomas, and Roger Waldinger. 1991. "The Changing Ethnic/Racial Division of Labor." In J. H. Mollenkopf and M. Castells, eds., *Dual City*, 43–78. New York: Russell Sage Foundation.

Borjas, George J. 1999. *Heaven's Door: Immigration Policy and the American Economy*. Princeton: Princeton University Press.

Brauer, David, and Mark Flaherty. 1992. "The New York City Recession." *Federal Reserve Bank of New York Quarterly Review* 17 (Spring): 66–71.

Ellis, Mark, and Richard Wright. 1999. "The Industrial Division of Labor Among Immigrants and Internal Migrants to the Los Angeles Economy." *International Migration Review* 33:26–54.

Ettlinger, Nancy, and Sangcheol Kwon. 1994. "A Comparative Assessment of the Role of Immigrants in U.S. Urban Labor Markets: A Case Study of Asians in New York and Los Angeles." *Tijdschrift voor Economische en Sociale Geografie* 85:417–33.

Fainstein, Norman. 1993. "Race, Class, and Segregation: Discourses About African Americans." *International Journal of Urban and Regional Research* 17: 384–403.

Granovetter, Mark. 1974. *Getting a Job: A Study in Contacts and Careers*. Cambridge: Harvard University Press.

Jaffe, Abram J., Ruth M. Cullen, and Thomas D. Boswell. 1980. *The Changing Demography of Spanish Americans*. New York: Academic Press.

Johnson, Kirk. 1997. "Black Workers Bear Big Burden as Jobs in Government Dwindle." *The New York Times*, Feb. 2, 1, 36.

Kain, John. 1968. "Housing Segregation, Negro Employment, and Metropolitan Decentralization." *Quarterly Journal of Economics* 82:175–97.

Light, Ivan, and Edna Bonacich. 1988. *Immigrant Entrepreneurs: Koreans in Los Angeles, 1965–1982.* Berkeley: University of California Press.

Light, Ivan, and Steven J. Gold. 2000. *Ethnic Economies.* San Diego, Calif.: Academic Press.

Porter, Michael E. 1990. *The Competitive Advantage of Nations.* New York: Free Press.

Portes, Alejandro, and Robert L. Bach. 1985. *Latin Journey: Cuban and Mexican Immigrants in the United States.* Berkeley: University of California Press.

Portes, Alejandro, and Julia Sensenbrenner. 1993. "Embeddedness and Immigration: Notes on the Social Determinants of Economic Action." *American Journal of Sociology* 98:1320–50.

Sassen, Saskia. 1988. *The Mobility of Labor and Capital.* New York: Cambridge University Press.

———. 1996. *Losing Control? Sovereignty in an Age of Globalization.* New York: Columbia University Press.

U.S. Bureau of the Census. 1973. *1970 Census of Population Public Use Sample.* Washington, D.C.: Government Printing Office.

———. 1983. *1980 Census of Population Public Use Micro Data Sample.* Washington, D.C.: Government Printing Office.

———. 1993. *1990 Census of Population Public Use Micro Data Sample.* Washington, D.C.: Government Printing Office.

———. 1996–1999. *Current Population Survey: Annual Demographic File.* Washington, D.C.: U.S. Department of Commerce.

Waldinger, Roger. 1992. "Native Blacks, New Immigrants, and the Post-Industrial Transformation of New York." In M. Cross, ed., *Ethnic Minorities and Industrial Change in Europe and North America,* 205–25. New York: Cambridge University Press.

———. 1996. *Still the Promised City?* Cambridge: Harvard University Press.

Warf, Barney. 1990. "Deindustrialization, Service Sector Growth, and the Underclass in the New York Metropolitan Region." *Tijdschrift voor Economische and Sociale Geografie* 81:332–47.

Wilson, William J. 1987. *The Truly Disadvantaged: The Inner City, the Underclass, and Public Policy.* Chicago: University of Chicago Press.

Wright, Richard, and Mark Ellis. 1996. "Immigrants and the Changing Racial/Ethnic Division of Labor in New York City, 1970–1990." *Urban Geography* 17:317–53.

———. 1997. "Nativity, Ethnicity, and the Evolution of the Intra-Urban Division of Labor in Metropolitan Los Angeles, 1970–1990." *Urban Geography* 18:243–63.

Zhou, Min, and Alejandro Portes. 1995. *Chinatown: The Socioeconomic Potential of an Urban Enclave.* Philadelphia: Temple University Press.

Soviet Jews: The City's Newest Immigrants Transform New York Jewish Life

Annelise Orleck

S oviet Jewish émigrés began to arrive in the United States during the early 1970s. From that time to the present, more than half of each year's new arrivals have chosen to stay in the New York metropolitan area. The social and cultural roots put down by the city's Soviet émigré population—which in the late 1990s numbered close to 300,000—are deep and permanent. Energetic entrepreneurial immigrants have transformed street life in much of Brooklyn and Queens, while young computer wizards and commercial artists have left a lasting imprint on the city's financial and design worlds. Soviet émigré painters, sculptors, playwrights, and dancers have made New York one of the world's most important centers of Soviet Jewish culture. At the same time, the immigration has both revitalized and transformed the flavor of New York Jewish life.

Most Soviet émigrés to New York have gotten their first taste of America in communities that were ethnic enclaves long before they arrived. From 1976 on, the vast majority have settled—at least for a while—in crowded Brooklyn and Queens neighborhoods among tens of thousands of elderly

East European Jews who were themselves once immigrants to the United States. Brighton Beach, Borough Park, Midwood, and Williamsburg in Brooklyn; Rego Park and Forest Hills in Queens; and Washington Heights in Manhattan all became home to Soviet émigrés. The new immigrants breathed fresh life into the withering economies of these old neighborhoods and enlivened fading commercial strips that had been built between the 1910s and the 1940s. Under elevated subway tracks in three-story walk-ups that had formerly housed kosher delicatessens and dairy restaurants, tailor shops, and glaziers, they opened black-and-silver-accented nightclubs, Georgian restaurants and sushi bars, state-of-the-art electronics stores, international groceries, and boutiques selling European designer clothes.

The new Russian émigrés reinforced the Jewish character of these communities by creating cultural institutions to replace those that had withered when earlier immigrants died or moved away. Still, there were tensions aplenty between the old and new Jewish immigrants, because the Soviet émigrés' expressions of Jewish identity were often unrecognizable to elderly East European Jews. These earlier immigrants had been raised speaking Yiddish and reading Hebrew religious texts. The new immigrants were raised under the antireligious regimes of Stalin, Khrushchev, and Brezhnev, during which time publications in Yiddish or Hebrew were virtually banned. As a result, the heritage that these new immigrants sought to pass on to their children was often neither expressly religious nor explicitly Jewish. During the long years of Communist rule, many Soviet Jews had carved out a sense of Jewish identity defined by their disproportionate representation in Russian theater, music, and literature. In New York many have tried to sustain that identity by opening schools of music, art, dance, and gymnastics. These schools mark both the change and the continuity in longtime Jewish communities as these immigrant academies appear in the mildewing shells of synagogues, yeshivas, and Yiddish cultural centers.

At the beginning of the twenty-first century, much of Brooklyn and Queens remains home to flourishing Jewish immigrant communities. That has been true for seventy-five years. But since the 1980s, Russian rather than Yiddish has become the lingua franca. It is the language of banter on street corners and in coffee shops, the language in which haggling takes place in groceries and at outdoor pushcarts. Store signs, newspapers, flyers taped on store windows are all in Cyrillic letters. As in many immigrant enclaves, these neighborhoods operate largely on a cash economy. Employers pay recent émigrés, leery of bureaucracy, in cash "under the table." And many consumer goods are sold for cash only. Illegal immigrants blend into a larger population of "legals" without attracting attention. Residents of Soviet ethnic enclaves in New York are able to find employment; purchase food and clothing; seek medical care; enjoy restaurants; and attend movies, weddings, and funerals without becoming citizens, and without learning more than a few words of English. Some immigrants never leave these comfortable ghettos. But for most Soviet émigrés, these ethnic enclaves have served as little more than launchpads into a more expansive American life. After a few years most have moved on to greener, more economically upscale communities. It is largely the elderly, the least educated, and the illegal immigrants who continue to need the emotional and economic buffer zone that the enclaves provide.

The most famous enclave created by Soviet émigrés is a tiny Brooklyn neighborhood called Brighton Beach (see Markowitz 1993). This crowded strip of Atlantic seashore soon became known as "Little Odessa" in recognition of the Ukrainian origins of most of the new arrivals. By 1980, it was the largest Soviet émigré outpost in the world—home to more than 30,000 Soviet Jews. But by 1991, when the collapse of the Soviet Union sparked a new wave of Jewish out-migration that dwarfed the exodus of the 1970s, Brighton had lost much of its allure to newcomers. Class condescension and regional snobbery among well-educated émigrés from Moscow and Leningrad have long generated cracks about "the Odessan riffraff" washing up on the shores of Brooklyn. The image of a rough-and-ready gangster ghetto was reinforced by sensational media coverage of "the Russian mob" and semiregular stories in both the local and national press about the neighborhood's "exotic, foreign flavor." Brighton's ghetto image repelled many new immigrants. To them it had become what the Lower East Side was to an earlier generation of American Jews and their immigrant forebears: an ambivalent symbol of immigration's early years, a place to shop, gather for family parties, visit one's elderly parents, maybe indulge in a bit of nostalgia for home, but not a place for ambitious new Americans to live. Whenever they could, the 1990s émigrés have settled elsewhere.

Jews from the former Soviet Union have now spread across the New York metropolitan area, revitalizing fading neighborhoods; making demands on educational, health, and social services; and riding the subways to work each day like millions of other new Yorkers, with briefcases and newspapers folded under their arms. At the dawn of the new millennium, a complex and highly diverse mix of Jewish immigrants from Moscow, Petersburg, Minsk, Kiev, and Tashkent have transformed large areas of Brooklyn, Queens, Manhattan, and, more recently, parts of The Bronx, New Jersey, and Long Island into a vast patchwork of Soviet émigré communities. (According to U.S. Immigration and Naturalization Service [INS] figures, approximately 35 percent come from Ukraine, 23 percent from Russia, 15 percent from Uzbekistan, and 8 percent from Belarus.) The numbers of Soviet immigrants waxed and waned over the 1990s, growing in response to anti-Semitic outbursts or economic convulsions in the former republics of the Soviet Union, declining at times when the INS has been strictest about reviewing their applications for refugee status. The immigration to New York City peaked in 1995–1996, with over 40,000 immigrants arriving in just two years. Eighty-five percent of these came with full refugee status, which meant that they received federal subsidies to ease housing, job training, and education costs. The Hebrew Immigrant Aid Society (HIAS), an organization that has help to resettle Russian Jews since the nineteenth century, records a falling off since that time, but with economic conditions still dire in much of the former Soviet Union and crime and ethnic violence out of control, there is no sign that this influx will end any time soon. It is likely to continue well into the twenty-first century (HIAS 1999; New York City Department of Planning 1999).

Background of the Immigration

Agitation by Soviet Jews for the right to emigrate from the USSR began, during the early 1960s, as part of a larger movement by Eastern bloc intellectuals for an end to human rights violations in the Soviet Union. Israel's military success in the Six Day War of 1967 had a great emotional impact on Jews in the USSR. Across the Soviet Union, Jews held unprecedented demonstrations demanding the right to emigrate to Israel. The government of Leonid Brezhnev responded with a flood of anti-Semitic pronouncements and publications, equating Israel with the Third Reich and the Israeli army with Hitler's S.S. (Low 1990; Levin 1988) This campaign encouraged longtime anti-Semites to be open about their feelings, creating an increasingly ugly atmosphere for Jews in many parts of the Soviet Union. Émigrés now living in New York recall those painful days. Physician Khaya Resnikov's[1] husband—whose dark hair and dark eyes distinguished him from his Russian neighbors—was regularly pushed and chastised on public trains and buses during those years. "They would say 'your place is in Israel. We don't need you here.'" Computer programmer Sophia Shkolnikov remembers children being asked at the beginning of each school year to stand and identify themselves by nationality. Those who self-identified as Jewish were then subjected to taunts and verbal abuse by other children, and sometimes by teachers as well.

Popular hostility against Jews was intensified by government reports about "overrepresentation" of Jews in universities and in the performing arts. Energetic government enforcement of ethnic quotas in Moscow, Leningrad, Minsk, Odessa, and Kiev forced even successful and assimilated Soviet Jews to question what would become of their children if they remained in the Soviet Union (Altshuler 1987:143–44). Jewish actors, directors, musicians, and even athletes felt the sting of discrimination. Actor and director Alexander Sirotin recalls being denied roles on Moscow television because he did not have "a Russian face," a not-so-subtle reference to his Jewish looks. Pianist Edith Shvartsmann, who now runs a dance, music, and gymnastics school on Ocean Parkway in Brooklyn, was working as an accompanist for the Russian gymnastics team in the 1970s. "It was the Olympic games in Montreal. I think it was 1976. And everybody knew, anyone who was Jewish they would never go. It didn't matter how much work you had put in or how much talent you had. This was true for coaches, athletes, everyone." With opportunities diminishing, Shvartsmann made plans to emigrate. "I had a small son," she says. "I just began to wonder what he could look forward to."

Despite growing protest among Jews inside the Soviet Union and in the West, few exit visas were granted before 1971. Most of those who tried to emigrate were dedicated Zionists who understood the dangers involved in simply asking for permission to leave. Almost everyone who applied to leave lost their jobs, and those who were refused permission faced years of unemployment as well as prosecution under a Soviet law prohibiting "parasitism." Applicants for exit visas to Israel were sometimes jailed on charges of Zionism, which Soviet prosecutors construed as a treasonous allegiance to an enemy state. Those denied permission to emigrate came to be known as *refuseniks*. Each year there were more of them.

Suddenly, during the spring of 1971, the Soviet government did an abrupt about-face. Claiming that "family reunification" had always been a state priority, they began to grant exit visas in the tens of thousands (Lewis 1978:356). There were several reasons for the stunning turnaround. First was a fear that the protests might continue to escalate and spread to other ethnic minorities who would themselves begin to demand the right to emigrate. Allowing people to leave was one effective way to get rid of the most visible and audible troublemakers. Second, appeals by Soviet Jews had generated political pressure from the United States, Western Europe, and even the Western Communist parties. And the beginnings of détente had sparked hope in top Soviet government officials that favorable trade agreements could soon be reached with Western powers (Gilbert 1985:74–76; Birman 1979).

Of the more than 100,000 Soviet Jews who emigrated to Israel before 1975, most came from Georgia, Bukhara, Uzbekistan, and Kirghizstan. These were among the most religious, least assimilated of Soviet Jews. Only one-third of Soviet Jewish immigrants to Israel in the early 1970s were from the Russian or Ukrainian republics, and fewer still came from the big cities of Moscow, Leningrad, Kiev, or Minsk. When emigration from those regions began in earnest in 1975, the desired destination of most émigrés changed. Most of these Western émigrés wished to settle in the United States. During the second half of the 1970s, more than 110,000 Soviet Jews emigrated to the United States, according to government statistics. Émigré organizations in New York put the number at nearly twice that. Eighty-five percent of these were from the largest cities of Russia and the Ukraine—Odessa, Moscow, Leningrad, and Kiev. Most of them were well educated, and few had strong attachments to the Jewish religion or to Israel.

This new emigration was made up of assimilated, successful urban professionals seeking to escape the anti-Semitism of the Soviet Union, the limitations placed on their professional development and their children's education, and the increasingly severe food shortages plaguing all Soviet citizens. Also, a decade of anti-Israel propaganda by the Soviet government had had its effect on these later émigrés. Though they recognized that official portrayals were biased, many had nonetheless come to believe that life in Israel was difficult and dangerous. Without a keen Zionist commitment, few wished to trade the hardships of Soviet life for the insecurities and dangers of life in the war-torn Middle East. They saw a brighter future for themselves and their children in America.

While this process of reevaluation was going on, an important shift occurred in settlement opportunities available to Soviet émigrés. Before 1976, HIAS allowed Soviet émigrés no choice but to go to Israel. Pressure to change this policy began to build in the United States. This caused great consternation and outrage among Israeli government officials, who insisted that the Jewish state badly needed the labor power and remarkable skills that Soviet Jews brought with them. Several Israeli leaders proposed that American Jewish charitable agencies cut off assistance to Soviet Jews who wished to settle outside of Israel. This prompted an angry response among American Jews. After 1976, HIAS changed its policy and began offering departing Soviet Jews the opportunity to choose where they wished to settle. For the next few years a majority chose the United States (Sawyer 1979:207–12; Weinstein 1988:610).

In 1982, Soviet authorities once again slammed shut the doors to further emigration. A handful of Jews were still granted exit visas each year, but after a high of 51,320 in 1979, just 522 were permitted to leave in 1984. This dramatic decline in Jewish emigration from the Soviet Union was accompanied by a renewed government campaign against the study and promotion of Jewish culture, and by official condemnations of Zionism that sounded eerily similar to the rhetoric of the post-1967 era. Arrests and show trials began again. Some Jewish activists were sentenced to long terms in labor camps that while not as lethal as those of Stalin's day, still bore a shocking resemblance to the conditions described in the writing of Alexander Solzhenitsyn. Soviet Jews living in the United States and Israel feared for the safety of relatives left behind. Nearly 400,000 Soviet Jews had asked for and received the "invitations" from relatives in Israel that were the required first step in the process of applying for exit visas. When the doors closed suddenly in 1982, they were stuck in the Soviet Union for the foreseeable future. Though not technically refuseniks, this huge pool of people experienced many of the same economic, personal, and legal difficulties that made the lives of refuseniks so trying and uncertain. The mid-1980s were as bleak a time for Soviet Jewry as any since the late 1960s. Then, again without warning, political winds began to shift (Gilbert 1985; Wiesel 1987; Friedgut 1989).

Mikhail Gorbachev became General Secretary of the Soviet Communist Party in 1985. At first, the government of this lifelong Communist Party *apparatchik* (functionary) held little promise for change. Within a year, though, his reformist tendencies became apparent. In 1986 he began releasing Jewish political prisoners. Simultaneously with these high-profile releases, which were calculated to capture the attention of the West, Gorbachev took steps that year to make emigration easier. In May 1987, 871 Jews were permitted to leave, nearly as many in one month as had been allowed out the year before. An unexpected side effect of Gorbachev's new policy of *glasnost* fueled a dramatic increase in Jewish emigration over the next few years.

Though the democratization of speech and the press in the Soviet Union certainly had its benefits for Jews, who could for the first time in more than half a century practice their religion, mount Jewish plays and exhibitions, and safely protest the imprisonment of Jewish activists, it also created space for deeply rooted Russian anti-Semitism to bubble to the surface anew. No longer sponsored by the government, anti-Semitic organizations proliferated at the grass roots. The most influential of these groups was *Pamyat,* which demonstrated in Moscow against alleged Jewish meat hoarding and alcohol dealing during the very same month that Gorbachev began to open the doors to Jewish emigration.

In 1989, on the 1,000-year anniversary of the Russian Orthodox Church, Jews across Moscow found violently hostile leaflets in their mailboxes threatening pogroms, and crosses painted on their apartment doors. One Jewish journalist described the poisonous climate, even among educated professionals: "At the editorial office of a progressive newspaper, two sweet women of my age approach me, hissing into my face, 'Leave amicably before we slaughter the lot of you'" (*Harper's* 1991:18). Rebecca Pyatkevich recalls that even small children were chased from neighborhood playgrounds by older neighbors shouting, "'Go back to your part of town. Go away.' It was not a pleasant thing to grow up with."

A panic emigration ensued. Even as the Soviet Union continued to liberalize, even after the Berlin Wall fell, hundreds of thousands of Jews applied for exit visas. Between 1989 and 1991, 106,677 Soviet Jews emigrated to the United States. By 1996 another 156,901 had come, well over a quarter-million people in six and a half years. These numbers count only legal immigrants. Activists in the U.S. Soviet immigrant community estimate that illegal immigration adds between 10 and 30 percent to the official count.

The reasons for continued migration of Jews from the republics of the former Soviet Union are both complex and simple. For the majority of these immigrants there are three answers: family reunification, resurgent anti-Semitism, and the aftermath of the 1986 Chernobyl nuclear reactor explosion, which created skyrocketing rates of thyroid cancer and myriad other diseases across Byelorussia and parts of Russia and the Ukraine. For the rest, many and varied reasons exist that affect not only Jews. Jewish émigrés are part of a flood of former Soviet citizens who headed for the West during the 1990s. Many have been driven out by housing and food shortages and by spiraling inflation that has placed basic foods almost out of reach of the average family. Others flee ethnic strife that has escalated into open warfare in some former republics. Still others seek refuge from an astonishing explosion of violent crime that has disproportionately hurt women and children.

To highlight the differences between those who left the Soviet Union in the 1970s and these post-1987 immigrants, I refer to them from here on as Third and Fourth Wave émigrés, respectively. This also places them in the context of earlier Jewish out-migrations from Eastern Europe, the First Wave beginning in the 1880s and lasting through the 1910s and the Second Wave coming after World War II. These designations reflect both the historical linkage between waves of Jewish emigration to New York and more personal connections. As one Brighton shopkeeper explained to me in 1980: "From this side of the Atlantic it may look like three different kinds of immigrants. From the other side I saw it this way. My grandfather left before the First World War. My uncle, who was in the Red Army, escaped after the Second. And I came thirty years after him." Family ties remain the most important reason for immigration. Jewish émigrés from the former Soviet Union who are continuing to arrive in New York are most often the siblings, cousins, children, and grandchildren of those who came in the 1970s. It is a chain migration that seems likely to continue until there are few Jews left in the lands that once made up the USSR.

Settling an Exodus

At least 300,000 Soviet immigrants now live in the New York area. Counting their American-born children, the numbers in that community reach closer to half a million. The parents in these families were not, like so many immigrants of the pre-1965 era, farmers or small-town craftspeople suddenly thrown into the roar of America's most urbanized city. Since World War II most Soviet Jews had been big-city dwellers, accustomed to subways and buses, the jostling and speed of urban life. And they came with skills to offer. In a 1990 survey of late 1980s arrivals in nine U.S. metropolitan areas, an astonishing 56 percent of Soviet émigrés described themselves as academics, scientists, professionals, or technical workers (Tress 1996:263–79) According to INS data, about a third of the Soviet immigrants entering New York City in the early 1990s had held professional occupations (Lobo, Salvo, and Virgin 1996). The youngest, strongest, and most adaptable were quickly absorbed into the booming economy of New York in the 1980s and 1990s. But many experienced dramatic downward mobility, at least initially. The downward slide was more common for Soviet immigrants in New York than in other cities (see Gold 1995 on the experiences of Soviet Jews in California).

There were several reasons for this. The first problem was simple competition. The 1980s and 1990s saw the largest influx of foreign-born immigrants into New York since the 1920s. This meant that Soviet Jews were competing with hundreds of thousands of other new arrivals. Indeed, in contrast to earlier waves of immigration, many of these newcomers, like the Soviet Jews, were well educated in technical and scientific fields. For those who arrived after 1987, the job situation was particularly difficult. New York's continued loss of manufacturing jobs further limited opportunities for new immigrants seeking well-paid work (Dugger 1997).

But competition and a changing economic base were not the only reasons that some Soviet Jews struggled financially in New York. Their slower adjustment and lower rate of employment also reflected three demographic trends particular to the New York Soviet Jewish immigration: greater numbers of elderly, people without college degrees, and new arrivals with no family in America.

Most of these immigrants found their way to ethnic enclaves in Brooklyn and Queens through the intercession of private Jewish resettlement agencies, the most important of which was the New York Association for New Americans (NYANA). Founded after World War II to offer counseling, job placement, and housing assistance for Jewish Holocaust survivors, NYANA has since that time aided many other Jewish refugees: Romanians, Greeks, Hungarians, and Egyptians in the 1950s and Cubans, Czechs, and Poles in the 1960s. During the 1970s it aided refugees, both Jewish and non-Jewish, from thirty-nine countries. But by far the largest project in its history was begun in the mid-1970s, when Soviet Jewish immigrants began to arrive in New York City at rates that soon reached more than 100 each day (HIAS 1999).

NYANA caseworkers decided to settle as many of these immigrants as they could in historically Jewish neighborhoods, where, they assumed, the local populations would be most welcoming and where a social service system was already in place to care for the Jewish elderly. Since affordability was a pressing concern (immigrants were not allowed to bring cash with them from the Soviet Union), NYANA looked for apartments in aging inner-city Jewish communities with good housing stock and high vacancy rates. The first settlement sites chosen for Soviet émigrés were Washington Heights in Manhattan; Rego Park and Forest Hills in Queens; and Williamsburg, Borough Park, and Brighton Beach in Brooklyn (Fisher 1975:267–69; Jacobson 1975:190–94).

Once new immigrants found permanent housing, NYANA assigned vocational counselors to each working-age adult, tested them for English proficiency, and enrolled them in English as a Second Language courses. The NYANA method of teaching English enabled many new arrivals to grasp basic conversational English in a few weeks. The agency then offered vocational training in business and accounting, industrial trades, carpentry, building maintenance, and food service. It also provided retraining and licensing courses for engineers, computer scientists, and health care professionals (NYANA 1996).

Unfortunately, only a small percentage of these immigrants were able to take full advantage of these programs. NYANA simply did not have the resources to reach such a large immigrant population. The vast majority of Jews arriving in New York from the former Soviet Union had to fend for themselves or try to make use of networks established by friends and family members who had been in New York longer. How successful immigrants were at making the transition to the American work world depended a great deal on their gender, age, and class. In short, younger émigrés have done better than their elders; men have fared better than women; and those with professional backgrounds, especially those from the largest cities, have acculturated more easily than their less-educated counterparts.

Class, Gender, and Generation

Class distinctions among the immigrants have carried over to the United States. Even in the "Worker's State," those with university degrees, particularly from the most prestigious schools, experienced a far higher standard of living than those who did not finish high school. Approximately one-third of Soviet émigrés to New York fall into the latter category. In addition, many of the less-educated émigrés were raised in rural areas or small towns. Overall, they have fared less well than better-educated émigrés, particularly those from Moscow, St. Petersburg, Minsk, Kiev, and Odessa. Age has been a factor as well. Most young adults with strong educational backgrounds were able to find work and move to comfortable homes. By the early 1980s they had begun to make their presence felt throughout New York as physicians, entrepreneurs, stock analysts, industrial researchers, accountants, and computer specialists. Older working-age immigrants, especially those who are fifty or older, have had a much harder time picking up their careers where they left off in the Soviet Union.

Less easily able to master English than younger émigrés, middle-aged professionals have still applied for competitive high-level positions commensurate with those they occupied in the former USSR. Rarely hired for such jobs, émigrés say that an "intellectual holocaust" has occurred, forcing physicians and lawyers, Ph.D.s and musicians to exchange their vocations for clerical work and manual labor. *Science* magazine estimates that approximately 15 percent of Soviet immigrants arriving in the United States between 1987 and 1990 came with Ph.D. or equivalent degrees in science and engineering. That 15 percent was above and beyond those who came with M.D.s or with Ph.D.s in the humanities and social sciences. (Statistics for New York City for the early 1990s show 15 percent of Soviet arrivals with an M.A. degree or higher.) The top Soviet mathematicians and theoretical physicists were quickly hired by U.S. universities, and some talented graduate students and recent Ph.D.s were also snapped up, mostly by corporations. But thousands of older Soviet Jewish scientists have been forced to drive taxis; walk dogs; or work as store clerks, doormen, or companions to the elderly. They are often denied even lower-level science positions because they are considered overqualified. "In Russia," one engineer commented bitterly, "we had to hide that we are Jews. Here, to get a job, we have had to hide that we have a Ph.D." Many also feel that they have to hide their age to find work in ever-changing high-technology fields where only the newest degrees count. After a few rejections, some greying émigré scientists in their thirties and forties began to dye their hair, eyebrows, and beards (Rubin 1975; Holden 1990; Cordero-Guzman and Grosfoguel 1998).

If the job market has been dismal for male professionals in their forties and fifties, it has been doubly difficult for older women, who face discrimination because of their sex as well as their age. According to a 1995 Office of Refugee Resettlement survey of all refugee groups, Soviet Jews have the largest gender-based wage gap nationally, with the median hourly wage of $9.75 per hour for men and $7 for women. Among those earning $15 per hour or more, men outnumber women by nearly two to one. For the large number of middle-aged women immigrants in New York who had worked as pediatricians in the Soviet Union, the loss of professional status has been particularly devastating. Pediatrics was seen in the Soviet Union as a "women's field," and the general perception among U.S. physicians is that the training these women received was of a lower grade than that of other Soviet doctors. Of all the émigré physicians to enter the United States since the 1960s, these women have had the least success in rebuilding their careers (Office of Refugee Resettlement 1995, cited in Tress 1996).

After thirty-two years of pediatric practice near Minsk, Bertha Klimkovitch, who came to Brooklyn in 1979, could find no job better than that of sewing machine operator in a Williamsburg garment sweatshop. "I cried so much. But I know that for the children it will be better here. Now I am happy because the children are working and the grandchildren go to college." Still, she allows herself some sadness about the premature end of her career. Sonya,[2] fifty-one when she moved to Brighton Beach from Leningrad, had also practiced medicine for decades prior to her departure. After several unsuccessful attempts to pass the language exams that are prerequisites for immigrants seeking medical training in the United States, she was forced to take a minimum-wage job as a companion and chore worker for an elderly woman. She too comforts herself with the thought that her son, an electronics engineer now living in Houston, has done far better for himself in the United States than he could have in Russia. Still, she often finds her life in Brighton Beach drab and boring. "As for myself," she sighs, "I could be more fulfilled."

Almost all Soviet Jewish women worked outside the home before emigration. And they were just as likely as men to have earned college degrees and achieved professional success. According to a 1994 federal government study of Soviet refugees nationally, 60 percent of Soviet Jewish women refugees in the United States reported having held jobs in the former Soviet Union that were classified as academic, scientific, professional, or technical. Once in the United States they have been far less likely than their male counterparts, even over time, to continue their careers. The same study, by the federal Office of Refugee Resettlement, found that only 31 percent of Soviet immigrant women, mostly the young, have found employment in their fields here. More than 55 percent have had to take jobs in service or clerical fields (Office of Refugee Resettlement 1994, cited in Tress 1996).

After the initial months of family elation following their arrival in New York, followed by an adjustment period when most mothers were too busy meeting the immediate needs of their families to worry about themselves, many adult women have gone through periods of profound depression, mourning the loss of respect, professional identity, and careers that they will probably never have again. Like Bertha Klimkovich, many formerly professional women in the Soviet immigrant community recall months, and even years, when they cried each day on their way to jobs that offered little pay and even less satisfaction when compared to the professions they had trained for (Halberstadt 1996).

Such dramatic loss of professional status, coupled with frustration over the inability to speak English and initial incompetence at such basic tasks as job hunting, shopping, and reading official mail, has caused severe emotional and psychological problems for many older working-age immigrants. Adele Nikolsky, coordinator of Russian immigrant services for a Brooklyn community health center, noted in 1996 that area mental health clinics were seeing "overwhelming numbers of middle-aged immigrants" with debilitating symptoms of depression and anxiety. Many have also complained of poor health, the result of an overtaxed and undersupported Soviet health care system, and stress caused by emigration or loss of status. Finally, for those from southwestern Russia, the Ukraine, and Byelorussia, the knowledge that they may have been exposed to fallout from the 1986 Chernobyl nuclear reactor accident has caused anxiety, possibly psychosomatic illnesses, and an array of very real illnesses that are just beginning to become apparent (Nikolsky 1996; Weinberg et al. 1995).

Mental health centers in Brooklyn and Queens must also serve tens of thousands of Soviet elderly. These elderly immigrants face many special problems. Past working age, the vast majority require housing subsidies if they are to live on their own. Many need some sort of home care. All require more regular attention from physicians than do younger immigrants. Almost all are dependent for their sustenance on Supplemental Security Income (SSI), Medicare, and food stamps. Because nearly one-third of the Soviet émigrés in New York are elderly, they are also the largest immigrant consumers of government assistance in the city. Despite former president Bill Clinton's restoration of SSI and disability benefits to legal immigrants in 1998, they must still become citizens if they wish to remain eligible for food stamps. During the summer of 1997, when the federal government prepared to cut off food stamps to large numbers of legal immigrants, panic gripped many of the city's poorer ethnic enclaves. City, state, and private Jewish charitable agencies scrambled to fill the needs of largely elderly immigrant communities (Dorf 1997; HIAS 1996; Solomon 1996).

Gaining access to these services is one reason that so many Soviet elderly have concentrated in the city's most visible ethnic enclaves, or, as some more affluent émigrés now refer to them, ghettos. Settlement in senior citizen–oriented urban Jewish enclaves like Brooklyn's Brighton Beach and the Forest Hills section of Queens eased the adjustment of many Soviet elderly. These neighborhoods offered familiar social and cultural environments, language accessibility, and an abundance of inexpensive subsidized housing that has enabled many Soviet elderly to live alone or with just a spouse for the first time in their lives. Living in housing complexes for the elderly, in neighborhoods with a high concentration of elderly Jewish immigrants, or both, many émigrés developed more active social lives and experienced a stronger sense of community in New York than they had in the Soviet Union. There are now many such Soviet Jewish communities strung across the city of New York, but the first one to be created remains the most visible—the crowded stretch of Brooklyn seafront called Brighton Beach.

"Little Odessa"

Memory and Community

The first Soviet Jews were settled in Brighton Beach in the mid-1970s by NYANA. The neighborhood quickly became a mecca for Russian and Ukrainian immigrants. The housing stock—mostly 1920s Art Deco apartment buildings—was inexpensive and in excellent condition. Commercial space was plentiful. And there were well-established services for the elderly. Brighton was also emotionally appealing. Its residents were almost all Eastern European Jews, many of whom spoke Yiddish as their first language. This meant that Soviet elderly could begin to communicate with their neighbors immediately. Unlike many other Jewish neighborhoods in New York, Brighton was culturally Jewish but not overwhelmingly religious. Finally, it was located on a narrow strip of land facing the sea, perfect for walking, for meeting neighbors, for breathing in the fresh salt air. Thousands of Odessans and other Ukrainians, pining for the Black Sea, found in Brighton Beach a little of the feel of home. By the 1980s it had come to be known both among émigrés and in the New York press as "Little Odessa," a reflection of the Ukrainian origins of nearly three-quarters of the new arrivals.

Though very different from Odessa, with its broad avenues and grand buildings, Brighton quickly came to feel like home for many émigrés, particularly the elderly. Fanya[3] emigrated from Odessa in 1978 with her daughter and two young granddaughters. "The first time I heard Yiddish spoken on the street here, I couldn't believe my ears," she recalled in an emotional whisper. "Then I saw little boys wearing yarmulkes, walking down the street, unafraid, and I cried." Although Fanya's daughter, who owns a small grocery store on Brighton's main commercial strip, speaks no Yiddish, her granddaughters learned it as students in a Brooklyn yeshiva (religious school). Fanya feels that she's come home. "In the First World War I lost my father, in the Second World War my husband. Since then I have had a bad heart. I could not cry at all. Here, for the first time I cried. Here, when my own little ones speak to me in Yiddish, my heart feels better."

With its fruit stands and street peddlers, barrels of pickles and swimming carp, haggling shoppers and bantering merchants, Brighton evoked the lost Jewish world of an earlier era: the crowded small-town marketplace, the courtyards and ghetto streets of urban Eastern Europe in the early twentieth century. Indeed, Brighton has been a Jewish immigrant enclave since World War I. It became popular among First Wave émigrés as a summer resort in the late 1910s. By the 1930s it was a thriving and diverse community of Jews from Russia, Poland, Czechoslovakia, and Rumania, most of whom were active in the city's two major garment unions. Brighton supported a dozen synagogues, myriad charitable and cultural organizations, branches of the Jewish Labor *Bund,* the Arbeiter Ring (Workmen's Circle), the Zionist *Farband,* and branches of the Democratic, Republican, Socialist, and Communist parties. A hotbed of radical political protest in the 1930s and 1940s, Brighton saw its Jewish immigrant culture become enriched and transformed after World War II by the arrival of thousands of survivors of the Nazi Holocaust. In the late 1960s the Amalgamated Clothing Workers' Union opened the Warbasse apartment houses, which were soon filled with thousands of immigrant garment union retirees who reinforced Brighton's immigrant feel and gave it the nation's second-largest concentration of senior citizens. Only Miami Beach had more.

By the mid-1970s, Brighton's large elderly population was fast diminishing as people died or moved to Florida, opening up an abundance of commercial and residential space. For that and other reasons, it seemed a logical place for NYANA caseworkers to settle some of the hundreds of Soviet émigrés arriving daily in New York. Since most of those already living in Brighton were also Eastern European Jews, many of them born in Russia, caseworkers hoped that the settlement process would proceed smoothly. But, as is so often the case when new immigrants come to live among older émigrés of the same ethnicity, tempers soon flared. Each group developed quick and strong impressions of the other as they interacted on Brighton streets, in the hallways of apartment buildings, in senior centers, shops, and synagogues. The new neighbors fell into a strained sort of intimacy like estranged cousins bound to one another by bloodlines in the distant past, related but uncomfortable. They had high expectations because each had nurtured idealized images of the other during the long struggle to "free Soviet Jewry." And so there were inevitable disappointments, turf wars, and misunderstandings.

The issue of Jewish identity among the Soviet Jews was perhaps the greatest bone of contention in the early years of the immigration, and it remains an issue to this day. In the 1970s, observant Jews throughout Brooklyn reached out to the newcomers, hoping to school them in the fundamentals of a religious practice that Jews in the Soviet Union had been prevented from observing for half a century. Brooklyn synagogues and yeshivas launched outreach programs to attract and teach the new immigrants. They leafleted apartment buildings with invitations to attend special Russian-language holiday services. Of the eleven synagogues in Brighton, only five were able to attract Soviet immigrants to join, and these were almost all people over sixty.

With such a lukewarm response, tempers flared among older Brighton residents. Many felt that the Soviets were pushy and unfriendly, unwilling to return greetings or wait their turn on line. With less justification, they also railed against the generous federal and private subsidies that the newcomers received, perhaps forgetting that they too had been aided by Jewish charitable groups when they arrived decades earlier. Their resentment was openly expressed. You could hear it on the streets, on the boardwalk, in synagogues, in stores: "Why did we fight to bring them here? Why did they want to come here? They're not even Jews. They don't want to be Jews."

Some strongly Jewish-identified members of the immigrant community tried to mediate. Alexander Sirotin, a playwright and director from Moscow, formed the

Jewish Union of Russian immigrants to sponsor activities with a Jewish theme among the new arrivals. Through the 1980s he was host of *Gorizont* (Horizon), a Russian-language radio show on the Lyubavitch Hasidic radio network. The message of Sirotin and other Jewish-identified leaders in Brighton was: let the Soviet immigrants nourish their Jewish identities in their own ways, in their own time. As examples, Sirotin pointed to an émigré Yiddish theater troupe and to gatherings of senior citizens at which Yiddish songs and poems were sung and recited by recent Soviet immigrants. "American Jews try to teach the Russian immigrant about Jewishness using a strange language, and then wonder why he does not understand," Sirotin noted. He saw Soviet émigrés as akin to concentration camp survivors, when it came to their Jewish identity. "We are not starving physically but we are starving for Jewishness," Sirotin wrote in 1981. "You can't shove food down a starving man's throat. It is the same with these Jews. They must be fed *Yiddishkayt* (Jewishness) with a teaspoon" (Sirotin 1981).

In truth, just like American-born Jews and earlier waves of Eastern European immigrants, Soviet Jewish émigrés embraced a wide range of Jewish identities. Among the new immigrants were some who were very religious and others who identified strongly with Yiddish language and culture but not with religion. Some had begun attending synagogue and studying Hebrew in the 1960s and 1970s as an act of resistance. Others, schooled in a Communist society, saw religion as a vestige of premodern superstition and so rejected it out of hand. Some identified themselves as both Russian and Jewish; others claimed Russian language and culture as their own. All knew that they were Jews. Living in the Soviet Union, where they were forced to carry internal passports with the letter *J* emblazoned on them, where appearing Jewish, bearing a Jewish name, revealing a Jewish ancestor might lead to all sorts of petty as well as serious harassment, all of these émigrés were keenly and always aware that they were Jews. Indeed, they had all paid a terrible price in the blood of family and friends for the crime of being Jewish.

Having survived decades of murder, torture, and imprisonment at the hands of Cossacks, Nazis, and Stalinists, Soviet Jewish immigrants were outraged that those who had lived comfortably in the United States for much of this time would dare to tell them that they were not Jews. Surveys of Soviet immigrants in the United States show that a large majority strongly identify as Jews, far more strongly than do most American Jews. More than one-third enroll their children in Jewish afternoon or Sunday schools. Like American-born Jewish families, the vast majority celebrate the more popular and less religious holidays like Passover and Hanukkah with family gatherings and ritual meals at home (Sawyer 1995). A staggering number of adult men have had themselves circumcised since their arrival in the United States, more than 10,000 in New York City alone (Sugarman 1992). But Soviet émigrés balk at what they see as coercive pressures by religious Jews. Despite offers of scholarships and tuition remission, a great many Soviet émigré families withdrew their children from New York religious yeshivas when school authorities demanded that uncircumcised immigrant boys submit to the operation.

After decades of repression, finding comfortable ways to express Jewishness has taken time for Soviet Jewish immigrants. Brighton storekeepers who at first offended the sensibilities of observant Jews by staying open on the Jewish High Holy Days—Rosh Hashana and Yom Kippur—soon began to close their businesses on Jewish holidays and post signs wishing their customers *mazl* (luck) and *shalom* (peace.) Hearing the language again on the streets of Brighton after half a century, many elderly and middle-aged Soviet immigrants revived the Yiddish of their youth. The *mamaloshn* (mother tongue) peppers the Russian repartee in crowded groceries, bakeries, and butcher shops. "Many years ago I used to hear my grandparents speak," one storeowner explained. "But I forgot it all until I moved here. Suddenly it came pouring back."

The refreshing of distant memories has not always been easy or comforting for Soviet émigrés. Like many Vietnamese, Cambodian, Salvadoran, and Haitian immigrants now living in New York, elderly Soviet Jews are a highly traumatized population. They have lived through Stalin's purges; the Nazi occupation, during which one of every two Soviet Jews was murdered; and the "black years" of Soviet Jewry after World War II when most of the Soviet Union's Jewish artists, intellectuals, and physicians were either executed or sentenced to hard labor in the gulag. Almost all have lost loved ones to violent deaths. Many feel crippling guilt at having survived—and at leaving family graves behind. The symptoms of posttraumatic stress disorder are common among them. Bits of random memories surface suddenly in the conversations of the aged immigrants who line benches in the asphalt parks that dot Brighton. Flashbacks and nightmares can easily bleed through the thin tissue separating a happy present from a more troubled past.

These traumatic memories sometimes make it difficult for elderly émigrés to meet their needs in a new and strange place. Sophie Spector, who worked for many years at the Shorefront Y and Senior Center in Brighton teaching English and helping elderly Soviet Jews to adjust, found that simply calling for an ambulance could evoke memories of the era in Soviet history when political dissidents were whisked off to hospitals and never heard from again. If a police car arrived before the ambulance, as is often the case in New York City, the elderly immigrant panicked. An uncomprehending medic, arriving moments later, would then try to push the terrified old man or woman into the vehicle. Far too often, Spector recalled, a simple ambulance call escalated into a hostile encounter between police, medics, and a crowd of immigrants.

Many émigrés find the health care system in New York cold and impersonal compared to small neighborhood clinics in the Soviet Union, where they received a great deal of personal attention. They grow frustrated and angry at not being able to find physicians near their homes who will accept Medicaid and, when they do, at waits of up to four hours (Caroll 1993). Having received substandard medical care at understaffed and overcrowded Soviet hospitals, some view Western medicine as a whole with suspicion, turning instead to herbal remedies. Brighton pharmacies now carry a bewildering array of dried herbs in hand-labeled bags.

Elderly women stand on neighborhood street corners selling everything from garlic skin pastes to powdered reindeer horn, assuring prospective customers that these "alternative antibiotics" can cure ills that bedevil physicians. The emergency room staff at Coney Island Hospital, the major public health facility in southern Brooklyn, keeps a Russian-language herbal remedy book so that they can figure out what patients may have taken (Garrett 1997).

Such confusions notwithstanding, most elderly Soviet émigrés have found Brighton Beach to be a place where they can begin to heal from the traumas of the past. Brighton's tradition of public communal mourning has helped them to voice openly long-suppressed pain at the loss of loved ones. Soviet immigrants have flocked to long-established Brighton commemorations of the Holocaust. Alongside Brighton's concentration camp survivors they pray and mourn, read poetry, sing Yiddish partisans' songs, light memorial candles, and say Kaddish (the Jewish prayer for the dead). For Soviet immigrants over the age of seventy, a vital part of the adjustment to Brighton has been a recognition that they are not only refugees of authoritarian Communism but also Holocaust survivors. For nearly half a century, the Soviet regime repressed facts about the Nazi occupation and destroyed sources. Through all of this time, Soviet Jewish survivors of World War II carried their memories with them as the only documentation of the murder of 1.5 million of their friends, family, and loved ones. Once in New York, they have begun to tell and to record their own family stories, marking the losses not in millions but in memories of individual loved ones—mothers, husbands, fathers, wives, children, friends.

As part of their recognition of themselves as a community of survivors, Soviet émigrés added to Brighton's communal calendar of mourning a day of remembrance for the tens of thousands of Jews shot to death by the Nazis in the forest of Babi Yar, near Kiev, in 1941. And a few blocks from the Y, they erected a sign marking Babi Yar Triangle, a tiny park of tarred ground, wooden benches, and a few stone tables with inlaid chessboards over which old men in berets bend low in concentration. A public marker of the kind that one could not find in Kiev, it represents freedom to mourn, freedom finally to name the dead aloud without fear of reprisal, freedom to cry in public, freedom even to laugh and remember the good times. As their grandchildren play around them, say Soviet émigrés, they have finally begun to heal.

Eating, Drinking, and Acculturating

Entrepreneurship is the lifeblood of all sorts of immigrant enclaves. Not surprisingly, Brighton Beach hums with the business of buying and selling. From the beginning of the Soviet Jewish immigration, small businesses have been a major source of income for new arrivals—both those who already had some experience with retail sales in the former Soviet Union and professionals who felt they needed some new way of making a living in the United States. One early study of New

York immigrants indicated that nearly three-quarters dreamed of opening their own businesses (Simon 1985). Partly this was an idealized vision of American capitalism. To own a business was to have no boss, no restrictions on where one could settle, and no limitations on what one could earn. It was also a recognition that with limited English, it might be difficult to find other work. Many new arrivals believed that they could create thriving businesses in a Russian immigrant neighborhood without becoming fluent in English. Brighton Beach Avenue is testament to their success.

The first Soviet immigrant–owned stores to appear on "the Avenue" were groceries: clean, bright, and modern, they stood in stark contrast to the old-fashioned corner stores of an earlier generation. These stores occupy a special place in the life of each immigrant family, for they offer daily reminders of the difference between the former Soviet Union and the land where they now live. Every day in Brighton is testimony to the miracle of abundance at the core of so many dreams of America. In Moscow, Leningrad, or Minsk, keeping a family fed meant standing in one line after another for hours each day just to purchase the essentials; bribing truckers, farmers, and grocery workers; and scouring the city for the latest black market shipments. In Brighton immigrants can choose between at least a dozen groceries offering Polish, Hungarian, German, Russian, and American meats, cheeses, juices, and chocolates. Bakeries, butcher shops, fish stores, and fruit stands compete with the groceries and with each other to create increasingly eye-catching displays of delectables. These stores have become informal community centers as a largely elderly clientele exchange news and congratulations or offer condolences. For some immigrants who now live in other parts of the city or the country, the stores have become places to assuage pangs of nostalgia—the smells, the packaging, the Russian banter all evocative of home.

Brighton's Russian restaurants and nightclubs, which reflect the geographic diversity of this immigration, also serve as important public gathering spaces where a sense of group identity is forged and reinforced. Ukrainian food, not surprisingly, is the most commonly served cuisine, along with traditional Ashkenazi (Northern European) Jewish specialties and an odd amalgam known as Odessan-style Continental. But Georgian restaurants are also popular, as are restaurants serving Uzbek and other Central Asian cuisines. Meat, cheese, and potato-filled dumplings are variously called *pirogi* (Ukrainian), *pelmeni* (Central Asian), and *vareniki* (Russian), but they can be found almost everywhere. So can *shashlyk* (shish kebab, made with lamb, chicken, or sturgeon and served on a swordlike skewer), and chicken Kiev (fried with butter and mushrooms at the center). Regional specialties include Odessan shrimp in garlic sauce, *lavash* (crusty round Georgian bread eaten hot and sliced like a pie), *chakokhokbili* (a Caucasian chicken stew with tomatoes), and *baklazhan* (eggplant) with pomegranate or walnut sauce. Whatever the restaurateurs' region of origin, groaning banquet tables are the norm, covered with *zakuski* (appetizers), flowers, and elaborate place settings. Plates of smoked fish, pickled vegetables, and cold vegetable salads greet arriving guests, with bottles of vodka, water, wine, and soda rising like islands in the sea of food.

Brighton restaurants vary greatly in size and grandeur. But they all share an extravagant taste in interior design that makes even the smallest eatery feel more like a stage set than a dining room. From the red walls of the Primorski restaurant, with its small colored lights and stained-glass sailing ships, to the marble bathrooms, crystal chandeliers, chrome-and-black-enamel banquettes, and strobe-lighted dance floors of the big nightclubs, these restaurants are soaked with fantasy. Blonde Russian torch singers in skintight, low-cut Spandex; a perfect Stevie Wonder impersonator at the Primorski; big bands with congas and horns; even full-scale floor shows like the pistol-packing dance number at the Rasputin, complete with dancers in fedoras and double-breasted pinstripes, suggest a sense of irony and a capacity for self-parody in the owners and patrons of these clubs. The fantasy, the irony, the food, the music, and the vodka all work together to create moments of shared emotional release that build intimacy and group feeling. They also make for great parties.

These restaurants have their roots in Soviet Jewish culture, where from the 1930s to the 1980s it was not only difficult but also dangerous for Jews to gather in groups. With the KGB on the steps of many synagogues, and gatherings in private homes subject to sudden police raids, restaurants were among the only places where Jews could gather in a relaxed atmosphere. "The spirit of Soviet Jewry really came to life in restaurants," says Alexander Sirotin (1981:10). "There, ordinary workers, by day forced to comply with Soviet officials, to submit to constant harassment, could finally become people of character, of unique identity. This was the only place where they could remove all masks to reveal openly a Jewish face. In the absence of other possibilities, the restaurant became the center of life for many Jews in Soviet cities. This custom was carried here." In the Soviet Union, these communal spaces were hidden from prying eyes of unfriendly officials. That custom, too, was carried here. For many years, Russian restaurants in Brighton hid their fabulous interiors with blank fronts, heavy curtains, and blackened street-facing windows. This camouflage, which reflected both a lingering distrust of strangers and a desire to discourage casual browsing by outsiders, was meant to mark the restaurants as off-limits to tourists. The lavishly decorated National removed a large plate-glass window and replaced it with a metal wall, broken only by a windowless wooden door. The owners of Sadko, a two-floor black-and-silver discotheque built on the site of an abandoned pizzeria, were even more intent on hiding. For years, the club owners preserved the pizzeria storefront as it was on the day that it closed, complete with white Formica counter and pizza ovens. Over the faded sign for *Mama Mia Pizzeria,* small black letters advertised Sadko. There was no indication that a chic, expensive club lay within those walls. Yet each weekend, dark cars and limousines pulled up at the side entrance to the former pizzeria, where a signless wooden door admitted those in the know. Some-time during the mid-1980s, the owners erected a more elaborate nautical facade, but the porthole windows were placed high above the street. Some habits die hard.

Twenty-five years after the immigration began, these restaurants have become more relaxed, more open to outsiders. The *Village Voice, The New York Times,* and other city newspapers regularly review the restaurants in Brighton. Even the infamous Rasputin, reputed gathering ground for the local Russian mob, attracts curious non-Russian customers. Outsiders may still be greeted with stares, as if they have crashed someone else's family gathering. But both restaurateurs and patrons have grown accustomed to the odd "American" family joining in the Sat-urday night festivities. Tourism in New York's ethnic enclaves is, after all, a time-honored part of American pluralism. Some restaurant owners have even begun to appreciate patronage by tourists because the youngest, most Americanized of So-viet émigrés have begun to abandon these immigrant hotspots in favor of Man-hattan dance clubs and American music.

One sort of gathering at the émigré restaurants still draws the younger gener-ation. As they have been from the beginnings of the immigration, Brighton's Rus-sian restaurants are the sites where émigrés hold bar and bat mitzvahs—Jewish coming-of-age rituals—for their children. Like earlier generations of Jewish im-migrants in New York, Soviet émigré families often use these celebrations to show friends and neighbors how well they have done for themselves in New York; the more extravagant, therefore, the better. More about affirming a cultural/com-munal Jewish identity than embracing religion, these Soviet émigré bar and bat mitzvahs offer an eclectic mix of traditional religious and cheerfully irreligious food, music, and dance. Shrimp (strictly forbidden under Jewish dietary laws) is served alongside gefilte fish (a traditional Jewish dish of ground carp and whiting with onions). Electric guitars accompany the bar mitzvah boy's recitation of prayers. Synthesizers approximate the violin and clarinet sounds of Eastern Eu-ropean Jewish music, with a disco bass booming beneath it all.

Increasingly, Brighton's Russian restaurants are showing signs of Americani-zation. By the summer of 1997 the band at Primorski restaurant insisted that they didn't know any *horas* (celebratory Jewish circle dances), though they had played them enthusiastically just a few months before. And, if the decor of Brighton's restaurants remains wild, the diners have toned down their style. Women wear less purple satin and pink chiffon. Fewer men wear shirts open at the chest. A strain of highbrow snobbism has crept into the Russian restaurants of Brighton Beach. Still, these gathering places continue to satisfy an emotional need among Soviet immigrants old and new for a sense of community and familiarity. For that reason the nightclubs will likely continue to play a central role in Soviet Jewish New York for years to come, even if the younger generation tags along only under protest.

Vorovskoy Mir (Thieves' World)

Organized crime, although less visible in Brighton in the late 1990s than it was a decade earlier, is also likely to remain a community fixture for some time to come. Since the 1970s, the "Odessa mob" has made the name of Brighton Beach infamous among law enforcement agents from New York to Moscow. This small group of primarily Ukrainian Jewish gangsters learned their trade in the wide-open port city of Odessa. Released from prison, they were granted exit visas in time to accompany the tens of thousands of honest citizens departing for Israel and the United States. They slipped into this country unnoticed by the FBI or local law enforcement. Some were non-Jews who used the identification papers and visas of deceased Jews.

Typical of these early gangster immigrants was Evsei Agron, a short Josef Stalin look-alike who listed his occupation as jeweler when he arrived at Kennedy Airport in 1975. He neglected to mention the seven years he had served in a Soviet prison camp for murder or the gambling and prostitution rings he had been running in West Germany. Agron became the first boss of a Brighton-based Soviet mob operation profiting from extortion, prostitution, and drug sales. A far more sophisticated organized crime syndicate was established in the late 1970s by Odessan black marketeer Marat Balagula, who masterminded multimillion-dollar gasoline frauds and created a crime network that stretched from Brighton to San Francisco. Though Balagula was convicted of fraud in 1994, his organization continues to run a network of corporations that invest illegally obtained cash in oil refineries, tankers, gas stations, and truck stops (Friedman 1994, 1996; Burstein 1986).

Brighton was a good spot for Russian mobsters for a variety of reasons. It was just a short drive from Kennedy Airport, air link to fellow gang members in Europe and the former Soviet Union. Its teeming streets gave perfect cover; it was easy to hide among the tens of thousands of Soviet immigrants already living in Brighton. During the 1970s there were still plenty of vacant apartments, some of which were bought up in large blocks by gang bosses and rented to street soldiers as needed. One immigrant who moved to Brighton in the early 1980s recalled that there were entire buildings in one part of the neighborhood—huge Art Deco edifices with turrets, mosaics, and long, dark hallways—that belonged to criminal families. Everyone knew where they were and steered clear of those blocks (Rosner 1986).

Like most criminals, the Russian mob preyed first on their own. Evsei Agron ran protection rackets in Brighton that by 1980 averaged $50,000 per week, extorted from local émigré shopkeepers with threats of violence. Loan sharks lent money at astronomical interest rates to naive aspiring entrepreneurs, new immigrants wary of official paperwork. Car-theft rings began to prowl the streets as well, sometimes recruiting children under the age of sixteen—who could not be sentenced to long prison terms—to commit the actual crime. The transformation of this neighborhood, which had always been one of the least violent in New York, came as a shock to longtime Brighton residents. The early 1980s were a particularly violent period. A mob boss was shot to death in his car in front of the Odessa restaurant late one night. A well-known former journalist was gunned down in a jewelry store. And one Yom Kippur (Day of Atonement), a man was shot to death at close range on the boardwalk. Stunned elderly Jews, First and Second Wave immigrants dressed in Holy Day attire, gathered around the scene of the crime. One angry voice could be heard above the crowd: "There is something very sick happening in this neighborhood. They shoot each other on the holiest day of the year. These cannot be Jews."

Since the collapse of the Soviet Union in 1991, many Soviet émigrés most active in the New York underworld are in fact not Jewish. The most powerful competitor to Balagula is a *gory* (crime boss) named Vyacheslav Ivankov, who moved to Brighton in 1992, masquerading as an ordinary Jewish immigrant. Sent by a consortium of crime syndicates that believed the U.S. market was too profitable to be left to Jewish gangsters alone, Ivankov established bases for more than two hundred Russian crime families in U.S. cities. In 1995 Ivanvkov was arrested in Brighton for extorting $3.5 million from two Soviet émigré investment bankers whom he had kidnapped at gunpoint in the bar at the New York Hilton.

The reputation of Soviet Jewish immigrants, particularly those who live in Brighton, has suffered as a result of adverse publicity generated by these criminals. By the mid-1990s, new Soviet émigrés shuddered angrily when asked if they lived or wanted to live in Brighton. "I am not like the people there," one woman said vehemently. "I work. Everyone in my family works. We are not like *that*." The 1994 film *Little Odessa* by Tim Roth exemplified the media stereotyping that makes Russian émigrés leery of association with Brighton Beach. In this grim portrayal, Brighton is populated almost exclusively by leather-jacketed, gun-toting thugs. Though most Russian émigrés reject that depiction, they fear that it still reflects badly on them and are quick to distance themselves from the neighborhood. What they don't talk about are the ways that Brighton continues to serve as an emotional and cultural home base for Soviet Jews across the New York area—a place to shop; to visit relatives; and to celebrate birthdays, weddings, and anniversaries at Russian restaurants. It is the symbolic portal through which many, if not most, Soviet immigrants pass, but like most immigrant ghettos, it has become a revolving door.

Other Soviet Jewish Enclaves in New York

Brighton Beach has been overcrowded for years now. Apartments are hard to come by, and rents are higher than in neighborhoods where housing is less in demand. With a flood of immigrants pouring into the city throughout the 1990s, what was once a fairly well contained ethnic enclave in Brighton has spread throughout the city. More recent immigrants have moved to Bay Ridge, Bensonhurst, and Borough

Park, among other parts of Brooklyn. And when apartments there became scarce in the 1990s, Jewish resettlement agencies began to look toward another longtime Jewish neighborhood: Co-op City, a massive thirty-five-building apartment complex in The Bronx. All of the areas settled by the most recent émigrés are working-class communities, solid neighborhoods with blocks of row houses, and substantial 1930s Art Deco buildings or modern apartment towers. The more urban, the better for many of the émigrés, who were almost all big-city dwellers in the Soviet Union. Many Americans would be put off by Co-op City, a 300-acre island jammed with towering high-rise dwellings. But the Moscow, Kiev, and St. Petersburg expatriates who have flocked there since 1987 are quite content with their urban aeries (Bryant-Friedland 1995).

New émigrés are proud of not living in Brighton and speak glowingly of the friendships they have made with non-Russian neighbors. In Bensonhurst, tough-talking Russian émigré shopkeepers develop strong white-ethnic urban identities, enhanced by their sense of kinship with Italian and Italian-American neighbors. Similar bonds have been formed in Borough Park, where Soviet Jews live in varying degrees of comfort with their intensely religious Hasidic neighbors. Among the older generation, friendships are often made in the stores and markets, where Russian and Hasidic women speak to each other in Yiddish. While many of the Hasidic customs bemuse and bewilder the Russians, some have proven quite helpful. On occasion, Hasidic women, in keeping with their religious mandate to visit the sick, have brought food and medicine to elderly Russian Jews living alone. While the Russians find it difficult to relate to the Hasidim's religiosity, they express pleasure that religious Jews can practice their faith openly.

Far removed from Brighton Beach culturally but similarly insulated and close knit is another large ethnic enclave created by Central Asian Jews from Uzbekistan, Tajikistan, and Kazakhstan. Since the 1970s, more than 35,000 of these "Bukharan" émigrés have created a bustling community in Forest Hills, with restaurants, barbershops, food stores, and synagogue that together have given 108th Street the nickname "Bukharan Broadway." Culturally, linguistically, and religiously distinct from their western Soviet counterparts, Bukharan émigrés believe themselves to be descendants of an ancient Persian Jewish community and trace their origins in Uzbekistan as far back as the fifth century. They have never spoken Yiddish but rather speak a dialect of Persian written in Hebrew characters. And they share in the cultural identity of Tadzhiks and Iranians, just as Jews from the western republics identify with Russian culture (Carr 1997).

Because Central Asian Jews have a long history of entrepreneurship even in the Soviet Union, their economic adjustment to New York has been rapid and successful. Family businesses, which rely on the combined labor of children, parents, and grandparents, are flourishing both in Queens and in Manhattan, where Bukharan émigrés run furniture stores on Lower Broadway as well as many of the Forty-seventh Street jewelry stores where Hasidic diamond cutters practice their trade. The cultural transition has been more difficult, especially for older Bukharans, who hold onto ancient traditions of prayer, food, and relations between men and women. From the ancient domed and pinnacled cities of Bukhara, Tashkent, and Samarkand, it is a vast geographic and cultural leap to the twenty-story apartment buildings and sprawling grid of numbered streets that dominate the landscape of Rego Park, Queens.

Bukharan Jews were deeply religious before emigrating—and they have retained that devotion. While Jews from the western Soviet Union have, in the main, rejected attempts to make them religious, Bukharan Jews have embraced Orthodox religious practice. Some have joined the Lyubavitch Hasidic sect. But the vast majority have continued to observe ancient Persian traditions; the language and melody of their prayers, holiday foods and customs, clothing, and mores are all quite different from those of Jews raised in the West. Those differences have not diminished in Queens, where even affluent Bukharans have faced prejudice and stereotyping, not only in dealings with American-born but also from fellow Soviet émigrés.

If Ukrainian immigrants in Brighton have bristled at charges that they are not "real Jews," Bukharans in Queens are angered by Russian and Ukrainian Jews who insist that Central Asians are not "real Russians." Such sentiments have created severe tensions in many Queens public schools, says Susan Sokirko, who runs a program for Russian-speaking students at Forest Hills High School. David, a thirteen-year-old Ukrainian Jew, insists that "we get offended when you call them Russians." Bukharan children in the public schools end up "outcasts because of their accents and backgrounds," Sokirko says. This contributes to a high dropout rate (Gorin 1995).

Adolescents and young adults also face problems at home, stemming from the insistence of religious parents that everyone in the family continue to observe traditional mores. Many parents still arrange marriages for their children, and *toys* (weddings) remain one of the central rituals in the life of the community. When a child resists such an arrangement, or insists on a greater degree of independence than Bukharan fathers are used to, conflicts arise. Battles between fathers and daughters have been especially intense, sometimes resulting in physical violence.

Anna Halberstadt of NYANA runs a support program for battered women from the Soviet émigré community. Although Bukharans represent just 15 percent of the total number of Soviet Jews in New York, they constitute more than 50 percent of the participants in NYANA's domestic violence program. Victoria Neznansky, a NYANA counselor, says that older Bukharan women will seek treatment and support, but few are willing to leave their marriages for fear of being cut off entirely from their communities and bringing shame on their children. Daughters of abused Bukharan women have gone further. After years of watching her father beat her mother, one seventeen-year old Bukharan girl began flouting his authority by wearing short skirts and red lipstick to school. She also told him that she would never marry a Bukharan man because they abuse their wives. When the father began beating her as well, she ran away from home. Fifteen-year-old Nellie called New York City Child Welfare Services and asked to be placed in foster care because she could no longer bear to watch her father beat her mother (Halberstadt and Nikolsky 1996).

Like the older women who have flocked to NYANA's battered women's groups, these young girls cling to the hope that intervention by social workers will bring an end to the battering of Bukharan women. NYANA caseworkers are also hopeful. The prevalence of domestic violence seems to be diminishing in the Bukharan community with time. Some traditional Bukharan elders have attempted to prevent change by rushing youngsters into adulthood, trying to marry off girls still in their teens, or pushing boys to drop out of school to begin work in the family business. But the most rigid parents have been those who themselves were having difficulty making the financial, social, or psychological transition to life in New York. In the Bukharan community, and across Soviet Jewish New York, most parents are proud of their children's accomplishments and believe that their children's achievements and happiness justify the sacrifices the family has made in moving to the United States.

Conclusion

The impact of Soviet Jewish émigrés on New York has been tremendous. Even with upward of one-third of their children in religious academies, Soviet Jews have become the second-largest group of foreign-born students in the New York City public schools. And the great number of elderly among them has made Soviet Jews the New York immigrant group most dependent on public assistance. But Soviet Jewish New Yorkers have been not only consumers of public resources. The long hours and tireless labor of immigrant shopkeepers has helped to revitalize flagging neighborhood economies across Brooklyn and Queens. With their superb educations in math and science, Soviet researchers, computer programmers, and medical technicians have made their presence felt in New York–area universities and hospitals, in the financial centers of Wall Street, and in the corporate offices of midtown Manhattan. Continued immigration to New York in the coming decades will reinforce all of these trends (Tress and Gold 1996).

Still, Soviet Jewish New York has changed dramatically over the past twenty-five years. Most of those who came in the 1970s have by now grown accustomed to New York life. Whether they speak flawless, barely accented English or continue to communicate primarily in Russian, they have come to feel settled in their American lives. "America is my country, not Russia," one Brighton businesswoman replied impatiently when asked whether she continued to follow the news from home. "I have no one left there to worry about. My family is all here or in Israel."

That comment illustrates one of the differences between Soviet Jews and many other immigrant groups who have arrived in New York since 1965. Like other waves of Jewish immigrants from Eastern Europe, most Jewish émigrés from the former Soviet Union feel that there is nothing left of the world they knew, nothing to go back to. Most don't even care to visit their old home. During the painful years of the 1980s, when the doors of the Soviet Union were bolted against those who wished to leave, Third Wave immigrants watched and listened for any sign of shifts in Soviet policy toward Jews, for many had family members still living there. But since the Gorbachev era, more than 300,000 Jews have emigrated and settled in the United States. Most immigrant families have been reunited with their loved ones. When asked why they came, more than a few Soviet Jews who emigrated in the mid-1990s replied: "Everyone I know is here."

The 1990s immigrants, though, are different in many ways from even their family members who emigrated twenty years earlier. One of the most important distinctions is political. The first émigrés were passionately anti-Communist. Many of them greatly admired Ronald Reagan for his hard-line stands on military preparedness and Soviet expansionism. They also saw the Republican party as being tough on crime in the streets, the experience of which shocked them profoundly after a lifetime in authoritarian Russia. These émigrés, when they became citizens, tended to register and vote Republican. With the arrival of hundreds of thousands of Fourth Wave immigrants during the late 1980s and the 1990s, this political profile began to shift. Soviet Jews began to vote Democratic (Lin 1992).

Traumatized by the economic chaos in the former Soviet Union, by the frightening rise in violent crime, and by the resurgence of anti-Semitism since the fall of the Communist state, Fourth Wave immigrants tend to be far less idealistic about capitalist democracy than their counterparts from the 1970s. Some even look back with a certain nostalgia to the Communist era, when at least the streets of Soviet cities were safe. Having witnessed the power vacuum and widespread suffering that followed Communism's end, many came to this country as strong supporters of government subsidies for housing, education, health care, and the elderly. These beliefs inclined them to vote Democratic. So did political developments in the United States in the 1990s.

Republican candidates vowed during the 1994 elections to gut social welfare programs that buffered tens of thousands of Soviet émigrés from poverty and to cut or end federal housing and health care subsidies, stipends for elderly immigrants, food stamps, and legal services. These campaigns terrified newly arrived, low-income, and particularly elderly Soviet immigrants. Extremely sensitive to any hint of a pogrom in the making, many Soviet Jews were also upset by Pat Buchanan's strident anti-immigrant rhetoric and by California governor Pete Wilson's support for Proposition 187 (prohibiting health care and educational services to illegal immigrants). After years of allying primarily with American Jews, Soviet émigrés began to make common cause with other immigrant groups. During the

1994 and 1996 election seasons, Soviet Jewish organizations joined with Latino and Asian groups to oppose politicians who called for new laws restricting legal immigration.

Welfare reform also moved Soviet émigrés to organize politically. The Personal Responsibility and Work Opportunity Act, signed by President Clinton in 1996, eliminated Supplemental Security Income (SSI) and cash benefits as well as food stamps for legal immigrants who did not become citizens after five years. This provoked all-out panic in New York's elderly immigrant communities. "This seems unbelievable," seventy-six-year-old Boris Leybovich screamed in Russian at an informational meeting held in the Forest Hills Senior Center. "How can they accept us here, then throw us to the garbage? If this happens, we will live in the street. This can't be happening" (Ramirez 1996). The New York City branch of United Jewish Appeal trained 7,000 elderly immigrants for the citizenship test during the summer of 1997 when the law was to take effect. The oldest immigrants, fearful of their ability to pass the citizenship exam, studied and worried furiously. Isylya Berdichevskaya, a retired Minsk bookkeeper living in Bensonhurst, made numerous appointments to take the exam but, sleepless with anxiety, never showed up, resigning herself to whatever fate befell her.

In the end, as part of a balanced-budget agreement passed early in August 1997, Clinton negotiated the restoration of cash assistance for elderly immigrants who were already receiving SSI at the time the bill was signed. For tens of thousands of Soviet elderly, the last-minute reprieve meant the difference between careful budgeting and homelessness. When Clinton failed to restore food stamps, New York and eight other states voted to continue supplying food stamps to legal immigrants (Dorf 1997; Ramirez 1996). In New York City, however, new welfare cuts hit the Soviet immigrant community hard. New York mayor Rudolph Giuliani enacted deep cuts in public assistance to the disabled. He also drastically reduced the numbers of welfare recipients exempted for health reasons from workfare programs. This created anger in many Soviet émigré communities in Brooklyn and Queens, where public assistance is an important means of support. The anger became vocal and organized when one Brooklyn émigré in his late fifties, whose exemption for heart trouble was revoked under the city's new welfare regulations, collapsed with a heart attack shortly after beginning his job with the city's Work Experience program.

During 1997 more than ten thousand Soviet Jewish immigrants, most of them from New York, even marched on Washington to protest government cuts in aid to legal immigrants. Speakers at the demonstration castigated the president and Congress in strong, angry language. This immigrant community had come a long way from its nearly uncritical adulation of Ronald Reagan twenty-five years earlier. During 1998 and 1999 community leaders voiced equally critical views of New York's mayor. Comfortable enough to express their dissatisfactions with elected officials, sure enough of their place in a pluralist society to join multiethnic coalitions, Soviet Jewish immigrants are beginning to seem more and more like New

Yorkers. And with a population, including their American-born children, of about half a million people spread throughout the city, much of New York is feeling decidedly more Russian. That may well change as the younger generation acculturates, but that's only if the immigration dwindles. If conditions in the republics of the former Soviet Union worsen or stay the same, the exodus of Jews is likely to continue. If that happens, the Russification of Jewish New York will continue as well.

Notes

1. Not her real name.
2. Not her real name.
3. Not her real name.

References

Altshuler, Mordecai. 1987. *Soviet Jewry Since the Second World War: Population and Social Structure.* Westport: Greenwood.

Birman, Igor. 1979. "Jewish Emigration from the USSR: Some Observations." *Soviet Jewish Affairs* 9 (September): 46–63.

Bryant-Friedland, Bruce. 1995. "Russians Perplex Their Bronx Brethren." *Bronx Beat Online,* November 13.

Burstein, Daniel. 1986. "The Russian Mafia: A New Crime Menace Grows in Brooklyn." *New York,* November 24.

Caroll, Linda. 1993. "Seeking Care in a Strange Land: Medical Culture Shock." *Newsday,* October 10.

Carr, Donna. 1997. "The Jews of Bukhara." *byblos@getnet.com.*

Cordero-Guzman, Hector, and Ramon Grosfoguel. 1998. "The Demographic and Socioeconomic Characteristics of Post-1965 Foreign Born Immigrants to New York City." Unpublished paper.

Dorf, Matthew. 1997. "With Food Stamp Loss, Emigres in Bay Area Worry About Hunger." *Jewish Telegraphic Agency,* August 22.

Dugger, Celia. 1997. "Immigrant Influence Surges." *The New York Times,* January 9.

Fisher, Leon D. 1975. "Initial Experiences in the Resettlement of Soviet Jews in the United States." *Journal of Jewish Communal Service* (March): 267–69.

Friedgut, Theodore. 1989. "Passing Eclipse: The Exodus Movement in the 1980s." In Robert Friedman, ed., *Soviet Jewry in the 1980s: The Politics of Anti-Semitism and Emigration and the Dynamics of Resettlement,* pp. 3–25. Durham: Duke University Press.

Friedman, Robert I. 1994. "The Russian Mob." *New York,* November 7.

———. 1996. "The Money Pit." *New York,* January 22.

Garrett, Laurie. 1997. "Crumbled Empire, Shattered Health." *Newsday,* October 28.

Gilbert, Martin. *The Jews of Hope.* New York: Viking.

Gold, Steven. 1995. *From the Worker's State to the Golden State.* Boston: Allyn and Bacon.

Gorin, Julia. 1995. "Along the Bukharan Broadway." *Newsday,* July 23.

Halberstadt, Anna. 1996. "A Model Assessment of an Emigre Family from the Former Soviet Union." *Journal of Jewish Communal Service* (Summer): 244–55.

Halberstadt, Anna, and Adele Nikolsky. 1996. "Bukharan Jews and Their Adaptation to the United States." *Journal of Jewish Communal Service* (Summer): 298–309.

Harper's. 1991. "I'm Not Fleeing, I'm Being Evicted." *Harper's,* June 1991.

Holden, Constance. 1990. "No American Dream for Soviet Refugees." *Science,* June 1.

Hebrew Immigrant Aid Society (HIAS).1999. *Annual Report 1997–1998.* New York: HIAS.

Jacobson, Gaynor. 1975. "Spotlight on Soviet Jewry: Absorption in the USA." *Journal of Jewish Communal Service* (December): 190–94.

Levin, Nora. 1988. *The Jews in the Soviet Union Since 1917,* 2 volumes. New York: New York University Press.

Lewis, Phillipa. 1978. "The Jewish Question in the Open, 1968–71." In Lionel Kochan, ed., *The Jews in Soviet Russia Since 1917,* pp. 349–65. London: Oxford University Press.

Lin, Wendy. 1992. "Immigrants Back Clinton." *Newsday,* November 3.

Lobo, Arun Peter, Joseph Salvo, and Vicky Virgin. 1996. *The Newest New Yorkers, 1990–1994.* New York: Department of City Planning.

Low, Albert D. 1990. *Soviet Jewry and Soviet Policy.* New York: Columbia University Press.

Markowitz, Fran. 1993. *A Community in Spite of Itself: Soviet Jewish Emigres in New York.* Washington: Smithsonian Press.

New York City Department of City Planning. 1999. *The Newest New Yorkers, 1995–1996.* New York: Department of City Planning.

Nikolsky, Adele. 1996. "An Adaptation Group for Middle-Aged Clients from the Former Soviet Union." *Journal of Jewish Communal Service* (Summer): 316–25.

New York Association for New Americans (NYANA). 1996. *Starting Over: The NYANA Resettlement Process.* New York: NYANA.

Office of Refugee Resettlement. 1994. *Report to Congress FY 1993 Refugee Resettlement Program.* Washington, D.C.: U.S. Department of Health and Human Services.

——. 1995. *Report to Congress FY 1994 Refugee Resettlement Program.* Washington, D.C.: U.S. Department of Health and Human Services.

Ramirez, Margaret. 1996."Welfare Fears: No Refuge for Elderly Refugees." *Newsday,* August 4.

Rosner, Lydia S. 1986. *The Soviet Way of Crime: Beating the System in the Soviet Union and the USA.* South Hadley, Mass.: Begin and Garvey.

Rubin, Burton. 1975. "The Soviet Refugee." *Journal of Jewish Communal Service* (December): 195–201.

Sawyer, Susan. 1995. "Apple Pie and Affiliation: Soviet Jews Try Religion American Style." *The International Jewish Monthly.* Online.

Sawyer, Thomas E. 1979. *The Jewish Minority in the Soviet Union.* Boulder, Colo.: Westview.

Simon, Rita J. 1985. *New Lives: The Adjustment of Soviet Jewish Emigres in the United States and Israel.* Lexington, Mass.: Lexington.

Sirotin, Alexander. 1981. "The Wandering Jew." Unpublished essay.

Solomon, Linda. 1996. "Providing High Quality Service to Elderly Soviet Emigres." *Journal of Jewish Communal Service* (Summer): 326–34.

Sugarman, Rafael. 1992. "The Kindest Cut of All." *Urban Gazette,* December 10.

Tress, Madeline. 1996. "Refugees as Immigrants: Revelations of Labor Market Performance." *Journal of Jewish Communal Service* 72(4) (Summer): 263–79.

Tress, Madeline, and Steven Gold. 1996. "Immigration, Acculturation, Integration and Other Questions: A Review of the Recent Literature on Soviet Jews in the United States." *Journal of Jewish Communal Service* (Summer).

Weinberg, Armin, Sunil Kripilani, Philip L. McCarthy, and Jack Schuli. 1995. "Caring for Survivors of the Chernobyl Disaster: What the Clinician Should Know." *Journal of the American Medical Association* 274(5) (August 2): 408–12.

Weinstein, Lewis. 1988. "Soviet Jewry and the American Jewish Community." *American Jewish History* (June).

Wiesel, Elie. 1987. *The Jews of Silence: A Personal Report on Soviet Jewry,* expanded edition. New York: Shocken.

Chinese: Divergent Destinies in Immigrant New York

Min Zhou

If you love her, send her to New York, because that's paradise; if you hate her, send her to New York, because that's hell.

> —*Prelude to the Chinese movie*
> A Native of Beijing in New York

New York offers many fortunes but unequal opportunities to newcomers. Not everyone can make it here. It [New York] is like a happy melting pot for some, a pressure cooker for many others, and still a dumpster for the unfortunate.

> —*A Chinese immigrant*[1]

In New York City, any rush-hour subway ride in the morning or evening gives a visitor a chance to rub shoulders with people of different ancestries and hear various languages spoken. New York has, of course, long been an immigrant city, but until recently the immigrants were overwhelmingly European. Time has washed off the "colors" of the old-timers from Russia, Italy, and Ireland, "melting" them into an indistinguishable "white." A new ethnic mosaic is in the making as a result of the arrival of hundreds and thousands of newcomers from Asia and the Americas.

This chapter has benefited from insightful discussions with prominent scholars, civic and business leaders, community organizers, and residents in the Chinese immigrant community in New York City. I wish to thank Nancy Foner, Paul Huang, John Logan, and Joyce Zhao for their helpful comments and suggestions. I also thank Jo-Ann Yap Adefuin and Amy Chai for their research assistance. The research is supported by the UCLA Asian American Studies Center.

Today, the visitor to New York inevitably encounters the world. As one Anglo traveler on the number 7 subway train through Queens reported, "I feel I am riding a train through the globe. There are so many different faces, so many strange languages, and so many unfamiliar mannerisms that I suddenly become an alien. Once the train gets past Shea Stadium and goes underground, I feel I am on the Orient Express."[2] Indeed, this traveler was getting off the train in Flushing with fellow passengers who were mostly Asian. Flushing is now known as the Chinatown of Queens. A traveler who takes the N train to Brooklyn and gets off at Eighth Avenue comes out of the subway station to find what seems to be a street in China. That is Sunset Park, but the Chinese call it *Bat Dai Do* (Eighth Avenue in Cantonese); it is the Chinatown of Brooklyn.

Chinese immigrants, though arriving in New York as early as the 1850s, now constitute one of the largest pieces of this new ethnic mosaic. Between 1982 and 1989, 72,000 Chinese immigrants (including 10,000 from Hong Kong and 9,000 from Taiwan) entered the City of New York legally, and between 1990 and 1996, about 71,500 added to the pool of Chinese newcomers (New York City Department of City Planning 1992a, 1999). Post-1990 arrivals from mainland China, Taiwan, and Hong Kong consistently rank third among the newest New Yorkers (New York City Department of City Planning 1999), not counting the thousands of undocumented Chinese immigrants (Chin 1997; Liang 1997). Together with their native-born coethnics, the number of ethnic Chinese in New York City grew more than sixfold in just three decades, from 33,000 in 1960 to 239,000 in 1990, and to an estimate of approximately half a million in 2000.[3]

How are these newest New Yorkers adapting to their new homeland? As this chapter explores the processes of transformation and adaptation among new Chinese immigrants in New York in the 1980s and 1990s, it illuminates the divergent destinies that these immigrants experience. I use a combination of quantitative and qualitative data, including U.S. census data, immigration statistics compiled by the U.S. Immigration and Naturalization Service and the New York City Department of City Planning, and my own field observations and interviews. Specifically I examine the changing trends of Chinese immigration, the distinct characteristics of the newcomers, the new patterns of settlement, and the impacts of immigration on the lives of new immigrants.

Changing Trends in Chinese Immigration to the United States

The Consequences of Chinese Exclusion

Chinese immigration to the United States dates back to the 1840s, initially driven by the capitalist expansion of the American West. Since then, more than 1.5 million Chinese immigrants have been legally admitted (U.S. Immigration and Naturalization Service 1997:28).[4] In the beginning, Chinese immigrants arrived on the West Coast in search of gold. Most came under labor contracts, working at first in the mining industry and later on the transcontinental railroads west of the Rocky Mountains. These Chinese laborers, predominantly male peasants from the Canton region of South China, intended to stay for only a short time and "dig" enough gold to take home. But few realized their gold dreams; many found themselves instead easy targets of discrimination and exclusion. Not only were their contributions to developing the West and to building the most difficult part of the transcontinental railroad unrecognized, their mere existence became a nuisance when the job was done (Chan 1991). In the 1870s, deep-seated anti-Chinese sentiment among white workers surfaced and turned into racist attacks against the Chinese. Whites accused the Chinese of building "a filthy nest of iniquity and rottenness" in the midst of the American society and driving away white labor by "stealthy" competition. They called the Chinese the "yellow peril," the "Chinese menace," and the "indispensable enemy" (McCunn 1979; Saxton 1971). Rallying under the slogan "The Chinese Must Go," the Workmen's Party in California successfully launched an anti-Chinese campaign for laws to exclude the Chinese. In 1882, the U.S. Congress passed the Chinese Exclusion Act, which was renewed in 1892 and later extended to exclude all Asian immigrants until World War II.

Legal exclusion, augmented by extralegal persecution and anti-Chinese violence, effectively drove the Chinese out of the mines, farms, woolen mills, and factories and forced them to cluster in urban enclaves on the West Coast that later evolved into Chinatowns (Nee and Nee 1973; Saxton 1971). The number of new immigrants arriving in the United States dropped substantially following the enactment of the Chinese Exclusion Act, from 123,000 in the 1870s to 14,800 in the 1890s, and then to a historically low number of 5,000 in the 1930s. This trend did not change significantly until the 1960s (see figure 5.1). Faced with Chinese exclusion, many Chinese laborers already in the United States lost hope of ever fulfilling their dreams and returned permanently to China. Others, who could not afford the return journey (either because they had no money for the trip or because they had no fortunes to bring home), gravitated toward San Francisco's Chinatown for self-protection, whereas others departed for the East Coast to look for alternative means of livelihood (Zhou 1992). As a result, Chinatowns in the Northeast and the Midwest, particularly in Chicago, grew as they absorbed those fleeing the extreme persecution in California (Lee 1960; Lyman 1974; Zhang 1998).

New York's Chinatown made its initial appearance in the four-block neighborhood across Canal Street from Little Italy in Lower East Manhattan in the 1870s (Sung 1987). During the era of free immigration between 1860 and 1880, 99 percent of the Chinese laborers that came to the United States lived and worked in the Pacific Northwest and more than 70 percent in California (Wong 1995). At the turn of the century, the proportion of Chinese living in California dropped to 39 percent while the proportion in New York increased to 6 percent. New York's Chinese population was relatively small but experienced steady growth; it grew

Figure 5.1 Chinese Immigrants Admitted to the United States, 1851–1996

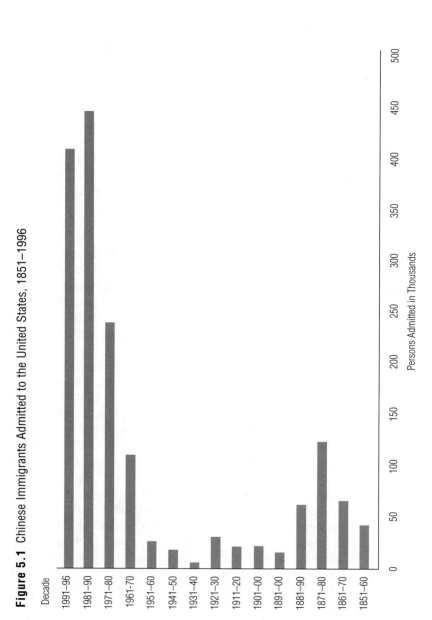

Source: U.S. Immigration and Naturalization Service 1996.

from 7,170 to 13,731 between 1900 and 1940 while California experienced population loss from 45,753 to 39,556.

During the exclusion era, immigrant Chinese in New York shared many common characteristics with their coethnics in California and elsewhere in the country. First, most were from villages in the Sze Yap area, speaking Taishanese (a local dialect incomprehensible even to the Cantonese), and from other villages in Sam Yap and the greater Canton region.[5] Second, most left their families behind in China and came to America as sojourners with the aim of making a "gold" fortune and returning home. Third, most were poor and uneducated and had to work at odd jobs that few Americans wanted. Laundrymen, cooks or waiters, and household servants characterized most of the workers in Chinatown. Fourth, they spoke very little English and seemed unassimilated in the eyes of Americans. In fact, as "aliens ineligible for citizenship," the Chinese were not allowed to naturalize. Pre–World War II Chinatowns across the country were bachelor societies. In 1890, there were 495 men per 100 women in New York's Chinese population; in California, 1,224 men per 100 women. By the 1940s, New York's Chinatown had grown into a ten-block enclave, accommodating almost all the Chinese immigrants in the city. As a typical bachelor society, the gender ratio in New York was even more skewed than before, with 603 men per 100 women, compared with a much more balanced ratio of 224 men per 100 women in California.

Post–World War II Trends

After the repeal of the Chinese Exclusion Act in 1943 and the passage of the War Bride Act in 1945, Chinese women were allowed into the United States to join their husbands and families, and they comprised more than half of the postwar arrivals from China. As a result, the bachelor society began to dissolve. However, the number of Chinese immigrants entering the United States each year was still very small because the annual quota was set at 105 (Sung 1987). According to the U.S. Immigration and Naturalization Service, legal admissions of Chinese immigrants averaged only 965 annually in the 1950s, a drop from 1,670 in the 1940s when many war brides came.

The surge of Chinese immigration, which began in the late 1960s, reflects the passage of amendments to the Immigration and Nationality Act, also referred to as the Hart-Celler Act. The act abolished the national quota system that restricted immigration from Southern and Eastern Europe, lifted the ban on immigration from Asia, and established the seven preference categories with an equal per-country limit of 20,000 in annual admissions. Since the Hart-Celler Act went into effect, immigration from China, Hong Kong, and Taiwan has grown at unprecedented rates. According to the U.S. immigration statistics (U.S. Immigration and Naturalization Service 1997), the number of legal immigrants admitted from China, Hong Kong, and Taiwan went from 110,000 in the 1960s to 445, 000 in the 1980s. Altogether from 1971 to 1996, approximately 1.1 million Chinese immigrants were legally admitted to the United States as permanent residents. In New York City, Chinese immigrants arrived at an average annual rate of 12,000 in the 1980s and 1990s, accounting for almost 20 percent of all Chinese immigrants legally admitted to the United States (New York City Department of City Planning 1992a, 1999).

Immigration has led to huge increases in the Chinese American population as a whole (see figure 5.2). Indeed, in 1990, foreign-born Chinese accounted for about two-thirds of the Chinese American population nationwide. By 1990, the ethnic Chinese population in the United States was 1,645,472, fourteen times its size in 1950 (118,000). In 1990, the state of California was home to 43 percent of the U.S. Chinese population; New York State came second, with 17 percent of the total. Compared to California's ethnic Chinese population, New York's is much more urban and concentrated: in 1990, about 84 percent of the Chinese in New York State lived in New York City, whereas only 19 percent of California's Chinese lived in San Francisco and another 10 percent in Los Angeles.[6] Overall, contemporary Chinese immigration has transformed the nation's old Chinatowns from bachelor societies to full-fledged family communities. In New York's Chinatown, over two-thirds of the adult residents are currently married, and in New York City as a whole, about 80 percent of the Chinese live in married-couple households.

Forces Behind the Surge of Chinese Immigration

Without question, the passage of the Hart-Celler Act has been critical in accelerating Chinese immigration since the late 1960s. Indeed, by stipulating that spouses and children of U.S. citizens are exempt from numerical limitations, the act has allowed Chinese immigration to exceed the 20,000 per-country limit. More than three-quarters of contemporary Chinese immigrants have come to the United States to join families, and many are immediate family members not subject to the per-country limit.

Broader geopolitical factors, independent of or interacting with the act, also account for the surge of contemporary Chinese immigration. Between 1949 and the end of the Great Cultural Revolution (1966–1976), China was sanctioned by the West and isolated from the rest of the world. Emigration was highly restricted, and communications with overseas relatives were regarded as antirevolutionary and subversive. For many years the government banned the movement of Chinese people across borders and severely punished those who attempted illegal border crossing. Since the 1970s, sweeping social, economic, and political changes have taken place in China. Several historical events are particularly important: China gained admission to the United Nations at the expense of Taiwan in 1971; President Nixon visited China in 1972, marking the first official Sino-U.S. contact since the founding of the People's Republic of China; the Chinese Great Cultural Revolution ended in 1976 upon the death of Communist Party chairman Mao Zedong and premier Zhou Enlai; China and

Figure 5.2 Ethnic Chinese population in the United States: 1950–1990

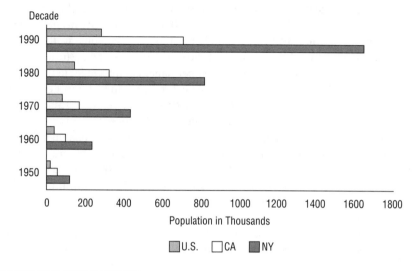

Source: U.S. Bureau of the Census 1950–1990.

the United States established normal diplomatic relations in 1979; the Chinese government began to implement an open-door policy in 1978 and launched nationwide economic reforms in 1984; also in 1984, China and Britain signed an agreement on the 1997 return of Hong Kong to China; and last but not least, the Chinese military put down a prodemocracy student movement in Beijing's Tiananmen Square in 1989. These historical events have had significant consequences for emigration from China, Hong Kong, and Taiwan.

In China, liberalized emigration policy, economic reform, and the new opportunity to study abroad are among the most significant factors contributing to emigration. As China opened its door in the late 1970s, it relaxed emigration restrictions. The normalization of Sino-U.S. relations with China made it possible for relatives of U.S. citizens or longtime U.S. resident aliens to apply for U.S. immigrant visas in China. Initially, most of the United States–bound emigrants were from the historically important sending regions in Guangdong Province. Later on, newly established migration networks facilitated emigration from other parts of China.

China's open-door policy has also unintentionally created pressure for emigration. Since 1978, China has aggressively pursued its modernization goal through scholarly and technological exchanges. Over the past thirty years, China has sent hundreds of thousands of students and visiting scholars to the United States, as well as to other Western countries, for postgraduate education and advanced professional training (Orleans 1988; see also *Chinese Education News,* August 23, 1997, p. 1). According to the Chinese Ministry of Education,

130,000 government-sponsored exchange visitors and students and 137,000 self-sponsored students went abroad to study or do research in the developed countries in the West in the 1980s and early 1990s, the majority headed for the United States. A significant proportion of the students who come to the United States, estimated at two-thirds or more, decide to stay rather than return to China (Orleans 1988). Many foreign students find permanent employment in the United States after completing their studies or practical training. In fact, most employer-sponsored immigrants from China have had their nonimmigrant student visas adjusted to permanent residency status in the United States. Moreover, the 1989 crackdown of the student prodemocracy movement in Beijing's Tiananmen Square led to special U.S. legislation, the Chinese Student Protection Act, granting permanent residency to more than 48,000 Chinese nationals (mostly students and visiting scholars) and their families between 1993 and 1994 (U.S. Immigration and Naturalization Service 1995, 1996:19).

In Taiwan and Hong Kong, political uncertainty and anxiety about the future have spurred emigration. The ousting of Taiwan from the United Nations and the normalization of China-U.S. diplomatic relations caused a huge volume of capital outflow, as well as an exodus of middle-class Chinese to the United States (Li 1997). The return of Hong Kong to the sovereignty of China in 1997 also triggered the exodus of thousands of capitalists and members of the middle and upper-middle classes who sought safe havens in the West. The flight of middle-class professionals and capitalists coincided with the globalization of the U.S. economy, which now attracts transnational capital investment and favors the importation of highly skilled foreign labor (Liu and Cheng 1994; Skeldon 1994). Starting in the early 1980s, capitalists from rapidly growing Asian economies saw the United States as a modern gold mine for investment. Many overseas Chinese from Hong Kong and Taiwan invested in old Chinatowns and new suburban Chinese communities (Li 1997; Lin 1998; Wong 1998).

Last but not least, the end of the Vietnam War in 1975 and subsequent political repression in Vietnam has pushed thousands of refugees out of their homeland. The United States resettled over 600,000 of them, including some 200,000 ethnic Chinese, whose admissions were not subject to the per-country limit. Many Sino-Vietnamese went to live in Chinatowns or in neighborhoods settled by other Chinese immigrants.

Chinese Newcomers to New York

Diverse Origins

During the past three decades, approximately one in five Chinese immigrants (and more than a quarter of those from the mainland) arriving in the United States has called New York City home. Unlike old-timers, most new Chinese immigrants to New York flew there directly from Asia, rather than remigrating after spending time in America's West. The majority came to join their families, others were sponsored by their U.S. employers, and still others were smuggled in without proper documents (Chin 1997; Kwong 1997; Liang 1997; Sung 1987; Wong 1987; Zhou 1992).

Whereas old-timers were typically Cantonese from rural villages in the southern areas of Guangdong Province, recent Chinese immigrants have come from a wider range of places. In 1990, 48 percent of Chinese New Yorkers were born in China, 11 percent in Hong Kong, 8 percent in Taiwan, 11 percent in other parts of the world, and 22 percent in the United States. The U.S. Immigration and Naturalization Service data attest to the concentration of mainland Chinese in New York City. Among new Chinese immigrants who entered New York City between 1982 and 1996, 77 percent were from the mainland, 13 percent from Hong Kong, and 10 percent from Taiwan (New York City Department of City Planning 1992a, 1999).

Even among mainland Chinese, diversity of origin is a distinct characteristic. In Canton, cities and towns have replaced rural villages as the major sending communities. Outside Canton, many regions that historically sent few emigrants to the United States have become important sources of emigration, including capital cities of Beijing, Shanghai, and Tianjin; coastal cities in Fujian, Zejiang, and Shangdong; and inland cities in Sichuan and Hunan. Today, few Chinese immigrants understand Taishanese, the dialect of the old-time peasants, and Mandarin speakers have become nearly as numerous as Cantonese speakers among the most recent arrivals. In Chinatown, Cantonese remains the most common language, but Fujianese has become increasingly common among coethnic residents and workers as the Fujianese subenclave expands (Kwong 1997). In recent years, Chinese immigrants from Southeast Asia and the Americas have also become visible in New York City.

Diverse Socioeconomic Backgrounds

Today's Chinese immigrants have a variety of socioeconomic backgrounds. Some arrived with little money, minimum education, and few job skills, which forced them to take low-wage jobs and settle in deteriorating urban neighborhoods. Others came with family savings, education, and skills far above the levels of average Americans. Table 5.1 shows that new Chinese immigrants have been disproportionately drawn from the highly educated and professional segments of their sending societies. Nationwide, levels of educational attainment are significantly higher than those of the general U.S. population in both 1980 and 1990, and skill levels have increased over time. Most remarkable are foreign-born Taiwanese, who were twice as likely as their mainland counterparts and three times as likely as average Americans, to have a college degree. Not surprisingly, a higher proportion of foreign-born Taiwanese hold professional occupations as compared to their coethnics as well as to average American workers, no doubt an indication of employer-

Table 5.1 Selected Characteristics of Immigrants from China, Hong Kong, and Taiwan in the United States: 1980–1990

	1980				1990			
	China	Hong Kong	Taiwan	U.S.[a]	China	Hong Kong	Taiwan	U.S.[a]
Total foreign-born persons	286,120	80,380	75,353	226,545,805	529,837	147,131	244,102	248,709,873
Males per 100 females	102	102	86	95	102	99	113	95
Length of residence less than 5 years (%)	27.2	34.9	54.6	—	31.9	25.2	33.6	—
Naturalized citizens (%)	50.3	38.3	28.9	—	44.2	54.4	38.5	—
College graduates or more (%)[b]	28.5	42.7	59.8	16.2	30.9	46.8	62.2	20.2
Professional occupations (%)[c]	16.8	19.1	30.4	22.7	29.0	40.9	47.4	22.3
Median household income	$18,544	$18,094	$18,271	$16,841	$31,000	$42,000	$39,000	$28,000

Source: U.S. Bureau of the Census 1983, 1993.
Notes: [a] The total U.S. population, including the native-born. [b] Persons 25 years or over. [c] Persons 16 years or over.

sponsored or investment migration among the Taiwanese. Chinese immigrants also have higher median household incomes than the national average, probably because Chinese immigrant households usually contain multiple wage earners.

What about New York City's Chinese? As table 5.2 shows, New York seems to attract a less diverse group of immigrant Chinese than Los Angeles. New Chinese New Yorkers are dominated by immigrants from the mainland (48 percent), whereas new Chinese Angelinos are more evenly distributed by place of origin, with a significant proportion (22 percent) from other Chinese diasporic communities around the world. New York's Chinese immigrants have lower socioeconomic status as measured by education, occupation, and median household income. Moreover, New York's ethnic Chinese population is residentially more concentrated at the neighborhood level, with one-fifth residing in Manhattan's Chinatown (Old Chinatown hereafter); only 4 percent of Los Angeles's ethnic Chinese population lived in Chinatown.

Although New York receives a disproportionate number of low-skilled Chinese immigrants, not all are confined to low-level occupations. Some have continued the time-honored route of mobility, starting out at the very bottom of the labor market, while others from the beginning have been able to move into professional occupations in finance, education, and even various levels of the government. Still others are self-employed. Immigrants with high levels of human capital (education and skill) and those with limited human capital but experience in a trade tend to be attracted to entrepreneurship, especially in business specialties where the Chinese are concentrated and that offer opportunities and resources for business creation. Today, Chinese immigrants in New York find themselves in various types of jobs, ranging from cooks, waiters, seam-

Table 5.2 Selected Characteristics of the Chinese American Population: New York and Los Angeles,[a] 1990

	New York	Los Angeles
Place of birth (%)		
U.S.	21.9	23.1
Mainland China	47.5	27.0
Taiwan	7.9	19.9
Hong Kong	11.4	8.0
Other	11.3	22.0
Socioeconomic status (among the foreign-born only)		
Average years of schooling	13.5	15.3
Managerial and professional occupations (%)	20.6	31.0
Median household income	$29,667	$36,224
Residence in Chinatown[b] (%)	19.8	3.5

Source: Adapted from tables 1, 3, 4, and 5 in Zhou (1998).
Notes: [a]Principal metropolitan statistical area. [b]New York's Chinatown includes fourteen tracts; 6, 8, 16, 18, 27, 29, 41, 2.01, 2.02, 14.02, 22.01, 43, 15.01, and 25. Los Angeles's Chinatown includes four tracts: 2071, 1971, 1976, and 1977.

stresses, and housekeepers to research and development scientists, computer engineers, laboratory technicians, Wall Street stockbrokers, midtown bankers, and "astronaut" (transnational) businessmen.

New Patterns of Settlement

Today's Chinese New Yorkers are diverse not only in the dialect they speak, the customs they practice, and their socioeconomic characteristics but also in their settlement patterns. Historically, the majority of Chinese immigrants who came to New York clustered in Old Chinatown. Today, about one in five settles there; many others bypass the century-old enclave to settle in new Chinatowns in outer boroughs or upscale neighborhoods in affluent suburbs. As shown in figure 5.3, ethnic Chinese New Yorkers are dispersed throughout the city, although they are highly concentrated at the neighborhood level. Ethnic Chinese clustering is visible in Manhattan, where Old Chinatown is located; in northeastern and north-central parts of Queens (Flushing and Jackson Heights); and in western and southern parts of Brooklyn (Sunset Park and Sheepshead Bay). There are relatively few Chinese (about 3 percent) and very little ethnic clustering at the neighborhood level in the Bronx.

Old Chinatown

Old Chinatown has been a long-standing immigrant community for over a century. The census of 1860 showed that only 120 Chinese lived in New York City, or 0.2 percent of the total Chinese population (63,109) in the United States at the time (Zhou 1992). Story has it that when a Chinese merchant, Wo Kee, opened a general store on 8 Mott Street in 1870, coethnic immigrants began to gravitate toward the place (Lee 1960; Sung 1987). The first East-bound group settled in a three-street area (Mott, Park, and Doyer) on the Lower East Side of Manhattan (Jackson 1983; Wong 1979). Until the 1970s, most Chinese immigrants entering New York made Chinatown their home. Although decentralization of the Chinese population began as early as the 1950s, substantial out-migration and outer-borough settlement were not common until much later. According to census counts in 1990, about 50,000 Chinese lived in the core (defined by fourteen census tracts[7]), up from 26,700 in 1970; 53 percent of the area's residents were Chinese, up from 32 percent in 1970; out of the fourteen tracts, five had a Chinese majority and another five contained 25 percent or more Chinese (Zhou 1992; Zhou and Kim 1999). Census counts are no doubt too low and miss many undocumented immigrants who are too scared to cooperate with census staff. Probably at least twice as many Chinese live in Old Chinatown and the surrounding area as census figures indicate.

The majority of Chinatown residents are Cantonese from the traditional sending regions in South China. In recent years, a noticeable group of Sino-Vietnamese

Figure 5.3 Residential Distribution of Chinese New Yorkers, 1990

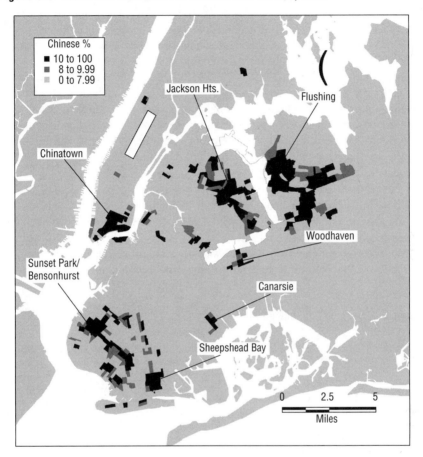

Source: Logan (1999). Courtesy of the Lewis Mumford Center for Comparative Urban and Regional Research, State University of New York at Albany.

has settled in Chinatown; most are fluent in Cantonese and share many cultural characteristics with the Cantonese, as they originally immigrated to Vietnam from Guangdong and Guangxi provinces. Another dialect group, the Fuzhounese from Fujian province, has also established a foothold in Chinatown. Because of cultural differences and coethnic stereotyping, Fuzhounese, who generally arrive as undocumented immigrants, do not mingle with the Cantonese; instead they have built their own subenclave in a three-block area on East Broadway under the Manhattan Bridge (Kwong 1997). Although Chinatown's residents are culturally diverse, they share similar socioeconomic status; many are recent arrivals, have low levels of education, speak little or no English, hold low-wage jobs, and live in poverty. As table 5.3 shows, the elderly are a significant presence in old China-town; 21 percent of the household heads in the core area of Chinatown were sixty-five years or older, compared to 15 percent citywide. Some of these elderly people have chosen to keep their residence in Chinatown even after their children and grandchildren have moved to the suburbs.

In Chinatown, walk-up tenement and loft buildings line the streets. Overcrowd-ing characterizes Chinatown living. Over 90 percent of residents live in rental housing, and many housing units are in poor and deteriorating condition. New immigrants arriving in Chinatown are often shocked by the squalid living that provides a striking contrast to the glamorous skyscrapers in the background. One middle-aged woman who arrived to join her daughter's family in Chinatown re-called,

I'd never imagined my daughter's family living in this condition. My daughter, who was about to give birth to her first child, lived with her husband in a one-room apartment. When I arrived in New York, my daughter had to squeeze me into their apartment. They had only one queen-size bunkbed that almost filled the room. I slept, and later with the baby, at the bottom, and my daughter and

Table 5.3 Selected Characteristics of the Lower East Side, Flushing, and Sunset Park,[a] 1990

	Chinatown Manhattan CD#3	Flushing Queens CD#7	Sunset Park Brooklyn CD#7	New York City
Total population	161,617	221,763	102,553	7,322,564
Age of household head 65 +	20.6	11.1	11.7	14.6
Housing				
Renter occupied	92.1	53.3	71.9	71.4
Year housing built before 1950	59.2	36.8	82.7	55.3
Racial makeup				
Non-Hispanic white	29.3	58.2	33.6	43.2
Non-Hispanic black	8.3	4.2	4.0	25.2
Hispanic	32.3	15.0	51.4	24.4
Asian	29.6	22.2	10.4	6.7
Chinese	95.8	41.4	77.6	48.8
Place of birth				
Foreign-born	35.5	39.8	29.2	28.4
Arriving after 1980	46.2	49.8	55.5	45.8
Education				
At least some college	14.5	20.6	16.2	19.0
Occupation				
Managerial and professional	18.4	29.0	15.4	30.5
Families below poverty level	25.5	6.5	21.0	16.3
Median household income	$20,007	$36,000	$25,875	$29,823

Source: New York City Department of City Planning 1992b, 1993.
Note: [a] Defined by New York City's Community Districts.

her husband on top. In China, I had a spacious three-bedroom apartment. It was just like hell living there.[8]

This woman's family eventually bought a house in Brooklyn. Like her, many immigrants came from relatively affluent middle-class backgrounds but were not wealthy enough to afford adequate housing when they got here. Others who came from the working class seemed more optimistic. One Chinatown man remarked, "Sharing a two-bedroom apartment with another family in Chinatown wasn't that bad. In China, I lived just like that and there were many people who lived in worse conditions. Here, you are pretty sure that this would change in a few years. But in China, you were not so sure."[9] Many Chinese immigrants reluctantly tolerate the dank and filthy cubicle dwellings in the hope that someday they will move out of Chinatown. Indeed, many have been able to do so. In Chinatown, most of the residents are either recent arrivals or elderly; very few second-generation young people are raising their families there.

For many Chinese immigrants, Chinatown's inferior living is offset by the easy access to jobs and services. With the continuous arrival of new immigrants and the tremendous influx of foreign capital, the physical boundaries of Chinatown have expanded so that it now covers a huge area in lower Manhattan. The ethnic enclave economy has also been transformed. During the 1930s and 1940s, Chinatown's ethnic economy was highly concentrated in restaurant and laundry businesses. By the 1970s, the laundry business had shrunk substantially and the garment industry had become one of Chinatown's backbone industries. In the 1980s, Chinatown's garment industry grew to more than 500 factories, run by Chinese entrepreneurs and employing more than 20,000 immigrant Chinese, mostly women. Today, the garment industry in Chinatown is showing some signs of shrinking as many factories move out of the enclave, but it remains strong as an ethnic niche for immigrant women. It is estimated that three out of five immigrant Chinese women in Chinatown work in the garment industry. The restaurant business, another backbone industry in Chinatown, has continued to grow and prosper. Listed restaurants run by Chinese grew from 304 in 1958 to 781 in 1988, employing at least 15,000 immigrant Chinese workers (Kwong 1987; Zhou 1992). In addition, various other businesses have also experienced tremendous growth, ranging from grocery stores; import/export companies; and barbershops and beauty salons to such professional services as banks; law firms; financial, insurance, and real estate agencies; and doctors' and herbalists' clinics. Chinatown's economic development is described by sociologist Jan Lin (1998) as a two-circuit phenomenon embedded in a postindustrial global city: sweatshops and tenements are the lower circuit, characterized by low-wage jobs, unskilled labor, sidewalk peddlers, and crowding or slum living; and finance and redevelopment are the upper circuit, characterized by high-skilled and professional service jobs, capital-intensive redevelopment, transnational businesses, and modern tourism.

Chinatown has also witnessed a growth of civic and religious institutions. In Old Chinatown, family or clan associations and merchants' associations (tongs) were the major community-based organizations. These organizations functioned primarily to meet the basic needs of sojourning workers, such as helping them obtain employment, offering different levels of social support, and organizing economic activities. Powerful tongs controlled most of the economic resources in the community and were oriented toward shielding Chinatown from outsiders and preserving the status quo within the community (Kuo 1977). The single most important social organization was the Chinese Consolidated Benevolent Association (CCBA). The CCBA was established as an apex group representing some sixty organizations in Chinatown, including different family and district associations, the guilds, the tongs, the Chamber of Commerce, and the Nationalist Party. Controlled by a few powerful tongs, the CCBA cooperated with all voluntary associations and operated as an unofficial government in Chinatown (Kuo 1977; Sung 1987).

Traditional organizations functioned to secure the standing of Chinatown in the larger society and to provide a refuge for sojourning laborers. Some of them formed underground societies to profit from such illicit activities as partitioning territories, extortion for business protection, gambling, prostitution, and drugs (Dillon 1962; Kuo 1977; Sung 1987). The rapid demographic change in the nature of Chinese immigration has created pressing demands for services associated with resettlement and adjustment problems that have overwhelmed the existing traditional organizations in Chinatown. To accommodate these changes, traditional organizations have been pressured to redefine their role, and various new organizations have been established in Chinatown. A glance at one Chinese business directory, for example, reveals over 100 voluntary associations, 61 community service organizations, 41 community-based employment agencies, 16 daycare centers, 27 career training schools, 28 Chinese- and English-language schools, and 9 dancing and music schools in New York City in the early 1990s (Chinatown Today Publishing 1993).[10] Most of these organizations are located in Manhattan's Chinatown; some are located in new satellite Chinatowns in Flushing, Queens, and Sunset Park, Brooklyn.

Traditional ethnic institutions have changed their orientation from sojourning to settlement and assimilation. To appeal to the settlement demands of new immigrants and their families, the CCBA has established a Chinese language school, an adult English evening school, and a career training center and has instituted a variety of social service programs, including employment referral and job training services. The CCBA-operated New York Chinese School is perhaps the largest children- and youth-oriented organization in Chinatown. The school annually (not including summer) enrolls about 4,000 Chinese children, from preschool age to twelfth grade, in its 137 Chinese language classes and over 10 specialty classes (e.g., band, choir, piano, cello, violin, tai chi, ikebana, dancing, and Chinese painting). The Chinese language classes run from 3:00 to 6:30 P.M. daily after regular school hours. Students usually spend one hour on regular school homework and two hours on Chinese language or other selected specialties. The school also has English classes for immigrant youths and adult immigrant workers (Zhou 1997).

The Chinese-American Planning Council (CPC), established in the late 1960s in Chinatown, is another important civic organization. The CPC has become a rival organization to the CCBA, representing an assimilationist and mainstream agenda similar to that of other labor organizations such as the International Ladies' Garment Workers' Union and the Chinese Staff and Workers' Association. Led by educated second- or 1.5-generation (foreign-born, arriving in the United States at young ages) Chinese Americans who are devoted to the community, the CPC challenges the traditional patriarchal structure and conservative stance of the CCBA through grassroots class mobilization and the support of federal and local governments and private foundations. The CPC offers a broader array of services to families and children than the CCBA (though the CCBA's Chinese school has a much larger enrollment than the CPC's). Its aim is to provide "access to services, skills, and resources toward the goal of economic self-sufficiency and integration into the American mainstream" (Chinese-American Planning Council 1993). During the 1970s, the CPC, then known as the Chinatown Planning Council, initiated a number of youth-targeted programs in such areas as drug prevention, outreach, and recreation to help immigrant children and youths adapt to their new environment. These programs targeted high-risk youths not only by offering counseling and opportunities for young people to voice their concerns and problems, but also by providing places for them to engage in recreational activities, such as reading, having parties, and playing pool or video games, and sponsoring free field trips, shows, and museum visits (Kuo 1977). Most of these programs have continued, expanded, and diversified in the 1990s.

Many smaller civic and voluntary ethnic organizations have also been established to address concerns and demands of new immigrants and their children. The Chinatown History Museum, now the Museum of Chinese in the Americas, was established in 1980 primarily as a history project for reclaiming, preserving, and sharing Chinese American history and culture with a broad audience. The member-supported museum offers historical walking tours, lectures, readings, symposia, workshops, and family events year-round, not only to Chinese Americans but also to the general public. The museum also provides school programs for grades K to 12, guided and self-guided visits for college-level students, and a variety of videotapes, slide presentations, and exhibits.

Ethnic religious institutions have also played an important role in helping immigrants adjust to life in the United States. Although Chinese immigrants are mostly nonreligious, many initially affiliate with religious institutions for practical support and later are converted through intense participation. In the larger Chinese community in New York City, the number of churches or temples has doubled since 1965, including over eighty Christian churches and eighteen Buddhist and Taoist temples; about three-quarters are located in Manhattan's Chinatown. While

Buddhist and Taoist temples tend to attract adults, including some college students and the elderly, Christian churches generally have well-established after-school youth programs in addition to their regular Sunday Bible classes.

Overall, the growth of the ethnic economy and community-based ethnic institutions has strengthened and expanded existing community social structures. The ethnic community, in turn, furnishes a protective social environment, helping immigrants cope with racism, unemployment, family disruption, school dropouts, drug abuse, and crime and providing access to resources that can help immigrants and their children to move ahead in mainstream American society (Zhou 1992). A counterargument is that Chinatown's enclave economy reinforces the traditional patriarchal social structure, privileging the elite while exacerbating intraethnic conflicts and trapping the working-class immigrants into permanent subordination (Kwong 1987, 1997; Lin 1998).

Flushing

Before the surge in contemporary immigration, the Flushing neighborhood in north-central Queens was mainly a white, moderate-to-middle-income area whose residents were of Jewish, Irish, Italian, and German ancestry. In 1960, 97 percent of the population was non-Hispanic white. Flushing shared in the postwar development that affected the entire borough of Queens, resulting in a mixture of housing types. The downtown area, especially the blocks within walking distance of the subway and the Long Island Railroad station, was a mixture of multifamily apartment buildings and low-density units, occupied by young-person households, families with small children, and elderly people. The prevalence of single- or two-family houses, originally built for middle-income families, increased with distance from downtown.

Before the 1970s, nonwhites were not welcomed into the neighborhood. A long-time Chinese resident who was married to a white American had arrived from China in 1946 to join him in Jamaica, Queens. When they decided to move to Flushing she had to send her husband to look for housing. She explained, ". . . because they [whites] didn't want to see Chinese here. At that time, there were few Chinese around in the community. I was not the only one, but there weren't many. . . ." According to this resident, the business district in Flushing had only one Chinese restaurant and one Chinese laundry in the early 1960s.[11] In more affluent parts of Flushing, there were incidents of neighborhood action as residents attempted to block Chinese families from moving into the area in the 1950s.

Today's Flushing has a different face. It is often referred to as the "second" Chinatown, the "satellite" Chinatown, or "Little Taipei." However, Flushing does not match Old Chinatown in ethnic density. Also, the ethnic label, whether "Chinatown" or "Little Taipei," is highly contested as Flushing is not dominated by a single ethnic group. In demographic terms, it is clearly a neighborhood that has experienced rapid transition and that contains a variety of ethnic and racial groups. Between 1970 and 1990, in the general Flushing area (defined as Queens' Community District #7), the non-Hispanic white population fell by 31 percent while the area's total population increased by 5 percent. As table 5.3 shows, in the general Flushing area, whites were still a majority in 1990, but the presence of Hispanics and Asians was noticeable. About 40 percent of the residents were foreign-born, half having arrived after 1980. Compared to those living on the Lower East Side, Flushing's residents displayed a better socioeconomic profile, with much higher levels of educational and occupational attainment, lower rates of poverty, and higher median household incomes. Overall, this is a relatively affluent urban area.

By 1990, the area surrounding downtown Flushing had become multiethnic. At the core (defined by eleven census tracts[12]), the proportion of whites in every census tract decreased drastically since the 1970s; only one tract still maintained a white majority. In 1990, whites constituted only 24 percent in the population of the eleven–census tract area, Asians 41 percent (Zhou and Kim 1999). Among the Asians, 41 percent were Chinese, 38 percent Koreans, and 15 percent Indians. Representatives of these three Asian groups are clearly visible in the central business district. The concentrations, however, are rarely more than a few blocks in extent. Indeed, only two of the eleven tracts had an Asian majority (no single ethnic group dominated); nine tracts in the core area contained 25 percent or more Asians.

Reflecting national trends, Flushing's Chinese immigrants come from three major regions: Taiwan, mainland China, and Hong Kong. Although most Taiwanese prefer Los Angeles—only 16 percent of the Taiwanese immigrants in the United States live in New York City—Taiwanese are very visible in Flushing. Among Chinese immigrants, those from Taiwan are significantly better educated and are concentrated more in professional occupations. Many Taiwanese immigrants first came to Flushing because they did not identify with Manhattan's old Chinatown, which is dominated by the Cantonese and by Cantonese culture. Moreover, Taiwanese had the educational backgrounds and economic resources to build their own enclave away from the existing center of Chinese settlement (Zhou and Logan 1991). Once the Taiwanese movement to Flushing began, other Chinese followed, and after a while a new type of immigrant enclave emerged that includes many from the mainland as well.

With the injection of massive amounts of capital and the influx of affluent, entrepreneurial, and highly skilled immigrants from Taiwan, Flushing's Chinese enclave economy began to develop in the 1980s. According to the Downtown Flushing Development Corporation, property values in Flushing increased 50 percent to 100 percent during the 1980s, and commercial vacancy rates plummeted from 7 percent in the late 1970s to less than 1 percent today (Parvin 1991a:22). Since 1975, new retail and office development has rejuvenated the downtown area. Today, the business center has expanded in all directions from the core. Commercial development is extraordinarily active, with new businesses springing up literally overnight. Modern office complexes house banks and service-oriented firms owned by Taiwanese immigrants and transnational Taiwanese, as well as subsidiary firms from the Asian Pacific. In the heart of the downtown commercial and transportation hub, the multilingual signs of several mainstream bank branches and Asian-owned banks stand at the busiest intersection. Just a few blocks from the subway station, in what was until recently an aging neighborhood rapidly falling into decay, is a fourteen-story pink granite and limestone tower— the Sheraton La Guardia East Hotel. Such a sight in downtown Flushing would have been unimaginable in the 1970s. The hotel is Taiwanese-owned and is the only full-service hotel in Queens outside the airports (Parvin 1991b:22). In the immediate vicinity of the subway station, stretching up and down Main Street and onto the side streets, Chinese restaurants and shops, interspersed with greengrocers, drugstores, and fast-food restaurants, give the area an unmistakable look of Chinatown.

But it is not quite a new Chinatown. Flushing's commercial core is also filled with Korean, Indian, Pakistani, and Bangladeshi restaurants and stores, packed into shop fronts along the main streets. Korean, Indian, Pakistani, and Bangladeshi immigrants think of Flushing as their own community, just as the Chinese view Flushing as a distinct Chinese community. Suburban Chinese come to the neighborhood for multiple purposes. For example, many suburban Chinese families bring their children to Flushing's Chinese Cultural Center for Saturday afternoon language classes and recreation. While children are at the center, their parents usually shop at the local grocery and specialty stores. Others come to Flushing to study or browse in the crowded municipal public library that owns books, magazines, and newspapers in different Asian languages, staying afterward to do some shopping and perhaps eating at one of the many ethnic restaurants.

The business expansion of the Chinese community is particularly noteworthy. A 1982 survey of Chinese-owned businesses in Flushing counted five grocery stores, three restaurants, two supermarkets, one real estate agency, a professional building, a drug and herbal store, and a beauty salon (Hom and Smith 1982:343). Just ten years later, Chinese businesses are booming, and the rate of turnover and expansion is so rapid that it is virtually impossible to keep an accurate count. No longer are Chinese restaurants the only or even the predominant form of business activity. There are as many Chinese realtors today, and two-and-a-half times as many doctors' offices and pharmacies, as restaurants. An ethnic market survey conducted by the Flushing Chinese Business Association in 1990 found that over half of the consumption needs of Chinese residents in the area were being met by local food and grocery stores. The development of Flushing as a comprehensive business center means that suburban Chinese residents no longer have to go to Manhattan's Chinatown to visit a restaurant, to shop, or to satisfy their need for Chinese cultural activities. Flushing's Chinese enclave economy also maintains strong ties to Old Chinatown. Although it is quite far from Old Chinatown, it provides convenient access to the subway, which makes the commute relatively easy. Many Chinese immigrants living in Flushing still commute to Chinatown to work or shop.

Flushing's Chinese community is relatively free from the constraints of traditional social structures in Old Chinatown. In recent years, the immigrant Chinese in Flushing have become more actively involved in local politics, mostly through direct political participation (Lin 1998). For example, they have formed various civic organizations, the most prominent being the Chinese American Voters Association, that work closely with ethnic businesses and other non-Chinese community-based organizations. Such efforts were initially prompted by specific business concerns such as the lack of municipal services, confusing rules and regulations, and insensitivity of public officials to specific needs of the business community. Common economic concerns also encouraged different immigrant groups to work together to improve the neighborhood's image and to mediate interethnic misunderstandings and conflicts. New ethnic associations organized street-cleaning campaigns and voter-registration drives and lobbied the city on a wide range of issues. In the early 1990s, eight of forty-eight members of Community Board #7 were Asians. The Chinese played an important role in the Downtown Flushing Development Corporation and other community organizations, such as the Friends' Reconciliation Project, which served to mediate and resolve neighbor disputes (Chen 1992).

Even though the Chinese are a visible presence in Flushing's economy and are the largest immigrant group, they have not been able to muster enough clout to exert much political influence. In 1990, Asians made up almost a third of the population of the 20th Council District but only 7 percent of registered voters. City Councilwoman Julia Harrison was twice challenged by Asian American candidates—one Korean and one Chinese—but won both elections in the 1990s (Dugger 1996; Lii 1996).

Over time, Flushing's Chinese community has become more diverse in terms of class. The ethnic economy has attracted growing numbers of low-skilled working-class immigrants. For example, many mainland Chinese, mostly of urban working-class background, have settled in Flushing because of the conveniences and job opportunities offered. Also, middle-class neighborhood pioneers have sent for their relatives, many of whom are less skilled and have fewer resources than their predecessors. The shift in class status has become increasingly visible since the mid-1990s. Nowadays, Chinese immigrants often refer to Flushing as the second Chinatown rather than "Little Taipei," implying the increasing visibility of immigrants from the mainland. The class diversity among Flushing's Chinese has a number of implications. For Chinese immigrants, class segmentation means greater social service burdens and higher risk of bearing a dual stigma—foreign and poor. For their part, more Chinese immigrants see Flushing as a temporary home on the route to suburbia. Since the mid-1990s, there is evidence of secondary migration among the more affluent Chinese immigrants from Flushing to bedroom communities in Long Island, New Jersey, and Connecticut.

Sunset Park

Sunset Park is a working-class neighborhood originally settled by European immigrants who lived in two-story houses and brownstones that line surrounding streets. It is conveniently located along the B, N, and R subway lines and is just about thirty minutes by subway from Old Chinatown. As in Flushing, the earlier European immigrants and their children have gradually moved to the suburbs since the late 1960s, leaving many absentee-owned houses and many vacant storefronts. As white residents slowly abandoned the neighborhood, ethnic minorities and new immigrants, first Dominicans, then Puerto Ricans, then Asians and Arabs, began to move in (Winnick 1990). The third column of table 5.3 indicates that Sunset Park, defined as Brooklyn Community District #7, is dominated by renter-occupied housing. Most of the housing structures were built before 1950. Unlike in Old Chinatown, there has been little new real estate development in the neighborhood. Like Flushing, Sunset Park is a new multiethnic immigrant neighborhood but with a different racial/ethnic makeup. Of some 102,000 residents in the district in 1990, about 34 percent were non-Hispanic white; 4 percent were black; 51 percent Latino; and 10 percent Asian, 78 percent of whom were Chinese. Between 1980 and 1990, the Chinese experienced a population growth of 319 percent, compared with a 26 percent loss among non-Hispanic whites (New York City Department of City Planning 1992b).

Sunset Park is more an outlet or extension of Old Chinatown than a newly founded Chinatown with its own unique character as in Flushing. It houses recent arrivals as well as Chinatown's out-movers, who are mostly of working-class background. Among Chinatown out-movers, some families resettled in Sunset Park as they attained a measure of economic mobility, whereas others were pushed out of Chinatown merely because of overcrowding and because of the fear that their teenage children might be pressured into joining gangs.

Sunset Park offers affordable housing and easy access to Chinatown. The more upwardly mobile immigrant Chinese are unlikely to move to Sunset Park because of the neighborhood's working-class characteristics, but they may purchase a home as rental property. Less upwardly mobile, hard-working immigrants are often able to buy a house in Sunset Park on the condition that they rent out part of it to coethnic immigrant families to help meet the hefty monthly mortgage payments. A former member of Brooklyn's Community Planning Board explained that with continued high immigration from China and Hong Kong, "more and more Chinese will be coming to New York. There is no more room in Manhattan, and Queens is too expensive for newcomers. Brooklyn, being affordable and easily accessible, is the logical place to be" (Zhou 1992:191–92). In fact, most immigrant Chinese in Sunset Park share similar socioeconomic characteristics with non-coethnic residents in the neighborhood. The arrival of immigrant Chinese families has helped revitalize the dying neighborhood by means of homeownership, and in turn this has attracted more immigrants from Old Chinatown and from abroad.

Today, most of Sunset Park's Chinese immigrants are Cantonese from the mainland and Hong Kong. A sizable number of Fuzhounese have also moved into the neighborhood, mostly in basement units rented from coethnic homeowners (Kwong 1997).

As increasing numbers of Chinese immigrant families moved into Sunset Park, so did ethnic businesses. The ethnic economy that has developed along Eighth Avenue between Thirty-ninth and Sixty-fifth Streets can trace its origin to the opening of Fung Wong Supermarket, owned by Hong Kong immigrant Tsang Sun (Sunny) Mui, on Eighth Avenue in 1986 (Aloff 1997; Mustain 1997). In recent years, the number of garment factories has grown along with ethnic service-oriented businesses such as restaurants, grocery stores, beauty salons, herbal medicine stores, health clinics, and accounting and legal offices. By the early 1990s, there were an estimated 300 stores and 250 garment factories in the neighborhood (Gladwell 1993). Immigrant Chinese now call Sunset Park "Bat Dai Do," a Cantonese translation of "Eighth Avenue," which means the road to good fortune and prosperity. Although Bat Dai Do is not as well developed as Flushing and the basis for ethnic social organization is not as solid as in Old Chinatown, Sunset Park has certainly served to accommodate the pressing needs of new immigrants for jobs, housing, and child rearing.

Causes and Consequences of Settlement

Chinese New Yorkers have consolidated and expanded their ethnic community in Old Chinatown, Flushing, and Sunset Park. Ethnic clustering is also visible in other neighborhoods of Queens and Brooklyn. As seen in figure 5.3, Chinese are found in Jackson Heights and neighborhoods south of Jackson Heights in Queens, and Sheepshead Bay and neighborhoods southeast of Sunset Part in Brooklyn. Several factors contribute to this paradoxical pattern of residential dispersion and concentration.

First, there is the class status of immigrants along with the availability of relatively decent and affordable housing. The more affluent segment of the immigrant Chinese population can often bypass Chinatown to buy homes in outer-borough middle-class neighborhoods with their family savings and with incomes secured by well-paying professional jobs in the mainstream economy. These affluent individuals are likely to purchase homes in Flushing or other Queens neighborhoods, where they can enjoy a semisuburban life while also living close to Manhattan. Those without well-paying jobs have to find places with multifamily housing units and apartment buildings so that they can rent out part of their homes to help pay monthly mortgages. For many Chinese immigrants, purchasing a home, rather than improving English or advancing to a more desirable occupation, is considered a major achievement and a symbol of success in life.

The second factor is ethnic networking. Where one lives depends on whom one knows. Because of limited English proficiency, many immigrants depend on family or friendship networks to find work and housing. Family members and friends can spread the word or obtain information about housing availability through informal social contacts. Chinese homeowners prefer Chinese renters because of language and cultural convenience and put advertisements in Chinese language newspapers to find renters. The reliance on family members and friends has a direct effect on the concentration of immigrant Chinese from the same dialect group. As mentioned previously, Chinese immigrants from different places of origin do not necessarily speak the same language. The language barrier often separates Cantonese speakers from Mandarin speakers from Taiwan and the mainland. As a result, few Taiwanese- and Mandarin-speaking mainlanders are interested in living in Old Chinatown. Mandarin speakers are also less likely to settle in Sunset Park than in neighborhoods in Queens. Ethnic realtors play an important role, too. For newcomers, coethnic realtors are indispensable in the housing business. Realtors not only help immigrants purchase housing but also steer them into particular neighborhoods.

A third factor explaining the residential patterns—dependency of immigrants on the enclave economy—is perhaps the most important. Regardless of where they live, most immigrant Chinese are tied to the opportunities offered by ethnic economic enclaves (Zhou and Logan 1991). An important consideration in residential location for many Chinese immigrants is convenient access to public transportation; the neighborhood must be within easy walking distance of bus and subway lines that can get them to work quickly. In the enclaves, immigrants can find jobs, information about jobs in other places, and even transportation to get to jobs elsewhere. Also, ethnic banks and credit institutions in the enclave facilitate home financing for coethnic immigrants. In terms of time and distance, Flushing, Sunset Park, and most of the neighborhoods with sizable Chinese populations are reasonably close to Manhattan's Chinatown and other job centers and ethnic communities in the city.

Contemporary patterns of Chinese immigration and settlement are quite distinct from those of the past. By sheer numbers, the arrival of the newest New Yorkers injects the old metropolis with new blood, contributing to the economic and social vitality of the city. Also, the settlement of new Chinese immigrants has brought large numbers of people with higher-than-average education and economic resources that enable them to create their own ethnic economy (Logan forthcoming). But growth is not without pain and potential risks.

The development of the ethnic economy in Chinatown, Flushing, and Sunset Park has been accompanied by rising house prices, overcrowding, noise, traffic congestion, and crime, causing one longtime resident in Flushing to lament that the new Flushing "looks like hell. . . . It's really a disaster. There is too much traffic, filth, and chaos."[13] Among established residents, there is a deep-seated fear that their neighborhoods are turning into another Chinatown or into a microcosm of Taipei, Shanghai, or Hong Kong, which they imagine are among the most crowded and polluted cities in the world. Established residents worry about

React

increased density and the destruction of what were once tranquil neighborhoods but now draw more and more crowds of cars and people. In Flushing, for example, some longtime shopkeepers in the neighborhood are openly angry about the changed business environment and waste no time telling the new immigrants what they think (nor do they spare a thought for political correctness in assigning blame). They complain not only about the soaring rents from heavy Asian real estate investment, but also that Asian customers often want to bargain over prices, which they say has forced many non-Asians out of business. The real estate frenzy has had still other impacts on the appearance and the physical character of the neighborhood. According to some residents, many churches, mosques, temples, old homes, and other community buildings have been either torn down or converted into private homes.

Ethnic networking, serving as a primary means to channel immigrants from diverse socioeconomic backgrounds into middle-class neighborhoods throughout the city, has contributed to class segmentation of new ethnic enclaves. Flushing started out as a new type of ethnic enclave: Mandarin-speaking and rich in financial and human capital. Most of the earlier Chinese immigrants into Flushing were from Taiwan. Investors from Hong Kong and mainland China, as well as non-Cantonese-speaking professional migrants from China (e.g., foreign exchange students who obtain permanent residency status through employment), gravitated to Flushing. These professional migrants or investors used their economic and human-capital resources to build up the area into the status of an enclave. The neighborhood pioneers invested heavily in real estate and business development, which helped to provide the finance capital, housing, and employment opportunities for subsequent immigrants who in turn paved the way for later arrivals. After a while, these middle-class neighborhood pioneers began to send for their families, many of whom were not as resourceful as their sponsors and experienced downward occupational mobility. Also, the ethnic economy drew in low-skilled working-class immigrants from Manhattan's Chinatown and Sunset Park. The class segmentation has reinforced the negative stereotypes of Chinese immigrants as foreign and poor and has added to social-service burdens in Flushing.

The development of new ethnic enclaves has also intensified interethnic relations. When immigrants and businesses cluster in ethnic enclaves, they impact coethnic members disproportionately but cause little concern among non-coethnic outsiders. Only when ethnic businesses expand outside the enclave is there the possibility of interaction and confrontation (Tseng 1994; Min 1996). Today, multiethnic neighborhoods are a central feature of the areas where Chinese concentrate outside Old Chinatown. With the increasing presence of Chinese immigrants, a certain amount of interethnic conflict has inevitably surfaced in community life. Longtime residents feel that they are being locked out of their own neighborhoods. Some complain bitterly about non-English signs on the local shops. In Flushing, blacks and Hispanics often report that they are automatically considered to be criminals by certain Chinese and Korean shopkeepers. Chinese immigrants also often complain that blacks and Hispanics are hostile. It is important to note that ethnic frictions manifest themselves differently in different neighborhoods. Flushing—a multiethnic neighborhood in the truest sense of the word—has not witnessed anything like the level of tension that has already exploded into pitched battles on the streets of other New York neighborhoods. This of course is good news for Flushing residents, but we would do well to remember that ethnic hostility is unpredictable and can flare up without much notice. In this sense, the existence of any level of interethnic tension is a cause for concern (Zhou and Kim 1999).

Discussion and Conclusion

In the past, Chinatown was a bachelor society sheltering immigrants from racism and discrimination, hence reinforcing the stereotype of "the unassimilable alien." Even today, many immigrants continue to cluster in Chinatown, work in the ethnic enclave economy, and socialize among their coethnics. Since the ethnic community provides jobs, housing, services, and a familiar cultural environment, immigrants can conduct their daily lives without learning English and communicating with the outside world. As a result, the stereotype of "unassimilability" has prevailed in the public mindset. However, today's Chinese immigrant community is not quite as isolated and immigrants are not quite as unassimilable as many think. There are several significant ways by which the ethnic community shapes the lives of Chinese immigrants as they strive to become American.

 First, participation in the ethnic enclave economy facilitates upward social mobility for immigrants while also keeping them at arm's length from the mainstream society. The experience of working women in Chinatown provides a prime example. In New York, immigrant Chinese women comprise over half of the workforce in the enclave garment industry. Most of the garment workers lack English proficiency, have few job skills, and are married to other immigrants similarly handicapped. Since their husbands alone cannot provide for the family, these women must work to support their families. They often find working in Chinatown a better option than working in low-wage jobs in the larger secondary economy, because enclave employment enables them to fulfill their multiple roles more effectively as wage earners, wives, and mothers. In Chinatown, jobs are not hard to find, working hours are flexible, employers are tolerant to children's presence, and private child care within walking distance from work is accessible and affordable. Chinatown also offers convenient grocery shopping and various takeout foods. These amenities enable women to juggle work outside the home and household responsibilities. Moreover, women socialize at work with other coethnic women, who come from similar cultural backgrounds and share similar goals and concerns about family, child rearing, and mobility. By the sewing machine, they can brag about children, complain about insensitive husbands or nagging relatives back in the homeland, share coping strategies, and comfort each other over hardships. These ties serve as a source of emotional support and psychological comfort.

The enclave economy is a double-edged sword, however. While it undoubtedly facilitates upward mobility for many immigrant families, enabling some to buy homes or set up their own businesses, and provides various resources, such as after-school programs that help children get ahead, working in the enclave economy does not help immigrants gain English proficiency or learn American ways. And many will be struck with low-wage jobs there. A good many who arrive with little knowledge of English and few transferable job skills and those arriving as undocumented may find themselves "trapped" in Chinatown, toiling in dead-end jobs under poor working conditions and seeing little hope of ever making it in America.

Second, involvement in the enclave economy heightens rather than reduces the salience of ethnicity. For one thing, jobs created in Chinatown, Flushing, and Sunset Park and goods and services provided there tie immigrant Chinese from diverse socioeconomic backgrounds together despite spatial dispersion. Put another way, the ethnic enclave has directly or indirectly increased the degree of ethnic cohesion that cuts across class lines, thereby sustaining a sense of ethnic solidarity. At the same time, living and working in the ethnic enclave reinforces common values and norms and creates new mechanisms for sanctioning nonconformity among Chinese immigrant workers from diverse class backgrounds.[14] As one immigrant worker replied to the question of why Chinatown workers were seemingly reluctant to stand up for their rights, "I don't think you people get it. In Chinatown, if you fight, you lose your job. Nobody will ever hire you. When factories close down, other workers will blame you, and your family will blame you."[15] In a sense, the survival and success of many ethnic businesses depend on cheap immigrant labor as well as unpaid family labor. In Chinatown, the economic behavior is embedded in an ongoing structure of social relations. Ethnic entrepreneurs depend on a motivated, reliable, and exploitable coethnic labor force. In return, they create job opportunities to serve the short-term goals of coethnic workers who must choose between low wages and joblessness (Zhou 1992). However, ethnic cohesion is not inevitable and does not inhere in the moral convictions of individuals or the value orientations in which they were socialized in the country of origin. Rather, ethnic cohesion is contingent on structural disadvantages that immigrants confront in the host society. Immigrant Chinese from various dialect groups, especially those from rival groups, do not display much solidarity in the homeland, nor did they need to stress the consciousness of being Chinese (Zhou and Kim 1999). On arrival in the United States, however, ethnic cooperation becomes a logical strategy for social mobility.

Third, the development of ethnic social organizations broadens the interaction between the ethnic community and the larger society while it also intensifies intraethnic competition over who governs the community. To many New Yorkers, Chinese immigrants seem to be socially isolated in their own ethnic circles with little interest and knowledge about metropolitan affairs. This is no longer true. In fact, Chinese immigrants are increasingly connected to other New Yorkers through Chinese-language newspapers, such as the *World Journal,* and Chinese-speaking television and radio stations that feature news and stories about America and international affairs. There is no shortage of information about the larger society that is particularly relevant to Chinese immigrant life thanks to the well-educated, well-informed, and dedicated members of the first and second generation who work with coethnic immigrants in various community-based organizations. Unlike the old ethnic associations, new civil organizations do not require membership based on family, kinship, or place of origin; they serve the entire Chinese community. Their leaders are interested not in translating power into economic self-gain, but in helping the ethnic community to integrate into the larger society and affecting public policy. However, new leaders and their civic organizations, with good intentions, often find themselves struggling with little money and the problems of generating grassroots support. The new leaders are sometimes criticized as being naïve; insensitive to cultural specific needs; and ignorant of the power of family, kin, and friendship bonds; they are also often accused of using white middle-class formulas to solve Chinese immigrants' social problems (Zhou and Kim 2001). Indeed, one reason that they have had so much trouble building their organizations is their transient status and dependency on outside funding. Residing outside of the community, the new leaders lack a shared identity with new immigrants based on a common struggle for survival (Kuo 1977).

In sum, recent Chinese immigration to New York City has led to dramatic changes in the metropolitan Chinese community, and these changes in turn have had far-reaching effects on the way the immigrants come to see themselves in New York and the way they relate to their coethnics and other New Yorkers. Many Chinese New Yorkers revere the Statue of Liberty with high hopes for a better life—sharing the same dream as those who came before them from Europe or other parts of the world. However, as the quotes cited at the beginning of the chapter indicate, the new life in New York involves divergent destinies. Many newcomers have continued to head to Old Chinatown as their first stop in the journey to attain the American Dream, but others have bypassed the traditional staging place, moving directly into outer-borough neighborhoods. This phenomenon challenges the conventional wisdom about immigrant assimilation, which has it that residential mobility is associated with acculturation. Chinese immigrant residential patterns also suggest that the newcomers are not birds of passage. Like most earlier European immigrants, they too want to become American. However, their sheer numbers and economic power do not automatically translate into social acceptance and political power. Indeed, Chinese immigrants' desire to assimilate, no less than ethnic succession, can be perceived as a threat to white middle-class neighborhoods. Resistance from established residents, intertwined with the Chi-

nese way of making it in America, reinforces immigrant ethnicity, complicating
the direction of assimilation.

Notes

1. Personal interview, August 1999.
2. Personal interview, January 1995.
3 The estimate is based on the 1990 census population plus the number of new
   arrivals recorded by the U.S. Immigration and Naturalization Service (INS), an
   estimate of natural births, and a rough estimate of undocumented immigrants.
4. The number of illegal immigrants would have offset that of the returnees, most
   of whom left the United States during the harsh years of Chinese exclusion.
5. Sze Yap includes four counties—Taishan, Kaiping, Enping, and Xinhui—and the
   people share a similar local dialect. Sam Yap (counties of Nanhai, Panyu, and
   Xunde) and the Pearl River Delta counties (such as Zhongshan) were main among
   sending communities in the Canton region.
6. These are the figures for principal metropolitan statistical areas in New York,
   N.Y.; Los Angeles–Long Beach, Calif.; and San Francisco, Calif.
7. Old Chinatown in 1980 and 1990 includes fourteen tracts: core area—6, 8, 16,
   18, 27 29, and 41, and extended area—2.01, 2.02, 14.02, 22.01, 43, 15.01, and
   25 (Zhou 1992). The total population in these tracts was in 92,873 in 1990; over
   half were Chinese.
8. Personal interview, November 1989; reinterview, May 1993.
9. Personal interview, May 1993.
10. The actual number of community organizations in Chinatown was approximately
    twice as many as this list because many were not listed in this particular directory.
11. Personal interview, May 1993.
12. Flushing in this chapter refers the core area in downtown Flushing, which is
    officially defined by the Queen's Community Board #7 as an area including eleven
    contiguous census tracts in both 1980 and 1990 censuses: 797, 845, 851, 853,
    855, 857, 859, 865, 867, 871, and 875.
13. Personal interview, May 1993.
14. The development of the enclave economy is of course full of cutthroat competition
    and intense internal conflicts, making the sanctioning of nonconformity one of
    the key functions of ethnic economic institutions. Whether this function is effec-
    tive or not, however, is the topic of another paper.
15. Personal interview, November 1994.

References

Aloff, Mindy. 1997. "Where China and Brooklyn Overlap." *The New York Times,*
    February 7, p. C1.
Chan, Sucheng. 1991. *Asian Americans: An Interpretive History.* New York: Twayne.
Chen, Hsiang-Shui. 1992. *Chinatown No More : Taiwan Immigrants in Contemporary
    New York.* Ithaca: Cornell University Press.

Chin, Ko-lin. 1997. "Safe House or Hell House? Experiences of Newly Arrived Undocumented Chinese." In Paul J. Smith, ed., *Human Smuggling: Chinese Migrant Trafficking and the Challenge to America's Immigration Tradition,* pp. 169–95. Washington, D.C.: Center for Strategic and International Studies.

Chinese-American Planning Council. 1993. *Chinese-American Planning Council: Program List.* New York: CPC.

Chinatown Today Publishing. 1993. *Chinese-American Life Guide.* Hong Kong: Chinatown Today Publishing.

Dillon, R. H. 1962. *The Hatchetmen: Tong Wars in San Francisco.* New York: Coward McCann.

Dugger, Celia W. 1996. "Queens Old-Timers Uneasy as Asian Influence Grows." *The New York Times,* March 31 (Sunday), p. 1.

Gladwell, Malcolm. 1993. "Rebirth in New York: Neighborhoods Growing Again in the City." *Washington Post,* September 18, p. A1.

Hom, David, and David G. Smith. 1982. "Chinese Ethnic Market and Banking." In Maris Starczewska-Lambasa, ed., *The Ethnic Markets in New York City: A Study of Italian, Jewish, Polish, Chinese and Korean Markets and Their Profit Potential for the Airlines, Banking and the Dailies,* pp. 287–380. Hempstead, N.Y.: Hofstra University Yearbook of Business (ser. 17, vol. 3).

Jackson, Peter. 1983. "Ethnic Turf: Competition on the Canal Street Divide." *New York Affairs* 7(4): 149–58.

Kuo, Chia-Ling. 1977. *Social and Political Change in New York's Chinatown: The Role of Voluntary Associations.* New York: Praeger.

Kwong, Peter. 1987. *The New Chinatown.* New York: Hill & Wang.

———. 1997. *Forbidden Workers: Illegal Chinese Immigrants and American Labor.* New York: New Press.

Lee, Rose Hum. 1960. *The Chinese in the United States of America.* Hong Kong: Hong Kong University Press.

Li, Wei. 1997. *Spatial Transformation of an Urban Ethnic Community from Chinatown to Chinese Ethnoburb in Los Angeles.* Ph.D. diss., Department of Geography, University of Southern California.

Liang, Zai. 1997. "From Fujian to New York: Understanding the New Chinese Immigration." Presented at the conference Transnational Communities and the Political Economy of New York in the 1990s, New School for Social Research, New York.

Lii, Jane H. 1996. "Neighborhood Report: Northern Queens: Common Heritage, but No Common Ground." *The New York Times,* April 21 (Sunday), p. 11.

Lin, Jan. 1998. *Reconstructing Chinatown: Ethnic Enclave, Global Change.* Minneapolis: University of Minnesota Press.

Liu, John M., and Lucie Cheng. 1994. "Pacific Rim Development and the Duality of Post-1965 Asian Immigration to the United States." In Paul M. Ong, Edna Bonacich and Lucie Cheng, eds., *The New Asian Immigration in Los Angeles and Global Restructuring,* pp. 74–99. Philadelphia: Temple University Press.

Logan, John R. 1999. "Global Neighborhoods: The New Diversity in Metropolitan America." Unpublished manuscript. Department of Sociology, State University of New York at Albany.

Lyman, Stanford M. 1974. *Chinese Americans.* New York: Random House.

McCunn, Ruthanne Lum. 1979. *An Illustrated History of the Chinese in America.* San Francisco: Design Enterprises of San Francisco.

Min, Pyong Gap. 1996. *Caught in the Middle: Korean Communities in New York and Los Angeles.* Berkeley: University of California Press.

Mustain, Gene. 1997. "Chinatown Grows in Brooklyn, Too." *Daily News,* October 27, p. 34.

Nee, Victor G., and Brett de Bary Nee. 1973. *Longtime Californ': A Documentary Study of an American.* New York: Pantheon.

New York City Department of City Planning. 1992a. *The Newest New Yorkers: A Statistical Portrait.* New York: Department of City Planning, City of New York.

———. 1992b. *Demographic Profiles: A Portrait of New York City's Community Districts from the 1980 and 1990 Censuses of the Population and Housing.* New York: Department of City Planning, City of New York.

———. 1993. *Socioeconomic Profiles: A Portrait of New York City's Community Districts from the 1980 and 1990 Censuses of the Population and Housing.* New York: Department of City Planning, City of New York.

———. 1999. *The Newest New Yorkers: 1995–1996, An Update of Immigration to NYC in the mid '90s.* New York: Department of City Planning, City of New York.

Orleans, Leo A. 1988. *Chinese Students in America: Policies, Issues and Numbers.* Washington, D.C.: National Academy Press.

Parvin, Jean. 1991a. "Immigrants Migrate to International City." *Crain's New York Business* 7 (27, July 8).

———. 1991b. "Flushing: Progress vs. Neighborhood." *Crain's New York Business* 7 (27, July 8).

Saxton, Alexander. 1971. *The Indispensable Enemy: Labor and the Anti-Chinese Movement in California.* Berkeley: University of California Press.

Skeldon, Ronald. 1994. "Hong Kong in an International Migration System." In Ronald Skeldon, ed., *Reluctant Exiles? Migration from Hong Kong and the New Overseas Chinese,* pp. 21–51. Armonk, N.Y.: M.E. Sharpe.

Sung, Betty Lee. 1987. *The Adjustment Experience of Chinese Immigrant Children in New York City.* New York: Center for Migration Studies.

Tseng, Yenfeng. 1994. Suburban Ethnic Economy: Chinese Business Communities in Los Angeles. Ph.D. Dissertation. Department of Sociology, UCLA.

U.S. Bureau of the Census. 1983. *1980 Census of Population: The Foreign Born Population in the United States.* Washington, D.C.: U.S. Government Printing Office.

———. 1950–1990. *Census of the Population, United States: Summary.* Washington, D.C.: U.S. Government Printing Office.

———. 1990. *Census of Population: The Foreign Born Population in the United States.* Washington, D.C.: U.S. Government Printing Office.

U.S. Immigration and Naturalization Service. 1995. *Statistical Yearbook of the Immigration and Naturalization Service, 1993.* Washington, D.C.: U.S. Government Printing Office.

———. 1996. *Statistical Yearbook of the Immigration and Naturalization Service, 1994.* Washington, D.C.: U.S. Government Printing Office.

———. 1997. *Statistical Yearbook of the Immigration and Naturalization Service, 1996.* Washington, D.C.: U.S. Government Printing Office.

Winnick, Louis. 1990. *New People in Old Neighborhoods: The Role of New Immigrants in Rejuvenating New York's Communities.* New York: Russell Sage Foundation.

Wong, Bernard. 1979. *A Chinese Community: Ethnicity and Survival Strategies.* Singapore: Chopmen Enterprise.

——. 1987. "The Chinese: New Immigrants in New York's Chinatown." In Nancy Foner, ed., *New Immigrants in New York,* pp. 243–71. New York: Columbia University Press.

——. 1998. *Ethnicity and Entrepreneurship: The New Chinese Immigrants in San Francisco Bay Areas.* Boston: Allyn and Bacon.

Wong, Morrison G. 1995. "Chinese Americans." In Pyong Gap Min, ed., *Asian Americans: Contemporary Trends and Issues,* pp. 58–94. Thousand Oaks, Calif.: Sage.

Zhang, Qingsong. 1998. "The Origins of the Chinese Americanization Movement: Wong Chin Foo and the Chinese Equal Rights League." In K. Scott Wong and Sucheng Chan, eds., *Claiming America: Constructing Chinese American Identities during the Exclusion Era,* pp. 41–63. Philadelphia: Temple University Press.

Zhou, Min. 1992. *Chinatown: The Socioeconomic Potential of an Urban Enclave.* Philadelphia: Temple University Press.

——. 1997. "Social Capital in Chinatown: The Role of Community-Based Organizations and Families in the Adaptation of the Younger Generation." In Lois Weis and Maxine S. Seller, eds., *Beyond Black and White: New Voices, New Faces in the United States Schools,* pp. 181–206. Albany, N.Y.: State University of New York Press.

Zhou, Min, and Rebecca Kim. 1999. "A Tale of Two Metropolises: Immigrant Chinese Communities in New York and Los Angeles." Presented at the conference "Los Angeles and New York in the New Millennium," LeRoy Neiman Center for the Study of American Society and Culture, University of California at Los Angeles, May 19–20.

——. 2001. "Elite Groups, Social Networks, and the Paradox of Ethnicity: Cohesion and Diversity Within the Chinese Immigrant Community in the United States." Unpublished manuscript. Department of Sociaology, University of California at Los Angeles.

Zhou, Min, and John Logan. 1991. "In and Out of Chinatown: Residential Mobility and Segregation of New York City's Chinese." *Social Forces* 70(2): 387–407.

Zhou, Yu. 1998. "How Do Places Matter? A Comparative Study of Chinese Ethnic Econimies in Los Angeles and New York City." *Urban Geography* 19(6): 531–52.

Koreans: An "Institutionally Complete Community" in New York

Pyong Gap Min

G o to any part of New York City where a sizable number of Koreans live and you are bound to find many Korean churches. This was apparent when I was house hunting in the Flushing-Bayside area of Queens this past winter. Virtually every neighborhood in the area, I found, has a Korean church within a two-mile radius. Altogether, there are ninety-two Korean churches in Flushing and another fifteen in Bayside.

And this is only one neighborhood in the city. *The Korean Churches Directory of New York* published in January 2000 listed 555 churches in the New York–New Jersey metropolitan area. Given that some recently established Korean Protestant churches and sixteen Korean Catholic churches are not included in the directory, there may be nearly 600 Korean churches in the metropolitan area serving a Korean American population (including the second generation) of perhaps as many as 180,000 people. In both their number and their social functions, Korean churches are the most important ethnic organizations in the New York Korean community. Yet many other important ethnic organizations flourish as well.

There are roughly 95 alumni associations, 60 Korean merchants' associations, 50 cultural organizations, 40 social service agencies, 40 professional associations, 40 nonchurch religious organizations, and 15 local Korean associations, along with the Korean Association of New York (an umbrella organization) and approximately 100 other ethnic organizations. In addition, three Korean-language dailies, TV stations, and radio stations integrate Koreans dispersed in different parts of the city by providing Korean-language programs and news about Korea as well as about the Korean community and the larger American society.

In the early 1960s, Raymond Breton (1964) coined the term "institutional completeness" to indicate the degree to which networks of social organizations dominate an immigrant/ethnic community. In his view, "The community with many formal organizations is said to be more institutionally complete than the one with only a few or none" (Breton 1961:28). Using Breton's definition, the Korean community in New York can be said to be more institutionally complete than any other immigrant or ethnic community in the city and perhaps in any American city. New York's Korean community is so tightly organized that no Korean immigrant in the city can live without being powerfully influenced by formal ethnic networks.

To date, four books focus on the Korean community in New York (Kim 1981; Min 1996, 1998; Park 1997), but only Kim's study examines community organization in detail. By now, it is badly out of date. The Korean community in New York in 2000 differs radically from what it was like in the 1970s when Kim collected his data, not only in the number of ethnic organizations but also in its community structure. This chapter brings the analysis of ethnic organizations up to the present; it also provides information on Koreans' immigration and settlement patterns and small-business activities. I mainly draw on data collected between 1997 and 1999 for a larger study comparing Chinese, Indian, and Korean communities in New York. I updated the numbers on different types of Korean ethnic associations in New York on the basis of ethnic and church directories published in 1999 and 2000. I also conducted personal interviews cited in this chapter in Spring 2000. This chapter covers Koreans in the New York–New Jersey metropolitan area, although it focuses on Koreans in New York City. I use "New York" to indicate the New York–New Jersey metropolitan area and "New York City" to refer to the central city.

Korean Migration to the United States and New York

Pre-1965 Migration and the Old Korean Community in New York

The first wave of Korean immigrants to the United States, approximately 7,200 Koreans, came to Hawaii to work on sugar plantations between 1903 and 1905. Approximately 40 percent of these predominantly male laborers were Christians (Choy 1979:77). Many chose to cross the Pacific for religious freedom as well as for a better economic life. The migration was short-lived, coming to a sudden end in the summer of 1905 when, in an effort to protect Japanese laborers in Hawaii from competition, the Japanese government pressured the Korean government to stop sending labor migrants to the United States. In 1905, Korea became Japan's protectorate as a result of Japan's victory in the Russo-Japanese War, putting Japan in a position to strongly influence Korea.

Between 1905 and 1924, approximately 2,000 additional Koreans came to Hawaii and California. The majority were picture brides of the 1903–1905 pioneer bachelor immigrants. About 600 of them were political refugees and students who were involved in the anti-Japanese independence movement. Japan annexed Korea in 1910 and colonized it until 1945. Most of the Korean political refugees/students studied at universities in New York and other East Coast cities, such as Columbia, Princeton, and New York University. These students constituted the core of the old Korean community in New York. Most of the political refugees/students who settled on the East Coast returned to Korea after Korea won its independence from Japan in 1945, and they played a leading role in the new government and in Korean universities. For example, Syng-Man Lee, who received a Ph.D. degree in theology from Princeton University and subsequently led the Korean independence movement in Honolulu, was elected the first president of South Korea in 1948.

Since Korean students at Columbia University and other schools composed the majority of New York's Korean residents in the first half of the twentieth century, Manhattan was the center of the old Korean community. Korean students in Manhattan often found jobs in Chinatown, and, heavily Christian, they established the Korean Church of New York in 1921. Initially, services were held in an American church building on Twenty-first Street and Madison Avenue, but in 1927 the Korean congregation purchased a building on 115th Street between Broadway and Riverside Drive, just across from Columbia University. The church became the center of the New York Korean community and its anti-Japanese political activities (Historical Compilation Committee of Korean Church of New York 1992). Many church members returned to Korea after completing their graduate education and assumed important positions in government, academia, religion, and business.

Post-1965 Mass Migration and Growth of the Korean Population in New York

The mass migration of Koreans to New York is a fairly recent phenomenon. Indeed, today's Korean Americans are, overwhelmingly, post-1965 immigrants and their children. During and after the Korean War (1950–1953), the close military, political, and economic connections between the United States and South Korea led to increased immigration. Approximately 15,000 Koreans emigrated to the United States between 1950 and 1964. The vast majority were Korean women married to U.S. servicemen stationed in South Korea and Korean orphans adopted by American citizens. Thus, most Korean immigrants during this period came as wives or children of American citizens and did not have direct connections to the small New York Korean community.

In general, the Korean population in the United States was negligible before 1970. The 1970 census counted about 69,000 Koreans in the nation. Admitting a great undercount, the number of Korean Americans in 1970 may have been no more than 100,000. By 1990, the figure was about 790,000. As of January 2000, people of Korean ancestry, including U.S.-born Koreans, may number well over one million.

In the wake of the liberalized 1965 Immigration Act, the annual number of Korean immigrants gradually increased in the late 1960s and early 1970s. By 1976, the 30,000 mark was reached, and throughout the 1980s there was an annual flow of over 30,000. Indeed, in that decade, South Korea was the second-largest source country of Asian immigrants, right below the Philippines. That both the Philippines and South Korea had close political, military, and economic connections with the United States explains their position as leading senders of immigrants. Indeed, in the 1970s and 1980s the U.S. military involvement in South Korea brought more than 3,500 Korean women to the United States annually as wives of U.S. servicemen.

In 1960, only about 400 Koreans lived in the New York–New Jersey area (Korean Association of New York 1985:54), a significant proportion of whom were Korean students enrolled at Columbia University, New York University, and other schools in the region. The Korean Foreign Students Association of New York, organized largely by Korean students at Columbia and New York University in 1955, led Koreans' community activities until the early 1960s.

After the 1965 immigration legislation, New York's Korean community mushroomed. Between 1970 and 1997, 8 to 13 percent of Korean immigrants entering the United States each year settled in New York State and 3 to 6 percent in New Jersey, the majority moving to the New York–New Jersey metropolitan area. By the late 1990s, according to current population survey estimates, the New York Consolidated Metropolitan Statistical Area was home to close to 100,000 foreign-born Koreans. As of 2000, the Korean population in the metropolitan area, including those born in the United States., is likely to be about 180,000. Interestingly, in the 1990s a higher proportion of annual Korean immigrants to the United States chose the New York–New Jersey metropolitan area than in the 1980s.

In the late 1960s, when the liberalized immigration law took full effect, the only Asian group in New York with a large number of residents who used family preferences to sponsor were the Chinese. The number of Koreans and Asian Indians—the other two major Asian groups in New York now—was so small that neither group could benefit much from family reunification preferences.

Initially, in the late 1960s and 1970s, most Koreans and Indians arrived using occupational preferences. Two factors made this possible. First, an expanding medical industry in the New York–New Jersey area at that time and a demand for health care professionals attracted many Korean as well as many Asian Indian and

Filipino medical professionals to the city (Kim 1981:153–56; Liu et al. 1991). Korean and other Asian medical professionals filled vacancies in the periphery specialties such as family practice and radiology and in low-income minority neighborhoods that were not attractive to native-born whites (Kim 1981:155–56; Rosenthal 1995; Shin and Chang 1988). More than one-third of the 6,200 Korean medical professionals admitted to the United States between 1965 and 1975 settled in the tristate area (Kim 1981:148–57). They included approximately 1,200 Korean physicians.

Second, many Korean foreign students who studied at major East Cost universities moved to New York to find professional/managerial jobs or start small businesses. They changed their legal status to become permanent residents in the late 1960s and the 1970s by marrying Korean nurses or through other mechanisms. In fact, the most successful Korean business owners in New York today typically arrived two to three decades ago as foreign students to pursue their graduate education in the United States. Many Koreans started businesses after earning a master's degree in the humanities or social sciences because the degree did not help them to find a professional or managerial job.

The economic recession in the early 1970s and lobbying by U.S. professional associations led the U.S. government to revise the 1965 Immigration Act in such a way that it severely curtailed the entry of occupational immigrants, especially professionals. The revisions included a requirement that prospective professional immigrants get employment offers from U.S. employers before entry into the United Stares (Harper 1979:2–3). The Health Professional Educational Act of 1976 required that foreign physicians and surgeons first had to pass the National Board of Medical Examinees' examination or its equivalent and a foreign-language test to gain admission to the United States (Harper 1979:5; Ong and Liu 1994:60–61). As a result of these revisions, the immigration of Korean medical professionals almost came to an end after 1976, with the proportion of Korean immigrants settling in New York and New Jersey also slightly decreasing after this year. An overwhelming majority of Korean medical professionals in New York are oldtimers who came to the United States before 1976.

However, by the late 1970s and 1980s, as Korean occupational immigrants admitted to New York in the late 1960s and the early 1970 became naturalized citizens, they were able to invite family members and relatives to the United States for permanent residence. Thus, the earlier Korean occupational immigrants and students created a chain that has perpetuated the family-based migration of Koreans to the New York area. Korean immigrants in New York who were admitted on the basis of family reunification since the 1980s represent a lower class and more diverse occupational backgrounds than the earlier professional and student immigrants.

This downward trend in Korean immigrants' class background, which is also true of New York's Indian community, has been further accelerated by changes in South Korea. South Korea's economic conditions have significantly improved over the last twenty years. Koreans experienced a growth in per capita income from $843 in 1977 to $2,199 in 1987, and then to $9,200 in 1995. Moreover, social and political insecurity, which pushed many middle-class Koreans to the United States in the 1970s and the early 1980s, has been substantially reduced recently. South Korea had a popular election in 1987, putting an end to the sixteen-year military dictatorship. The breakdown of the Cold War between Western countries and Eastern European Communist countries also reduced tensions between North and South Korea.

The significant improvements in economic, social, and political conditions, along with the increasing publicity of Korean immigrants' adjustment difficulties in the United States, have reduced the influx of Korean immigrants during recent years. The number of annual Korean immigrants, which peaked in 1987 with 36,000, has gradually declined, reaching the lowest point (16,000) in 1994. Better economic opportunities are no longer a pull factor for middle-class Koreans' migration to the United States; instead, "a better opportunity for children's education" is the major motivation for their United States–bound migration. It is now working-class Koreans who seek to move to the United States. Most Korean foreign students who have recently completed a master's or Ph.D. program have returned to Korea to find professional and managerial jobs.

Koreans' Settlement Patterns in New York

Queens is known as the borough of Asian immigrants, as 47 percent of Asian Americans in New York City settle there (U.S. Bureau of the Census 1993, table 55). The tendency to concentrate in Queens is most conspicuous among Korean immigrants. In 1990, 70 percent of Korean Americans in New York City resided in Queens. Bayside, Little Neck, Douglaston, Flushing, Woodside, and Elmhurst/ Corona are the areas of high Korean concentration in the borough, the areas that have also attracted a large number of Chinese immigrants. Thus, Korean and Chinese immigrants in Queens tend to cluster in the same areas, the phenomenon that is understandable considering many similarities in culture, physical characteristics, and socioeconomic status between the two groups.

Flushing is the home to about a quarter of New York City's Korean Americans. Already in 1990, nearly 20,000 Koreans lived in Community District 7, which encompasses Flushing, Whitestone, and College Point (New York City Department of City Planning 1992:228). As of January 2000, more than 25,000 Koreans were estimated to live in Flushing. They have established a residential and commercial center in a dozen blocks of downtown Flushing, an area known as "Flushing Koreatown," with its core at the intersection of Roosevelt Avenue and Union Street. Several apartment complexes located along Roosevelt Avenue between Union Street and 147th Street house many Korean families, including elderly Koreans who often remain in Flushing when their adult children move to New

Jersey or Long Island in search of better schools for their own children (Min 1998, chapter 6).

Flushing Koreatown has about 450 Korean businesses with Korean-language signs that cater exclusively to Korean customers with distinctive ethnic tastes. These businesses include about 30 Korean restaurants, 40 nail salons/barber-shops, 25 clothing shops, 18 travel agencies, 20 after-school institutes, and 10 coffee shops/bakeries. Korean restaurants in New York City, and Flushing in particular, are in strong competition with one another in serving Korean customers. They serve an excellent lunch menu with several side dishes for a special price of $5.99, less expensive, by the way, than in Seoul. Flushing Koreatown houses about fifteen Korean social service agencies, including the Flushing Korean Association, the Korean YMCA and YWCA, two Korean youth centers, the Korean American Senior Citizens Center of Greater New York, and the Korean Family Counseling and Research Center.

Fewer than 10 percent of New York City's Koreans live in Manhattan. Most are long-time immigrants or 1.5- and second-generation Koreans who are employed in American companies located there. However, there is one place in Manhattan that Korean immigrants and Korean tourists frequent, and where Korean stores with Korean-language signs are visible. This is the "Broadway Korean Business District," a rectangular ten-block area from Twenty-fourth Street and Thirty-fourth Street between Fifth and Seventh Avenues. Approximately 400 Korean import and wholesale companies with Korean-language commercial signs are located in this area. They import wigs, hats, leather bags, clothing, toys, and other manufactured goods from South Korea and other Asian countries and then distribute the merchandise mainly to Korean retailers in New York and other cities. Many Korean importers started retail and wholesale businesses dealing in Korea-imported manufactured goods in the 1960s and the 1970s. Because they facilitated Korean exports, the Korean government partially capitalized their businesses through loans from branches of the Korean Foreign Exchange Bank in New York.

Also located in the Broadway Korean Business District are a large number of Korean professional businesses, such as accounting firms, law firms, travel agencies, and real estate offices that mainly serve Korean importers and wholesalers. There are also about twenty-five Korean restaurants, several nightclubs, two bakeries, a few bookstores, and other businesses in the Broadway area that meet Korean ethnic tastes. Although Korean restaurants in Flushing serve exclusively Korean immigrant customers, those in Manhattan's Broadway area cater to many second-generation Korean and non-Korean customers. The intersection of Thirty-second Street and Broadway is considered the heart of the Broadway Korean Business District. In October 1995, the city named the district "Koreatown" and posted an official sign at the intersection. This was a result of intensive lobbying activities by the Broadway Korean Businessmen's Association, a group of Korean importers and wholesalers in the area. A Korean-owned hotel (Stanford Hotel), mainly accommodating Korean tourists from Korea and other parts of the United States, is located in the heart of the Broadway Korean Business District.

The Korean population in New York's suburbs has witnessed a phenomenal increase in the last two decades. This is due to three factors: remigration of Korean immigrants initially settled in Flushing and other Korean enclaves in Queens; the increase in the number of 1.5- and second-generation Korean American families; and the growth in the number of nonresident Koreans, including employees of overseas branches of Korean companies. Many Korean immigrants who initially settled in Korean enclaves in Queens and established a good economic position have remigrated to suburban areas with better schools for their children and lower crime rates. Bergen County in New Jersey, Long Island, and Westchester County are popular destinations of remigrating Koreans. Also, a growing number of 1.5- and second-generation Korean Americans who hold professional and managerial jobs in the mainstream economy live in suburban counties, especially Bergen County and Westchester County, as well as in Manhattan. Korean residents in Bergen County also include many nonresident Koreans, such as employees of New York branches of Korean firms, and diplomats and other Korean government employees working for the Korean Consulate and other government agencies located in Manhattan.

Bergen County, across the Hudson River from Manhattan, is the New York metropolitan suburban county with the largest Korean population. In 1990, approximately 16,000 Koreans resided there, making the county's Koreans the largest Asian immigrant group there. I estimate, based on the number of Kims listed in the Bergen County public telephone directory (201 area code) published in January 2000,[2] that approximately 33,600 Koreans now live in the county. This suggests that the county's Korean population more than doubled between 1990 and 2000. Korean immigrants in Bergen County are most visible in the Fort Lee and Palisades Park downtown areas, where they have established suburban Korea-towns. In January 2000, I counted 130 Korean stores with Korean-language signs in the Fort Lee downtown area and another 120 Korean stores in Palisades Park that cater exclusively to Korean customers. Korean merchants in both areas have conflicts with local city governments over posting Korean-language commercial signs and keeping Korean stores open until late at night.

Korean Immigrants' Concentration in Small Business

It is widely known that Korean immigrants in the United States are concentrated in several types of labor-intensive small businesses. Although other immigrant groups, such as Iranians and Israelis in Los Angeles, also have high self-employment rates (Light and Roach 1996), no other immigrant group active in small business has attracted as much media attention as Koreans. Publicity about Korean immigrant merchants is due mainly to the fact that many of them play a middleman minority role, distributing products made by large corporations to low-income minority customers, and that this role has led to a great deal of intergroup conflict. Korean immigrants' middleman role may be more conspicuous in New York than in any other Korean community.

An analysis of the 1990 census (public use sample) data reveals that 27 percent of foreign-born Korean workers in the New York–New Jersey metropolitan area were self-employed. Because census data greatly underestimate the self-employment rate, an independent survey is needed to provide a better measure for the Korean immigrant population. According to a 1988 survey I conducted of Korean married immigrant women in New York City, 49 percent of Korean wives and 61 percent of their husbands (56 percent of the sampled wives and their husbands combined) were self-employed; 55 percent of Korean immigrant families represented in the sample owned at least one business (Min 1996:48). Because unmarried, younger Korean workers, many of whom received a college education in the United States, are likely to have a lower self-employment rate, the self-employment rate of all Korean immigrant workers in the New York metropolitan area at the end of the 1980s was probably lower than 56 percent. Nevertheless, nearly half of Korean immigrant workers may well have been self-employed in small businesses.

For many, and perhaps most, Korean immigrants, running a small business is a step down from their occupations in Korea. Many have college degrees and held professional jobs in Korea but have set up shop in New York because their professional certificates are not recognized here and they lack proficiency in English (Min 1984). Given the alternatives, a small business is preferable to low-level service or factory jobs. The story of Won-Chul Shin illustrates the three-way occupational transitions from a professional/managerial job in Korea to the initial blue-collar job and to self-employment in a small business in the United States, common to most Korean immigrant men in the 1970s. Giving up a managerial position in a branch of Korean Exchange Bank, Shin decided to emigrate to the United States when his wife qualified as a nurse for an immigrant visa. Arriving in Atlanta in 1974, he found a blue-collar job in a lumber company while his wife, who was unable to get a registered nursing certificate due to the language barrier, worked as an aide in a nursing home. After working in a Majic Market grocery chain store as a cashier for two years, Shin started his own grocery in 1979, with his wife joining the family business.

Lacking business capital, training, and information, the Korean immigrants in the early 1970s took several years to establish their own businesses. In contrast, recent Korean immigrants have been better prepared, since they know before they leave Korea that self-employment is the only option for most of them and usually expect to run small businesses in the United States.[3] Thus, most recent Korean immigrants have brought a large amount of money with them to use as their business capital. Once they arrive, Korean immigrants easily acquire business information and training through employment in Korean-owned businesses. After they get business training and save money through this initial employment, they usually open their own stores that specialize in the same type of business. As is clear from the foregoing analyses, Korean immigrants' ethnic and class resources help them establish and operate businesses effectively, while the language barrier and other disadvantages for employment in the general economy force them to turn to those businesses (Light 1984; Min 1984, 1988; Yoon 1991).

The 1988 survey showed that about 30 percent of Korean workers in New York City were employed in Korean-owned businesses, and that only about 15 to 20 percent of the Korean immigrant workforce is in the general economy (Min 1996:48). Korean immigrants who find work in the general economy have usually received a graduate education in the United States and hold professional or managerial jobs. Most are longtime, first-wave professional and student immigrants who came to the United States in the 1960s and the 1970s. Many have found employment in the general economy because of their bilingual fluency. For example, many major American banks with branches in the Flushing-Bayside area have hired dozens of Korean immigrants as managers to attract Korean customers. About twenty Korean teachers and counselors working in public schools have also benefited from their bilingual background.

Korean businesses in New York are highly concentrated in several labor-intensive retail and service business specialties: wholesale and retail of Korean- and Asian-imported manufacturing goods; produce, grocery, and fish retail; dry-cleaning; nail salons; and garment subcontracting (Min 1996:54). The wig industry and sale of other Korean-imported manufactured goods were the first Korean enterprises that started in the 1960s. Today more than 500 Korean-owned wholesale businesses in the New York–New Jersey metropolitan area import manufactured goods not only from South Korea but also from other Asian countries. These importers distribute merchandise to Latino as well as Korean retailers. Korean retailers in this specialty get preferential treatment from Korean wholesalers in terms of purchases on credit, price and speed of delivery of items, and information on "trendy" items.

Produce retail is probably the best-known Korean business in New York. The New York–New Jersey metropolitan area is home to approximately 2,000 Korean-owned produce retail stores, including many in black neighborhoods. There are also the same number of Korean-owned grocery stores in New York. Because many Korean stores sell both produce and grocery items, it is not easy to count the number of Korean-owned stores in the two specialties separately. Initially, in the 1970s, Korean immigrants in New York purchased produce and grocery retail stores from Jewish and Italian American retirees. This is a good example of ethnic succession in business niches. Before Korean immigrants came to New York in large numbers, Jewish and Italian Americans dominated the city's produce and grocery retail businesses. By the 1970s, many Jewish and Italian storeowners were reaching retirement age, and their upwardly mobile children had no interest in minding the store. Jewish and Italian Americans in New York still, however, dominate the wholesale end of the produce and grocery business, and Korean retailers depend on them for supplies of retail items.

Middleman minorities play an intermediary economic role by providing a bridge between minority customers and producers from the dominant ethnic/racial groups (Blalock 1967; Bonacich 1973; Zenner 1991). Jews in medieval Europe, Chinese in Asian countries, and Indians in Africa have been cited as typical examples of middleman minorities. Korean immigrants in the United States play a similar role as they distribute products made by large white corporations to low-income black and Latino customers (Kim 1981; Min 1990, 1995, 1996; Min and Kolodny 1994; Waldinger 1989). Korean-owned grocery and liquor stores in major American cities are heavily concentrated in low-income black neighborhoods while they depend entirely on white manufacturers for supply of grocery and liquor items. Thus Korean grocery and liquor retail businesses are typical middleman businesses. Although New York's Koreans are not active in the liquor business, they are prominent in a third type of middleman business—produce retail stores. Many Korean produce retail stores are located in white middle-class neighborhoods, but large numbers are in low-income black neighborhoods in Harlem, Jamaica, and Brooklyn while they depend entirely on white, mostly Jewish, wholesalers.

Historically, middleman merchants specializing in retail businesses in minority neighborhoods have met with hostility and rejection from their customers in the form of boycotts, arson, and riots (Eitzen 1971; Palmer 1957; Porter 1981). Like middleman merchants in other societies, Korean merchants in black neighborhoods in many U.S. cities have encountered boycotts, destruction of stores in riots (as in the Los Angeles riots of 1992), and other forms of rejection (Min 1996). As far as long-term boycotts of Korean stores are concerned, no other city can match New York City. Between 1981 and 1990, Korean merchants in black neighborhoods in Harlem, Jamaica, and Brooklyn encountered five long-term boycotts that lasted at least a month each. As discussed in detail elsewhere (Min 1996:74–78), four of the long-term boycotts involved Korean produce stores whereas one targeted a Korean grocery store. In all cases, the boycott started with a dispute between a Korean store owner or employee and one or more black customers, which black nationalists quickly turned into a long-term boycott. The longest boycott, which occurred in Brooklyn's Flatbush area in January 1990 and ended in May 1991, drew international media attention.

The literature on middleman minorities has focused on host hostility, especially hostility from minority customers, but has neglected the effects of hostility on ethnic solidarity among middleman minorities. The middleman literature has also described middleman merchants as almost totally controlled by producers and government agencies. As I have documented in detail (Min 1996), boycotts and other forms of hostility have strengthened solidarity not only among Korean merchants but also among all Korean Americans. Moreover, Korean merchants have effectively used collective strategies to protect their economic interests against white suppliers (Min 1996).

Koreans' solidarity in reaction to business-related intergroup conflicts and Korean merchants' collective actions against white suppliers have been especially noteworthy in New York City. Consider the effects of the 1990–1991 black boycott of two Korean-owned produce stores in Brooklyn on Korean ethnic solidarity. In the early stage of the boycott, the Korean Produce Association of New York and the Flatbush Korean Merchants Association raised funds, mostly from members, to help the two store owners being targeted by the boycot. Later, the Korean ethnic media joined the fund-raising campaign, asking all Koreans to donate money and to make visits to shop in the two stores. In addition, many Korean ethnic churches raised funds from their members for the two store owners. Approximately $150,000 was raised during the first year of the boycott, providing each store owner with about $7,000 per month. In September 1990, the Korean Association of New York organized a mass demonstration in front of City Hall to show Koreans' dissatisfaction with Mayor David Dinkins's "lukewarm effort" to terminate the boycott. Approximately 7,000 Koreans, including Korean elders and second-generation Koreans, participated in the demonstration.

Although most New Yorkers are aware of boycotts of Korean stores in black neighborhoods, few may be familiar with Korean merchants' boycotts of and demonstrations against white suppliers. Korean business associations have organized some fifteen boycotts, demonstrations, or combinations of the two against white suppliers to protest unreasonable treatment of Korean merchants (see Min 1996:193–202). All but three boycotts, demonstrations, or both were organized by the Korean Produce Association of New York against produce suppliers at Hunts Point Markets, the site of frequent confrontations, which often included physical violence, with employees of wholesalers. In almost all the boycotts, the Korean Produce Association of New York succeeded in making the supplier formally apologize and promise to improve their services to Korean merchants. The Korean-American Grocers Association of New York has used price bargaining and collective purchasing to protect its members' interests against grocery suppliers and manufacturers.

Churches as the Most Important Ethnic Organizations

Christian churches are the most important Korean ethnic organizations in New York as well as in other American cities. The significance of Christian congregations is evidenced by the fact that more than 75 percent of New York City's Korean immigrant families are affiliated with a Korean church and that the vast majority (80 percent of them) attend church once or twice a week. The presence of approximately 600 Korean churches, including a Korean Catholic church with 6,000 members, forty other religious organizations, and thirty theological schools in the

New York area, further demonstrate the importance of Christian life among Korean immigrants in the region.

American missionaries—mostly Presbyterian—brought Protestantism to Korea at the end of the nineteenth century by establishing Christian schools and hospitals, while French missionaries had introduced Roman Catholicism to Korea one century earlier. However, both Christian religions were not popular until the 1960s partly because their Christian religious faiths and rituals collided with ancestor worship, the core of Confucian customs, and partly because the Japanese colonial government repressed the Christian religions during the colonial period (1910–1945). In 1962, only 2.8 percent of the Korean population was Protestant and 2.2 percent Catholic (Park and Cho 1995:119). The proportion of Christians gradually increased in conjunction with economic growth in South Korea. According to a survey conducted in 1991, approximately 25 percent of people in South Korea were Christians, 19 percent were Protestants, and 6 percent were Catholics, while the proportion of Buddhists was 28 percent.

Christians have been especially numerous among those migrating to the United States. Several surveys reveal that most Korean immigrants attended a Christian church before immigration (Hurh and Kim 1990; Min 2000b; Park et al. 1990). Korean immigrants have been largely drawn from the urban middle-class segments of the Korean population in which Christians are heavily concentrated. This is the major reason that Christians are overrepresented among Korean immigrants, although regardless of their class or urban-rural background, Korean Christians are more favorably disposed to emigrate than non-Christians. Although Buddhists outnumber Christians in Korea, fewer than 10 percent of Korean immigrants say they were Buddhists prior to migration (Hurh and Kim 1990; Min 1999; Park et al. 1990).

What is striking is that non-Christian Korean immigrants, including Buddhists, participate in Korean churches as the latter have become the Korean community centers. Thus, whatever their previous religious preference in Korea, the vast majority of Korean immigrants are affiliated with a Korean church. My own survey conducted in 1997 and 1998 reveals that 79 percent of Korean immigrants in Queens reported that either Protestantism (62 percent) or Catholicism (17 percent) was their current religion (Min 2000b).[4] All but two Korean Christian immigrant respondents (98 percent) were affiliated with a Korean church. Moreover, the vast majority of Korean immigrants affiliated with a Korean church participate in a congregation regularly—once or twice a week. My Queens data show that 83 percent of Korean immigrants affiliated with a Korean church go there at least once a week. This is a much higher rate than among other Christian groups in the United States. According to national studies of Presbyterians, 78 percent of Korean Presbyterians attend Sunday worship service every week in comparison to 28 percent of white, 34 percent of African American, and 49 percent of Latino Presbyterians (Kim and Kim 2001).

What explains Korean immigrants' exceptionally high rate of affiliation with ethnic congregations and their exceptionally high rate of participation? For one thing, Korean immigrants included a large number of pastors. Second, because of their severe language barrier, Korean immigrants find it more difficult to participate in a white American or ethnically mixed congregation than many other immigrant groups. At the same time, their cultural homogeneity draws them to Korean congregations. Indeed, Koreans' monolingual background means that Koreans—and their churches—are not splintered by their language divisions. Almost all Indian Christian immigrants in the United States attend a white American or ethnically mixed congregation mainly because they do not have ethnic pastors and partly because they are divided by several different languages (Min 2000b).

Third, regularly attending a Korean church meets important psychological needs. Because of great adjustment difficulties, including a language barrier, long hours of work, and experiences of downward occupational mobility, most Korean immigrants turn to religion to find a new meaning to life. Although many completed college and held a professional occupation in Korea, they now engage in a blue-collar small business in the United States that demands long hours of work and is associated with low social status. Not surprisingly, they are frustrated with their low status, which has led some to return to Korea. Until very recently, most Korean immigrants found satisfaction in being able to maintain a higher standard of living in New York than their relatives and friends did in Korea. However, economic growth in South Korea in recent years has meant that most Korean immigrants no longer have an edge over their friends and families in Korea, which is a further source of frustration.

Finally, most Korean immigrants go to a Korean church every week out of their desire for communal ties. In 1989, I interviewed by telephone 131 Korean pastors in New York City to examine the major social functions of Korean immigrant churches (see Min 1992). According to what the pastors in the survey told me, Korean churches provide all kinds of services for their members: immigration orientation, job referral, business information, a Korean-language and/or after-school program for children, educational counseling, *hyodo kwangkwang* (providing "filial trips" for elders), and even marriage counseling. A small church usually provides services mainly through the head pastor's personal contacts with members, while a large church helps members through various formal programs. Korean churches are the most important social service agencies in the Korean community.

Although they provide multifaceted services, they have not responded to the welfare needs of the community as a whole. To my knowledge, only two church programs have been designed to help all Koreans in New York. One is the Korean Youth Center, established in Flushing in 1991 by the Council of Korean Churches of Greater New York to help solve Korean youth gang and other juvenile problems. The other is a program established by the Korean Catholic Apostle Church of Queens to provide legal and family counseling to any Korean in New York.

Professional lawyers and counselors, mostly members of the 6,000-member church, take turns in giving free counseling.

Korean churches help Korean immigrants maintain fellowship and friendship networks—an important reason that they go to a church every week. Almost all Korean churches in New York provide an extended fellowship hour for members after the Sunday worship service with refreshments or a full lunch served. The results of my 1989 telephone survey show that about one-fourth of Korean churches in New York provide a full lunch for members. Each family, on a rotating basis, usually brings Korean food cooked by commercial places *(janch'ijip)* to church. The churches also hold parties after Sunday worship services to celebrate important Korean national and Christian holidays.

Large Korean churches are less effective than small churches in meeting immigrants' need for primary social interactions, which is why a Korean church is often split into two (Shin and Park 1988). However, even large Korean churches have made adjustments to facilitate the immigrants' primary social interactions. Korean churches usually divide members into several different groups by area of residence, and each group is encouraged to hold regular district meetings called *kuyuk yebae.* A district meeting combines a religious service and a dinner party at a member's private home, which provides district members with ample opportunity for informal social interactions. Church members in the same district rotate hosting the meetings. District meetings are usually held once a month, but in some churches they are held twice a month or more often.

Another major social function of Korean immigrant churches is that they help immigrants maintain their cultural traditions. All Korean churches celebrate not only Christian religious holidays but also Korean national holidays such as Lunar New Year and Korean Independence Day, when a variety of Korean traditional foods are served. Many church members wear traditional Korean dress on important holidays. Almost all Korean churches hold a year-end party at a member's private home on New Year's Eve, with church members usually playing *yoot,* a traditional game. About half of New York City's Korean churches have established Korean-language schools to teach children the Korean language, history, and culture. In addition to these formal programs, Korean children also learn the Korean language and manners informally through interactions with other children. Indeed, a major reason that Korean parents with school-age children attend a Korean church is for the benefit of ethnic education.

Ethnic Media

In his study of the Korean community in New York in the 1970s, Illsoo Kim wrote that Korean immigrants maintained a nonterritorial community centered on "organizational and institutional activities" (Kim 1981:316). However, as I have noted, since the late 1970s Korean immigrants in the New York metropolitan area have established several ethnic enclaves in Queens and New York suburbs as the

Korean population has increased. Both practically and symbolically, territoriality now plays a far more important role in Korean immigrants' ethnic retention and identity than it did in the 1970s.

Nevertheless, even now most Korean immigrants in New York are residentially widely dispersed, living in predominantly white or multiethnic neighborhoods rather than a Korean enclave. The ethnic media play a central role in integrating geographically dispersed Korean immigrants in the New York area. Five Korean-language TV programs, two radio programs, three Korean-language dailies, and several weeklies provide Korean immigrants in the New York area with news and all kinds of information on a daily and hourly basis. Great improvements in media technologies since the early 1980s have enabled all immigrant/ethnic communities to develop and improve their ethnic media. Yet because of their monolingual background, Korean immigrants have been able to develop their native-language media far more effectively than other immigrant groups.

Hankuk Ilbo is the largest and oldest Korean ethnic daily newspaper (founded in 1967) in the New York–New Jersey metropolitan area. *Choong Ang Ilbo* (founded in 1975) is the second-largest, with a circulation of 34,000 (38,000 on the weekend), while *Sae Gae Ilbo* ranks behind the other two in circulation and influence. All three Korean-language dailies, as branches of major dailies in Korea, duplicate each issue that is published in Seoul. In the 1970s, *Hankuk Ilbo* and *Choong Ang Ilbo* photocopied (on an electronic copier) each issue airmailed from the Seoul headquarters daily. The result was that Korean immigrants read newspapers several days after they were published in Korea. Now, they can read newspapers the same day they are published in Korea as each branch duplicates newspapers from its Seoul headquarters via satellite. According to my 1997–1998 survey, 68 percent of Korean immigrant families in Queens subscribe to at least one Korean-language daily, while 33 percent subscribe to an English-language newspaper. The majority read a Korean daily delivered to their homes by second-class mail, although many buy them at newsstands in Flushing, the Broadway Korean Business District in Manhattan, or Fort Lee and Palisades Park in New Jersey.

Each Korean ethnic daily includes a Korean-American section that carries news about the Korean community and the larger American society. The Korean-American section has several pages of classified advertisements that are the major source of revenue for each ethnic daily. Classified advertisements provide information about employment in, and sale of, Korean businesses. New immigrants usually find employment in a Korean business through either their personal networks or an advertisement in an ethnic daily. In most cases, Korean immigrants purchase their businesses from coethnic owners, and they often depend, at least in part, on advertisements carried in Korean ethnic media to learn of business opportunities. Most Korean churches also advertise their worship services in Korean dailies to attract more members; these advertisements, in addition to business-related ones, are an important source of revenue for each newspaper.

As of March 2000, there were two Korean-language TV stations in Flushing and one in Palisades Park, New Jersey. The Korean TV stations in Flushing, CH17 KTV and the Korea (Cable) Channel, air programs twenty-four hours a day, with several programs aired twice a day. CH17 KTV, with twenty-five employees, covers the city's five boroughs and portions of Long Island and Bergen County; the cable TV station, with ten employees, covers Queens and portions of Brooklyn and Manhattan. They can provide round-the-clock programming with so few employees mainly because they make extensive use of videotaped TV dramas and other programs produced by two Seoul TV stations. In fact, the New York City–based TV stations produce only about 10 percent of their programs. Both provide evening news from the Korean Broadcasting Station in Seoul via satellite at 8:30 every evening. Thus Koreans in New York have access to news from Korea on the same evening that it is broadcast in Korea, although they get it fourteen hours later because of the time difference. Mountain Broadcasting Corporation, located in Palisades Park, New Jersey, offers a Korean TV program for only two hours a day, between 8:00 and 10:00 P.M. for Koreans in Bergen County, upstate New York, and New York City.[5] In addition, two other Korean TV programs in Bergen County air six hours a day on American channels (Time Warner and Cablevision).

The two Korean radio stations in New York, Radio Seoul and Christian Broadcasting, air programs twenty-four hours a day: . Radio Seoul is an AM station (1480) located in Flushing. Korean immigrants in New York can listen to Radio Seoul programs anywhere, anytime: in the bedroom, the car, the workplace, a Korean grocery store or barbershop. Thus it reaches a wider Korean audience and has a more powerful influence on Korean immigrants than any other ethnic medium. Whereas New York's Korean TV stations mainly show videotaped programs produced by Korean TV stations in Seoul, *Radio Seoul,* with thirty-five employees, creates its own programs tailored to Korean immigrant life. This is another reason Radio Seoul has gained a great deal of popularity. It has developed a number of programs in which Korean professionals directly provide Korean immigrants with practical information and counseling about health, family, education, real estate, economy, law, tax returns, and so forth.[6] I participated in a Friday program for the radio station, talking about American society and the Korean community for about ten to fifteen minutes. Radio Seoul also provides news from Korea several times a day at regular intervals, often relaying the headline news from the Korean Broadcasting Station in Seoul. Thus, *Radio Seoul* helps Korean immigrants get information from South Korea on an hourly basis.

Christian Broadcasting is a nonprofit Korean broadcasting station (FM subcarrier) established in 1990 in Manhattan mainly for Christian missionary activities. It is largely supported by donations from Korean Christian immigrants and Korean churches in the New York area. In the main, it airs Korean pastors' sermons and hymns with intermittent news and classical music to an audience in the tristate area. A Korean immigrant has to buy a special receiver to listen to the subleased Christian station. Approximately 40,000 Korean families in the tristate area subscribe to the station, which indicates the significance of Christian religions to the Korean community. Many Korean churches pay fees to Christian Broadcasting to publicize their pastors' sermons to the Korean Christian population, which provides important revenue for the station.

Other Ethnic Organizations

Alumni Associations

In addition to Korean churches and ethnic media, a wide range of ethnic organizations flourishes in the New York–area Korean community. Chinese and Japanese immigrants in the nineteenth and early twentieth centuries organized ethnic associations based largely on clan ties and locality of origin (Kitano 1976:94; Lyman 1974:32–37). However, clan and provincial ties in Korea are not important for contemporary Korean immigrants' ethnic networks, and there are only fifteen kin- or locality-based associations in the New York Korean community. Instead, premigrant ties based on the same school are important for Korean immigrants' formal and informal ethnic networks. *The Korea Central Daily Business Directory* published in January 1999 listed ninety-two alumni associations, sixty-one of them middle or high school based and thirty-one college based. Considering those not included in the directory, there may be over a hundred alumni associations in the Korean community in New York. With the exception of several associations whose members had graduated from U.S. theological schools, all alumni associations were based on ties to high schools and colleges in Korea.

Alumni associations usually hold outdoor picnics for alumni and their family members in the spring and fall, with traditional Korean foods cooked outdoors. Most alumni associations have a major party for members and their spouses at the end of the year, usually held in a hotel ballroom. Several university alumni associations in the New York metropolitan area have recently organized year-end parties for college-attending children of alumni members to provide young men and women with an opportunity to get together. Each alumni association is further divided into subgroups based on year of graduation. Members of each subgroup often maintain strong friendships, going beyond the formal activities of the organization to provide each other with aid. They often organize a rotating credit association and meet monthly at a designated restaurant for friendship and to collect money to be drawn by each member on a rotating basis. Many Korean immigrants give preferential treatment to alumni members when hiring employees, transacting businesses, and making private loans. Thus they use alumni connections effectively for their business purposes.

Social Service Agencies

There are approximately forty social service agencies in the Korean community in the New York metropolitan area. These include seven elderly centers, four youth centers, three family and counseling centers, and a small-business service center. Most of these social service agencies are located in Korean neighborhoods in Flushing, Fort Lee, and Palisades Park. Three Korean elderly centers are located in Queens, and the other four are in Brooklyn, The Bronx, Staten Island, and Fort Lee (New Jersey). Korean elderly centers provide a number of services, including health clinics, translation services, and assistance in filling out applications for welfare programs. Moreover, they provide the Korean elderly with a meeting place and many recreational programs. In addition, they offer a number of educational programs, including English and citizenship test classes. The (Korean) YWCA in Flushing has also established a Korean elderly college. Korean elderly immigrants settled in Korean enclaves in Queens and other parts of the city feel so comfortable living in the United States that they are reluctant to go back to Korea even if their adult children return to Korea for career reasons (see Min 1998, chapter 6).

In addition to four youth centers, the Korean YMCA and YWCA in Flushing have developed youth programs, an indication of youth problems in the community. Youth centers were established in the late 1980s and early 1990s in response to many gang-related and juvenile problems in the Korean community. Korean immigrant students' language barrier and their sense of alienation in school, second-generation children's conflicts with their parents, and Korean immigrant parents' long hours of work are at the root of young people's problems. In addition, the many Chinese youth gangs in New York City often appeal to Korean problem children. In fact, Chinese gangs actively recruit Korean children.

Business Associations

About sixty specialized business associations and local merchants' associations exist in the Korean community in New York. Korean business associations initially had two general objectives: maintaining friendship and exchanging information among members. Most business associations have added three more specific objectives to protect their economic interests against outside groups: collectively handling business-related intergroup conflicts, lobbying governments and politicians to protect Korean business interests, and moderating competition among Korean merchants (see Min 1996:209). They have also developed programs to provide services to the Korean community as a whole, in part because they have the financial resources to do so. Most Korean trade associations get big donations from their suppliers (a major source of revenue), some of which they spend for services to the Korean community.

The Korean Produce Association of New York annually holds the Korean Harvest and Folklore Festival just after *Choo Seok,* the Korean equivalent of Thanksgiving. About 30,000 Koreans—20 percent of Koreans in the New York–New Jersey metropolitan area—usually participate in this festival to enjoy Korean folk songs, dances, and games and traditional Korean food. The association spends $25,000 to $30,000 for the festival each year. Both the Korean Produce Association of New York and the Korean-American Grocers Association of New York have established scholarship funds for Korean and black students, annually awarding $1,000 to each of several students. The Broadway Korean Businessmen's Association operates the Broadway Korean-American Bank and the Broadway Korean School (which holds sessions on Saturdays). Twenty percent of its budget goes toward providing services to the Korean community, including scholarships for Korean students in need.

Political Organizations and Ethnic Politics

Several Korean political organizations are active in the New York area. The Korean Association of New York is an umbrella organization that represents the New York–area Korean community to the larger society and the home country. Since the organization was established in 1960, its president has been chosen through direct election every two years. In most elections, two or three candidates have been in strong competition. In campaigning for this two-year position that pays no salary, candidates have spent a great deal of money (usually over $200,000) mainly because of the high social status attached to the office. Representing the Korean community in New York, the president can meet New York City's mayor, other community leaders, and even high-ranking government officials from Korea. Many successful Korean immigrant businessmen are ready to spend money for status, and thus almost all who have served as the president have been successful businessmen. Three or four candidates who have lost the presidential election have taken the election results to American courts to try to prove election fraud.

Of the many political and intergroup activities in which the Korean Association of New York (KANY) has been involved, its efforts to moderate Korean-black conflicts are perhaps most noteworthy. The umbrella organization intervened in all of the major black boycotts of Korean stores in New York. It also made efforts to reduce Korean–African American conflicts by bringing the two communities closer together (see Min 1996:133–35). For example, in December 1988, when the Korean community was struggling to end a four-month-long boycott of a Korean store in Brooklyn, KANY leaders attended a dinner party for racial harmony organized by the *New York Voice,* a major African American daily in New York City. At the party, Koreans and blacks performed their traditional music and dances, and KANY donated $5,000 to the daily. In April 1990, when a black boycott of two Korean produce retail stores was receiving international media attention, the newly elected president of the KANY organized a twenty-five-member interracial team for a ten-day visit to Korea, called a goodwill mission. The team consisted of ten Koreans and fifteen African American, Latino, Jewish, and Italian American religious, educational, and political leaders. The ten New York Korean community and business leaders who accompanied the non-Korean leaders paid for the non-Korean participants' airfare as well as their own travel expenses. In July 1990, after the community leaders returned from visiting Korea,

KANY turned the interracial team into the Ethnic Committee for Racial Harmony and Outreach (ECHO), designed to provide a permanent forum to contribute to interracial harmony.

KANY, in close coordination with the Korean Consulate, provides a bridge between the Korean community in New York and the Korean government. Whenever a member of the assembly or a high-ranking government official from South Korea (even the president) visits New York, he or she will drop in at the KANY office in Manhattan. The KANY president often lobbies the consulate, the Korean government, or both to change policies pertaining to Korean Americans. In 1995, KANY sent a twenty-person team to South Korea for a forum to pressure the Korean government to recognize dual citizenship for Korean Americans.[7] It annually recommends a dozen Korean Americans to the Korean government for prestigious awards for contributing to the Korean community or Korean society. It also annually presents awards to a dozen Korean and non-Korean citizens who contribute to the Korean American community.

Most of the political organizations in the Korean community in New York are concerned with democratization or unification in Korea. Yet three organizations engage in lobbying and political activities in New York to protect Koreans' political and economic interests there. One is the Coalition of Korean-American Voters, made up of 1.5- and second-generation Korean Americans. Created in the aftermath of the 1990 black boycott of two Korean stores, it has been involved in organizing voter registration drives among Koreans, supporting Korean American political candidates, presenting Korean community issues to non-Korean political candidates, and surveying Koreans' political attitudes.

Another is the Korean-American Democrats of New York, whose office is located in Flushing. Created in 1993 to protect Korean political interests through the Democratic Party, the organization is made up of first- and 1.5-generation Korean community leaders from different occupational categories: lawyers, merchants, professors, activists, and government officials. It has organized a number of fund-raising parties to support various Democratic Party candidates, including Mario Cuomo, David Dinkins, Gary Ackerman, Bill Clinton, and Al Gore. It has also recommended several Koreans for influential positions in the New York City government. In addition, it has organized voter registration drives and political seminars.

The third organization involved to protect Korean interests in New York is the Korean Small Business Service Center (KSBSC). Established in 1986, it serves as the representative for all Korean trade associations in dealing with local government agencies. KSBSC has negotiated with city and other governmental officials to help Korean merchants who have violated business regulations and to lobby lawmakers and government agencies to make business regulations less strict. Staff members from KSBSC visit City Hall at least three times a week, meeting with city government officials to protect Korean merchants both individually and collectively. As I have examined elsewhere (Min 1996:183–92), KSBSC, in close coordination with other Korean business associations, has intensely lobbied government officials and politicians to protect Korean merchants' economic interests. For example, in 1991, KSBSC successfully lobbied the New York City Consumer Affairs Department to get the Trade Waste Association to lower the commercial waste disposal fee, helping nearly 10,000 Korean merchants save a considerable amount of money. Another instance involved the regulation of sidewalk stands. New York City had long stipulated that stores located on streets sixteen or more feet wide could display a stand on the sidewalk up to four feet wide and ten feet long. Sung Soo Kim, KSBSC director, lobbied city government administrators relentlessly, arguing that such a strict rule made it difficult for small produce and flower retailers to survive in New York City. His lobbying activities were central to the passage of a bill by the City Council that, effective July 1993, increased the allowable width from four to five feet.

So far, no Asian American has been elected to the New York City Council, which is a reflection of the short history of the Asian American community and the lack of Asian American political power there. Yet several Asian Americans have been elected as school board members over the last several years. Altogether, seven Koreans now serve as school board members in the New York–New Jersey metropolitan area, four in New York City and three in various New Jersey school districts. The Chinese community, which has a much longer history in the region and four times as large a population as the Korean community, has six school board members, all serving in New York City community school districts. Even though the New York–area Indian community is twice as large as the Korean community and although Indian immigrants, as a group, can speak English much better than Koreans, only two Indian Americans are currently school board members. If number of elected school board members is any measure of an Asian community's political development, and I think it is, the Korean community is ahead of the other New York–area Asian communities.

Ad hoc committees established in the Koran community for each school board election played an important role in raising money and publicizing the election through the ethnic media. Yet it was the Korean parents' associations that mobilized votes. Three Korean parents' associations in New York City (one each in Community Districts 24, 25, and 26) and three in New Jersey school districts are mainly concerned with preventing discriminatory treatment against Korean students and promoting ethnic education in public schools. Having Korean school board members, Korean parents feel, is essential in achieving both aims. In New York City, parents of students enrolled in any school in the district can participate in the school board election regardless of their legal status. Moreover, a very small fraction of white American citizens (usually less than 5 percent) participate in school board elections. Korean parents have realized that if they mobilize other Korean parents to cast ballots, they can elect Korean candidates. Thus, each Korean parents' association has utilized small-group networks to bring as many Korean parents to voting booths as possible.

Conclusion

The New York Korean community has an exceptionally large number of ethnic organizations that provide formal and informal social networks, and a variety of services. Moreover, the ethnic media have integrated geographically dispersed Korean immigrants in the New York area, making news and information about the community and the home country available on a daily basis. Korean immigrants are also heavily concentrated in several types of small businesses, which offers the community another important basis for ethnic attachment. The result is that Korean immigrants in New York are strongly integrated into their ethnic community culturally, socially, and psychologically. Most speak Korean at home and in the workplace and practice Korean customs most of the time. They maintain social interactions mainly with other Koreans. They identify as Korean, expressing loyalty to their home country.

Three major factors account for Korean immigrants' high degree of ethnic attachment: cultural homogeneity; the significant role of the ethnic church; and concentration in small businesses (Min 1991 and 1998, chapter 4). Although Korean immigrants elsewhere in the United States also maintain high levels of ethnic attachment, because of the larger population base and presence of several ethnic neighborhoods in the New York area, the Korean community there is more tightly organized than in many other parts of the country.

Assimilation and ethnic attachment are not necessarily mutually exclusive. Members of a group can achieve a high level of assimilation while preserving their cultural traditions and social networks, as is clear from the mode of adaptation of Jewish Americans. In the Korean immigrant community, however, the factors that contribute to ethnic attachment also hinder assimilation into American society. Put in another way, Koreans' monolingual background, along with the extensive development of their ethnic media, segregation in their own religious congregations, and their economic segregation, isolate them from the larger society.

One might expect that this kind of segregation from the larger society would hinder involvement in mainstream political activities. However, this has not been the case among Korean immigrants in New York. In fact, as it turns out, ethnic resources have actually facilitated collective action and political development. Korean community leaders have effectively used the ethnic media to educate Koreans about the importance of participating in school board elections and the 2000 U.S. census. To give two examples, Korean-language media have been able to widely publicize community political issues because all Korean immigrants speak the same language. Korean immigrants' participation in ethnic churches provides an institutional basis for ethnic collective and political activities. For example, Korean church vans took church members to City Hall for a large-scale demonstration against New York City mayor David Dinkins in September 1990. Finally, Korean immigrants' middleman economic role and their business-related intergroup conflicts have helped them develop lobbying and political skills. Although many Korean business and community leaders speak broken English, they know how to lobby government agencies and politicians because they have already done so for their economic interests.

New York's Korean community, as well as other Korean communities, is slowly undergoing the generation transition as an increasing number of 1.5- and second-generation Koreans complete their education and participate in the labor force. To what extent will second-generation Koreans follow the mode of their parents' adjustment, characterized by high levels of ethnic attachment and segregation from the larger society? Currently available data, although limited, strongly suggest that the second generation will not encounter the same structural factors that contribute to Korean immigrants' high levels of ethnic attachment and social segregation. Thus, I predict they will achieve assimilation into the mainstream society to a much greater extent than their parents did, while losing much of their ethnic attachment.

To elaborate, Koreans' monolingual background and Confucian customs and values are the two major factors that make Korean immigrants culturally homogeneous. However, second-generation Koreans, like other second generations, are achieving a high level of linguistic assimilation, with only a small proportion being fluent in the mother tongue (Hong and Min 1999; Min 2000a). Second-generation Koreans also reject exactly the Confucian elements of Korean culture characterized by age-based authoritarianism and patriarchy (Kim and Yu 1996; Min 1999). Moreover, Korean Christian congregations are much less important for second-generation Koreans' ethnic attachment than for their parents'. Many second-generation Korean Christians attend white or pan-Asian congregations, and those who attend Korean congregations participate less frequently than their parents (Min 1999). More significantly, second-generation Koreans have revised Koreanized, especially Confucianized, Christian religions so much that their religious practices may be more similar to those of white Americans than to those of their parents (Chai 1998; Min 1999, 2000b). Finally, while the vast majority of Korean immigrants participate in the Korean ethnic economy, second-generation Korean adults mainly participate in the general economy, with their self-employment rate lower than white Americans' (Min 1996:52). In a nutshell, culturally, religiously, and economically, second-generation Koreans are far more assimilated into the mainstream society than their immigrant parents.

Notes

1. The increase in the number of unemployed people in South Korea in the aftermath of the financial crisis that started at the end of 1997 pushed many Koreans to the United States and discouraged Korean immigrants to return to Korea. However, under the strong leadership of President Kim Dae-Joong, South Korea had achieved economic stability by the end of 1998.

2. According to the Korean census, Kims account for 21.8 percent of the Korean population. Since Kim is a uniquely Korean name, we can assess the Korean population in a particular city or county by counting the number of Kims listed in one or more public telephone directories. See Shin and Yu (1984).

3. In one "predeparture survey" conducted in Seoul in 1986, 61 percent of all respondents and 71 percent of male respondents reported that they would go into business when they came to the United States (Park et al. 1990:86).

4. I conducted a telephone survey of Korean households in Queens using the "Kim sample technique" (randomly selecting Kims listed in a public telephone directory), and 187 Korean adult immigrants were successful interviewed. For details of the Kim sample technique, see Shin and Yu (1984).

5. A Korean immigrant owns this station, but he leases air time to other ethnic TV programs for the remaining hours.

6. Korean professionals such as medical doctors and accountants provide information and counseling free to the audience because it helps them gain more customers.

7. The Korean government does not give dual citizenship to overseas Koreans mainly because it believes that doing so will lead many Koreans in China and the former Soviet Union to repatriate to Korea for permanent residence. But it has revised laws pertaining to overseas Koreans in such a way that Korean Americans can own property in Korea and can visit with no visa as well as hold jobs there.

References

Blalock, Herbert. 1967. *Toward a Theory of Minority Group Relations.* New York: Wiley.

Bonacich, Edna. 1973. "A Theory of Middleman Minorities." *American Sociological Review* 35:583–94.

Breton, Raymond. 1961. "Ethnic and Personal Relations of Immigrants." Ph.D. diss., Johns Hopkins University.

——. 1964. "Institutional Completeness of Ethnic Communities and the Personal Relations of Immigrants." *American Journal of Sociology* 70:193–205.

Chai, Karen. 1998. "Competing for the Second Generation: English-Language Ministry in a Korean Protestant Church." In Stephen Warner and Judith Wittner, eds., *Gatherings in Diaspora: Religious Communities and the New Immigration,* pp. 295–332. Philadelphia: Temple University Press.

Choy, Bong-Youn. 1979. *Koreans in America.* Chicago: Nelson Press.

Eitzen, D. S. 1971. "Two Minorities: The Jews of Poland and the Chinese of the Philippines." In N. R. Yetman and C. Hoy Steele, eds., *Majority and Minority: The Dynamics of Racial and Ethnic Relations.* Boston: Allyn and Bacon.

Harper, E. J. 1979. *Immigration Laws of the United States, 1978 Supplement.* Indianapolis: Bobbs-Merrill.

Historical Compilation Committee of Korean Church of New York. 1992. *70 Years of History of Korean Church of New York* [in Korean]. Seoul: Kipeunsaem.

Hong, Joann, and Pyong Gap Min. 1999. "Ethnic Attachment Among Second-Generation Korean Adolescents." *Amerasia Journal* 25:165–78.

Hurh, Won Moo, and Kwang Chung Kim. 1990. "Religious Participation of Korean Immigrants in the United States." *Journal of the Scientific Study of Religion* 29:19–34.

Kim, Elaine, and Eui-Young Yu. 1996. *East to America: Korean American Life Stories.* New York: New Press.

Kim, Illsoo. 1981. *New Urban Immigrants: The Korean Community in New York.* Princeton: Princeton University Press.

Kim, Kwang Chung, and Shin Kim. 2001. "The Ethnic Roles of Korean Immigrant Churches in the U.S." In Ho-Hyon Kwong, Kwang Chung Kim, and Stephen Warner, eds., *Korean Americans and Their Religions: Pilgrims and Missionaries from a Different Shore.* College Park, Penn.: Penn State University Press.

Kitano, Harry. 1976. *Japanese Americans: The Evolution of a Subculture,* 2d ed. Englewood Cliffs, N.J.: Prentice-Hall.

Korean Association of New York. 1985. *History of the Korean Association of New York.* New York: Korean Association of New York.

Light, Ivan. 1984. "Immigrant and Ethnic Enterprise in North America." *Ethnic and Racial Studies* 7:195–216.

Light, Ivan, and Elizabeth Roach. 1996. "Self-Employment: Mobility Ladder and Economic Lifeboat." In Roger Waldinger and Mehdi Bozorgmehr, eds., *Ethnic Los Angeles,* pp. 193–214. New York: Russell Sage Foundation.

Liu, John, Paul Ong, and Carolyn Rosenstein. 1991. "Dual Chain Migration: Post-1965 Filipino Migration." *International Migration Review* 25:487–513.

Lyman, Stanford. 1974. *Chinese Americans.* New York: Random House.

Min, Pyong Gap. 1984. "From White-Collar Occupations to Small Business: Korean Immigrants' Occupational Adjustment." *Sociological Quarterly* 25:333–52.

——. 1988. "Korean Immigrant Entrepreneurship: A Multivariate Analysis." *Journal of Urban Affairs* 10:197–212.

——. 1990. "Problems of Korean Immigrant Entrepreneurs." *International Migration Review* 24:436–55.

——. 1991. "Cultural and Economic Boundaries of Korean Ethnicity: A Comparative Analysis." *Ethnic and Racial Studies* 14:225–41.

——. 1992. "The Structure and Social Functions of Korean Immigrant Churches in the United States." *International Migration Review* 26:1370–94.

——. 1995. "Korean Immigrants and Their Entrepreneurial Adaptation." In Silvia Pedraza and Ruben Rumbaut, eds., *Origins and Destinies: Immigration, Race, and Ethnicity in the United States.* Belmont, Calif.: Wadsworth.

——. 1996. *Caught in the Middle: Korean Immigrants in New York and Los Angeles.* Berkeley: University of California Press.

——. 1998. *Changes and Conflicts: Korean Immigrant Families in New York.* Boston: Allyn and Bacon.

——. 1999. "The Intergenerational Transmission of Religion and Ethnicity: Korean Immigrants in New York." Paper presented at the annual meeting of the Metropolitan Conference. Washington, D.C., October.

——. 2000a. "Korean Americans' Language Use." In Sandra Lee McKay and Sau-Ling Cynthia Wang, eds., *New Immigrants in the United States: Readings for Second Language Educators,* pp. 306–32. Cambridge: Cambridge University Press.

——. 2000b. "Religion and Ethnicity: A Comparison of Indian Hindu and Korean Christian Immigrants." *Bulletin of the Royal Institute for Inter-Faith Studies* 2:121–40.

Min, Pyong Gap, and Andrew Kolodny. 1994. "The Middleman Minority Characteristics of Korean Immigrants in the United States." *Korea Journal of Population and Development* 23:179–202.

New York City Department of City Planning. 1992. *Demographic Profiles: City's Community Districts from the 1980 & 1990 Censuses of Population and Housing.* New York: New York City Department of City Planning.

Ong, Paul, and John Liu. 1994. "U.S. Immigration Policies and Asian Migration." In Paul Ong, Edna Bonacich, and Lucie Cheng, eds., *The New Asian Immigration in Los Angeles and Global Restructuring,* pp. 45–73. Philadelphia: Temple University Press.

Palmer, Mabel. 1957. *The History of Indians in Natal.* Natal Regional Survey, vol.10. Cape Town: Oxford University Press.

Park, In-Sook Han, and Lee-Jay Cho. 1995. "Confucianism and the Korean Family." *Journal of Contemporary Family Studies* 26:117–34.

Park, In-Sook Han, James Fawcett, Fred Arnold, and Robert Gardner. 1990. *Korean Immigrants to the United States: A Pre-Departure Analysis.* Papers of the East-West Population Institute no. 114. Honolulu, Hawaii: Population Institute, East-West Center.

Park, Kyeyoung. 1997. *The Korean American Dream: Immigrants and Small Business in New York City.* Ithaca, N.Y.: Cornell University Press.

Porter, Jack N. 1981. "The Urban Middleman: A Comparative Analysis." *Comparative Social Research* 4:199–215.

Rinder, Irwin. 1958–59. "Stranger in the Land: Social Relations in the Status Gap." *Social Problems* 6:253–60.

Rosenthal, Elizabeth. 1995. "Competition and Cutbacks Hurt Foreign Doctors in the U.S." *The New York Times,* November 7.

Shin, Eui-Hang, and K.S. Chang. 1988. "Peripherization of Immigrant Professionals: Korean Physicians in the United States." *International Migration Review* 22:609–26.

Shin, Eui-Hang, and Hyung Park. 1988. "An Analysis of Causes of Schisms in Ethnic Churches: The Case of Korean American Churches." *Sociological Analysis* 49:234–48.

Shin, Eui-Hang, and Eui-Young Yu. 1984. "Use of Surname in Ethnic Research: The Case of Kim in the Korean-American population." *Demography* 21:347–59.

U.S. Bureau of the Census. 1993. 1990 *Census of Population, General Population Characteristics, New York* (CP-1–27). Washington, D.C.: U.S. Government Printing Office.

Waldinger, Roger. 1989. "Structural Opportunity or Ethnic Advantage? Immigrant Business Development in New York." *International Migration Review* 23:48–72.

Yoon, In-Jin. 1991. "The Changing Significance of Ethnic and Class Resources in Immigrant Businesses: The Case of Korean Immigrant Businesses in Chicago." *International Migration Review* 25:303–32.

Zenner, Walter. 1991. *Minorities in the Middle: A Cross-Cultural Analysis.* Albany, N.Y.: SUNY Press.

Jamaicans: Balancing Race and Ethnicity

Milton Vickerman

O ver the past four decades, more than half a million Jamaicans have migrated to the United States, the majority settling in New York City. Jamaicans, along with other West Indian immigrants, have put a distinctive stamp on several of the city's neighborhoods, which have taken on a definite West Indian flavor.[1] In Crown Heights, East Flatbush, The North Bronx, and Laurelton, visitors sometimes feel as if they are in Kingston, Bridgetown, or Port of Spain. The people on the street speak English with a West Indian accent, restaurants advertise patties and roti, and calypso and reggae music blare from car radios. Because of their large numbers, because they are concentrated in particular neighborhoods, and because of their race and distinctive culture, West Indians are having a decided impact on race relations in the city. In turn, their own lives are affected by American society's perception and treatment of blacks. Race—a social identity based on perceived physical features—takes on a whole new meaning for West Indians when they move to the United States. This chapter focuses on Jamaicans, the largest segment of the West Indian immigrant population. I argue that Jamaicans' adaptation to American society is strongly influenced by contradictory pressures—or cross-pressures—

generated by the conflicting demands of holding both a racial identity and a cultural (or ethnic) identity. These cross-pressures and Jamaicans' economic activities determine their place in New York City.

This essay is based on two studies I conducted, one in the 1980s, the other in the 1990s. Between 1988 and 1990, I interviewed, at length, a nonrandom ("snowball") sample of 106 male Jamaican immigrants in New York City. Mainly, I conducted these in-depth interviews in the respondents' homes, although I did some in their workplaces, in my own home, and in other settings such as churches. The respondents, who ranged in age from twenty-two to seventy-two, had lived in the United States an average of 11.5 years. Sixty were in white-collar occupations, forty-six in blue-collar work. I also draw on a study I conducted in 1999 with a snowball sample of thirty-seven second-generation West Indians who were interviewed using a structured questionnaire.[2] Most of the second-generation West Indians originally came from New York City. I should note that I am a Jamaican immigrant, and this background (as a Jamaican New Yorker) has, I believe, deepened my understanding of the Jamaican migrant experience.

Migration Patterns

Jamaicans and other West Indians have a long history of migrating to other countries in the search for a better life (Palmer 1990:3). This is not surprising. West Indians come from societies with small, resource-poor economies that are very dependent on more developed societies. Income, wealth, and land are distributed very unequally, and their societies are marked by high levels of unemployment. At the same time, because of tourism, the proximity of North America, and the predominance of America media throughout the region, West Indians are well aware of American affluence and American standards of living. Moreover, U.S. and Canadian investment in the region, as well as the American economy's demand for individuals with particular skills, have also contributed to the flow from the West Indies. In fact, migration is a "flight" response that has become ingrained in the culture of West Indian societies (Brodber 1989). This includes not only internal migration from rural to urban areas, but—much more significant—international migration. Once begun, migration also is network driven, a dynamic that is reinforced by the family reunification provisions of U.S. immigration law.

Large-scale Jamaican migration to the United States dates from the beginning of the twentieth century, with these nationals predominating among the 138,615 West Indians who migrated to this country from 1899 to 1928 (Reid 1939:235).[3] New York City—especially Harlem in the first third of the twentieth century— was the destination of choice. The Great Depression virtually halted emigration from Jamaica, but after World War II, several thousand Jamaicans—along with other West Indians—migrated to Britain. This movement to the "mother country" was severely curbed when the British government passed the Commonwealth Immigration Act in 1961. Not long after, in 1965, the Hart-Celler Immigration Act shifted West Indian immigration back to the United States, ushering in the present wave, which still is going strong.

A look at data from the U.S. Immigration and Naturalization Service (INS) shows the dramatic increase in numbers after the 1965 Immigration Act. In the ten years before 1965, approximately 1,500 Jamaicans per year migrated to the United States; in the decade 1966–1975, Jamaican immigration averaged 12,400 annually. Between 1976 and 1985, the numbers increased further, to about 18,000 per year, in large part a result of the political turmoil, high crime rate, and economic recession that characterized Jamaica through much of the 1970s and into the early 1980s.[4] Although the crime rate has declined and the political situation on the island is more stable, the difficulties of making a living continued to lead large numbers of Jamaicans to migrate in the 1990s. One reflection of these difficulties is that the overall Jamaican unemployment rate averaged 16 percent between January 1997 and April 1999. The situation is far worse for women than for men in that 23 percent of Jamaican females but only 10 percent of Jamaican males experienced unemployment during this time (Statistical Institute of Jamaica 1999a, 199b). Quite likely, this marked difference in unemployment rates helps account for the fact that the post-1965 immigration includes a higher proportion of women than men; on the receiving end, it has also often been easier for female immigrants to obtain jobs than men—especially as domestics (see, for example, Foner 1998).

Presently, immigration from Jamaica to the United States continues at a high level. In 1998, 15,146 Jamaicans officially migrated to this country—a figure that placed Jamaicans as the eighth-largest group admitted that year and the largest of all West Indian groups. Considering Jamaica's small size, this figure is particularly impressive. An examination of Jamaica's immigration rate (the number of legal immigrants divided by the nation's population) shows that it far outstrips the rate of other large sending countries. In 1992, for example, China's immigration rate stood at 33 per 10,000 of the Chinese population; Jamaica's immigration rate was 76. Only Guyana, at 113 per 10,000, had a higher immigration rate (Heer 1996:86–88). Bear in mind that INS figures underestimate the number of Jamaicans in the United States since they include only legal immigrants. The INS estimates that in 1996, 50,000 Jamaicans resided in the United States illegally. Overall, in that year, at least 300,000 foreign-born Jamaicans lived in the United States.[5]

Although New York City does not draw as many new Jamaican immigrants as it used to, it remains the destination of choice for most Jamaicans who move to the United States. Between 1990 and 1994, 40 percent of Jamaican immigrants settled in New York City, compared to 50 percent in the 1972–1979 period (New York City Department of City Planning 1996, 1999). In the late 1990s, according to census data, some 150,000 foreign-born Jamaicans— approximately half of all Jamaicans in the United States—were living in the five boroughs. Most congregate in the West Indian enclaves of Crown Heights and Flatbush in Brooklyn, in The

North Bronx, and in sections of eastern Queens (Crowder 1999). Occupationally, Jamaican New Yorkers are heavily concentrated in service-sector jobs. English facility has clearly given Jamaicans, and other West Indians, advantages over non-English-speaking immigrants in competing for personal service, clerical, and re-tailing jobs. Health care is a major employer, particularly of women. In 1990, of the Jamaican women aged 16–65 in New York City who reported an occupation to the census, nearly a third were in the health care field as nurses' aides, orderlies, attendants, or nurses. Many Jamaican women are also found in clerical jobs or as domestic workers. Jamaican men are much less occupationally concentrated than women and are found in a variety of jobs including security guards, truck drivers, construction workers, janitors, and carpenters (see Kasinitz and Vickerman forth-coming for a fuller account of Jamaicans' role in New York's economy).

A few words are in order about the serial migration pattern that characterizes the movement of Jamaicans to New York. Typically, one spouse moves to New York first and then sends for other family members after becoming established in the city. This migration pattern has implications for immigrants in New York as well as those left behind. When a parent migrates, children are often left in the care of the nonmigrating spouse or with extended family members. To help care for these children and family remaining in Jamaica, Jamaicans routinely send back large barrels stocked with food, clothing, and consumer items ranging from bat-teries to television sets. In fact, a whole industry catering to shipping barrels to Jamaica (and elsewhere in the West Indies) has grown up in New York's West Indian neighborhoods. Although serial migration clearly evolved as an adaptation to economic necessity, because usually it's not feasible for all the members of a Jamaican family to migrate at once, and as a consequence of U.S. immigration law that emphasizes family reunification, the fact is that the pattern has drawbacks. It ends up splitting apart families for indeterminate lengths of time, ranging from months to years. Marriages often dissolve as spouses grow apart from each other. And the effects on children can be devastating since they may feel abandoned and develop behavioral problems. Indeed, these problems may continue after children migrate to New York because emotional bonds with parents are often strained when families reunite after years of separation (see Prescod-Roberts 1980; Palmer 1990; Bonnett 1990; Moses 1996).

Race and Ethnicity in New York City

Jamaicans' racial identity as "blacks"—at least in the terms that race is thought of in the United States—and American society's focus on black skin color have criti-cal implications in shaping Jamaicans' sense of themselves, and their social rela-tions, in New York. Indeed, the interaction of Jamaicans' race and their ethnicity creates cross-pressures that influence all aspects of their lives.[6] The concept of cross-pressures refers to situations in which individuals find themselves being pulled in opposite directions, simultaneously, by forces that are equally powerful.

Because they are subject to cross-pressures concerning race, influenced by both homeland views and American views of race, their behavior is hard to predict. In some situations, their attitudes and behavior are dictated by values and beliefs they bring with them from home; in other situations, they are influenced by new notions about race that they confront in New York.

Among Jamaicans—and West Indians in general—cross-pressures are created on the one hand by their socialization in a society that deemphasizes race and extols achievement as a cultural ideal, especially through education. This ideal, although only partially realizable, is strongly held by many Jamaicans and shapes their aspirations for themselves and their children (see, for example, Smith 1965; Foner 1973; Kuper 1976; Austin 1987). The process of immigration tends to strengthen this idealization of achievement by selecting out those Jamaicans who are most motivated. Moreover, the growth of distinct West Indian enclaves in New York City in recent years has allowed Jamaicans and other West Indians greater opportunities than in the past to replicate West Indian culture in New York City. In short, Jamaican immigrants in New York City tend to be individuals who have been shaped by the peculiar history, culture, and social structure of their homeland to view life as a series of challenges that, with enough self-effort, can be overcome to attain success at the end. However, once they arrive in America, many Jamaicans find that race presents a much greater challenge than anything they have been accustomed to. They begin to understand that being "black" is perceived much more negatively here than in Jamaica. The gradual and painful process of learning, firsthand, about everyday discrimination against blacks is the other side of the cross-pressures equation. Whereas Jamaica's history, culture, and social structure, and the very act of immigration, lead Jamaicans to idealize achievement, the realization that blacks—including Jamaicans—experience routine discrimination in the United States makes them understand that this achievement cannot be divorced from the larger struggle for social justice for all blacks.

The Jamaican Background

To better understand the nature of the cross-pressures that Jamaican immigrants experience, it is helpful to briefly examine the factors in Jamaica that have shaped their ideas about race and the kind of ethnic identity they bring with them to New York. Essentially, cross-pressures for Jamaican immigrants develop because Jamaican society deemphasizes ascribed characteristics—race being the most important one—and stresses achievement through education. That this should be the case is ironic given Jamaica's history. Historically, race has been central to Jamaican society because Jamaica developed as a plantation colony based on African slavery, and even after emancipation, the British dominated the political and economic order for over a century more. This long period of imperial domination left its mark on a social structure in which blacks have long been subordinated— as slaves until 1834 and afterward as a struggling peasant class. The social structure resembled a pyramid in which subordinated blacks—the mass of the population—formed the base, and a small white elite enjoyed wealth, power, and prestige. In between these two groups was a mulatto group that, though of mixed biological ancestry, was culturally European (Lewis 1968; Curtin 1970). The Jamaican population also contains three other minority groups—Jews and other people of Middle Eastern descent, Chinese, and East Indians.

Although slavery in Jamaica led to the development of antiblack stereotypes and discrimination, these have not been as all-encompassing as those experienced by African Americans. In fact, powerful forces in Jamaica have tended to offset black subordination in such a way as to make race seem unimportant. First, from a demographic point of view, blacks far outnumber any other group on the island, constituting anywhere from 75 percent to 90 percent of the population.[7] This demographic dominance by blacks is very significant, in that it means that the average Jamaican is accustomed to seeing blacks at all social levels—from prime ministers to homeless people on the street. Moreover, since World War II blacks have increasingly been upwardly mobile because of foreign investment in Jamaica and the gaining of independence from Britain in 1962. Because of these realities, Jamaicans tend not to link achievement with race. Also, demographic dominance of the population means that Jamaicans see black skin as "normal," in the way that white skin is "normal" in America. It also means that present-day Jamaicans do not usually experience the blatant discrimination that was more apparent in Jamaica under colonialism and that blacks in the United States still routinely face.

In addition to demographics, a second important factor deemphasizes race in Jamaica: political leaders officially promulgate the notion that Jamaica is a diverse society in which different races coexist peacefully. The most concrete manifestation of this is the national motto: "Out of many, one people." The Jamaican political system reinforces these sentiments because it is based on a two-party model that draws its strength from a coalition of different classes. The system studiously avoids appeals to race, thereby helping to prevent the subject from becoming a public issue (see, for example, Stone 1972, 1973; Nettleford 1978; Palmer 1989). The other side of this official subordination of race is the institutionalization of education as the major means for attaining upward mobility. In the Jamaican context this refers not simply to book learning but also to characteristics such as speaking standard English, good grooming, and being law abiding. The main importance of "education" so conceived is that despite its obvious ideological connotations, many—if not most—Jamaicans accept and try to practice this cultural ideal (see, for example, Norris 1962; Kuper 1976).

A third factor also serves to downplay race in Jamaica. Unlike in the United States, Jamaicans never accepted the view that race is a question of being "black" or "white"; nor have they embraced a "one-drop rule" that posits that all individuals of even remote African ancestry are "black." Instead, as noted before, the mixed-race segment of the population has always been accepted as distinct from either blacks or whites. Moreover, in defining race, Jamaicans have tended to consider not simply physical features but also ancestry, education, social class, occupation, and wealth (see, for example, Henriques 1957). A person with dark skin who is highly educated, is wealthy, and holds a prestigious occupation is recognized for these characteristics—and is not stigmatized on the basis of his or her skin color. This multifaceted approach is reflected in a tendency to focus on skin shade instead of differences between distinct "racial" groups. The upshot is that despite Jamaica's history of subordinating its majority black population, Jamaicans generally dislike viewing the world in racial terms. An unspoken taboo exists about speaking out forcefully on racial issues, and individuals who break this taboo find themselves subject to harsh criticism (see, for example, Nettleford 1978; Post 1978).

Jamaican Ethnicity in New York City

Jamaican immigrants' ethnic identity in New York City is strongly conditioned by their premigration experiences in Jamaica and their concentration in New York neighborhoods with other West Indian immigrants. Their sense of "Jamaican-ness" overlaps, to a great extent, with a sense of being West Indian. For instance, in my research many respondents used the term "Jamaican" and "West Indian" interchangeably. That they continually rub shoulders with other West Indians in New York City—especially those from the English-speaking Caribbean—shows Jamaicans their commonalities with these other West Indians. Whereas in the West Indies people often think of themselves in nationalistic terms as "Jamaicans," "Barbadians," or "Trinidadians," in New York City the similarities between these groups become very evident. The reality that Jamaicans share a common history, language, and university[8] as well as cultural elements with other Anglophone Caribbean immigrants, combined with their living in the same New York neighborhoods, creates a feeling that, in New York City, cultural differences among West Indians pale in comparison to their cultural similarities. Perhaps the single best example of this shared sense of ethnicity is the annual Labor Day parade along Eastern Parkway in Brooklyn, which draws participants from every country in the West Indies. The flip side of the coalescing of a West Indian identity is the realization that Jamaicans and other West Indians differ, in significant ways, from African Americans, whites, and other groups.

The most important element in Jamaican (and West Indian) ethnicity in New York City is a self-perception that Jamaicans are hard-working, goal-oriented, success-driven individuals—in short, achievers. At the same time, because of their premigration experiences, Jamaicans often wish to downplay race. It is not that they try to shy away from their African ancestry. Rather, they usually try to point out that they have a different, more positive, view of what it means to be "black" than Americans. Whereas Americans often have a generalized negative view of "blackness," Jamaicans are accustomed to seeing blacks occupy all levels of their society and, especially among recent immigrants, they tend not to perceive race as a bar to upward mobility. Indeed, the process of migration usually causes Jamaicans to focus very intently on achieving upward mobility and, consequently, they often view American society's tendency to consider race first as being a hindrance to their goals. The opinions of one middle-aged engineer are a good example of these orientations. He expressed disgust at the prevalence of racial stereotyping of blacks in America and argued, instead, that people should be judged strictly on the basis of their qualifications:

> I think a man should be qualified for a job. . . . I don't want a job because I'm black. I want a job because I'm qualified. . . . If you make an application here [for a job], they want to know your race. What the hell with my race! I feel right away that you're going to judge me off of that and I am at a disadvantage there. I'm a man! Do I have the qualifications? That [is what] you must find out.

This emphasis on qualifications is typical of Jamaican immigrants and consistent with Jamaican society's stress on education as the legitimate means for attaining upward mobility. Another respondent—a chemist—put the situation this way:

> I think we [West Indians] refuse . . . to really get caught up in the whole racial issue . . . although we are being treated the same way racially. Our thing is . . . to forge ahead just the same. . . . Since . . . we . . . grow up . . . [with] a more socioeconomic issue in the West Indies—we are not that sensitive to racism; although some, you know, is pretty blatant that you just can't refuse from knowing that it is racism.

Jamaicans measure achievement in New York City in educational, occupational, and material terms; not only in comparison to others in America but, perhaps more importantly, in comparison to Jamaican standards. In other words, they always compare where they are now with where they were, or could have been, in Jamaica. Because of this (recall Jamaica's high unemployment rates), despite the hard work that is necessary to get ahead in New York City, many Jamaicans believe that migrating to New York City was the right decision. To some extent, official data support this optimism. According to 1990 census data, the median household income of New York resident Jamaicans stood at $45,088 compared to $30,700 for African Americans.[9] However, it is important to note that these data hide a great deal of variation. Not all Jamaicans are doing well economically in New York, and no doubt what accounts for the relatively high Jamaican figure is the many people working in each family. For Jamaican immigrants home ownership is the most tangible sign of economic success. In 1990, according to the census, nearly a third of Jamaican New Yorkers were home owners (Grasmuck and Grosfoguel 1997), and indeed some of the people I interviewed prided themselves on owning several houses. Not surprisingly, Jamaicans in The North Bronx and eastern Queens, who are better off economically than their compatriots in Brooklyn, are also more likely to own their own homes.[10]

Another important aspect of Jamaican ethnicity is a tendency toward conservatism on social issues. This dovetails with Jamaicans' general desire to deemphasize race and, to some extent, stems from the colonial-influenced values that have become ingrained in Jamaican culture.[11] This social conservatism is ironic because of the common portrayal of Jamaicans as hedonists and troublemakers, but it manifests itself in a variety of ways.[12] For instance, their attitudes toward law and order issues tend to be conservative, since Jamaican culture emphasizes respect for authorities and the police. This reflects the need under colonialism— and in present-day Jamaica—to manage conflict between "haves" and "have-nots" (manifested in high crime rates) in a society with high levels of social inequality.[13] State-sanctioned violence (i.e., police violence) has been one way of accomplishing this goal;[14] patronage, directed toward the lower classes through the established political parties, has been another. Socialization to accept the status quo has been a third, and very significant, mechanism for containing social conflict, and respect for law and order has been a crucial component of this socialization. Of course, such socialization is more readily apparent among middle- and upper-class Jamaicans, and the prevalence of poverty means that many poorer Jamaicans continually challenge the legitimacy of the status quo. Nevertheless, the society also socializes these Jamaicans to respect the status quo, and the measure of the success of this socialization—and of the other means for suppressing social conflict—is Jamaica's relative stability as a society.[15] Some of the Jamaicans I interviewed displayed a decidedly law-and-order bent when they argued that some young Jamaicans who had migrated in the 1980s were ruining the image of Jamaicans through their criminal activities. In the view of these respondents, the police rightly target such individuals for prosecution.

A second example of Jamaicans' social conservatism is that male Jamaican immigrants often hold a "traditional" view of family life since they perceive themselves as heads of their households and expect their wives to do such household chores as cooking, washing, and cleaning. Though not as easy to link to colonial-influenced values, these attitudes are definitely premigration in origin. As in Jamaica, male Jamaican immigrants expect their partners to do household chores (see, for example, Osofsky 1966:134). These attitudes came through when some of my respondents complained that American women are too "independent minded" and not good housekeepers. Note, however, that Jamaican women's roles are more complex than the men I spoke to indicate. In Jamaica, women have a long tradition of working outside the home, although they are expected to perform "women's work" in the home. Though male immigrants have the same expectations of their female partners in this country, immigration tends to give Jamaican women more autonomy relative to men—especially since they often migrate first. Women's increased income in New York (relative to Jamaica) translates into greater power within the household, and this, in turn, can cause conflict within immigrant families where males experience difficulty adjusting to their partners' new status (see, e.g., Foner 1986; Bonnett 1990; Gordon 1990; cf. Hondagneu-Sotelo 1994).

Jamaicans' conservative social values also come out in parents' expectations and treatment of their children. The prevailing attitude among Jamaican immigrant parents is that children should be seen and not heard, and, contrary to American mainstream values, corporal punishment is seen as an appropriate, indeed a desirable, disciplinary tool. As one second-generation Jamaican high school student put it: "West Indian parents do not tolerate . . . raising your voice [to them]. . . . You must respect your elders and things of that nature—no matter what: always respect them." Not surprisingly, parents' attempt to maintain this kind of "traditional" authority and to transfer "old-world" values to children often leads to conflict within immigrant families, particularly since the children generally have an attenuated relationship with Jamaican culture and in some cases have been separated from their parents for long periods.

The Impact of Race

Jamaican immigrants' ethnic identity in New York City develops within the context of a society that is highly racialized. In fact, to a large extent, their ethnic identity develops in response to American society's racialization, as they attempt to distance themselves from unflattering assumptions about blacks. In reaction to racism, ethnic identity becomes an alternative avenue of self-definition. The problem is that Jamaicans can only partially extract themselves from American society's generalized negative view of blacks. Even Jamaicans who have lived in the United States for many years have trouble coming to terms with the fact that their skin color has such a negative impact on their daily lives and aspirations. Although, as I have noted, antiblack stereotypes exist in Jamaica, they are relatively mild and have been weakening with time because of the self-confidence engendered by—among other things—black numerical and political dominance, a culture that preaches self-reliance, and the cultural force of strong problack ideologies such as Rastafarianism and Garveyism. Race, in Jamaica, is not a publicly debated issue; in the United States, race is a public and pressing question. Blacks are a minority group in this country (and in New York City), and, whereas Jamaicans define "blackness" loosely, Americans adhere to a much stricter definition. Perhaps most problematic is that while Jamaicans do not associate race with achievement, Americans tend to view blacks as low achievers. This is particularly painful because the idea that Jamaicans are achievers lies at the core of their ethnic identity in this country.

Because of these contrasts in ideas and experiences with race in Jamaica and the United States, many Jamaicans I interviewed expressed puzzlement, frustration, and even astonishment at their encounters with racism in New York. As other writers have noted, Jamaicans often do not realize what it means to be "black" until they migrate to America; this, of course, refers to the stronger negative sentiments attached to African ancestry in this country compared to Jamaica (see, for example, Foner 1987). As one Jamaican letter writer to the ethnic newspaper the *Jamaica Weekly Gleaner* put it:

> "I'm Jamaican," I say. To which the response is, "But . . . aren't you Chinese?" Well, yes, but what has that got to do with being Jamaican? Jamaicans have a rich heritage, with ancestors of many nations, including Europe, China, Africa, and India. But we have mixed and integrated in such a way that no matter what our color, our primary identity is Jamaican. . . . In fact, most Caribbean people are hardly even aware of racism in their everyday lives. As one Caribbean woman put it, "Imagine, I had to come all the way to Canada to discover I was Black!"[16]

I encountered similar sentiments in my research. For instance, a young computer programmer told me:

> Race was important [in Jamaica] but not on a day-to-day basis. The difference I find is that when you get to America, you have to start thinking about race when you walk into the store. . . . In Manhattan you walk into a store; you'll find that people will be following you around. Things like that you have never been accustomed to. To me, what has been a shocker here is to walk on the train and for women to clutch their handbags. . . . That has been, to me, my worst problem to overcome since I have been here.

Another respondent—a truck driver—put it this way: "I am just here four years now [and] . . . I am going to honestly tell you—America is not what I expected. . . . I am having a problem getting adjusted to the American system, per se. Because up here . . . the lifestyle that is America is not me, honestly. . . . It might be too fast for me or maybe it's the city I am in. Maybe it's because I am in New York."

These sentiments result from frequent episodes of antiblack racism—ranging from subtle to blatant—that Jamaicans encounter in New York City.[17] Subtle racism is problematic because it is difficult to prove or to fight. Nevertheless, many of the Jamaican men I interviewed complained that people avoided them on the street or that women clutched their purses when they approached. They also complained of being watched in stores and of being glared at when, on account of their jobs, they found themselves in white neighborhoods. My Jamaican respondents spoke of more blatant discrimination as well—being refused service in public places and threatened or assaulted for racial reasons. (They were certain that race was the motive for the incidents of violence that they reported because their attackers preceded the incidents with racial insults.)[18] Some men reported being stopped and issued racial insults by the police; many feared that such encounters could result in physical abuse, and as a result they tended to be wary of the police.[19]

For most of the Jamaican men in my study, the most troubling form of racism involved discrimination in the workplace. Such racism directly attacks their economic well-being, the main reason for migrating to the United States. It also directly attacks an aspect of their ethnicity on which they pride themselves: their competence because of qualifications. Because they come from a society that puts so much stress on educational and occupational qualifications for attaining upward mobility, Jamaicans find it very galling when, despite their qualifications, they are discriminated against in New York. Among my Jamaican respondents, racial incidents in the workplace varied in detail, but all left a bitter taste. For instance, one accountant reported being fired because he refused to sanction his company's discrimination against its lower-level black employees. Another—the truck driver I mentioned earlier—told me of confrontations with his immediate superior over the latter's treatment of black customers. Still other Jamaicans reported being denied promotions for racial reasons. One man summarized the reasons for his difficulties in obtaining promotion: "I was doing the work but I would be in charge of all whites. . . . They didn't want me to do that."

Jamaicans' Impact on New York City

The influx of several hundred thousand Jamaican immigrants has obviously had a significant impact on New York City. New West Indian neighborhoods have emerged—and are expanding. And the growing Jamaican and West Indian presence in the city has consequences for race and ethnic relations, for the economy, and for the dynamics of New York City politics.

Relations with African Americans

The conflicting demands of holding an ethnic identity as Jamaicans/West Indians and a racial identity as blacks—the cross-pressures I have referred to—particularly affect relations with African Americans. The effects of cross-pressures show up most clearly in Jamaicans' tendency to alternate between distancing themselves from and identifying with black Americans. While much has been made of apparent conflicts between these two groups—and certainly they do exist—the conflicts have to be understood within the context of a society that discriminates against all people of African ancestry. In fact, Jamaicans and other West Indians also feel strong solidarity with African Americans on many issues.

First, consider the distancing side of the equation. For Jamaicans, cross-pressures are particularly acute because most Americans make few distinctions among people of African ancestry, regardless of their origins. In response to this, Jamaicans assert their ethnic identity to show that they are different from African Americans. Some Jamaicans even assert that they are "superior" to African Americans.

Typically, distancing centers around questions of race and achievement, personal behavior, and family issues. My Jamaican respondents often stressed that they differ from many African Americans, especially poorer ones, in being hard and consistent workers. They also claimed that they make the most of the opportunities for upward mobility that present themselves in America. Moreover, they expressed disdain for welfare and were critical of those young blacks—including West Indians—who commit crimes. With respect to family issues, as I have noted, Jamaicans, particularly Jamaican men, emphasize traditional gender roles, arguing that Americans in general—including African Americans—have too readily abandoned these roles. The result, in their view, has been a breakdown in the traditional family.[20] In fact, most of the Jamaicans I interviewed had married women from Jamaica or other parts of the West Indies.

Despite these beliefs, a number of factors also bring West Indians and African Americans together. Strong cultural affinities exist between the two groups. For instance, black American music, both popular and religious, has long been popular in Jamaica;[21] the Black Power movement exercised a powerful influence on Jamaican young people in the 1960s; and American heroes of the black struggle against discrimination such as Martin Luther King Jr. and Malcolm X are widely admired in Jamaica (see, for example, Palmer 1989).

Even more important than these cultural affinities are the firsthand experiences of racial discrimination that Jamaicans encounter in New York City. Jamaicans and African Americans tend to live in the same neighborhoods—that in itself largely a result of discrimination in the housing market—and commingle to form close friendships. They experience similar episodes of racial discrimination in public (see, for example, Feagin and Sikes 1994; Vickerman 1999) and from the police, and both groups often perceive important social institutions—e.g., the media—as being biased against blacks. In short, Jamaicans find that usually, race trumps ethnicity. Indeed, the longer Jamaicans live in the United States, and thus the longer they are exposed to racial discrimination, the more they identify with African Americans (although they still maintain a sense of distinctiveness as West Indians). One powerful demonstration of this emerged in my research when Jamaicans who were longtime residents of New York City expressed scathing criticism of coethnics who disparage African Americans. They explained that living in a society pervaded with antiblack attitudes and experiencing discrimination had led them to reevaluate their premigration attitudes about race. As one Jamaican put it: "Some of us . . . say we are different . . . but don't fool yourself, you are judged basically on this [skin color]. . . . So I don't . . . get carried away; say, well, I am West Indian, I am treated differently. That's nonsensical!"

As for second-generation Jamaicans, they feel a closer identification with African Americans than their immigrant parents because they are American by birth and because they have assimilated into the African American community. This assimilation is not tension free, since Jamaican immigrants, seeking to counter antiblack stereotypes, try to transmit their own emphasis on achievement and pride in their ethnic identity to their American-born children. However, research shows that these attempts are successful only when parents can solidify them by sending their children to good schools, which in the New York context usually means a magnet school or a parochial school.

On one hand, second-generation Jamaicans who end up attending substandard and racially segregated inner-city schools typically become "American"-identified in the sense that they take on attitudes of discouragement that are prevalent among their impoverished African American peers. To protect themselves against racial discrimination, these Jamaicans identify as "black" and may adopt an adversarial stance toward whites. On the other hand, second-generation Jamaicans from better-off families who are able to go to good schools assimilate into the African American community more slowly, as their parents convince them of the advantages of maintaining a distinct Jamaican/West Indian identity. This happens because well-off West Indian immigrant parents exercise relatively greater influence over their children than do less-affluent West Indian parents, whose children are more influenced by their peers. Also, well-off parents can make a more plausible argument that if their children behave in certain ways, socioeconomic success will follow. These children observe that their parents often have prestigious jobs and therefore see obtaining similar jobs as a distinct possibility.[22] Like their parents, these ethnic-identified second-generation Jamaicans try to downplay race and stress achievement (Waters 1996; Vickerman 1999).[23] Inevitably, though, they do assimilate into the African American community, and this assimilation is apparent in their close friendships with African Americans, in their perception of racism as being an important (though not overpowering) issue, and in the way they identify themselves. In my research, most second-generation West Indians insisted that their American birth must be registered in their self-identity and identified themselves as "West Indian-American."[24]

Considerable cross-fertilization occurs between second-generation West Indians and African Americans on the level of popular culture. Two variants of reggae, especially—toasting[25] and dance-hall reggae—directly influenced the development of rap music in New York City, and several well-known hip-hop artists—including Busta Rhymes, Eric B, Heavy D, and Shinehead—trace their ancestry to Jamaica. Moreover, over the past few years, hip-hop artists such as the Fugees and Lauryn Hill (the mother of Bob Marley's grandchildren) have introduced a younger American audience to the music of classic reggae artists—notably Bob Marley—by performing cover versions of this music. At the same time, it should also be noted, rap is currently among the most popular musical genres in Jamaica (Manuel 1995; Goldman 2000).

Politics

Jamaicans have affected New York City politics in a number of ways: by swelling the size of the black population and by seeking to establish themselves, along with other West Indians, as a distinct ethnic voting bloc. Size is important in the shifting demographics of the city, which has seen the gradual rise in the minority population and the relative decline of the white population. In fact, New York City is now a majority-minority city, and West Indians have contributed to this change by their influx into the city in such large numbers. Overall, foreign-born West Indians comprise more than a quarter of New York City's black population.

The growth of New York City's West Indian population makes black politics more volatile. Because Jamaicans and other West Indians operate under cross-pressures, their political responses tend to be more variable than that of African Americans (Kasinitz 1987, 1992; Noel 1998). Admittedly, West Indians do often resemble African Americans in their voting patterns and in their support for candidates who they perceive will advance the interests of blacks as a group. Indeed, for much of their history, West Indian immigrant politicians have presented themselves not as West Indians but as blacks. Among the Jamaican immigrants I interviewed, approximately 75 percent identified themselves as Democrats and voiced strong support for black leaders such as Jesse Jackson and David Dinkins. Polling data show that in the 1989 mayoral elections, 90 percent of residents in highly West Indianized Crown Heights voted for Dinkins (McQueen 1989:6). The Jamaicans I studied advanced three main reasons for supporting black political leaders and the Democratic Party: Black candidates are especially sensitive to the needs of people of African ancestry, whatever their origin; West Indians are proud that blacks are attaining higher office; and Democrats tend to address issues—racial and economic issues, for example—that affect blacks.

Yet West Indians' political behavior does not simply echo that of most African American New Yorkers. Because West Indians tend toward social conservatism, they also feel pulled to issues—such as those relating to "family values" and "law and order"—that are often associated with Republicans.[26] Additionally (and like some African Americans), a minority of the Jamaicans I interviewed argued that bloc voting by blacks for the Democratic Party is counterproductive in that it eliminates the need for politicians to take black votes seriously. In addition, ethnic politics has become increasingly important in West Indian New York. The concentration of such large numbers of West Indians in city neighborhoods has opened up the possibility of political mobilization along ethnic lines (see Kasinitz 1992). A good example of this was the spirited 2000 Democratic primary race in the Eleventh Brooklyn Congressional District between Jamaican-born city councilwoman Una Clarke and the African American incumbent, Major Owens, which exposed fissures between the two communities (Hicks 2000).

West Indians use ethnic mobilization especially effectively when they perceive that their interests as West Indians are being threatened. A case in point occurred in 1996 when three separate laws, each of which contained negative repercussions for immigrants, were passed. The Antiterrorism and Effective Death Penalty Act of April 24 facilitated the easier removal of criminal aliens from the United States by, for instance, expanding the category of crimes of "moral turpitude" for which aliens can be deported. The Personal Responsibility and Work Opportunity Reconciliation Act of August 22 among other things barred most legal immigrants from obtaining Supplemental Security Income and food stamps; the Illegal Immigration Reform and Immigrant Responsibility Act of September 30 increased detention space for deportable aliens and instituted three- and ten-year bars to readmission for aliens deported for living in the country illegally.

Traditionally, Jamaican immigrants have adopted a casual attitude toward becoming citizens. Although they have intended to naturalize at some point, they often have not felt the need to rush the process. For instance, although 35 percent of the Jamaicans I interviewed had become citizens, they had taken an average of twelve years to do so once they were eligible (after five years of residence in the United States). One man had lived in the United States over thirty years before naturalizing. INS data show that 44 percent of the Jamaicans who naturalized in 1996 entered the country before 1985 (U.S. Immigration and Naturalization Service 1996). Many Jamaicans have a sentimental attachment to Jamaican citizenship (see Vaughn 1997:19)—and many are confused about the law, not knowing that Jamaicans can be dual citizens and therefore do not have to give up Jamaican citizenship if they naturalize. Also, some Jamaicans, like a few of the men in my study, deliberately avoid becoming citizens as a protest against racial discrimination

As the cumulative effect of the three 1996 immigration laws sank in, Jamaicans and other West Indians began to change their attitudes toward naturalization. Community activists urged West Indians to discard their ambivalence about naturalizing because citizenship is, among other things, protection against deportation and can potentially give West Indians more clout in city politics through the ballot box.[27] As one newspaper story in the ethnic press put it, West Indians "raise their families, pay taxes and make no demands on the elected officials. Because they do not vote in sufficient numbers, they do not command attention" (*Weekly Gleaner* 1995:19).[28] Just how effective the pronaturalization campaigns have been in the West Indian community is unclear, but more citizens means more voters—and thus more support for West Indian politicians. In fact, even before the mid-1990s, West Indian political power was on the rise, with the 1991 election of Una Clarke to the city council.

The Economic Impact of Jamaicans

Jamaican immigrants affect New York City economically by concentrating in distinct occupational niches. These niches have grown up over time and result from a complex combination of the skills, human capital, and cultural preferences they bring with them; the structures of opportunities available to them in the New York economy (including employer discrimination); and the operation of ethnic networks through which employment information and referrals flow (see Kasinitz and Vickerman forthcoming). Health care, as I mentioned, is a major ethnic niche for Jamaicans (especially women), as anyone who has spent time in a New York City hospital or nursing home knows well.

Private household workers, who care for affluent white New Yorkers' young children or see to the needs of New York's growing frail elderly population, are also often Jamaican or West Indian. A look at the domestic work niche clearly shows the effects of ethnic networking. Many Jamaicans who emigrated in the early days of the post-1965 influx were women who went into private household jobs. Sometimes these women were sponsored directly by white families, or they were induced to take domestic jobs by friends who were already working as domestics in the New York area. Once these Jamaicans were established, they typically passed on to their employers the names of relatives and friends (Jamaicans and other West Indians) who were also looking for private household work. This created networks of immigrant domestic workers that, despite the relative decline of this niche, have endured for long periods. These networks are sustained by the continued arrival of newcomers from Jamaica looking for work and by the close emotional and financial bonds that develop among West Indian domestics.[29] These bonds are often expressed in the formation of rotating credit associations ("partners" in Jamaican terminology), which give Jamaican immigrants ready access to small amounts of capital for emergencies, purchasing consumer items, or even funding businesses (see, e.g., Bonnett 1981; Kasinitz 1992; Johnson 1995; Louis 2000).

West Indians have created another niche for themselves in recent years—the jitney van industry, which provides a service to their own community. To some extent, New York jitney vans are a continuation of a West Indian tradition. In Jamaica and other parts of the West Indies, where public transportation is not as efficient as it should be, an alternate, privately owned transportation system has emerged consisting of small vans ("robots" in Jamaica) that ply the same routes as state-owned vehicles. In New York City, West Indians face a similar situation; New York City transit buses and trains are seen as expensive and not frequent or fast enough, especially in outlying areas of Brooklyn and Queens. To meet customer demand for better service, West Indian men have brought the concept of a privatized network of passenger vans to New York City.[30] Not surprisingly, given their large numbers and previous experience, many of these drivers are Jamaican. But if the jitney van industry illustrates immigrant initiative in the creation of occupational niches, it also illustrates the difficulties that can accompany such initiative. Jitney vans may be faster, cheaper, and more frequent than buses and trains, but they have also been criticized—even by some West Indian immigrants—as being unsafe. Consequently, the city council long resisted their legalization and van drivers have been subjected to police harassment, but the newfound political clout of West Indian politicians has led to the legalization of these vans (see, e.g., Tierney 1997:22; *Wall Street Journal* 1997; Dao 1999).

Although jitney drivers are an example of Jamaican self-employment, the fact is that Jamaicans have not gone into small business in a big way. Much has been made in the literature about the West Indian genius for business, but actually West Indians have very low rates of self-employment. According to 1990 census data, only 3 percent of New York City's West Indians are self-employed (and 4 percent of Jamaicans)—figures that are below the citywide average (5 percent) and not much higher than the rate for African Americans (2 percent) (Model 1999:17). That this should be the case makes sense in light of Jamaican history and culture, which, traditionally, have promoted education and the professions rather than small business ownership as the vehicle to upward mobility. Also, many Jamaicans report difficulty in obtaining credit, which they perceive as the result of racial discrimination. And racial segregation has concentrated most Jamaicans in the inner-city residential areas, with weak local markets and strong competition from other immigrants (Kasinitz and Vickerman forthcoming).

Finally, a word about whether employers discriminate in favor of Jamaicans—an issue that often comes up in the literature, partly because Jamaicans so often perceive this to be the case. My Jamaican respondents, for instance, often argued that employers favor them over African Americans because employers view Jamaicans as harder and more competent workers than African Americans (cf. Foner 1987).[31] Although evidence exists to support this position (see, for example, Kaufman 1995; Gladwell 1996; Waters 1999), it is also true that West Indians and African Americans often face similar obstacles in the labor force. As Waldinger (1996) has noted, in New York City's labor market, West Indians—especially males—and African Americans are generally more similar than different, and West Indians' ethnic niches only partially insulate them from racial discrimination. Moreover, as others have pointed out, some of the niches in which West Indians operate—for example, public-sector and personal service employment—are shrinking (see, for example, Johnson 1997; Model 1999). If, as some statistical indicators suggest, Jamaicans and other West Indians do well in New York's labor market, this probably stems less from positive discrimination than from their high labor force participation rate, high incidence of multiple family members in the workforce, the tendency for West Indians to hold multiple jobs, and an immigrant ethos that places a premium on achieving success in America. Census data for working-age immigrants in New York City show that in 1990, 81 percent of Jamaican men and 80 percent of Jamaican women were in the labor force, and a quarter of Jamaican households had three or more individuals in the labor force.

Conclusion

Jamaicans (like other West Indians) are still, in many ways, an invisible minority, often seen as part of the broader black population. Yet they are becoming an increasingly visible and important part of the fabric of New York City life. As I have argued in this chapter, dualities such as this are an intrinsic part of Jamaican life in the city. Sociologist Roy Bryce-Laporte put it well when he argued that "Black immigrants operate—as blacks and immigrants—in the United States under more levels of cross-pressures, multiple affiliations, and inequalities than either native blacks or European immigrants" (1972:48). The cross-pressures that Bryce-Laporte refers to, and that I emphasized throughout this chapter, stem from the intersection in the United States of contending Jamaican and American social patterns—especially the different views of what it means to be "black." Jamaicans are torn between the views of race they grew up with and the views of race they confront in New York.

As I have argued in this chapter, although race has always been important in Jamaica, powerful forces diminish its impact on daily life. These include the predominance of people of African ancestry in the population, which makes "blackness" "normal" the way "whiteness" is "normal" in the United States. Moreover, traditionally Jamaicans have focused their racial concerns on skin shade rather than on gross physical differences between people. Third, political ideology—especially in the postindependence period—consciously downplays race, in holding that Jamaica is a harmonious multiracial/multiethnic democracy. Furthermore, it posits that social inequality stems not from racial differences but rather from relative degrees of achievement—especially as manifested in educational attainment. Taken together, these factors mean that, for the most part, Jamaicans dislike conceiving of the world in racial terms; and to the extent that they do, they view race as complex and not an insuperable barrier to black achievement. In contrast to this muted view of race (as seen, for example, in little media discussion of the issue in Jamaica), race is a very public and pressing issue in America. In this country, Jamaican immigrants learn that African ancestry is more stigmatized than in Jamaica, and this stigma carries life-shaping consequences.

Because the most highly motivated and achievement-oriented Jamaicans are the ones who immigrate, the cross-pressures produced by these disparate views of race are particularly keenly felt by Jamaican New Yorkers. Cross-pressures shape who Jamaicans are in New York City, but Jamaicans also help shape the city, or, more accurately, the emerging city, because they are living in a New York with a steadily growing minority population. In fact, the new New York City is unprecedented in that, for the first time, the city's various minority groups now comprise the majority of the population (Waldinger 1996).

Along these lines, it is important to note that though present-day Jamaican migration to the city has declined relative to the 1980s, Jamaicans continue to migrate there in large numbers. Indeed, New York City remains the number-one destination for Jamaican immigrants. That this will continue to be the case stems from myriad factors, including Jamaica's continuing economic difficulties; the vibrant New York economy; the ease of travel between Jamaica and New York City; and the city's large, settled West Indian population (the largest in the United States), which helps to ease the difficult process of adjusting to life in America. Some writers view the latter two factors as particularly significant, since they show that West Indian immigration is increasingly transnational. In this view, immigration is becoming increasingly bidirectional, such that immigrants routinely engage in social and economic transactions that typically transcend national boundaries (see, for example, Sutton 1987; Schiller, Basch, and Szanton Blanc 1994; Portes, Guarnizo, and Landolt 1999).[32] An important implication of this is that transnationalism, by orienting immigrants back to their homelands, strengthens ethnicity and slows the process of assimilation. Among Jamaican immigrants, this would imply a strengthening of their ethnic identity as West Indians, as the size of their population grows through immigration.

The ramifications of these changing dynamics—demographic and immigrant— on New York City are unclear. As I have noted, in some ways Jamaicans and other minority groups seem destined to gain more freedom to express their distinctive ethnicities. But it also seems true that alongside this greater openness, people of African ancestry will continue experiencing many of the restraints that American society has always placed on them. The likelihood is that Jamaicans will continue to identify with the city's black population on many issues—indeed, second-generation Jamaicans assimilate into the black population. As sociologist Roger Waldinger (1996) has noted, the fates of West Indians and African Americans diverge only partially since, in fundamental ways, both are quite similar because of race. Jamaicans' lives in the New York City of the future will play out against the background of these polarizing and constraining forces.

Notes

1. By "West Indies" I am referring to the English-speaking islands in the Caribbean Sea and to territories in South America (Guyana) and Central America (Surinam and, to some extent, Panama) that are linked to these islands historically and culturally.

2. The second-generation individuals traced their ancestry to several Caribbean nations, including Jamaica, Guyana, Barbados, St. Marten, Grenada, Haiti, Trinidad and Tobago, and Panama. Averaging twenty-five years of age, 62 percent of the respondents were female, 85 percent were single, and 79 percent were college educated. Sixty-three percent identified themselves as "West Indian-American" and 60 percent came from families in which the annual household income was $55,000 or over. The telephone interviews (only one interview was face-to-face) were tape-recorded (with permission) and, on average, lasted about forty minutes each, although some went on much longer. Twenty-six of the respondents were originally from New York City, and the others lived in Glen Ridge, Long Island; Los Angeles; New Jersey; and Washington, D.C. The parents of these second-generation respondents had lived in the United States for decades, with mothers averaging twenty-eight years and fathers thirty-one years of residence.

3. Note, however, that large-scale Jamaican migration dates from shortly after the emancipation of slaves in 1834, when thousands of Jamaicans migrated within the Caribbean and, later, to Central America in search of work (see, for example, Eisner 1961; Richardson 1983; Thomas-Hope 1986; Fraser 1990; and Kasinitz and Vickerman 1999).

4. For instance, in two polls conducted in November 1977, Jamaican political scientist Carl Stone found that 60 percent of Jamaicans responded affirmatively to the following question: "Suppose you got an opportunity to go to the U.S.A. to live; would you go?" Similarly, 59 percent expressed favorable attitudes toward well-off Jamaicans who had migrated to Miami (Stone 1982:63–65).

5. The exact number of West Indians—and subcomponents of that population—in the United States is difficult to calculate exactly because the various methods available do not correspond exactly with group boundaries. For instance, although place of birth is an example of "hard" data collected by the Census Bureau, it is possible that some individuals who were born in Jamaica do not identify as "Jamaican." Moreover, some individuals with Jamaican connections who have lived in other foreign countries—notably the United Kingdom—could identify themselves as Jamaicans but would not be regarded as such. Also, place of birth does not capture second-generation individuals who identify themselves with their Jamaican ancestry. Similarly, the census' ancestry question does not give an exact count of the number of Jamaicans in that some individuals of Jamaican ancestry may hold other identities.

6. Although not necessarily employing the term cross-pressures, the literature on West Indians in the United States has long noted that they are subject to contradictory forces stemming from the peculiar features of their home societies and the prevalence of racism in the United States. For instance, see Reid (1939) and Basch (1987).

7. This variation arises because the socially constructed nature of race makes it difficult to strictly categorize people into fixed groups called "races." As I point out below, several factors affect where boundaries are drawn between groups, and one of the most important of these is social trends. For instance, although mixed-race individuals in Jamaica have long been seen, and see themselves, as a distinctly separate group, the growth of black racial pride has caused many of these people to rediscover their African roots. On a long-term basis the most important causes for this trend have been Garveyism and its offshoot, Rastafarianism. However, in the late 1960s, the American black power movement also influenced Jamaican society. One reflection of these problack trends is that from 1844 to 1960, the proportion of the Jamaican population identified as mixed race on various censuses averaged 18.5 percent. However, the 1970 census records that only 5.8 percent of the population were of mixed ancestry, and the 1980 census reported this figure at 12.8 percent. This fluctuation in the mixed-race population was accompanied, in 1970, by a surge in the percentage of Jamaicans identifying themselves as black (see Braithwaite 1956; Nettleford 1972; Lewis 1977; Vickerman 1999:25).

8. The University of the West Indies is a regionwide institution with campuses in Jamaica, Barbados, and Trinidad.

9. The figure for Jamaicans is found in Grasmuck and Grosfoguel (1997) and that for African Americans was calculated from 1990 printed census data (Social and Economic Characteristics) for New York City (U.S. Bureau of the Census 1990).

10. In 1990, 51 percent of Jamaican households in the Williamsbridge-Wakefield section of the Bronx (which contains the highest concentration of foreign-born

Jamaicans in New York City) earned over $35,000 and 37 percent of Jamaicans owned their own homes. In Queens, the median household income of blacks in 1990 ($34,314) slightly outpaced that of whites ($34,075), and some analysts argue that the large numbers of West Indians in the borough help account for the relatively high figure for blacks (Nossiter 1995; Roberts 1994). In contrast, only 40 percent of Jamaican households in Brooklyn's Crown Heights section earned more than $35,000 and only 14 percent of Jamaicans owned their own homes.

11. Some writers have argued that despite Jamaica's political independence, centuries of British rule continue to influence how modern-day Jamaicans perceive the world around them. For instance, historian Gordon Lewis (1968:193) noted that "independent Jamaica, despite the formal transfer of sovereignty, remained at heart a society still shaped by the colonial heritage. . . . Its values were still imported; for all of the ideas the new national bureaucracy praised—fair play, the rule of law, parliamentary government, and the rest—were ideas imparted by the colonial pro consuls." To support his position, Lewis cited Katrin Norris (1962), who concluded in her survey of early 1960s Jamaica that colonialism had imposed a mentality that went deeper than political domination. Jamaica, she argued, "has hardly begun to free herself from this inheritance, from the habit of trying, however successfully, to look at the world through British eyes" (71). David Lowenthal (1972) arrived at similar conclusions in his survey of West Indian societies, as did Diane Austin (1984) in her study of two neighborhoods in Kingston, Jamaica. She described the attitudes of some of her middle-class respondents as stemming from "British influenced norms" (e.g., page 165). My argument is not that such norms necessarily dominate Jamaicans' outlook on life but that they influence Jamaicans to put a conservative slant on many social issues—for example, their support for the police on questions of law and order (see Rohter 1997 for a good discussion of West Indians' social conservatism). Of course, I am referring only to tendencies, and the influence of colonialism wanes more and more as Jamaica grows in its status as an independent nation. As this takes place, other aspects of Jamaican culture are significantly affecting Jamaicans' worldview. Without a doubt, the most important of these other influences is the Afrocentrism of Rastafarianism and Garveyism. Foreign influences are also important, because of the heavy volume of Jamaican migration and America's political, economic, and cultural (through tourism and media) penetration of the West Indies.

12. See, for example, the portrayal of Jamaica on the "E" entertainment channel's program "Wild on Jamaica"; in films such as *Club Paradise, The Mighty Quinn,* and *Marked for Death*; and in newspaper articles such as "Jamaican Drug Gangs Thriving in U.S. Cities" (Volsky 1987).

13. In 1994, the bottom 20 percent of the Jamaican population earned only 6 percent of yearly income, compared to 48.4 percent of yearly income earned by the top 20 percent of the population (World Bank 1994).

14. For instance, Rastafarians have long faced repression in Jamaican society because their appearance, beliefs, and practice of smoking marijuana deviate from norms and values that the society deem appropriate (see, for example, Smith, Augier, and Nettleford 1960; Rubin and Comitas 1976).

15. Crime, of course, is a major issue in Jamaican society and is the main expression of conflict between "haves" and "have-nots." However, since the 1940s Jamaican

politics has alternated, predictably, between the left-leaning Peoples' National Party and the more conservative Jamaica Labour Party. The Westminster model of parliamentary democracy on which the political system is based has not faced serious challenge—even from the socialist Peoples' National Party of the 1970s.

16. See "Just Call Me Jamaican" (*Weekly Gleaner* 1995:19).

17. Second-generation West Indians also experience racial discrimination. For instance, in my research, a female college student reported being harassed by the white manager of a grocery store in the town where she attended college. Another reported being refused service in a restaurant; others reported racial harassment from schoolmates as they were growing up.

18. Many had paid special attention to the Howard Beach incident of December 1986 in which a white mob attacked three West Indians, causing one to be run over and killed by a car.

19. The brutalization by New York City police officers of Haitian immigrant Abner Louima in 1997 is a worst-case scenario of what many of the Jamaicans I interviewed feared.

20. It is important to remember that this argument represents a Jamaican male point of view and refers to tendencies. Among Jamaicans, many exceptions to these tendencies can be found.

21. In fact, American rhythm and blues has influenced the development of such Jamaican musical styles as ska, rock steady, and reggae (see, for example, Manuel 1995).

22. This trend emerged clearly in my research. Also, as Waters (1996) notes, well-off West Indian immigrant parents, as well as their poorer coethnics, attempt to inculcate traditional "West Indian" values into their children. The difference is that the children of the latter tend to dismiss these values as irrelevant given the bleak situations in which they live their lives. Waters implies that their peers are influential in helping these "American-identified" West Indians arrive at this viewpoint. This tussle for influence over the values and behavior of children recalls Elijah Anderson's discussion (1994) of the conflict between "decent" inner-city parents and inner-city residents who live by a "street" code. He argues that the former attempt to transmit values and behaviors to their children that will help them fit into mainstream society. However, these children are constantly being tempted, and often succumb to, peers who denigrate these values and behavior and reject mainstream society.

23. Many of the second-generation West Indians I interviewed in 1999 reported that their immigrant parents constantly emphasized the importance of achievement.

24. Mary Waters (1996) has argued that a key difference between American- and ethnic-identified second-generation West Indians is that the former feel overpowered by racism whereas the latter view racism as being a problem that can be overcome through self-effort. Waters alludes to the assimilation of ethnic-identified second-generation individuals into the African American community when she questions their ability to maintain, over the long term, an ethnic self-identity.

25. Toasting, a variant of reggae in which artists talk over preexisting rhythm tracks, originated in Jamaica in the late 1960s/early 1970s (Goldman 2000).

26. This is not to posit a neat dichotomy between "liberal" Democrats and "conservative" Republicans since political attitudes are complex. Instead, I am referring to broad trends among Jamaicans and other West Indians.
27. For examples of mistreatment of Jamaicans and other West Indians under the new immigration laws see Williams (1996) and Sachs (2000).
28. See also Richards (1988:26) for the results of a 1988 Gallup Poll of New Yorkers showing that in that year, only 34 percent of foreign-born blacks (mostly West Indians) in the United States were registered to vote.
29. These networks may also include women who started out as domestics but who have achieved a form of upward mobility by obtaining higher-paying jobs as nurses' aides or nurses.
30. Jitney vans evolved from the "gypsy cab" (unlicensed taxi) industry, in which West Indians have played a key role. See Kasinitz (1992) for a discussion of gypsy cabs.
31. This was particularly true of working-class Jamaicans. The professionals I interviewed usually expressed more skepticism about black/white relations.
32. Note that transnationalism, per se, is not a new phenomenon. What is new is the extent to which modern technology facilitates the process (see, for example, Portes, Guarnizo, and Landolt 1999). West Indians have long been transnational because, historically, their migration has been persistently circular. In many islands—Jamaica included—it has been accepted that people would routinely leave, seek employment abroad, and return home again (see, for example, Richardson 1983; Mintz 1998). However, it is also possible that transnationalism has limits, since some of the Jamaican immigrants in my study expressed little need to routinely interact with the West Indies. Instead, they argued explicitly that the culture that has been created by New York City's large West Indian population is an acceptable substitute for actual interaction with the West Indies (Vickerman 1999, 2000).

References

Anderson, Elijah. 1994. "The Code of the Streets." *Atlantic Monthly* (May): 80–94.

Austin, Diane J. 1987. *Urban Life in Kingston, Jamaica: The Culture and Class Ideology of Two Neighborhoods.* New York: Gordon and Breach.

Basch, Linda. 1984. "The Politics of Caribbeanization: Vincentians and Grenadians in New York." In Constance Sutton and Elsa M. Chaney, ed., *Caribbean Life in New York City: Sociocultural Dimensions,* pp. 160–81. New York: Center for Migration Studies of New York.

Bonnett, Aubrey W. 1981. *Institutional Adaptation of West Indian Immigrants to America: An Analysis of Rotating Credit Associations.* Washington, D.C.: University Press of America.

——. 1990. "The New Female West Indian Immigrant: Dilemmas of Coping in the Host Society." In Ransford Palmer, ed., *In Search of a Better Life: Perspectives on Migration from the Caribbean,* pp. 139–50. New York: Praeger.

Braithwaite, Lloyd. 1956. "Sociology and Demographic Research in the British Caribbean." *Social and Economic Studies* 6(4): 523–71.

Brodber, Erna. 1989. "Socio-cultural Change in Jamaica." In Rex Nettleford, ed., *Jamaica in Independence,* pp. 55–74. Kingston: Heineman Publishers (Caribbean).

Bryce-Laporte, Roy. 1972. "Black Immigrants: The Experience of Invisibility and Inequality." *Journal of Black Studies* 3(1): 29–56.

Crowder, Kyle. 1999. "Residential Segregation of West Indians in the New York/New Jersey Metropolitan Area: The Roles of Race and Ethnicity." *International Migration Review* 33(1): 79–113.

Curtin, Philip. 1970. *Two Jamaicas: The Role of Ideas in a Tropical Colony, 1830–1865.* New York: Atheneum.

Dao, James. 1999. "Immigrant Diversity Slows Traditional Political Climb." *New York Times,* 28 December, A1.

Eisner, Gisela. 1961. *Jamaica: 1830–1930.* Manchester: Manchester University Press.

Feagin, Joe, and Melvin P. Sykes. 1994. *Living with Racism.* Boston: Beacon.

Foner, Nancy. 1973. *Status and Power in Rural Jamaica: A Study of Educational and Political Change.* New York: Teachers College Press.

———. 1987. "The Jamaicans: Race and Ethnicity Among Migrants in New York City." In Nancy Foner, ed., *New Immigrants in New York,* pp. 195–218. New York: Columbia University Press.

———. 1986. "Sex Roles and Sensibilities: Jamaican Women in New York and London." In Rita James Simon and Caroline B. Brettel, ed., *International Migration: The Female Experience,* pp. 133–51. Totowa, N.J.: Rowman and Allanheld, 1986.

———. 1998. "Towards a Comparative Perspective on Caribbean Migration." 1998. In *Caribbean Migration: Globalised Identities.* London: Routledge.

Fraser, Peter D. 1990. "Nineteenth Century West Indian Migration to Britain." In Ransford Palmer, ed., *In Search of a Better Life: Perspectives on Migration from the Caribbean,* pp. 19–38. New York: Praeger.

Gladwell, Malcolm. 1996. "Outsiders Getting the Jobs in One Inner-City Revival." *Washington Post,* 10 March, A1.

Goldman, Vivien. 2000. "How Jamaica Changed the World's Music." *CommonQuest* 4(3): 20–31.

Gordon, Monica. 1990. "Dependents or Independent Workers:? The Status of Caribbean Immigrant Women in the United States." In Ransford Palmer, ed., *In Search of a Better Life: Perspectives on Migration from the Caribbean,* pp. 115–38. New York: Praeger.

Grasmuck, Sherri, and Ramon Grosfoguel. 1997. "Geopolitics, Economic Niches, and Gendered Social Capital Among Recent Caribbean Immigrants in New York City." *Sociological Perspectives* 40(3): 339–63.

Heer, David. 1996. *Immigration in America's Future.* Boulder: Westview.

Henriques, Fernando. 1957. *Jamaica: Land of Wood and Water.* London: Macgibbon and Kee.

Hicks, Jonathan. 2000. "Bitter Primary Contest Hits Ethnic Nerve Among Blacks." *The New York Times,* August 31, A1.

Hondagneu-Sotelo, Pierette. 1994. *Gendered Transitions: Mexican Experiences of Immigration.* Berkeley: University of California Press.

Jamaican Weekly Gleaner. 1995. "Caribbean Immigrants Defining their Future." *Jamaican Weekly Gleaner,* June 30–July 6, 19.

———. 1995. "Just Call Me Jamaican." *Jamaican Weekly Gleaner,* October 20–26, 19.

Johnson, Kirk. 1997. "Black Workers Bear Big Burden As Jobs in Government Dwindle." *The New York Times,* February 2, A1.

Johnson, Violet. 1995. "Culture, Economic Stability, and Entrepreneurship: The Case of British West Indians in Boston." In Marilyn Halter, ed., *New Migrants in the Marketplace,* pp. 59–80. Amherst: University of Massachusetts Press.

Kasinitz, Philip. 1987."The New Black Immigrants." *New York Affairs* 10(1) (Winter): 44–58.

——. 1992. *Caribbean New York: Black Immigrants and the Politics of Race.* New York: Cornell University Press.

Kasinitz, Philip, and Milton Vickerman. 1999. "West Indians/Caribbeans." In Elliott Robert Barkan, ed., *A Nation of Peoples: A Sourcebook on America's Multicultural Heritage,* pp. 520–42. Westport, Conn.: Greenwood Press.

——. Forthcoming. "Ethnic Niches and Racial Traps: Jamaicans in the New York Regional Economy." In Robert Smith, Hector R. Cordero-Guzman, and Ramon Grosfoguel, eds., *Ethnicity, Immigration and the Changing Political Economy of New York.* Philadelphia: Temple University Press.

Kaufman, Jonathan. 1995. "Immigrants' Businesses Often Refuse to Hire Blacks in Inner City." *Wall Street Journal,* June 6, A1.

Kuper, Adam. 1976. *Changing Jamaica.* London: Routledge and Kegan Paul.

Lewis, Gordon. 1968. *The Growth of the Modern West Indies.* New York: Monthly Review Press.

Lewis, Rupert. 1977. "Black Nationalism in Jamaica in Recent Years." In Carl Stone and Aggrey Brown, eds., *Essays on Power and Change in Jamaica,* pp. 65–71. Kingston: Jamaica Publishing House.

Louis, Meela. 2000. "Pooled Savings Help Jamaicans Build Businesses." *Wall Street Journal,* October 17, B1.

Lowenthal, David. 1972. *West Indian Societies.* London: Oxford University Press.

Manuel, Peter. 1995. *Caribbean Currents: Caribbean Music from Rumba to Reggae.* Philadelphia: Temple University Press.

McQueen, M. P. 1989. "Enthusiasm in Bed-Stuyvesant." *New York Newsday,* November 9, 6.

Mintz, Sidney W. 1998. "The Localization of Anthropological Practice." *Critique of Anthropolog* 18(2): 117–33.

Model, Suzanne. 1999. "Where New York's West Indians Work." Paper presented at the conference "West Indian Migration to New York: Historical, Contemporary and Transnational Perspectives." Research Institute for the Study of Man, New York City, April 16–17.

Moses, Knolly. 1996. "The 'Barrel Children'." *Newsweek,* February 19, 45.

Nettleford, Rex. 1972. *Identity, Race and Protest in Jamaica.* New York: Morrow.

——. 1978. *Caribbean Cultural Identity: The Case of Jamaica.* Kingston: Institute of Jamaica.

New York City Department of City Planning. 1996. *The Newest New Yorkers 1990–1994.* New York: Department of City Planning.

——. 1999. *The Newest New Yorkers 1995–1996.* New York: Department of City Planning.

Noel, Peter. 1998. "When Justice Was the Rage." *Common Quest* 3(1) (Winter): 32–39.

Norris, Kathleen. 1962. *Jamaica, the Search for an Identity.* London: Oxford.

Nossiter, Adam. 1995. "A Jamaican Way Station in the Bronx." *The New York Times,* October 25, 1B1.

Osofsky, Gilbert. 1966. *Harlem: The Making of a Ghetto.* New York: Harper Torchbooks.

Palmer, Colin. 1989. "Identity, Race, and Power in Independent Jamaica." In Franklin W. Knight and Colin A. Palmer, eds., *The Modern Caribbean,* pp. 111–28. Chapel Hill: University of North Carolina Press.

Palmer, Ransford. 1990. "Caribbean Development and the Migration Imperative." In Ransford Palmer, ed., *In Search of a Better Life: Perspectives on Migration from the Caribbean,* pp. 3–18. New York: Praeger.

Portes, Alejandro, Luis E. Guarnizo, and Patricia Landolt. 1999. "Introduction: Pitfalls and Promise of an Emergent Research Field." *Ethnic and Racial Studies* 22(2) (March): 217–37.

Post, Ken. 1978. *Arise Ye Starvelings: The Jamaican Labour Rebellion of 1938 and Its Aftermath.* The Hague: Martinus Nijhoff.

Prescod-Roberts, Margaret. 1980. "Bringing It All Back Home." In Margaret Prescod-Roberts and Norma Steele, eds., *Black Women: Bringing It All Back Home,* pp. 13–40. Bristol, U.K.: Falling Wall Press.

Reid, Ira D. A. 1939. *The Negro Immigrant.* New York: Columbia University Press.

Richards, Clay F. 1988. "NY Poll Finds a Kinship." *New York Newsday,* April 15, 26.

Richardson, Bonham. 1983. *Caribbean Migrants.* Knoxville: University of Tennessee Press.

Roberts, Sam. 1994. "In Middle-Class Queens, Blacks Pass Whites in Household Income." *The New York Times,* June 6, A1.

Rohter, Larry. 1997. "The Real Caribbean: Paradise Stops at the Beach's Edge." *The New York Times,* February 16, Section 4, 1.

Rubin, Vera, and Lambros Comitas. 1976. *Ganja in Jamaica: The Effects of Marijuana Use.* New York: Anchor Press/Doubleday.

Sachs, Susan. 2000. "INS Inspectors Are Judge, Jury, and Deporter, Report Says." *The New York Times,* October 6, B5.

Schiller, Nina Glick, Linda Basch, and Cristina Szanton Blanc. 1994. *Nations Unbound.* Basel: Gordon and Breach.

Smith, M. G. 1965. *The Plural Society in the British West Indies.* Berkeley: University of California Press.

Smith, M. G., Roy Augier, and Rex Nettleford. 1960. *The Ras Tafari Movement in Kingston, Jamaica.* Kingston: Institute of Social and Economic Research.

Statistical Institute of Jamaica. 1997a. *Main Labor Force Indicators 1995–1996.* http://www.statinja.com/97yrbook13b.htm.

——. 1997b. *Latest Information at a Glance* http://www.statinja.com/97yrbook 13b.htm.

Stone, Carl. 1972. *Stratification and Political Change in Trinidad and Jamaica.* Beverley Hills: Sage.

——. 1973. *Class, Race, and Political Behaviour in Urban Jamaica.* Kingston: Institute of Social and Economic Research.

——. 1982. *The Political Opinions of the Jamaican People (1976–81).* Kingston: Blackett.

Sutton, Constance. 1987. "The Caribbeanization of New York City and the Emergence of a Transnational Socio-cultural System." In Constance Sutton and Elsa Chaney, eds., *Caribbean Life in New York City: Sociocultural Dimensions,* pp. 15–30. New York: Center for Migration Studies.

Thomas-Hope, Elizabeth. 1986. "Caribbean Diaspora—the Inheritance of Slavery: Migration from the Commonwealth Caribbean." In Colin Brock, ed., *The Caribbean in Europe,* pp. 15–35. London: Frank Cass.

Tierney, John. 1997. "Man with a Van." *New York Times Magazine,* August 10, 22.

U.S. Bureau of the Census. 1990. *Census of Population, New York.* Washington, D.C.: U.S. Government Printing Office.

U.S. Immigration and Naturalization Service. 1996. *Statistical Yearbook of the Immigration and Naturalization Service, 1996.* Washington, D.C: U.S. Government Printing Office, 1996.

———. 1999. *Statistical Yearbook of the Immigration and Naturalization Service, 1997.* Washington, D.C.: U.S. Government Printing Office.

———. 1999. *Statistical Yearbook of the Immigration and Naturalization Service, 1997.* Washington, D.C.: U.S. Government Printing Office.

Vaughan, Sarah. 1997. "Taking the Vow of Citizenship." *Jamaican Weekly Gleaner,* April 17–23, 19.

Vickerman, Milton. 1999. *Crosscurrents: West Indian Immigrants and Race.* New York: Oxford University Press.

———. 2000. "West Indian Transnationalism and Immigrant Identity." Paper presented at the conference "Diaspora and Diversity Within the Black Experience." Colgate University, Hamilton, N.Y., June 2–4.

Volsky, George. 1987. "Jamaican Drug Gangs Thriving in U.S. Cities." *The New York Times,* July 19.

Waldinger, Roger. 1996. *Still the Promised City? African-Americans and New Immigrants in Post Industrial New York.* Cambridge: Harvard University Press.

Wall Street Journal. 1997. "Dream On." *Wall Street Journal,* July 21, A22.

Waters, Mary. 1996. "Ethnic and Racial Identities of Second-Generation Immigrants in New York City." In Alejandro Portes, ed., *The New Second Generation,* pp. 171–96. New York: Russell Sage.

———. 1999. *Black Identities: West Indian Immigrant Dreams and American Realities.* Cambridge: Harvard University Press.

Williams, Lena. 1996. "Aimed at Terrorists, Law Hits Legal Immigrants." *The New York Times,* July 17, A1.

World Bank. 1994. *World Development Report.* Washington, D.C.: World Bank.

West Africans: Trading Places in New York

Paul Stoller

In February 1999 four members of the New York Police Department's (NYPD) Street Crimes Unit gunned down Amadou Diallo, an unarmed West African immigrant. The killing, which took place in the vestibule of Diallo's apartment building, triggered a still unresolved controversy. Many of the details of the senseless police killing remain obscure. A few facts are clear. The police fired forty-one shots, nineteen of which struck Diallo, who died immediately. Before the fatal incident, Diallo, who was only twenty-two years old, lived quietly in the Bronx. The four plainclothes police officers mistook Diallo for a local serial rapist, whom, they said, Diallo resembled (Cooper 1999).

The ongoing research on which this article is based has been generously supported through grants from the Wenner-Gren Foundation for Anthropological Research, West Chester University, and from the National Science Foundation (Law and Social Behavior Program). Parts of this article have appeared in different form in *Anthropology and Humanism* 7(1) (1997) and in *American Anthropologist* 96(4) (1996). I thank Nancy Foner for asking me to contribute this essay to *New York's New Immigrants* and to Jasmin Tahmaseb McConatha for her critical reading of the present essay. The names of the traders mentioned in this article have been changed to protect their privacy. The quotations attributed to the various traders are derived from ethnographic interviews conducted in New York between 1993 and 1998.

A lethal mix of linguistic confusion, cultural misinterpretation, and racism probably led to the killing. Much of the press coverage of the Diallo tragedy has focused on the brutality of the killing and on the increasingly racist contours of NYPD-minority community relations. Mayoral press conferences and interviews defended the overall professionalism of police behavior. Mayor Giuliani, in fact, called for calm so that the "facts" of the case might be determined. Opponents of the mayor's police policies staged a demonstration in which speaker after speaker condemned police brutality against minorities. Triggered by the media's tunnel vision, the political implications of the Diallo incident quickly eclipsed the young man's personal tragedy.

Even so, careful readers of the coverage might have gleaned a glimpse of the young West African immigrant's life in New York City. Sidebar articles described Diallo's life. He was born in Lelouma, Guinea, a Fulani village situated on the Fouta Toro plateau of that West African nation. He came to New York City in 1997, one of thousands of single young West African men who in the past ten years have left their homelands to come to New York City to seek economic opportunity. Like many West Africans in New York City, Diallo settled in The Bronx among relatives: first with his uncle and then with two of his cousins. Work consumed much of Diallo's time. "The three roommates hardly saw each other, because they all worked so many hours, striving to make their way in a new country. Amadou Diallo, who peddled socks, gloves, videotapes, and other goods on Fourteenth Street in Manhattan, usually left each day by noon and did not return until midnight" (Waldman 1999). Coverage of memorial services and demonstrations presented brief portraits of the West African presence in New York City. Readers learned about such voluntary associations as the Guinean Association of America. They also learned that Diallo's parents had long been associated with international commerce. His father, in fact, manages businesses in Vietnam (see Weir 1999; Sachs 1999a, 1999b, 1999c).[1] And so for a fleeting moment the Diallo tragedy brought into focus the city lives of West African merchants who occupy trading places in America.

The surprisingly detailed media attention to the Diallo case, however, was short-lived. Journalists made limited mention of the fact that Diallo was one of thousands of street traders in New York City who established small vending businesses during the 1990s. Their reportage also omitted that Diallo's journey to New York is a contemporary version of the centuries-old tradition of long-distance trading in West Africa. In fact, the Fulani from Fouta Toro, the region where Diallo came from, have long mixed commerce, religion, and politics (Boville 1995 [1958]; Curtin 1974; Gregroire 1992) And so it is not at all surprising that like his forebears, Diallo, a pious Muslim, would leave Guinea at twenty years of age to seek commercial opportunities in a distant and exotic land.

This essay, which describes and analyzes the city lives of recent West African immigrants to New York, is based on field research conducted in Manhattan from 1992 to 1998. During those years I was a participant observer at street markets on 125th Street and on 116th Street, both in Harlem, and along Canal Street between Broadway and West Broadway. Field research in New York resulted in more than 100 informal interviews and twenty life histories. The research was a natural extension of roughly seven years of fieldwork conducted intermittently among Songhay-speaking peoples in the Republic of Niger between 1976 and 1990. That experience enhanced my capacity to grasp many of the nuances of contemporary West African social life in New York.

In the essay I attempt to describe the multifaceted city lives of men like Amadou Diallo. What global forces, if any, led West African long-distance traders to come to New York City? What has been the history of their immigration? What are the political, economic, and social dimensions of their social lives in New York City? The remainder of the essay consists of two parts: (1) a short history of recent West African immigration to New York City, and (2) a description that focuses on how West African immigrants have adapted to the political, economic, and sociocultural realities of life there.

West African Immigration to New York City

Small numbers of West Africans, mostly students, have been migrating to New York City for more than fifty years. In the 1990s West African immigration expanded significantly. Although most of the recent immigrants from West Africa, according to immigration statistics, come from Ghana and Nigeria, the focus of this essay is on the increasingly visible community of Francophone African immigrants, many of whom are street vendors in Harlem and in midtown and lower Manhattan. (New York City Department of City Planning 1999) These vendors come from Senegal, Mali, Guinea, Burkina Faso, and Niger. Some of the Nigerien vendors, in fact, come from villages where I conducted fieldwork between 1976 and 1990.

It is impossible to know just how many West African immigrants live in New York City. Figures from the U.S. Immigration and Naturalization Service (INS), which refer to legal immigrants intending to settle in New York City, are usually too low; figures from the various African immigrant associations are often inflated. These figures, no matter their source, make no reference to the thousands of West African itinerant traders, who are either import-exporters or African art dealers, who come to the United States for three to six months at time.

Between 1990 and 1996, according to estimates in *The New York Times,* the number of West Africans in New York City increased from 44,000 to near 88,000 (Jacobs 1999).[2] Even if this estimate is perhaps a bit high, it can be said that hundreds, if not thousands, of the Francophone West African immigrants to New York City work not as highly paid diplomats, but as unskilled wage laborers. Although census figures, which refer mostly to Ghanaian and Nigerian immigrants, show Africans to be a highly educated group, many of the recent Francophone immigrants come from families of long-distance traders who usually don't possess specialized technical skills or university diplomas. Most of them have become, like Amadou Diallo, street traders in Harlem, Brooklyn, and Lower Manhattan, where they share market space with African Americans, Jamaicans, Koreans, Chinese, Vietnamese, Ecuadorians, Mexicans, Pakistanis, and Afghans. Some of the Francophone immigrants who are literate and have obtained Employment Authorizations Permits from the INS drive medallion cabs, which are licensed; others, who are also literate, drive so-called gypsy cabs, which are often not regulated by City Hall. The more successful Francophone West African traders have used their profits to open restaurants or boutiques like Kaarta Textiles, a shop on West 125th Street in Harlem that sells cloth and clothing from West Africa. Other merchants operate thriving import-export businesses. Unlike other recent immigrants to New York City, the Francophone African street vendors have a dispersed pattern of residence. They live in small clusters in Harlem, The South Bronx, and Brooklyn and therefore have not constructed communities that dominate a particular neighborhood. They often keep to themselves and have little to do with the Ghanaians and Nigerians who comprise more numerous and more tightly knit communities.

From spring through fall groups of mostly Francophone West African traders pack vans with exotic leather goods and jewelry made in Africa and baseball caps and T-shirts—with the logos of American sports teams—made in China and Korea. They travel through what they call the "bush"—Indianapolis, Kansas City, Detroit—following the circuit of African American cultural festivals and trade shows.

Not all Francophone West Africans living in New York City, however, are merchants. Many of them work as store clerks, security guards, and grocery store delivery people. On the Upper West Side of Manhattan, for example, stock clerks in Price Wise Discount Drug Stores—along Broadway—often speak Wolof, the major Senegalese language, as they take inventory. In 1997 their boss, the manager, was also Senegalese. At Lexington and Ninety-second Street on the Upper East Side of Manhattan one can sometimes overhear a sidewalk conversation in Songhay, a major language in the Republic of Niger, as several Nigeriens take a break from delivering groceries. In November 1999 a loosely organized group of West African deliverymen staged a demonstration in front of the Food Emporium at Sixty-eighth and Broadway on the Upper West Side. They protested poor work conditions and low pay and talked to the media about their difficult lives in America (Jacobs 1999).

Although the West African contribution to New York City's exponential explosion of multiculturalism may be little known, the recent expansion of social diversity in New York City is widely acknowledged. New York City is one of the principal destinations of recent immigrants—documented and undocumented—to the United States. As new groups of recent immigrants have established communities, many urban, suburban, and even rural areas have become "suddenly" diverse and different. The emergence of difference, in turn, has undermined the myth of the American "melting pot," which, for some Americans, has made the specter of new immigration a bitter political issue of national scope. By the same token, the new immigration has sparked much political debate in local contexts. The West African presence in Harlem, for example, has sparked a great deal of political discussion, which ultimately triggered the dissolution of the African Market on 125th Street in October 1994 (see Stoller 1996; Portes and Stepick 1993; Davis 1990; Dugger 1996).

Global Restructuring and West African Migration to New York City

The increased migration of Francophone West Africans to North America devolves directly from global restructuring. As a complex of economic, political, geographic, and sociocultural phenomena, global restructuring has spurred the growth of multinational corporations, imploded notions of space and time, triggered the outplacement of manufacturing from the First to the Third World, prompted the outsourcing of industrial parts and the downsizing of corporate payrolls, stimulated the emergence of globalized financial markets, brought on the feminization of the workforce in rapidly proliferating export-processing zones, eroded large sectors of the American middle classes, and induced the exponential growth of the informal economies (see Coombe and Stoller 1994:251; see also Harvey 1989; Sassen 1991; Mollenkopf and Castells 1991).[3]

This complex of relations, however, has led less to the global integration of human and economic resources than to the polarization of rich and poor (Sassen 1991, 1996; Mittleman 1996). This polarization is quite evident in sub-Saharan Africa, a region of the world in which the number of poor had been expected to rise by 85 million to roughly 265 million by 2000 (Mittleman 1996). Economic problems in West Africa, for example, have recently been exacerbated by the World Bank's program of insisting that credit-hungry West African governments live within their means no matter the votility of international currency markets (Callaghy and Ravenhill 1993). One result of these policies was the 1994 devaluation of the West African franc that in one day lowered the Francophone West African standard of living by 50 percent. The devaluation affected the lives of millions of people, including traders who liquidated their inventories in West Africa and headed to New York City.

To demonstrate how these global forces influenced individual migration patterns, consider the case of Idrissa Dan Inna, a Nigerien trader on 125th Street. After obtaining a tourist visa from the American Embassy in Niamey, Niger, Idrissa arrived in New York City in February 1994, two weeks after the World Bank orchestrated the devaluation of the West African franc by 50 percent. Idrissa said that the devaluation had ruined his business in Niger. With twelve children to feed, he liquidated his inventory, obtained a visa, and bought a round-trip ticket to New York City. With the return portion of his ticket, he bought inventory. Several days after his arrival he was conducting business on 125th Street.

Idrissa Dan Inna, who spoke French and a smattering of English, came to New York City for two reasons. First, he wanted to avoid working in France, where new immigration laws provoked the harsh treatment of African aliens. Second, compatriots who had spent time New York told him of unrivaled opportunities there.

West African Traders in Harlem

Attracted by the global lights of New York City, many West African traders, like Idrissa Dan Inna, came to New York not to settle, but to make as much money as possible and then return home. After arriving they soon found that their lack of English, limited technological knowledge, and murky immigration status made working in the regulated economy almost impossible. Facing this brute reality, they entered the informal economy, many of them becoming street vendors.

Before 1990, the primary West African practitioners of informal street trading were Senegalese men vending from tables set up along midtown Manhattan sidewalks. Given the regulatory difficulties of obtaining a vending license from the City of New York, the majority of Senegalese conducted unlicensed operations (Ebin and Lake 1992; Coombe and Stoller 1994; Stoller 1996). By 1985 scores of Senegalese had set up tables in front of some of Manhattan's most expensive retailers along Fifth Avenue. Such a cluttered Third World place in a First World space soon proved intolerable to the Fifth Avenue Merchants Association. Headed by Donald Trump, the association urged City Hall to crack down on the unlicensed vendors.

Following the cleanup, Senegalese vendors relocated to less-precious spaces in midtown: Lexington Avenue and Forty-second Street near Grand Central Station and Thirty-fourth Street near Penn Station, to name two locations. They worked in teams to protect themselves from the authorities and criminals. One person would sell goods at a table. His compatriot partners would post themselves on corners as lookouts. Another compatriot would serve as the bank, holding money safely away from the trade. In this way midtown side streets became Senegalese turf.

As more Senegalese arrived in New York City, the vending territory expanded north to Eighty-sixth Street on the Upper East Side and south to Fourteenth Street near Greenwich Village and to Canal Street in Lower Manhattan. In some areas the Senegalese replaced vending tables with attaché cases filled with "Rolex" and other "high-end" watches. By 1990 the Senegalese had a lock hold on informal vending space in most of Manhattan. Backed by the considerable financial power of the Mourids, a Muslim Sufi brotherhood in Senegal to which many of the vendors belonged, the Senegalese soon became the aristocracy of West African merchants in New York City (Ebin and Lake 1992; Coombe and Stoller 1994; Stoller 1996). When merchants from other West African countries (Mali, Niger, Guinea, Burkina Faso, and Cote d'Ivoire) began to immigrate to New York City in 1989 and 1990, the Senegalese had already saturated the lucrative midtown markets, compelling them to set up their tables along 125th Street, the major commercial thoroughfare in Harlem.

Although African Americans have a long history of vending on the streets of Harlem (Bluestone 1991; McCay 1940; Ofsofsky 1971), the 125th Street informal market gradually took on more and more of an African character. Between 1990 and 1992 the so-called African market grew substantially. Although vendors reported the business along 125th Street to be fair during the week, on weekends the market swelled with shoppers. By 1992 the African market had become one of New York City's tourist attractions—one of the photo opportunities for tourists on double-decker tour buses following uptown routes.

The success of the market provoked a spate of political problems. Harlem business and political leaders lobbied the Dinkins administration to disperse the "illegal" market. Dinkins attempted to disband it but backed down when confronted with a raucous demonstration. The beginnings of the Giuliani administration, however, meant the end of the African market on 125th Street. On October 17, 1994, Mayor Giuliani declared street vending illegal on 125th Street. Although the 125th Street Vendors Association staged a protest, the vendors did, indeed, disperse. Many of the West African vendors moved their operations to the new Harlem market of 116th Street and Lenox Avenue. Owned and managed by Malcolm X's Masjid (mosque) Malcolm Shabazz, the majority of this market's vendors were from West Africa.[4] Still others who had obtained employment authorization permits from the INS found work as security guards or in low-skill factories, restaurants, liquor stores, or drugstores. Following the market's demise, some of the traders moved away from New York, seeking wage labor in more rural areas where the cost of living was lower. Several vendors returned to West Africa.

Like Amadou Diallo, the majority of West African street vendors live in apartments with one or two of their compatriots. Vendors who work the 116th Street market usually live in Harlem or The South Bronx. Traders who work in Lower Manhattan often live in Brooklyn in buildings where the occupants are exclusively West Africans. None of the vendors that I have met live outside the New York City limits.

A Profile of West African Traders in New York

As the brief journalistic portraits of Amadou Diallo suggest, the population of West African street vendors is almost completely male. Most traders, young and middle-aged alike, are either single or leave their wives and children in West Africa. No matter their marital status, they wire home as much money as they can. Several of the hundreds of vendors that I have met since 1992, however, have married American women and have started North American families, which usually means that they support families on two continents.

In Islam these transcontinental family practices present no moral or legal problems even if they sometimes increase the instability of marriages. In fact, the practice of settling in an exotic land, if only for a period of years, and starting a family extends the longstanding West African tradition of long-distance trading in foreign lands (see Rouch 1956; Cohen 1969; Brenner 1993; Gregoire 1993). A generation ago, for example, large numbers of Nigeriens settled in Ghana, married Ghanaian women, and raised families. Most of them returned to their already well-established families in Niger, leaving their new families in Ghana. From Niger, they would try to send money regularly to Ghana and would periodically visit their Ghanaian families. The vast majority of contemporary traders in New York City, however, do not marry American women.

There are also an increasing number of female traders, mostly Senegalese, who have sold dolls, jewelry, and cooked food at both the 125th Street and 116th Street markets in Harlem. Some of these women are middle-aged entrepreneurs who divide their time between Senegal and New York City. Others accompanied their husbands to New York. A number of Senegalese women have also opened thriving hair salons in Harlem and Brooklyn.

The West African traders are almost all practicing Muslims. If they are able, most of them pray five times a day and follow Muslim dietary restrictions, meaning that they avoid pork products and buy lamb and beef from Muslim butchers. Traders at the 116th Street market attend Friday Sabbath services, called *jumma,* at the Masjid Malcolm Shabazz on 116th and Lenox. They also observe Ramadan rituals, fasting from sunup to sundown during one prescribed month of the year. During Ramadan in 1996, the Masjid Malcolm Shabazz, managers of the 116th Street Harlem market, prohibited the daytime sale of cooked foods in their market space. Muslim clerics from West Africa, many of whom are Islamic healers who treat the traders' physical disorders with herbal medicines, routinely visit New York City. Traders also seek their advice about social and/or psychological problems.

The traders often face a bevy of social and economic problems in New York City. They usually live in outrageously expensive substandard housing located in crime-infested neighborhoods. Like all peddlers, their fortunes rise and fall with the seasons. In summer they can make a good deal of money; in winter sales usually plummet with the temperatures. Although they have some access to medical care, few, if any, of the traders have medical insurance. Although many of the traders have confidence in Western medicine, they sometimes find it linguistically as well as culturally difficult to explain their problems to medical staffers who often have difficulty understanding their limited English.

For most of the traders the defining social problem, however, is their immigration status. Traders with permanent resident status (holders of green cards) are a very small minority indeed. Their status enables them to travel and work more or less as they please. Traders with employment authorization permits, which are issued to immigrants who have married American women or who have been granted political asylum, are also free to work in either the formal or informal sector. They must renew their authorizations every year. Sometimes the INS restricts travel to the work permit holder's country of origin. A Senegalese trader in Lower Manhattan who possesses an employment authorization card told me how the INS turned down his request to visit his ailing mother in Senegal. They required official documentation of her illness.

Many West African traders in New York City, however, remain undocumented immigrants. This status makes many of them hesitant to travel outside of New York City, where, according to many people I've talked to, they are more fearful of American law enforcement. Lack of documentation means that traders often avoid going to physicians, postpone English instruction at night schools, keep their proceeds in cash rather than bank accounts, and fail to report the theft of their inventories. Although I don't know of any undocumented West African traders who have been deported, many of them fear being placed in detention and sent home—in disgrace.[5] They spend much of their time trying to obtain what they call "papers." They hire immigration brokers to fill out forms and immigration lawyers to represent them at INS hearings. As one undocumented trader from Niger put it: "Life in New York is full of uncertainties." Like most of his compatriots, he does not plan to settle in the United States; he will remain until "the time is right" to return.

West African City Life in New York

So far it is evident that the community of West African traders in New York City is profoundly fluid. Although many of the men who migrated to New York City in the early 1990s have returned home, they have literally traded places with younger relatives—brothers and cousins—who have maintained businesses set up by a pioneering kinsperson. As previously mentioned, only a small percentage of traders have married American women and have started families. Many of these men, who are among the most successful traders, hope to raise their children in both New York City and West Africa. The vast majority of traders say that they've come to New York City to exploit an economic situation and will return to West Africa when they've made enough money to return home with dignity. It sometimes takes years for many traders to reach this goal.

Given this set of priorities, few of the traders aspire to American citizenship. They also feel little social connection to the communities in which they live. As a result they contribute little to community life in places like Harlem, where I've often heard shoppers grumbling about how the African traders have exploited them. The ongoing expression of this attitude has reinforced a low-grade fever of resentment between West African traders and African American shoppers. The sociocultural, legal, and political tensions of living in New York City have also hardened negative impressions that many West Africans hold of American society. Many traders perceive America as a violent, insensitive, time-constrained place in which morally depleted people (non-Muslims) don't have enough time to visit one another. To buffer themselves from social privation and cultural alienation, West

Africans have formed informal credit groups or more formal mutual assistance groups like the Guinean Association of America. Many traders are also links in international economic networks, the cores of which are based in Senegal, Cote d'Ivoire, Mali, Niger, Guinea, and The Gambia. These cartels, based on real or fictive kinship ties, have existed in West Africa for centuries; they have been the foundation of long-distance trading throughout West Africa. During the past ten years, they have been extended to North America. It is to these networks that many West African traders in New York City owe their economic or social allegiance, or both.[6] These socioeconomic realities mean that the dynamic community of West African traders in New York City has little social stability and few formal institutions.

This brief outline of West African social life in New York City lacks a human face. Who are these traders? What specific problems do they face, and how do they resolve them? What is the quality of their lives in New York City? In describing some of the life issues faced by West African traders, I attempt to demonstrate how they confront and resolve—with varying degrees of success—medical problems, regulatory dilemmas, and cultural alienation. As will become evident, these problems are inextricably linked.

Health, Fear, and Politics in New York City

Moussa Boureima, who has lived and worked on the streets of New York City for more than five years, suffers from rheumatism. The condition, which makes his knees ache, his ankles swell, and his joints stiffen, is aggravated by the fact that he sells his merchandise outside—in the damp chill of fall and winter as well as the stifling humidity of summer—at the Malcolm Shabazz Harlem Market. Despite his continuous discomfort, Moussa has been hesitant to see a physician.

"I don't speak much English," he says. "Not enough to explain what's wrong with me. Last year I found a doctor on Seventy-second Street who spoke French. He gave me a shot and my pain went away, but it came back. I don't want to go to a hospital. I have no papers. I don't want any trouble."

Aside from his health, Moussa has a number of other very serious concerns about city life. With the money he earns from the sale of baseball hats, gloves, and scarves, he has to pay $450 per month to rent an apartment in a substandard building in the South Bronx. He also has to pay for his electricity, gas, and telephone. His daily transportation on the subway, food costs, the price of medication as well as necessary investments in new inventory quickly sap his financial resources. After he has paid his bills, he sends the remainder of his money to Tahoua, Niger, to support his wife and eight children.

Moussa migrated to America in 1994 because the economy was bad in Niger and there was little work in West Africa. He came to America without "papers." After three years of working outside at Harlem street markets, he had worries about his health. Given the approach of cold in the fall of 1997, for example, he dreaded the possible medical consequences.

Traders like Moussa Boureima often avoid hospitals, doctors, and nurses. One reason may well be cultural. A few traders have expressed a distrust of Western medicine. Several traders I know consult itinerant West African healers, herbalists who are Muslim clerics, to deal with both physiological and psychological problems. These healers travel to New York every four months or so, bringing with them fresh medicines from West Africa. Between 1994 and 1998, one such healer, Alpha Loga, traveled between Niger and New York City fourteen times.

For the great majority of West African traders, avoidance of public hospitals has less to do with a distrust of Western medicine than with a fear of the INS. Despite relatively light harassment from the INS, every West African trader I've met has expressed fears of detention and detainment. The fear of being turned into the INS ebbs and flows with the intensity of political debate about immigration.

In the summer of 1995, for example, there was much talk at the Malcolm Shabazz Harlem Market about Congress's proposals that would bar children of illegal immigrants from public schools and force public hospitals to report undocumented aliens seeking medical treatment. Although traders tend to be critical of Mayor Giuliani's police policies, his sharp criticism of these proposals won their praise. Mayor Giuliani said that refusing to treat sick people in public hospitals was morally wrong. "It's just out of a sense of decency," he said. "I can't imagine, even in parts of the country where views are harsher than they might be in New York, that they're basically going to say, let people die" (Firestone 1995). Indeed, Mayor Giuliani sued the federal government to uphold Executive Order 124, signed by Mayor Ed Koch in 1985, that prohibits city agencies from supplying information on a particular immigrant to the INS unless he or she is accused of a crime.

Given Mayor Giuliani's public assurances about maintaining the confidentiality of undocumented immigrants seeking New York City services—especially at public hospitals—why would a fairly well informed man like Moussa Boureima continue to avoid public services? The vast majority of West African traders that I've met take such assurances with a grain of salt. Despite Mayor Giuliani's federal lawsuit on behalf of New York City and Executive Order 124, the U.S. District Court found in favor of the federal government, which in effect repealed the executive order. Giuliani appealed the lower court decision to the U.S. Court of Appeals, which in May 1999 also found in favor of the federal government. Put another way, if Moussa Boureima, an undocumented immigrant, goes to the public hospital in New York City, he may well be reported to the INS. This sequence of events reinforces an overriding concern of most West African traders in New York City: can they trust outsiders—people whom they think misunderstand them? Although several public officials seem to support the rights of immigrants, most Americans, from the standpoint of West African street vendors, think immigrants pay no taxes and use up the ever-shrinking pot of public service resources—all of which contribute to Moussa Boureima's aversion to New York City public services.

Cultural Isolation

Although the vast majority of West African street vendors I've met in New York City express profound appreciation for the economic opportunities they enjoy and exploit in the United States, they invariably complain of loneliness, sociocultural isolation, and alienation from mainstream American social customs. These conditions, which lead to a diminished sense of control over one's life, have had an impact on the subjective well-being of men like Moussa Boureima and his compatriots Boubé Mounkaila and Issifi Mayaki (Mirowsky 1995; Mirowsky and Ross 1991).

Intensified by cultural differences, feelings of isolation from the larger sociocultural environment can have a significant impact on physical and psychological being. This kind of social isolation limits the range of activities and interaction in which people participate; it also reduces feelings of control and competence. Indeed, cultural alienation—living in a social environment where one cannot control, impact, or shape one's surroundings—can lead to feelings of powerlessness and helplessness (Mirowsky and Ross 1991; Tahmaseb-McConatha and Obudiate, 1998). This lack of control compels Moussa Boureima, who is sick, to avoid hospitals; it convinces Boubé Mounkaila, that he can do little to resolve regulatory dilemmas provoked by the City of New York and the INS.

The presence of family, however, may well diminish some of the negative effects of immigration. Accordingly, the absence of family is one of the greatest detriments to securing a sense of well-being among many West African traders in New York City. Constructed as lineages, the families of traders are usually their primary source of emotional and social support. Caught in the regulatory limbo of being an undocumented immigrant, Issifi Mayaki is unable to return to West Africa to see his family, whom he longs for. He says this situation frustrates him and sometimes makes him mean-spirited. For most West Africans in New York City, family is paramount. Even though they feel isolated and lonely in New York City, they have come to America, they say, to support their families back home.

> For the African psyche, the collective or the group is the ideal. For the African, the clan, the ethnic group is the base for unity and survival. The unit of identity among Africans is "we" and not "I." According to an Ashante, Ghana proverb, "I am because we are; without we I am not and since we are, therefore I am." Therefore all shame, guilt, pain, joys and sorrows of any particular individual are partaken by the group. The major source of identity is, therefore, for the African, the group, beginning with the smallest unit: the family. (Nwadiora 1996:118)

Although this statement oversimplifies Africa and Africans and misses the tensions that arise when individuals are routinely subjected to group pressures and responsibilities, it nonetheless captures an essential cultural difference between West Africans and most Americans (see Hofstede 1980). For most West Africans the ideal, if not the reality, of a cohesive family that lives and works together is paramount. This ideal, however remote, has survived regional, national, and international family dispersion. It leads men like Moussa Boureima, Issifi Mayaki, and Boubé Mounkaila to regularly phone their kin in West Africa; it compels them to send as much money as possible to help support their wives; their children; their cousins; and their aging parents, aunts, and uncles.

The absence of family has several psychological ramifications for many West African traders in New York City. Besides support, families provide a sense of trust and feelings of competence. As Issifi Mayaki has said, one can usually trust her or his blood kin. Generally speaking, the closer the blood ties, the greater the degree of trust. Absence of family therefore creates an absence of trust that leads, according to the traders I've talked to, to a considerable amount of stress and anxiety. For young men the absence of wives also means that they are in a kind of social and sexual limbo. They share profound cultural and social bonds with their wives, in whom they place great trust. In Niger, for example, marriage, which is sometimes between such close blood kin as cousins, family relations tie individuals into webs of mutual rights and obligations. Men expect wives, even during their long absences, to remain faithful to them. To avoid opportunities for infidelity, long-distance traders—who are also long absent—often insist that their wives live in the family compound. In this way, observant relatives—in-laws—not only enforce codes of sexual fidelity but also help raise the family's children. Many of the men, however, believe it is their inalienable right to have sexual relationships with other women—especially if they are traveling. As Muslims, moreover, they have the right, if they so choose, to marry up to four women, though this practice is increasingly rare. These are some of the cultural assumptions that many lonely and isolated West African traders bring to the social/sexual relationships with women they encounter in New York City. To say the least, these assumptions clash violently with contemporary social/sexual sensibilities in America.

Like many Nigeriens and Maliens in New York City, Moru Sifi talked of being lonely and feeling socially and culturally isolated during his time in New York City. A rotund man well into his fifties, Moru hailed from Dosso in western Niger. As one who had made the Muslim pilgrimage to Mecca, he was addressed by the title El Hadji. In his discussions of life in New York El Hadji Moru complained incessantly about city life. He did not like the food, detested what he considered American duplicity, and distrusted non-Africans. Between 1992 and 1994 he sold sunglasses on 125th Street in Harlem. Like Amadou Diallo, work and sleep constituted much of his life. El Hadji supported two devoted wives in Niger. "Our women," he said in August 1994, just before his departure, "know respect for their men. They also know how to cook real food. None of these Burger Kings and Big Macs. Rice, gumbo sauce with hot pepper, and fresh and clean meat. That is what I miss. I want to sit outside with my friends and kin and eat from a common bowl. Then I want to talk and talk into the night. I want to be in a place that has real Muslim fellowship."

During his two years in New York City, El Hadji said that he had remained celibate—by choice. He did not trust the women he met. The women, he said, often took drugs, slept with men, and sometimes even gave birth to drug-addicted babies. "Some of these women even have AIDS. Soon I will be in Niger in my own house surrounded by my wives and children." There are many West African traders in New York City who share El Hadji Moru's attitudes. Like him, they have remained celibate.

Boubé Mounkaila, by contrast, has been anything but celibate during his time in New York City. Like his brother traders, he misses his family, including a wife he has not seen in eight years and a daughter born several months after his departure. Sometimes, when he thinks of his family, says Boubé, "my heart is spoiled. That's when I listen to *kountigi* [one-stringed lute] music."

From the time he arrived in New York City in 1990 as a twenty-eight-year-old undocumented immigrant, Boubé has had many girlfriends and is well known among fellow traders as a ladies' man. He is a tall, good-looking, and charming man. He has also become fluent in what he calls "street English." Because he sells handbags, most of his clients are women, old and young. On any given day a young woman might be sitting in Boubé's stall waiting patiently for him.

Boubé's girlfriends, however, are not limited to local women. Several female tourists who have come to the Malcolm Shabazz Harlem Market have been much taken with him. In particular, two European women, both in their mid-twenties, have visited on several occasions. One of them lived with him for three months in 1997.

Boubé's domestic circumstances are exceptional among West African traders in New York City. For most traders, life is much less dramatic; it follows a course experienced by men like El Hadji Moru Sifi or Amadou Diallo—one works, eats, and sleeps. In some cases a trader might have occasional interludes with women or develop a long-standing relationship with one woman. Issifi Mayaki's situation is more typical. He is a handsome and well-dressed man of forty years who speaks good English. Between 1994 and 1997 he developed a relationship with a single African American woman with a ten-year-old daughter. The woman is a social worker. Issifi met the woman when he sold African print cloth on 125th Street in 1994. She expressed interest in him. He told her that he had a wife and children in Africa. She said that she didn't mind. They began to see each other but maintained separate residences.

When Issifi began to travel to African American trade shows far from New York City, his relationship began to unravel. His girlfriend did not want him to travel to festivals. She became jealous of his wife in Niger. When he told her of plans to travel home, she did not want him to go. As a result, Issifi began to believe that American women wish to totally consume their men, which, he said, is not the African way. This cultural clash became the source of unending contention, and eventually Issifi and his girlfriend drifted apart.

In the fall of 1997 Issifi asked for advice about his immigration situation. He had met an African American woman in Chicago who had agreed to marry him. This marriage would be an arrangement in which she would receive a lump sum payment and monthly infusions of money in exchange for a marriage that would qualify Issifi for an employment authorization permit and, he hoped, permanent resident status (the green card). He had been following changes in immigration regulations and knew that he would have to take action by January 15, 1998, if he eventually wanted to become a permanent resident. He wanted to know if he would be able to return to West Africa to visit his family after he had obtained a work permit. Such travel would be quite difficult and risky under the new regulations, and he might have to wait three or perhaps ten years before he would be able to return to the United States.

As previously mentioned, Issifi, like many West African traders, distrusted the establishment, which is why he chose not to consult an immigration lawyer about his situation. He eventually decided not to go through with the marriage.

"When the time is right," he said, "I will go home and start a business. My younger brother will come to run things here."

Other West Africans have made other domestic arrangements. Abdou Harouna, who, like El Hadji Moru Sifi, comes from Dosso, Republic of Niger, is not a trader but a "gypsy" cab driver. Abdou, who now calls himself "Al," came to New York City in 1992. In 1994 Al married an African American woman, not simply because he wanted to obtain immigration papers, but because he had fallen in love. His wife is a primary school teacher, and they now have a five-year-old daughter and live in Harlem.

One of the Nigerien traders, Sidi Sansanne, has two families: one in the South Bronx and another in Niamey, Niger. At the young age of thirty-eight, Sidi has become a prosperous merchant who runs a profitable import-export business that requires him to travel between Niger and New York City seven to ten times a year. Sidi is perhaps the ideal model of West African trader success. He came to the United States in 1989 and sold goods on the streets of midtown Manhattan. He invested wisely and realized that the American market for Africana was immense. He saved his money and went to Niger to make contact with craft artisans. In short order, he began to import to the United States homespun West African cloth, wool blankets, leather sacks, bags, and attaché cases as well as silver jewelry.

After obtaining an employment authorization permit, Sidi established a family in America by moving one of his two African wives (and her children) to New York City. In 1994 he became a permanent resident. As a permanent resident, Sidi is able to travel between the United States and West Africa with few restrictions. Because he travels to African so frequently, Sidi has become a private courier. For a small fee, he takes to Africa important letters or money earmarked for the families of various traders. From Africa he carries letters and small gifts to his compatriots in New York City. The freedom to travel also enables Sidi to find new craft ateliers in Niger. During his six-week sojourns in Niger he of course tends to his other family.

This pattern is a contemporary version of West African polygynous marriage practices. In Western Niger, for example, prosperous itinerant traders establish residences in the major market towns of their trading circuit. According to many Nigerien husbands, they try to pay equal attention to their wives and children in order to minimize the inevitable disputes that arise, especially when cowives live in one compound.[7]

Sidi is particularly proud of his youngest son in New York City. The boy, Soumana, attends public school in the South Bronx and has been put in a program for gifted students. In the summer of 1995, Sidi boasted of his son's performance. "He is so smart. He's very good in math, and never forgets anything. He was the top student in his class. The school gave him a certificate. I speak to him in Songhay," he continued, "so he can visit Niger soon. He does not yet know his country. But I will send him there when he is old enough for middle school. I don't want him to go to middle school in New York. The schools are not good, and he'd be exposed to bad people. I'll send him to my family in Niger so that he will learn discipline from his relatives. I want to send him to an American school in Niamey. That way, he'll know French as well as English and he'll be able to choose a university in Africa, France, or the United States. He'll be a real citizen of the world." Many of the traders share similar aspirations for their children.

Fellowship and Religion

Whatever the family circumstances of the traders, they invariably complain about the lack of fellowship in America. This lack takes on many dimensions. Traders often complain, for example, of the formality of American social interchange. In March 1998 a Malian trader said that for him America was almost like a prison:

> There are so many rules, here. Your time is scheduled. You cannot just drop by and see someone; you have to make an appointment. People are in too much of a hurry. They take no time to talk with one another. Everything is so tight. In Africa we are freer. Even if you are a stranger, people will invite you into their house and talk to you. Here that never happens. America is a prison. In Africa there is more fellowship.

The search for companionship among compatriots leads many West Africans to endure deteriorated conditions so that they may live in a "vertical village" like the Park View Hotel, "Le Cent Dix," at 110th and Lenox in Harlem. The majority of the Park View's tenants are Francophone West Africans. There are similar "villages" in high-rise as well as garden apartments in the Bronx and Brooklyn.

West Africans have also attempted to generate fellowship through the establishment of "national" associations. There are such groups as L'Association des Guineans aux USA, L'Association des Maliens aux USA, L'Association des Senegalais aux USA, and L'Association de Nigeriens de New York. The associations are usually connected in some way or fashion to the diplomatic missions of the various Francophone African countries. Meetings are held once a month, often at a particular nation's United Nations mission. During the meetings, issues of mutual concern are discussed. The associations hold receptions for major Muslim and national holidays. They sometimes collect funds to defray a compatriot's unexpected medical expenses. In the case of a compatriot's death, they also contribute funds to ship the body back to West Africa for burial.

Although West African traders speak highly of their particular associations, their participation in the regular activities of the organizations—the monthly meetings—is infrequent. Only a few traders among Nigeriens, for example, are active members. The vast majority of Nigerien traders have neither the time nor the inclination to attend association meetings or events. One reason for this infrequent participation has to do with a fault line that runs deep in Nigerien society—between the educated elite who run the associations in New York and the less educated traders and peasants who are "represented" by the associations.

Many West African traders in New York City seem to derive their greatest sense of fellowship and social support from Islam. The religion of Muhammad unquestionably structures their everyday lives and keeps alive their sense of identity in what, for most, remains an alien and strange place. During my seven years of ongoing conversations with West African traders in New York City, the subject of Islam has been invariably raised, especially when the conversation turns to the quality of life in the United States. They say that in the face of social deterioration in New York City, Islam has made them strong; its discipline and values empower them to cope with social isolation in America. It enables them to resist the divisive forces that they believe ruin American families. The great buffer to their cultural dislocation is the perception, held by almost all the traders that I have met, that Islam makes them emotionally and morally superior to most Americans.

El Hadji Harouna Soulay is a forty-five-year-old Nigerian who made the expensive pilgrimage to Mecca when he was thirty-four years old. El Hadji Harouna embodies the aforementioned sense of Islamic moral superiority. Between 1994 and 1997 he sold T-shirts, baseball caps, and sweatshirts from shelves stuffed between two storefronts on Canal Street in Lower Manhattan. He works hard to support one wife and fourteen children. He also sends money to his three brothers and four sisters. His mother and father are both dead.

On a rainy day in December 1995 El Hadji Harouna sat under an awning on the steps of Taj Mahal, a radio and electronics store on Canal Street near West Broadway. He pointed out two seemingly down-and-out street hawkers, both African Americans, employed by the owners of Taj Mahal.

"You see those men there," El Hadji Harouna said, referring to the hawkers. "They know only their mother. Sometimes they don't even know who their father is. That's the way it often is in America. Families are not unified. Look at him," he said, referring to the older of the two hawkers. "He is from Georgia. His family sends him money every month, and as long as I've known him he has not once returned there to visit them. Why do people here not honor their parents? Why do families here not stick together—at least in spirit? I want to get back to my family compound where we can all live together," El Hadji Harouna stated emphatically. "Can parents here depend on their children to take care of them when they are old? I do not think so. I have seen children who sit at home and eat their parents' money, but they think they owe their parents no obligation. My children phone me every week and ask me to come home. When I am old even if I have no money, my children will look after me. I will do no work. I will eat, sleep, and talk with my friends."

El Hadji continued his conversation but now concentrated on religion. "My Muslim discipline gives me great strength to withstand America. I have been to Mecca. I give to the poor. I rise before dawn so that I can pray five times a day, every day. I fast during Ramadan. I avoid pork and alcohol. I honor the memory of my father and mother. I respect my wife. And even if I lose all my money, if I am able, Inshallah, to live with my family, I will be truly blessed." Like most of the traders I've encountered, El Hadji's faith is inviolable.

Membership in the community of the faithful—the community of Muslims in New York City—creates for many West Africans a spiritual bond, provides a source of social support, and constructs a buffer against the stresses of city life in New York. Like any religion Islam provides explanations about the existential absurdities of life. It supplies an always already set of explanations for the sociocultural problems of Muslims living in societies in which Islam is not a major sociopolitical force. For many traders in New York City, Islam as a way of life is seen as morally superior to other faiths practiced in the United States. And yet, being a member of the community of the faithful does not dissipate a West African trader's financial difficulties, nor does it eliminate the stress of potential illness or the existential doubts brought on by cultural alienation.

A number of writers have recently depicted West Africans in New York as uniformly savvy entrepreneurs who easily solve the economic, political, and social problems they confront in America (see Millman 1997; Perry 1997). These heroic portraits are at best partial. There are certainly many West African traders who flourish in New York City; there are just as many, I think, who, for any number of reasons, continue to lose ground in their ongoing battles with economic privation and cultural isolation.

Even if traders adapt successfully to city life in New York, very few of them have expressed a desire to settle permanently in the United States. Even so, they want to preserve their economic gains and maintain the flow of money from the streets of New York City to the dusty paths of their West African villages. How to solve this dilemma? Recently, many of the more successful traders, both documented and undocumented, have brought their brothers to New York City. They live together, during which time the younger brothers work and learn the business. In time the older brother will return to West Africa, leaving the business in the trustworthy hands of kinsmen. They will have, in every sense of the phrase, engaged in the process of trading places.

Notes

1. Press coverage of the Diallo tragedy was surprisingly thorough. *The New York Times* sent a reporter to Guinea to cover Amadou Diallo's funeral. Since then, reporters have seemed to be more sensitive to issues of African immigrants in New York. A case in point was the November coverage of a strike by West African grocery deliverymen.
2. The New York City Department of City Planning, Population Division reports that for 1990–1996, 10,914 West Africans were admitted to New York City as permanent residents. The statistic does not include temporary migrants (students, exchange visitors, government officials) or undocumented migrants. This total is considerably smaller than the estimate reported in *The New York Times,* which considers West Africans excluded in the official total.
3. The expansion of the gulf between rich and poor in New York City has created space for the rapid growth of the informal economy, which is unregulated. Lack of regulation means that the informal sector includes street vendors as well unlicensed day care service. It also includes a craftsperson who builds furniture in an area not zoned for manufacturing. See Coombe and Stoller 1994; Castells and Portes 1989
4. In November 1998, the Masjid moved the market from the busy corner of 116th Street and Lenox to a space on the south side of 116th Street near Fifth Avenue.
5. There is a trader ethos that is well depicted in Jean Rouch's wonderful film *Jaguar.* Although Rouch may have romanticized the adventurous aspects of long-distance trading in West Africa, he is quite right about the trader's expectations of respect. After a long sojourn in foreign lands traders are accorded local reverence if and only if they return home with goods and perhaps enough money to "retire" to the village as a respected elder.
6. The Mourids, a Senegalese-based Sufi brotherhood, are well organized in New York City. Many Senegalese street vendors are members and owe their allegiance to their sheik in Touba City, Senegal. Less well organized purely economic networks exist among non-Senegalese. See Malcomson 1997; O'Brien 1971.
7. Women in polygynous marriages tended to avoid discussions about the internal dynamics of their households—especially with a male researcher. Accordingly, I have no data on their attitudes to polygynous arrangements—national or transnational.

References

Bluestone, Daniel. 1991. "The Pushcart Evil: Peddlers, Merchants and New York City's Streets, 1880–1940." *Journal of Urban History* 18:68–92.

Boville, E. W. 1995 [1958]. *The Golden Trade of the Moors.* Princeton, N.J.: M. Weiner.

Brenner, Louis, ed. 1993. *Muslim Identity and Social Change in Sub-Saharan Africa.* Bloomington: Indiana University Press.

Callaghy, Thomas, and John Ravenhill, eds. 1993. *Hemmed In: Reponses to Africa's Economic Decline.* New York: Columbia University Press.

Castells, Manuel, and Alejandro Portes. 1989. "The World Underneath: The Origins, Dynamics and Effects of the Informal Economy." In A. Portes et al., eds., *The Informal Economy,* pp. 11–33. Baltimore: Johns Hopkins University Press.

Cohen, Abner. 1969. *Custom and Politics in Urban Africa: A Study of Hausa Migrants in Yoruba Towns.* Berkeley: University of California Press.

Coombe, Rosemary, and Paul Stoller. 1994. "X Marks the Spot: The Ambiguities of African Trading in the Commerce of the Black Public Sphere." *Public Culture* 15:249–75.

Cooper, Michael. 1999. "Police Fire 41 Shots, and an Unarmed Man is Dead." *The New York Times,* February 5, A1, A25.

Curtin, Phillip. 1974. *Economic Change in Precolonial Africa: Senegambia in the Era of the Slave Trade.* Madison: University of Wisconsin Press.

Davis, Mike. 1990. *City of Quartz.* London: Verso.

Dugger, Celia. 1996. "Woman, Seeking Asylum, Endures Prison in America." *The New York Times,* April 15, A1.

Ebin, Victoria, and Rose Lake. 1992. "Camelots a New York: Les pionniers de l'immigration Senegalaise." *Hommes et migrations* 1160:32–37.

Firestone, David. 1995. "Giuliani Criticizes a US Crackdown on Illegal Aliens." *The New York Times,* August 23, A1, B2.

Gregoire, Emmanuel. 1992. *Alhazai of Maradi: Traditional Hausa Merchants in a Changing Sahelian City.* Boulder: Lynne Rienner.

——. 1993. "Islam and Identity of Merchants in Maradi (Niger)." In Louis Brenner, ed., *Muslim Identity and Social Change in Sub-Saharan Africa,* pp. 106–16. Bloomington: Indiana University Press.

Harvey, David. 1989. *The Condition of Postmodernity.* London: Basil Blackwell.

Hofstede, George. 1980. *Culture's Consequences.* Beverly Hills, Calif.: Sage.

Jacobs, Andrew. 1999. "African Deliverymen Complain, Gently, of a Tough Job."*New York Times,* November 10, B1.

Malcolmson, Scott. 1997. "West of Eden: The Mourid Ethic and the Spirit of Capitalism." *Transition* 79:24–44.

McCay, Claude. 1940. *Harlem: Negro Metropolis.* New York: Dutton.

Millman, Joel. 1997. *The Other Americans: How Immigrants Renew Our Country, Our Economy and Our Values.* New York: Viking.

Mirowsky, J. 1995. "Age and the Sense of Control." *Social Psychology Quarterly* 58(1): 31–34.

Mirowsky, J., and C. E. Ross. 1991. "Eliminating Defense and Agreement Bias from

Measures of a Sense of Control: A 2X2 Index." *Social Psychology Quarterly* 52(2): 127–45.

Mittleman, James, ed. 1996. *Yearbook of International Political Economy 9.* Boulder: Lynne Rienner.

Mollenkopf, John, and Manuel Castells, eds. 1991. *Dual City: Restructuring New York.* New York: Russell Sage Foundation.

New York City Department of City Planning. 1999. *The Newest New Yorkers 1995–1996.* New York: New York City Department of City Planning.

Nwadiora, Emeka. 1996. "Therapy With African Families." *Western Journal of Black Studies* 20(3): 117–25.

O'Brien, Conor Cruise. 1971. *The Mourids.* London: Oxford University Press.

Osofsky, Gilbert. 1971. *Harlem, the Making of a Ghetto: A History of Negro New York, 1900–1920.* New York: Harper and Row.

Perry, Donna L. 1997. "Rural Ideologies and Urban Imaginings: Wolof Immigrants in New York City." *Africa Today* 44(2): 229–60.

Portes, Alejandro, and Alex Stepick. 1993. *City on the Edge: The Transformation of Miami.* Berkeley: University of California Press.

Rouch, Jean. 1956. "Migrations au Ghana." *Journal de la Société des Africanistes* 26(1–2): 33–196.

Sachs, Susan. 1999a. "Guineans Still See Opportunity in U.S." *The New York Times,* February 21, 39.

———. 1999b. "Wanderings Over, a Son Is Laid to Rest." *The New York Times,* February 18, 1 B5.

———. 1999c. "Slain Man's Mother Is Center of Attention in Guinea." *The New York Times,* February 17, B1.

Sassen, Saskia. 1991. *The Global City: New York, London, Tokyo.* Princeton: Princeton University Press.

———. 1996. "Whose City Is It? Globalization and the Formation of New Claims." *Public Culture* 8:205–23.

Stoller, Paul. 1996. "Spaces, Places and Fields: The Politics of West African Trading in New York City." *American Anthropologist* 96(4): 776–89.

———. 1997. "Globalizing Method: Doing Ethnography in Transnational Spaces." *Anthropology and Humanism* 17(1): 81–95.

Tahmaseb-McConatha, J., and F. Obudiate. 1998. "Immigrant Women and Well-Being." Paper presented at the Annual Meetings of the Association for Women in Psychology. Baltimore, March.

Waldman, Amy. 1999. "Slain Man Is Remembered as Shy and Hard Working." *The New York Times,* February 5, A25.

Weir, Richard. 1999. "Start Off for a Final Journey." *The New York Times,* February 21, sec. 14, p. 6.

Dominicans: Transnational Identities and Local Politics

Patricia R. Pessar and Pamela M. Graham

From the late 1960s to the present, the Dominican Republic has consistently ranked among the top ten countries sending immigrants to the United States; and by the 1980s this small Caribbean nation was the leading source of emigration into New York City (New York City Department of City Planning 1992). An estimated 412,000 foreign-born Dominicans resided in the city in 1998,[1] with the majority living in upper Manhattan (Foner 2000:12).

Most studies of Dominicans in New York have concentrated on their economic incorporation (Pessar 1987; Grasmuck and Pessar 1991; Guarnizo 1992; Gilbertson and Gurak 1993; Hernández et al. 1995). Clearly, this is an important perspective. Dominicans themselves sometime say, "No hay vida en Nuevo York, solamente trabajo" (there is no life in New York, only work). Yet the focus on economic issues detracts from the rich social, cultural, and political lives Dominicans have fashioned (Duany 1994; Pessar 1995; Graham 1996; Torres-Saillant and Hernández 1998).

To contribute to a fuller and more balanced picture, this chapter focuses on Dominican New Yorkers' political development over the course of the last few decades.[2] In doing so, we will describe Dominicans' simultaneous incorporation into the political systems of New York *and* their country of origin. Such a binational perspective is essential for understanding a population that has been noted for its manifold transnational identities, social relations, and institutions (Georges 1990; Grasmuck and Pessar 1991; Guarnizo 1992; 1994; Graham 1996, 1997; Levitt 1999). We contend that a dual political engagement with the country of origin and the country of settlement has been an ongoing reality for Dominicans for some time now; moreover, it is an engagement that involves neither a zero-sum game nor mutually exclusive strategies. Our analysis considers the ways in which the political lives of Dominicans in the United States and in the Dominican Republic have been impacted by the unique characteristics of New York City's political processes and how, in turn, the city's political landscape has been altered by the contributions and presence of a large Dominican-origin population.

The research for this chapter draws on fieldwork conducted by the two authors in the Dominican Republic and in New York City over the course of the 1980s (Pessar) and 1990s (Graham) as well as on secondary source materials. A brief introductory history of Dominican immigration to the United States and a socioeconomic sketch of Dominican New Yorkers precede our discussion of Dominicans' political development.

Dominican Immigration to the United States

Although Dominicans did not begin emigrating to the United States in large numbers until the mid-1960s, the conditions that promoted this massive displacement were initiated almost a century earlier when significant political, economic, and sociocultural ties developed between the United States and the Dominican Republic. Indeed, in the early 1870s serious debates took place in the U.S. Congress over the possibility of annexing the newly independent Dominican nation to the United States. Over the years, the mounting interdependency between the two countries has supported a pattern of foreign investment that has enriched American business interests and a small coterie of Dominican elites while leaving the bulk of the growing Dominican population with insufficient access to land and wage employment (Grasmuck and Pessar 1991). This interdependency also managed to instill the lure of American culture, products, and consumerism far in advance of the actual mass emigration abroad (Moya Pons 1995). Moreover, two periods of U.S. military intervention (1816–1824 and 1965) and almost continuous U.S. political involvement in the country's internal affairs has severely limited progressive Dominicans' abilities to institute much-needed political and economic reforms (Calder 1984; Vega 1992; Moya Pons 1995).

From 1930 to 1961, dictator Rafael Trujillo severely curtailed emigration, a measure intended to strictly control the national labor force and to prevent the creation of threatening exile communities abroad (Georges 1990). When mass migration commenced in the early 1960s following Trujillo's assassination, there were clearly pressing economic problems on the island, but out-migration was initially spurred far more by political motivations than by economic need. Juan Bosch, the exiled leader of the Dominican Revolutionary Party (PRD), returned home and was elected president in 1962 on a platform calling for moderate economic reform and a reduction in U.S. control. After only seven months in office, Bosch was deposed in a coup supported by members of the Dominican elite, the military, and the U.S. government. This strong-arm action precipitated several years of unrest and popular uprising. When it appeared as if the popular forces might emerge victorious, the United States decided to intervene militarily, allegedly to prevent the establishment of a second Cuba in the United States's backyard (Gleijeses 1978). When "peace" was restored and elections were held in 1966, Bosch, who was again the PRD candidate, was so terrorized that he could not leave his house to campaign, and more than 350 of his PRD supporters were killed (Moya Pons 1995). The victor was Trujillo supporter Joaquín Balaguer, who had himself resided in exile in New York City between 1962 and 1965, where he "rebuilt his power base on 57th Street in a Horn and Hardart Cafeteria" (Hendricks 1980:386).

Dominican emigration to the United States soared during these politically volatile years, going from an annual average of 990 registered immigrants in the 1950s to 9,330 per year in the 1960s. Initially the emigrants were largely conservative, middle-class people fearful, at first, of the progressive Bosch regime and then of the popular unrest that gripped the country following Bosch's defeat (Guarnizo 1992). During this politically unstable period, the U.S. government's strategy for issuing visas changed, as migration was seen as serving American foreign policy interests. The then-U.S. ambassador to the Dominican Republic advocated granting wider access to visas as a safety valve to reduce political unrest (and to rid the island of political agitators) and as a way to improve relations between the two countries (Martin 1966; Mitchell 1992). The new visa policy made it possible for many progressive participants in the revolution of 1965 to get visas, including members of left-wing and social-democratic parties, labor organizers, and dissident students from the University of Santo Domingo (Georges 1987). This proved to be an exceedingly important episode in Dominican immigrant history, and one, as we shall see, that left its mark on the politics of the diaspora. Nonetheless, it did not take long before emigration came to be shaped far more by the economic needs of the Dominican populace and by a demand for a relatively cheap and vulnerable labor force in New York than by U.S. foreign policy concerns.

Although not officially organized or promoted by the Dominican state, since the mid-1960s out-migration has been a central feature of the country's economic and political development (Grasmuck and Pessar 1991). Ambitious development programs based initially on import substitution and, later, on export-led industrialization have fallen far short of projected revenues and job creation. In fact, in the 1980s and 1990s the Dominican Republic faced escalating oil prices, a sharp decline in exports, and massive foreign debt that it could no longer afford to repay.

Moreover, national growth rates were negative for the first time in decades. In order to renegotiate its foreign debt, the Dominican government adopted severe structural adjustment measures in 1982 under the tutelage of the International Monetary Fund. These policies dictated a wage freeze that lasted two years and contributed to drastic increases in the cost of basic consumer goods. Not surprisingly, the 1980s witnessed a general pauperization of the population and a shrinking of the middle class (Guarnizo 1992). Indeed, by 1992, per capita income was below levels reached in the early 1970s (when adjusted for inflation); unemployment rose from 15 percent in 1971 to 30 percent in 1991 (Hernández et al. 1995:14, 16).

Meanwhile, the salary differential between the Dominican Republic and the United States continued to widen. In 1980 the minimum monthly salary for full-time work in the United States was four times that in the Dominican Republic; by 1987 the difference had increased to six times, and by 1991 to thirteen times the republic's minimum wage (Grasmuck and Pessar 1991:46; Guarnizo 1992: 63). Any Dominican contemplating a move to the United States could only be encouraged by these calculations—and encouraged they were, as the sustained high rates of emigration throughout this period attest. Whereas only 11,655 Dominicans were legally admitted to the United States in 1977, this figure more than doubled throughout much of the 1980s and quadrupled in the 1990s (U.S. Immigration and Naturalization Service reports 1977–1999). Not only has the volume of migration increased, but its socioeconomic diversity has as well. The Dominican immigrant stream in the 1960s and 1970s was largely drawn from the middle sectors of Dominican society, but in the 1980s and 1990s it broadened to include many less-skilled workers and highly skilled professionals (Guarnizo 1992; Grasmuck and Pessar 1996). Nonetheless, the very poorest segment of the Dominican population is still underrepresented within this immigrant population.

Socioeconomic Incorporation in New York

> Here life is not worth
> a rotten guava.
> If a hoodlum doesn't kill you
> the factory will.
> > —*Sandy Reyes*
> > *and Karen Records,*
> > *cited in Georges 1990*

Although, as we have noted, initially many Dominicans emigrated owing to political necessity, over time the vast majority have departed in pursuit of economic advancement. Thus hopes of attaining (or sustaining) a secure middle-class standard of living have been uppermost in the minds of many. This was a far more attainable goal for the early waves of immigrants who arrived in New York in the 1960s and 1970s, when manufacturing jobs were more plentiful and when competition within the Dominican ethnic economy was less intense. Since then, most Dominican New Yorkers have struggled against daunting odds to hold down jobs and to accumulate modest savings. Indeed, compared to other New Yorkers, including other Hispanics, Dominican New Yorkers have not been faring well. According to the Current Population Survey of 1997, the Dominican population had the highest poverty rate, 46 percent compared to 24 percent for the entire city, and 37 percent for all Hispanics (Hernández and Rivera-Batiz 1997:34). Similarly, per capita household income among Dominicans was substantially lower than the New York City average at $6,094 for Dominicans compared to $19,043 for all New Yorkers and $16,560 for all New York City immigrants (Hernández and Rivera-Batiz 1997:34, 41). The unemployment rate for Dominicans was close to double the rate for the overall New York City population (Hernández and Rivera-Batiz 1997:44).

What accounts for this poor performance? Dominicans are unfortunately concentrated in two sectors, manufacturing and wholesale/retail trades, which have been marked by deteriorating wages and massive job loss over the last few decades. Also, the recent arrival of new populations of immigrants from Mexico and Central America who are willing to work for even lower wages under far inferior working conditions than many Dominicans deem acceptable has negatively affected the employment picture. Although some Dominican business owners have prospered in New York—a few boast a large workforce and assets of over one million dollars (Guarnizo 1992:261)—generally the growing ethnic enclave has turned out to be little more than a safety net for many owners. Moreover, jobs in Dominican-owned businesses tend to pay less and provide less adequate health and retirement benefits than those in native-owned firms (Grasmuck and Pessar 1991; Gilbertson and Gurak 1993).

Other factors also explain why Dominican New Yorkers are doing poorly. Many possess social handicaps, such as low levels of education and membership in female-headed households, which inhibit their prospects for advancement. In 1990, more than 60 percent of Dominicans over age twenty-five in New York City had not completed high school (Grasmuck and Pessar 1996). The impact of education on earnings becomes quite clear when we observe that Dominicans with less than a high school education showed no improvement in their earnings (adjusted for inflation) during the 1980s. By contrast, Dominican college graduates in New York earned 29 percent more in 1989 than in 1979 (Hernández et al. 1995:39–40).

A well-established link exists between female-headed households and poverty. Dominicans are no exception. Almost 40 percent of all Dominican households with children under the age of eighteen in New York City are female-headed and more than half (52 percent) of these are living below the poverty line (Hernández et al. 1995:39–40). By comparison, only 19 percent of married Dominican households are below the poverty line. Dominican women face a substantial gender gap in earnings; in 1989 the annual earnings of Dominican male workers was $15,088 while the comparable figure for women was only $11,347 (Hernández et al. 1995:49). Female-headed households are also more likely to be dependent on public assistance, another factor contributing to the high poverty rates of these households (Rosenbaum and Gilbertson 1995:246).

Racial discrimination is yet another serious obstacle confronting Dominican immigrants. In the 1990 census, the vast majority of Dominicans in New York City identified themselves as either mulatto, specified as "other" (50 percent), or "black" (25 percent). Skin color is a significant predictor of poverty among Dominicans, black and mulatto Dominicans having strikingly higher poverty levels than white Dominicans (Grasmuck and Pessar 1996). Dominicans perceived as "white" by potential employers appear to enjoy a relative advantage in the labor market over darker-skinned workers. One fair-skinned Dominican woman explained, "When I got my job in the laundry, the owners said that even though I spoke Spanish, they would hire me because they didn't want any Blacks working for them" (Pessar 1995:42–43).

In a manner paralleling their incorporation into the lowest tiers of New York City's labor market, Dominicans have settled into declining sections of the city. They are concentrated in Washington Heights/Inwood and Hamilton Heights in northern Manhattan and in parts of The South Bronx. These are neighborhoods characterized by overcrowded housing and schools, drug-related violence, tense police-community relations, inadequate access to health care services, and poorly maintained parks and physical facilities. Tolerance for such conditions may have been higher among earlier Dominican immigrants who were focused on returning to the Dominican Republic, and who viewed the deprivations associated with life in New York as temporary (Grasmuck and Pessar 1991). However, in the face of persistent, if not worsening, neighborhood conditions—and, in the context of continued inflows of Dominican immigrants alongside new generations of U.S.-born Dominicans—Dominican New Yorkers have mobilized to achieve local political representation and empowerment.

The Political Development of Dominicans in New York City

There was little in the early history of Dominican mass migration to New York City that augured the expanded political role Dominicans were to assume.[3] In the 1960s and 1970s, Dominicans received little attention in the media and were often mistaken for Puerto Ricans. As "invisible immigrants," Dominicans lacked a political presence as an identifiable immigrant group. The belief that Dominicans were unlikely to become citizens,[4] or if they did naturalize were unlikely to vote, meant that candidates for office paid little attention to Dominicans as an electoral constituency. In addition, few mechanisms existed for incorporating new immigrants into the mainstream political process, unlike the case of earlier eras of immigration when major political party organizations served as mobilizers of immigrant voters (Jones-Correa 1998; Erie 1985). Although reform movements in New York City in the 1960s and 1970s sought to lessen the power of traditional political party organizations and clubs and to encourage more minority participation, Dominicans were largely outside the circles of black and Puerto Rican political empowerment movements at that time (Arian et al. 1991).

Although they received little recognition within broader political circles in the city, Dominicans began to create an extensive organizational life within their own communities in the 1960s and 1970s. The earliest organizing efforts focused on cultural, recreational, and professional activities. By the late 1970s, at least thirty-six such clubs and associations existed in Washington Heights alone (Sassen-Koob 1979; see also Sainz 1990). Branches of Dominican opposition parties, such as the PRD and the Dominican Liberation Party (PLD), were also located in New York City; these organizations channeled exiles' efforts to gain control of the Dominican state. The political parties did not focus on conditions or issues affecting Dominicans in New York, but they set an important precedent of organizing immigrants on the basis of Dominican national origin. They also increased the visibility of what was becoming New York's fastest-growing immigrant community.

Beginning in the early 1980s, a cohort of Dominican-born and U.S.-educated leaders emerged who were intent on claiming resources and vying for power within New York City politics. They did so in the context of a growing Dominican presence in the city and against the backdrop of deteriorating economic and political conditions back in the country of origin, which made return a far less attractive option than before.[5] These new leaders spearheaded drives aimed at gaining representation for Dominicans on local advisory boards that determined funding for local antipoverty programs (Lescaille 1992; Jordan 1997) and on neighborhood school boards. Yolanda López, a longtime resident of Washington Heights, still speaks passionately about the campaign in the 1980s to gain greater community control over the neighborhood schools (in Community School District 6) and to make the schools more responsive to the needs and aspirations of their Dominican residents. "Even in the early eighties, our kids made up the bulk of students in the schools. But at that time our schools were the most overcrowded in the city, and many of our children left school without knowing how to read. We realized no one would help our kids if we Dominican parents did not struggle to take control."

The movement for empowerment and control in District 6 began in the 1980s when the Community Association of Progressive Dominicans confronted the school board and superintendent to demand bilingual education and programs for newly arrived immigrant families. Since then Dominicans have gained majority representation on the school board and have been able to shape programs to meet the community's changing needs. Their success has been the product of an aggressive program of voter registration; the creation of a parents' network throughout the district (based on the parent associations in each school); and the formation of a coalition of parents, community organizations, churches, and educators (Linares 1989). The result is a clear example of ethnic succession as Dominicans have replaced members of Washington Height's Jewish population, who despite their relatively small numbers had previously dominated the district's school board (Lowenstein 1989). Educator Guillermo Linares was elected president of the school board in 1986, and a few years later he wrote: "The education struggle and Community Board elections are important vehicles for empowering the community, especially Dominicans and Latinos, who cannot vote in regular elections, [if they are not citizens] but who can vote in school board elections" (Linares 1989:4).

As a result of these achievements, by the end of the 1980s Dominicans had ceased being "invisible" in public affairs. Their new visibility proved significant when in the late 1980s New York City and state governments embarked on a process of redistricting aimed, in large part, at maximizing chances for representation of previously underrepresented populations.[6] Already seasoned in ethnic politics, Dominican activists in northern Manhattan prepared proposals for a new district that would represent a predominantly Dominican constituency. They noted the great strides Dominicans had made in local school board elections, and they argued that Dominicans led all other groups in investments in Washington Heights and thus deserved the rewards of fair representation (Hernández and Lescaille 1991). Impressed by such arguments, the New York City Districting Commission created District 10 in northern Manhattan with a much greater percentage of Dominican residents than what previous districts covering the neighborhood had possessed. Since 1991 the district has been represented by Dominican-born former school board president Guillermo Linares.

Features of the 1993 Linares campaign, encompassing both the United States and the Dominican Republic, illustrate the binational nature of the emerging political community of Dominican New Yorkers. Linares's endorsements from powerful New Yorkers, like then-mayor David Dinkins, were matched by endorsements from prominent island politicians, such as high-ranking officials of the PLD. During the break between the primary and general elections, Linares returned to the Dominican Republic for a brief stay; there he raised funds for his campaign and participated in rallies that were covered by Spanish-language newspapers in New York. He even enlisted his mother to write a letter in Spanish from her home in the Dominican Republic urging voters in New York to vote for her son. The letter, deposited in scores of residential mailboxes throughout Washington Heights, read:

> As a mother of 9 children and 10 grandchildren, I have had many occasions to be proud in my life. But never have I felt as I do at this moment. Next Thursday, my son Guillermo will have the opportunity to become the first Dominican to serve as a member of the New York City Council.

She went on to appeal to the sentiments of many Dominican New Yorkers who were living far from loved ones when she wrote, "Unfortunately I cannot be there personally on Thursday to share this important moment in Guillermo's life. (I will be in Cabrera, Dominican Republic, from where I am writing you this card.)" But she reminded them that telephone lines do connect a people divided only by geography, not kinship, sentiment, or national pride.

> I will be waiting for the phone call to hear the good news. Please remember to vote for Guillermo Linares. . . . You will have a member of the City Council who will make you proud. And you are going to contribute to the phone call from Guillermo to his mother that will be very, very special!

Dominicans also gained politically as a result of the 1992 redistricting for the New York State Assembly: a regularly mandated process that also sought to reverse the political marginalization of underrepresented groups. Taking into account the pattern of Dominican settlement throughout northern Manhattan, District 72 was redrawn to increase the odds of the election of Latino candidates (Hanson and Falcón 1992). In 1996, Dominican-born Adriano Espaillat capitalized on the growing political involvement of Dominicans in District 72 when he successfully unseated the longtime Irish American incumbent, John Brian Murtaugh.[7]

At the same time that Dominicans began to win elected offices in New York, Dominican New Yorkers started to organize to gain more recognition and status within the Dominican Republic. The acquisition of dual nationality rights had long been a goal, but not until the 1980s did a group of leading entrepreneurs in New York begin to lobby vigorously for such rights. In the early 1990s, in response to these efforts and in recognition of the key role that remittances and investments of the overseas community had played in sustaining the country through difficult economic times,[8] the Dominican Senate decided to form the Committee on the Affairs of Dominicans Living Abroad. This official group dispatched members to the United States to discuss nationality and other political concerns.

Discussions over nationality rights were linked to the emerging role of Dominicans within New York City. Dominican politicians on the island and activists in New York agreed that it was advisable for larger numbers of Dominican immigrants to naturalize and to vote in the United States to increase the attention paid to Dominican causes on both sides of the border. This position gained popularity once anti-immigrant sentiments intensified in the latter half of the 1990s as federal and state governments legislated cutbacks in social and economic benefits available to legal immigrants. Indeed, Dominicans involved in a recent study of naturalization in New York referred to the changing laws and their sense of vulnerability when explaining their decisions to adopt U.S. citizenship (Singer and Gilbertson 2000). For their part, proponents of dual citizenship argued that Dominicans would be more inclined to become U.S. citizens if they had the option to continue being Dominican, not just symbolically but legally as well. A change in the Dominican constitution permitting the reacquisition of nationality rights was ultimately adopted in 1994 (Jiménez Polanco 1999b).[9]

The election in 1996 of New York–raised lawyer Leonel Fernández to the presidency of the Dominican Republic paved the way for further changes in the status of Dominicans living abroad. Electoral reform laws were passed in 1997 that permitted voting in presidential elections from outside the country by the year 2000. Debates over the logistics of managing voting from abroad has stalled its implementation, and the future availability of this right was still in doubt at the time of this writing. Although the Dominican government has yet to institutionalize a formal process for the congressional representation of Dominicans living abroad, de facto measures already exist. A PLD candidate for the Dominican city of Santiago was actually a member of the New York section of the party; he was included on the party's candidate rosters in the 1996 elections to offer a more formal political role to those living abroad (Itzigsohn et al. 1999).

Less-institutionalized political relationships between Dominican immigrants and the country of origin also endure. Major political parties continue to retain their prominence in northern Manhattan, and public forums and rallies are regularly held for presidential candidates during election years. Dominican immigrants have participated in the Diálogo Nacional program launched by Fernández early in his administration to gather popular input on state reform proposals. In one such meeting in Washington Heights, then-Dominican consul in New York Bienvenido Pérez stated that the meeting was convened with the purpose of assuring the participation of Dominicans living abroad: "Because we are the Dominican Republic overseas and the whole country should participate in the meeting" (Organo de Difusion Digital del Gobierno Dominicano 1998).

New Trends in Politics

Over the past few decades Dominicans have begun to disperse in large numbers away from New York City toward other growing centers of Dominican settlement such as Union City, New Jersey; Providence, Rhode Island; Lawrence, Massachusetts; and Miami, Florida. This demographic trend has started to shift Dominican political agendas away from local issues and toward those that affect Dominican immigrants throughout the United States. In these efforts, umbrella groups such as the Dominican American National Roundtable have sought the support of Dominicans in New York while hoping to redirect the concentrated political resources in the city toward other locales so as to address broader challenges faced by all Dominicans in the United States such as education, economic and business development, immigration reform, and political empowerment.

Though Dominican New Yorkers have proven successful in organizing around their Dominican identity, signs exist that strategic alliances are also being forged around more expansive identities based on pan-ethnicity (i.e., Latinos) and race (i.e., "blackness"). Racially based alliances are particularly striking for a population that brings from the Dominican Republic denigrating notions of blackness (based in large part on a highly contested history with neighboring Haiti) and the belief that to be partly white (the case for most Dominicans) is to be nonblack (del Castillo and Murphy 1987; Torres-Saillant 1998). The willingness to form racially based alliances reflects the fact that, regardless of their own understandings, Dominicans are frequently perceived by Americans as black and are thus subjected to biases and prejudices in this country. Recent accusations of police brutality with respect to the Abner Louima and Amadou Diallo cases have galvanized Dominican politicians and activists to protest alongside fellow Latinos, African Americans, and West Africans. In these acts of civil protest, Dominican participants have recalled the names of their own dead who have been the victims of questionable police tactics (Soto Bouzas 1999). Moreover, in their efforts to focus broader attention on racial problems in New York, some Dominicans have concluded that it would be hypocritical to do so without also pointing to the plight of badly discriminated against Haitian workers and their Dominican-born offspring back in the Dominican Republic. In this we see early signs that Dominican immigrants are beginning to extend their struggles against racism and appeals for racial tolerance across national boundaries.[10]

Although Dominican national identity has been a powerful mobilizer, it cannot and does not mask differences that exist among Dominicans. Both Democratic and Republican parties have supported different Dominican candidates, and there have been both personal and political differences among such candidates. For example, in 1997 City Councilman Linares was unsuccessfully challenged in his bid for reelection by another Dominican candidate who was strongly supported by State Assemblyman Espaillat. Many Dominicans have expressed concerns over the negative effects of such rivalries on the public image of Dominican New Yorkers as a unified group, and on the overall process of empowerment. Though these concerns are valid, more optimistic interpretations do not see these rivalries as limiting political empowerment. Instead, as a variety of Dominican candidates emerge, future electoral contests will focus less on the ethnic loyalties of voters and more on the general content and character of a given candidate's leadership (Torres-Saillant and Hernández 1998:99).

We also see a transition in the wings as a new cohort of young Dominican-born and U.S.-born leaders comes of age. Many of these youthful leaders have participated in the Unión de Jovenes Dominicanos (Dominican Youth Union) and in the organization it helped spawn, Dominicanos/Dominicans 2000. Formed as a nonprofit organization in 1997, the small network of young Dominican activists worked for three years to sponsor a national (and international) conference that would lead to the construction of "a national agenda for the advancement of the Dominican community in New York City and the United States" (Dominicans/Dominicanos 2000 Web site). The conference, held at the City College of New York in February 2000, attracted more than 1,500 registered participants. It consisted primarily of workshops on health care, youth, law, interethnic relations, politics, economic empowerment, women and social change, the "diaspora and the island," the media, and the arts. Linares and Espaillat led a political workshop in which they emphasized the importance of unity among Dominicans and the need to pursue naturalization and participation in U.S. elections. While other local Latino political figures were also in attendance, the emergence of a new and youthful Dominican leadership was the most noticeable feature of what was probably the largest nationally organized political meeting of Dominicans and Dominican Americans to date.

Dominicans are not only divided occasionally along generational lines; divisions along gender and class lines also exist. Over the years women have demanded a more visible and growing role in forging the destiny of the Dominican New York community. Women like Democratic district leader María Luna have been active in formal politics while others have stepped forward to found social service agencies and community activist groups. Still others have created their own publications, such as *Mujer Latina* ("Latin Women") and *Mia* ("Mine") to disseminate information on the achievements of Dominican and other Latino women in the United States (Torres-Saillant and Hernández 1998). The founders of early women's groups often focused their attention on issues of importance to women in both the Dominican Republic and the United States. A second wave of Dominican women's organizations, like Colectivo de Mujeres Dominicanas (Collective of Dominican Women), emerged in New York in the mid-1980s. Mirella Cruz, one of the founding members of that group, argued for focusing on Dominican women in the diaspora on the grounds that in the Dominican Republic women were in the vanguard organizationally whereas in the United States, Dominican women were "still dealing with such basic issues as demanding the right to legitimacy, or gaining acceptance as spokespersons for the Dominican community" (Torres-Saillant and Hernández 1998:84).[11] One hopeful sign that women leaders are gaining greater community acceptance was the active participation of young women leaders in the events of Dominicans/Dominicanos 2000.

Matters of gender equity unite Dominican women in the city and across the diaspora, but class differences among women condition the day-to-day challenges they confront and may choose to organize around. In New York City the larger and more formal women's associations were founded by better-educated and more financially secure women. For the most part, these women direct their efforts toward female empowerment (e.g., job training and referral) and toward redressing all forms of discrimination against Dominican women (both in the United States and in the country of origin). To attain these goals, the women sometimes forge alliances with activists in the Dominican Republic and with other minority women's groups in the United States. Certain poorer and more vulnerable Dominican women in New York City have created more informal groups targeted at resolving immediate survival matters. Mothers Against Violence is one such group. Comprised of eighteen women and founded in 1989, it has appealed to the mayor's office to focus on neighborhood problems of crime and drugs, and the women themselves have picketed the premises of known crack dealers in Washington Heights. Another group of women has organized around housing concerns related to the privatization of public housing in their neighborhoods and an increase in rental fees due to gentrification in Washington Heights (Monreal Requena n.d.). Recognizing the need to acknowledge class differences among Dominican women while also affirming common ground, Dominican female leaders have worked to forge interclass ties within their organizations and among diverse women's groups.

Dominicans and New York Politics: Reciprocal Influences

How, then, have Dominicans' political identities and practices been influenced by their residence in New York? And, at the same time, how have political processes in New York been impacted by a large Dominican presence? Although many Dominican immigrants were deeply involved in political struggles at "home" (and in some cases came to New York due to political persecution), few of the skills they developed in the Dominican Republic were actually transferable to the New York City political context. Elections in the Dominican Republic have slowly become more competitive and legitimate, but electoral outcomes have frequently been subject to charges of fraud and corruption. The country's semiauthoritarian style of presidential leadership under Joaquín Balaguer and its political party structure built on patriarchal and charismatic leadership created few access points for citizens seeking to influence the political system (Hartlyn 1998; Jiménez Polanco 1999a).

New York afforded a very different political landscape that required the development of different political skills. These have included an understanding of the city's ethnic politics and the need to mobilize Dominican residents as an identifiable national group, grassroots organizing around specific issues, and strategies for either countering existing mainstream political machines (e.g., gaining control of the Upper Manhattan school board) or claiming spaces within them (e.g., assuming district leadership positions). Dominicans' residential concentration in northern Manhattan has been a major asset in a system based on mediating competing claims of ethnic politics. The ability to gain majority-Dominican districts has lessened the need to engage in interethnic coalition building, although elected officials in "Dominican" districts have also had to seek the electoral support of voters of other national or ethnic backgrounds. The role Dominicans will come to assume in the city's Latino politics, as the number of Puerto Ricans residing there continues to decline, is unknown (Navarro 2000). What is clear is that relations between the two groups have sometimes been problematic. For example, in 1992 Dominican leaders complained that their community was being held back in politics and community organization by a Latino leadership that pursued a narrowly Puerto Rican agenda. In the words of Guillermo Linares, "We all sit at the table when it comes time to draw lines. When the time comes to determine who represents all of us, we no longer find ourselves at the table" (González 1992:B4).

As the city's largest immigrant group, Dominicans are not yet represented in political office in proportion to their overall population, but they have clearly left their mark on local politics. As we noted, Dominicans began vying for power in the 1980s when two Dominicans were elected as Democratic district leaders, six were elected to the Washington Heights Area Policy Board, four were appointed to the Community Planning Board in Washington Heights, and Dominicans replaced Jews as the majority members of District 6's school board. These advances were extended in the 1990s as Dominicans actively participated in the politicking surrounding the redrawing of the city's and state's electoral districts. Having successfully created "Dominican" districts, they went on to elect the first Dominican city councilman and state assemblyman. Dominicans have been naturalizing to U.S. citizenship at an increasing rate in response to reforms in the Dominican constitution permitting dual citizenship and the punitive U.S. immigration and welfare legislation passed in 1996.[12] Community organizations have been active in promoting naturalization and have provided assistance to immigrants requesting citizenship (Singer and Gilberson 2000:8). Prominent Dominican leaders in New York have openly encouraged community members to naturalize; at the Dominicans/Dominicanos 2000 conference the issue came up repeatedly.

Though Dominican New Yorkers have made strides in state and municipal politics, many remain disenfranchised from more formal forms of politics—in some cases due to their recent arrival, their undocumented legal status, or both factors. Despite this type of disenfranchisement, many Dominicans have insisted on asserting full membership within their communities. In doing so they, alongside other naturalized and U.S.-born Dominicans, have begun to define "the political" in more expansive ways to include problems of family survival; neighborhood crime and police brutality; and deteriorating schools, housing stock, and public services (Monreal Requena n.d.). As in poor and immigrant communities in New York City and elsewhere, women (like the Dominican members of Mothers Against Violence) have frequently spearheaded these struggles (Susser 1986; Hardy-Fanta 1993; Benmayor et al. 1997).

Cultural citizenship—that is, employing cultural expression to claim public rights and recognition, and highlighting the interaction between citizenship and culture (Rosaldo 1997)—is yet another way in which Dominican New Yorkers have extended the boundaries of "the political." It was matters of cultural citizenship that helped to animate the 1980s school board elections as Dominicans sought more funding for bilingual education. Since that time Dominicans have accounted for the largest share of the students entering New York City public schools; accordingly, Dominican community leaders have demanded that curriculum design, instruction, and leadership training remain responsive to the experiences and needs of these children. Important advances in cultural citizenship have also been achieved through the efforts of Dominican scholars. The creation in 1994 of the Dominican Studies Institute, located on the campus of the City College of New York, is exemplary. The institute calls for a greater presence for

Dominican studies within the curricula of regional colleges and universities. Its members maintain that the creation "of instruments of knowledge . . . will enhance the possibility of communication and will diminish the chances of tensions between Dominicans and non-Dominicans in the United States" (Torres-Saillant and Hernández 1998:88). Scholars affiliated with the institute and other New York academic institutions have also played an important role in assembling Dominicanists resident in the Caribbean, North America, and Europe. Their collaborative efforts contribute to transnational as well as national understandings of Dominican identity, Dominican literature, Dominican history, and so on.

Matters of representation of the Dominican immigrant experience have also concerned many scholars of Dominican ancestry. Accordingly, they have sought to redress discriminatory stereotypes, such as those that characterize Dominicans as drug dealers or welfare queens. A case in point is the powerful rebuttal advanced by scholars Genettta Candelario and Nancy López, who assert: "The mythical welfare queen who looms so large in media and political discussions" is a discursive move that manages to shift "public attention away from real problems of structural social stratification and to dissections of individual pathology" (1995:20). In place of this majority discourse that focuses blame on the victims, they call for policies aimed at providing the Dominican community with "access to jobs that are better paying, more secure, and provide social benefits" (19).

Struggles over representation are also being waged within the contexts of literature, visual arts, performing arts, and music.[13] Advances have been made in recent years as Dominican authors Julia Alvarez and Junot Díaz have managed to reach wide audiences through their novels, poetry, and short stories. Nonetheless, there is still a pressing need to bring other contemporary Dominican literary figures to the attention of a broader audience and to gain recognition of a Dominican literary presence in the United States dating back to the early 1900s.[14] On another front, Latino music has grown in popularity and is assuming an ever-increasing role in forging American popular culture. Dominicans have contributed to this cultural movement through their production of merengue and bachata. In many instances their lyrics serve as vehicles for expressing Dominican immigrants' experiences on both sides of the border. The music has also opened a space for new cultural expression and forms of empowerment, as when the lead singer in the 1980s group Milly, Jocelyn y Los Vecinos, became "the first woman to sing downhome merengue commercially . . . mostly about ladies leaving their *machista* men" (Hanley, cited in Torres-Saillant and Hernández 1998:136). Moreover, young Dominican American musicians are drawing on Dominican and Latin sounds and mixing them with elements of hip-hop urban culture to stake claims to identities that are simultaneously Dominican, Latino, diasporic, and Afro Caribbean.

Perhaps one of the more visible symbols of the Dominican presence in New York is the Dominican Day Parade, which has been held in Upper Manhattan since the early 1970s. By the mid-1980s, the City of New York officially recognized the parade and collaborated with community leaders; a Dominican Day was declared for August of each year, and the parade route in Manhattan moved downtown to follow the traditional Fifth Avenue route of all major ethnic parades in the city (Jordan 1997). Hardly surprising, it is Washington Heights, the heart of the Dominican New York community and Dominican American culture, that is most inscribed with symbols of Dominican nationality and pride. For example, several of the neighborhood's public schools have been named after Dominican heroes (such as Juan Pablo Duarte, Salomé Ureña de Henríquez, and the Mirabal sisters), and in February 2000 the City Council approved the renaming of a main thoroughfare in northern Manhattan from St. Nicholas Avenue to Juan Pablo Duarte Avenue. Interestingly, a speech by Councilman Linares promoting this renaming effort referred to the fact that the main streets in Santo Domingo are named for U.S. presidents Kennedy and Lincoln, so in his view it was only fitting to rename some streets in New York City for Dominicans (viewed on the program "Community in Action/*Enterese* with Councilman Linares," February 21 2000, Manhattan Neighborhood Network public access cable). On a more sober note, we find yet another example of the use of popular culture to claim public space and public voice in the pieces of memorial art depicting the tragic loss of Dominican youth killed in territorial drug wars (Camacho 1996).

Linking National Participation Across Borders

The increasing visibility of Dominicans in local New York City and New York State politics during the 1990s has led some observers to wonder whether immigrant interest in politics in the "home" country can be sustained in a context of increasing integration into the U.S. political system, especially among successive generations of Dominican-ancestry residents. These dilemmas of political identification have been central to 1.5- and second-generation Dominicans. At the Dominicanos/Dominicans 2000 conference, a leading organizer ended an energetic speech with the statement "We came here to stay!" A recent book on Dominican Americans addressed this issue of coexisting political loyalties, stating, "One could fear that the need to remain focused on multiple goings-on in divergent political systems of separate geographies may cause Dominicans to spread themselves thin" (Torres-Saillant and Hernández 1998:156).

Political actors on different sides of the border have tended to highlight the importance of participation in the United States as a strategy of engagement with *both* nations. Speaking before a workshop at the Dominicanos/Dominicans 2000 Conference, Assemblyman Espaillat stated that Dominicans in the United States had two choices: to remain exclusively involved in politics in the Dominican Republic, or to support Dominican causes by becoming U.S. citizens and working to affect change there via participation in U.S. politics. Espaillat clearly favored the latter approach. This strategy has also been endorsed by Linares, who, speaking a few years ago about his own political role, stated, "The Dominican Republic is the land and the people that I left with the hope that someday I would return to help. I'm still committed to that hope, but it will not happen through my physical return. As I work for my community here, I am working toward a better future for the Dominicans that I left behind" (*New York News* 1993).

The Dominican president Fernández also touched on this issue, stating shortly after his election:

> If you, young mother, or you, elderly gentleman, or you, young student, feel the need to adopt the nationality of the United States in order to confront the vicissitudes of that society stemming from the end of the welfare era, do not feel tormented by this. Do it with a peaceful conscience, for you will continue being Dominicans, and we will welcome you as such when you set foot on the soil of our republic. (Rohter 1996:A8)

The linking of participation in both national contexts was also broached by two of the best-known participants in the closing session of the Dominicanos/Dominicans 2000 Conference: Santo Domingo mayor Johnny Ventura, and U.S. Senate candidate/first lady Hillary Rodham Clinton. In his speech, Mayor Ventura praised the accomplishments of Dominicans living abroad, expressed gratitude for their contributions to the Dominican Republic, and emphasized that Dominicans in the United States were an "indisputable part of us," and that "we are two parts of one community." Mrs. Clinton, after commenting that the young organizers certainly would have a future in politics, assured them that their work was important not only to Dominican Americans, but also to Dominicans in the Dominican Republic. The appearance and comments of these two political figures symbolized the importance of the Dominicanos/Dominicans 2000 effort and of Dominican New Yorkers in both national contexts.

As Dominicans continue to construct a greater political presence in both the Dominican Republic and New York, important questions will require exploration: these include the viability of such a binational path in the medium or long term, and its benefits for different segments of the Dominican community. Over the years, male entrepreneurs have led the drive for dual nationality and dual citizenship. And, as we have seen, poorer Dominican immigrant women seem more inclined to struggle at the local, neighborhood level for pressing matters of family and community survival than to expend their limited resources to make common cause with their compatriots back on the island. This may change, however, as these women grow older and find that meager retirement benefits can be stretched farther in the Dominican Republic or through a strategy of alternating residence between the island and New York (Singer and Gilbertson 2000). Whatever the ultimate configuration of political allegiances and practices in the future, it is necessary to map the transnational political field in which Dominicans currently operate to understand the contexts and the nature of how this new immigrant group in New York has undergone the processes of becoming Dominican New Yorkers.

Notes

1. This figure is based on the March 1998 Current Population Survey.
2. For an annotated bibliography of works on Dominican migration to the United States, see Aponte (1999).
3. For an account of the small Dominican immigrant and exile communities in New York City before 1960, see Graham (1996).
4. Only 7.8 percent of those Dominicans admitted as permanent residents between 1960 and 1970 elected to naturalize by 1980. This rate increased to 17.7 percent one decade later for all Dominicans and to 21.7 percent for those residing in New York City (Grasmuck and Pessar 1996). By contrast, immigrants from many Asian countries had naturalization rates well above 50 percent during this same period (Grasmuck and Pessar 1996).
5. The poor performance of the Dominican Republic's economy in the 1980s was echoed in the political disillusionment of many who hoped that the presidential victory of the opposition PRD in 1978 and 1982 would bring about significant political change. The eight years of PRD government proved disappointing as the party grappled with international economic crises, legacies of the previous government's inefficient state apparatus, internal party discord, and ideological loss of focus. For many, Balaguer's return to the presidency in 1986 was the final episode in their disillusionment with the PRD (Hartlyn 1998; Jiménez Polanco 1999a).
6. Silvio Torres-Saillant and Ramona Hernández (1998) claim that Dominicans as a community became known to many Americans after Washington Heights broke out in three days of disturbances and civil disobedience just a few days before the scheduled Democratic National Convention. At that time many Dominicans protested the killing by New York City police of a young Dominican man who was accused of selling drugs. Fearing that the Democratic National Convention might be disrupted by the protests, the police commissioner, many elected officials, and the mayor himself managed to appease Dominican New Yorkers by promising a complete investigation into the incident and adopting such measures as offering classes in cross-cultural sensitivity training for New York City police officers.
7. Murtaugh won reelection in 1994, following the redistricting. In 1996, Espaillat's victory was not a landslide; he won by only 196 votes out of a total of 6,400 cast in the primary. While data on the ethnic composition of the vote is not available, the new district's high Latino population and the registration of 2,400 new voters in 1996, along with Espaillat's strong emphasis on his Dominican ethnicity (and Murtaugh's lack of the same) during the campaign suggest that the issue of ethnic identity had become an important political factor (Tilove 1996).
8. The Dominican economy has become dependent on a relatively informal and diffuse process of remittances of money by Dominicans residing in the United States. By the late 1990s these amounted to close to US$1.25 billion per year (Garcilazo 1997).

9. This change in the Dominican constitution occurred in the context of disputed presidential elections of that year. Charges of fraud and corruption leveled at once-again victor Joaquín Balaguer led him to sign a political pact that mandated several constitutional reforms.

10. On this score Dominican immigrant and scholar Silvio Torres-Saillant (1998) writes: "The long struggles for equality and social justice by people of color in the United States have yielded invaluable lessons from which Dominican people in the diaspora and in the native land have drawn empowerment. The diaspora will render an inestimable service to the Dominican people if it can help rid the country of white supremacist thought and negrophobic discourse" (143).

11. Women in the Dominican Republic continue to enjoy more official recognition and participation in formal politics than is the case for their Dominican counterparts in the United States. Nonetheless, some conclude that women's representation in such governmental bodies as the Dirección General de la Mujer is a measure aimed far more at official co-optation than true empowerment (Jacqueline Jiménez-Polanco, personal communication, May 2000). Recently, Dominican women activists and politicians have come together across party lines to gain approval of a quota law to establish a minimum number of female candidates that must be listed on parties' electoral slates in future Dominican elections.

12. In 1993 Dominicans accounted for 2 percent of all registered voters in New York City (Torres-Saillant and Hernández 1998:96).

13. For an excellent overview of Dominican American Arts, see Torres-Saillant and Hernández 1998.

14. Dominican authors are notably missing from such compendiums of U.S. Hispanic literature as *The Hispanic Literary Companion* (Kanellos 1997) and *The Latino Reader* (Augenbraum and Fernández Olmos 1997).

References

Aponte, Sarah. 1999. *Dominican Migration to the United States, 1970–1997: An Annotated Bibliograraphy.* Dominican Research Monographs. New York: City University of New York Dominican Studies Institute.

Arian, Asher, Arthur S. Goldberg, John H. Mollenkopf, and Edward T. Rogowsky. 1991. *Changing New York City Politics.* New York: Routledge.

Augenbraum, Harold and Margarite Fernández Olmos, eds. 1997. *The Latino Reader: An American Literary Tradition.* Boston: Houghton Mifflin.

Benmayor, Rina, Rosa M. Torruellas, and Ana L. Juaribe. 1997. "Claiming Cultural Citizenship in East Harlem: 'Si Esto Puede Ayudar a la Comunidad Mía . . .'" In William W. Flores and Rina Benmayor, eds., *Latino Cultural Citizenship: Claiming Identity, Space, and Rights.* Boston: Beacon.

Calder, Bruce. 1984. *The Impact of Intervention: The Dominican Republic During the U.S. Occupation of 1916–1924.* Austin: University of Texas Press.

Camacho, Jhovanny. 1996. "Dominican Memorial Art: Testimonials of Pain in a Diaspora." *Punto 7 Review: A Journal of Marginal Discourse* 3(1): 126–34.

Candelario, Ginetta E. B., and Nancy López. 1995. "The Latest Edition of the Welfare Queen Story." *Phoebe: Journal of Feminist Scholarship, Theory, and Aesthetics* 7(1–2): 7–22.

"Councilman Guillermo Linares." 1993. *New York News Sunday Magazine Supplement, Viva New York,* February 28, 6.

del Castillo, José, and Martin F. Murphy. 1998. "Migration, National Identity, and Cultural Policy." *Journal of Ethnic Studies* 15(3): 49–69.

Duany, Jorge. 1994. *Quesqueya on the Hudson: The Transnational Identity of Dominicans in Washington Heights.* Dominican Research Monographs. New York: City University of New York Dominican Studies Institute.

Erie, S. P. 1985. "Rainbow's End: From the Old to the New Urban Ethnic Politics." In J. W. Moore and L. A. Maldonado, eds., *Urban Ethnicity: A New Era.* Beverly Hills: Sage.

Foner, Nancy. 2000. *From Ellis Island to JFK: New York's Two Waves of Immigration.* New Haven: Yale University Press.

Garcilazo, Miguel. 1997 "Dominicans Get a Breath of Fresh Air: New Consul a Big Hit." *Daily News* (New York), August 9, 11.

Georges, Eugenia. 1987. "A Comment on Dominican Ethnic Associations." In Constance Sutton and Elsa Chaney, eds., *Caribbean Life in New York City: Sociocultural Dimensions.* New York: Center for Migration Studies.

——. 1990. *The Making of a Transnational Community: Migration, Development, and Cultural Change in the Dominican Republic.* New York: Columbia University Press.

Gilbertson, Greta, and Douglas Gurak. 1993. "Broadening the Enclave Debate: The Labor Market Experiences of Dominican and Colombian Men in New York City." *Sociological Forum* 8(2): 205–20.

Gleijeses, Piero. 1978. *The Dominican Crisis: The 1965 Constitutionalist Revolt and the American Intervention.* Baltimore: Johns Hopkins University Press.

González, David. 1992. "Dominican Immigration Alters Hispanic New York." *The New York Times,* September 1, A1.

Graham, Pamela M. 1996. *Re-imagining the Nation and Defining the District: The Simultaneous Political Incorporation of Dominican Transnational Migrants.* Ph.D. diss., University of North Carolina at Chapel Hill.

——. 1997. "Re-Imagining the Nation and Defining the District: Dominican Migration and Transnational Politics." In Patrica Pessar, ed., *Caribbean Circuits: Transnational Approaches to Migration.* New York: Center for Migration Studies.

Grasmuck, Sherri, and Patricia R. Pessar. 1991. *Between Two Islands: Dominican International Migration.* Berkeley: University of California Press.

——. 1996. "Dominicans in the United States: First and Second Generation Settlement of 1960–1990." In Silvia Pedraza and Rubén Rumbaut, eds., *Origins and Destinies: Immigration, Race, and Ethnicity in America.* Belmont, Calif.: Wadsworth.

Guarnizo, Luis. 1992. *One Country in Two: Dominican Owned Firms in New York and the Dominican Republic.* Ph.D. diss., Johns Hopkins University, Baltimore.

——. 1994. "Los Dominicanyorks: The Making of a Binational Society." *Annals of the American Academy of Political and Social Sciences* 533:70–86.

Hardy-Fanta, Carol. 1993. *Latina Politics, Latino Politics.* Philadelphia: Temple University Press.

Hanson, Christopher, and Angelo Falcón. 1992. *Latinos and the Redistricting Process in New York City: An Assessment and Profiles of the New Latino Assembly, State Senate and Congressional Districts.* New York: Institute for Puerto Rican Policy.

Hartlyn, Jonathan. 1998. *The Struggle for Democratic Politics in the Dominican Republic.* Chapel Hill: University of North Carolina Press.

Hendricks, Glenn. 1980. "La Raza en Nueva York: Social Pluralism and Schools." In Carlos G. Cortés, ed., *Latinos in the United States.* New York: Arno.

Hernández, Julio, and Fernando Lescaille. 1991. "A Proposal for a Dominican-Based District in Washington Heights and Inwood." Paper presented by the North Manhattan Committee for Fair Representation to the New York City Redistricting Commission.

Hernández, Ramona, and Francisco Rivera-Batiz. 1997. *Dominican New Yorkers: A Socioeconomic Profile, 1997.* Dominican Research Monographs. New York: CUNY City University of New York Dominican Studies Institute.

Hernández, Ramona, Francisco Rivera-Batiz, and Roberto Agoni. 1995. *Dominican New Yorkers: A Socioeconomic Profile, 1990.* Dominican Research Monographs. New York: City University of New York Dominican Studies Institute.

Itzigsohn, José, Carlos Dore Cabral, Esther Hernández Medina, and Obed Vázquez. 1999. "Mapping Dominican Transnationalism: Narrow and Broad Transnational Practices." *Ethnic and Racial Studies* 22(2): 316–39.

Jiménez Polanco, Jacqueline. 1999a. *Los Partidos Políticos en la República Dominicana: Actividad Electoral y Desarrollo Organizativo.* Santo Domingo, Dominican Republic: Editora Centenario.

——. 1999b. "El pactado acenso al poder de Leonel Fernández en la elección presidencial de 1996: la emergencia del liderazgo contingente y la construcción de una poliarquía consultiva." In Ramonina Brea, Rosario Espinal, and Fernando Valerio-Holguín, eds., *La República Dominicana: El Umbral del Siglo XXI Cultura, Política y Cambio Social.* Santo Domingo, Dominican Republic: Pontificia Universidad Católica Madre y Maestra.

Jones-Correa, Michael. 1998. *Between Two Nations: The Political Predicament of Latinos in New York City.* Ithaca: Cornell University Press.

Jordan, Howard. 1997. "Dominicans in New York: Getting a Slice of the Apple." *NACLA Report on the Americas* 30(5):37–42.

Kanellos, Nicolás, ed. 1997. *The Hispanic Literary Companion.* Detroit: Visible Ink.

Lescaille, Fernando. 1992. *Dominican Political Empowerment,* New York: Dominican Public Policy Project.

Levitt, Peggy. 1999. "Social Remittances: A Local-Level, Migration-Driven Form of Cultural Diffusion." *International Migration Review* 32(4): 926–49.

Linares, Guillermo. 1989. "Dominicans in New York: The Struggle for Community Control in District 6." *Centro de Estudios Puertorriqueños Bulletin* 2(5): 77–84.

Lowenstein, Steven. 1989. *Frankfurt on the Hudson: The German-Jewish Community of Washington Heights, 1933–1983.* Detroit: Wayne State University.

Martin, John. 1966. *Overtaken by Events: The Death of Trujillo to the Civil War.* New York: Doubleday.

Mitchell, Christopher. 1992. *Western Hemisphere Immigration and United States Foreign Policy.* University Park: Pennsylvania State University Press.

Monreal Requena, Pilar. n.d. "Associaciones de mujeres, racismo y pobreza en una ciudad global." Unpublished manuscript.

Moya Pons, Frank. 1995. *The Dominican Republic: A National History.* New Rochelle, N.Y.: Hispaniola.

Navarro, Mireya. 2000. "Puerto Rican Presence Wanes in New York." *The New York Times,* February 28, A1, B7.

New York City Department of City Planning. 1992. *The Newest New Yorkers: An Analysis of Immigration into New York City During the 1980s.* New York: Department of City Planning.

Pessar, Patricia. 1987. "The Dominicans: Women in the Household and the Garment Industry." In Nancy Foner, ed., *New Immigrants in New York.* New York: Columbia University Press.

———. 1995. *A Visa for a Dream: Dominicans in the United States.* Boston: Allyn and Bacon.

Rohter, Larry. 1996. "U.S. Benefits Go: Allure to Dominicans Doesn't." *The New York Times,* 12 October, A8.

Rosaldo, Renato. 1997. "Cultural Citizenship, Inequality, and Multiculturalism." In William W. Flores and Rina Benmayor, eds., *Latino Cultural Citizenship: Claiming Identity, Space, and Rights.* Boston: Beacon.

Rosenbaum, Emily, and Greta Gilbertson. 1995. "Mothers' Labor Force Participation in New York City: A Reappraisal of the Influence of Household Extension." *Journal of Marriage and the Family* 57:243–49.

Sainz, Rudy Anthony. 1990. *Dominican Ethnic Associations: Classification and Service Delivery Roles in Washington Heights.* Ph.D. diss., Columbia University School of Social Work, New York.

Sassen-Koob, Saskia. 1979. "Formal and Informal Associations: Dominicans and Colombians in New York." *International Migration Review* 13:314–32.

Singer, Audrey, and Greta Gilbertson. 2000. "Naturalization in the Wake of Anti-Immigrant Legislation: Dominicans in New York City." *Working Papers, no. 10.* International Migration Policy Program. Washington, D.C.: Carnegie Endowment for International Peace.

Soto Bouzas, Juan. 1999. "Ayer le tocó el turno a lideres hispanos." *El Diario/La Prensa,* March 23, 5.

Susser, Ida. 1996. "The Construction of Poverty and Homelessness in U.S. Cities." *Annual Review of Anthropology* 25:411–35.

Tilove, Jonathan. 1996. "Immigrant Voters Shaking Up Big-City Politics: Latinos Forming New Power Base." *Times-Picayune* (New Orleans), October 27, A12.

Torres-Saillant, Silvio. 1998. "The Tribulations of Blackness: Stages in Dominican Racial Identity." *Latin American Perspectives* 25(3): 126–46.

Torres-Saillant, Silvio, and Ramona Hernández. 1998. *The Dominican Americans.* Westport, Conn.: Greenwood.

U.S. Immigration and Naturalization Service. 1977–1999. *Annual Report of the Immigration and Naturalization Service.* Washington, D.C.: U.S. Government Printing Office.

Vega, Bernardo. 1992. *Trujillo y las forcas norteamericanas.* Santo Domingo, Dominican Republic: Fundación Cultural Dominicana.

Internet Resources

Organo de Difusión Digital del Gobierno Dominicano. "Dominicanos de EEUU presentan propuestas para el Diálogo Nacional." *Boletín de Noticias* 20 February 1998, *http://www.presidencia.gov.do/boletines/200298/cuarta.htm.*

Dominicanos/Dominicans 2000, *http://www.dominicans2000.org.*

Dominican American National Roundtable, meeting agendas, and participants, *http://danr.org.*

Mexicans: Social, Educational, Economic, and Political Problems and Prospects in New York

Robert C. Smith

What made me realize it? Well, my family, like most of my family from the girls' side, they like—[got] pregnant, have kids, and I don't want to go through that. . . . Half my friends are gone . . . like half that group is locked up, half of that group already has two or three kids. . . . And I don't wanna go through that.

Juana, now a college student, made these comments in 1999 to explain how she realized she was putting her future at risk and why she stopped cutting classes and started studying in high school. The choice that Juana made

This chapter was written while the author was a Fellow at the Oral History Research Office at Columbia University, in a program supported by the Rockefeller Foundation. It also draws on research and writing done with the support of the following institutions: the Social Science Research Council (SSRC), Program in International Migration, with funds provided by the Andrew W. Mellon Foundation; the National Science Foundation (NSF), Sociology Program; the Barnard College Project on Migration and Diasporas; and the Barnard College Small Grants Program. The author very gratefully acknowledges these sources of support. Excellent research on the projects funded by NSF, Barnard, and SSRC was done by three graduate students, Sandra Lara, Sara Guerrero Rippberger, and Antonio Moreno; and several undergraduates: Agustin Vecino, Griscelda Perez, Carolina Perez, Lisa Peterson, Sandra Sandoval, Linda Rodriguez, Katie Graves, Brian Lucero, and Judit Vega. Errors of fact or interpretation in this article are mine alone. I also thank Nancy Foner for inviting me to contribute to this volume, and for the help of John Mollenkopf of City University of New York and Joseph Salvo of the New York City Department of City Planning in getting some of the census and Current Population Survey (U.S. Bureau of the Census, various years a, b) figures.

reflects both one person's ability to overcome the difficult conditions of her own life and a larger reality among Mexicans in New York. Though a significant minority of Mexicans and Mexican Americans in New York are upwardly mobile, a larger number have not been able to overcome the obstacles they face. Juana's past and current groups of Mexican friends include teen mothers, young men in jail, and young men stuck in low-paying "immigrant" jobs as well as college students and others in well-paying jobs. The varied fates of this small group of people offer a microcosm of the larger Mexican population in New York. This chapter analyzes some of the causes of the varied fates among Mexicans in New York and suggests some ways these disturbing trends might be addressed. Approximately 250,000–275,000 Mexicans lived in New York City in 2000, constituting approximately 13 percent of the city's Latino population; in the greater New York there were probably 500,000 Mexicans.[1]

The importance of the Mexican-origin population in New York and the Northeast stems from several of its characteristics, including its great potential for growth; its continued engagement with Mexico; its ambiguous social location in New York's racial and ethnic hierarchies; and its varied and contingent futures in education, the labor market, and politics. This variation and contingency are of particular interest because they give us analytical insight into larger processes of assimilation, incorporation, and differentiation. Why, for example, did Mexicans in New York experience larger decreases in nominal per capita income in New York City than any other Latino group between 1980 and 1990, while at the same time important segments of their population experienced considerable economic and educational upward mobility? These trends seemed to continue through the 1990s and up to the present. What are the prospects for political action in New York for what some predict will soon be the largest minority group on the East Coast? The answers to such questions enable us to better understand the larger processes involved.

Analytically, this chapter attempts to present an overview and introduction to the Mexican community and uses their story to gain new insights into larger patterns of assimilation, incorporation, and social differentiation. The chapter does not take a categorical theoretical position on how incorporation works but rather seeks to analyze the variation and contingency in Mexican futures using relevant scholarly work. The variety and contingency observed cannot be fully explained by any of the most often used theoretical frameworks. These include assimilation theory (the favorite straw man of current immigration studies), which stresses the need to conform to mainstream norms to succeed (Warner and Srole 1945; see Alba and Nee's 1999 revival of the concept or Gordon's 1964 version); pluralist approaches with their view that ethnic organization is reinforced by the political system in New York (Glazer and Moynihan 1968); "culture of poverty" theories that view poverty as the outcome of bad work habits and other cultural traits (Mead 1997); "oppositional" views that see minority resistance to dominant institutions as "doomed resistance" that trades safeguarding a particular ethnic or racial identity in exchange for the potential benefits in these institutions, such as school (Willis 1977; Ogbu 1974, 1987); "segmented assimilation," which posits upward assimilation to the mainstream, downward assimilation to an inner-city culture, or the use of immigrant ethnic social networks and resources to circumvent discrimination, avoid doomed resistance, and succeed (Portes and Zhou 1993; Zhou and Bankston 1998; Zhou 1999); "racialization," which posits that a group's relationship to the color line and the structural conditions surrounding it largely determine life chances (Roediger 1991; Omi and Winant 1986); and the "minority culture of mobility" concept, which sees African American paths to upward mobility as an adaptation to the structural circumstances they confront (Neckerman et al. 1999). I return to these issues briefly in the conclusion. For now, I begin with a discussion of the history of Mexican immigration to New York and the East Coast, followed by a short analysis of the Mexican population's social, economic, and educational life. I then consider the problems and prospects for political mobilization among Mexican New Yorkers, concluding with some speculation as to what lies ahead in the years to come.

Data for this chapter come from ethnographic research and interviews done in New York and Mexico since 1987. I draw on my dissertation and related work on transnational communities conducted in the early and late 1990s, research on the second generation in the late 1990s, and continued engagement with the New York Mexican community over more than a decade. I also draw on some analyses of census and other public data.

Mexican Migration to New York and the East Coast

The Mexican-origin population in New York City, including both immigrants and native-born Mexican Americans, was somewhere around 250,000–275,000 in 2000, with about half of this number between the ages of twelve and twenty-four (Valdes de Montano and Smith 1994; Smith 1995). This figure represents a vast increase from the approximately 35,000 to 40,000 Mexicans in 1980 and the 100,000 in 1990.[2] Moreover, there was a 232 percent increase in births to Mexican mothers in the city between 1988 and 1996, according to the New York City Department of Health. "Little Mexicos" have sprung up in several places in New York: Jackson Heights in Queens; El Barrio, or Spanish Harlem, in Manhattan; Sunset Park and Williamsburg in Brooklyn; and in The South Bronx. Even Staten Island now has its complement of Mexican sports leagues and settlers. Outside the city, in the wider metropolitan area, Mexicans have become a presence in Hudson Valley towns like Newburgh and Mount Kisco and in New Jersey cities like Paterson and Passaic in the north and Bridgeton and Hammonton in the south. Mexican consular officials offer a "soft estimate" that another 300,000 reside outside the city in New Jersey, Connecticut, and the New York suburbs. Moreover, the whole of East Coast agriculture and related industries now rely mainly on Mexican labor: from Pennsylvania mushroom fields to Delmarva peninsula chicken-processing plants, to tomato picking near the Canadian border to peach picking in Athens, Georgia. Census experts estimate that Mexicans will soon become the largest Latino minority on the East Coast (Alonso-Zaldivar 1999), and in some of the places just named, they already are.

The potential for growth in the Mexican population in and around New York City is tremendous. By 2000, an estimated 2.2 million Latinos lived in New York City, and while Puerto Ricans are a declining proportion of the Latino population, other groups—including Mexicans—are increasing. Mexican population growth in New York is astounding—its is the fastest of any group in the city—and several factors point to continued growth. Mexico has a huge population: 95 million in 1998, as compared to about 8 million for the Dominican Republic. Moreover, two trends in Mexican population dynamics and migration suggest continued high levels of migration to the United States, and New York in particular. Mexico, at least through the medium term, will have new annual labor market entrants of between 800,000 and 1,000,000, far in excess of its economy's ability to produce jobs. Also, migration is likely to increase from nontraditional sending regions, thereby initiating new migration chains and networks. There is a growing tendency as well for migrants, including first-timers, to stay for longer and to settle in the United States (Durand et al. 1999; Cornelius 1994).

The tremendous potential for growth in New York's Mexican population makes the future of Mexicans and their children extremely important to the city's future. There are causes for both optimism and concern—optimism because of the success of some Mexicans, but concern because of a mismatch between mechanisms of integration in New York and the demographic and settlement characteristics of the Mexican population. In short, although many Mexicans have experienced upward mobility in the first and second generations, more have not. Challenges to Mexican incorporation in New York stem from their geographical dispersal and resulting problems in political mobilization, their non-niched insertion into the economy, and the uneven educational settings into which they move and from which they come.

History of Mexican Migration to New York City

"We opened the road," said Don Pedro, sitting at his kitchen table in 1992 in a town I call (for confidentiality) Ticuani as he looked back at the fifty years of Mexican migration from the Mixteca to New York City that started when he and his brother Fermin crossed the United States–Mexico border on July 6, 1943.[3] Indeed, most Mexican migration to New York can be traced to a historical accident. Don Pedro and his brother and cousin had been unsuccessful in bribing their way into a bracero contract, that is, a contract to a government labor program that recruited Mexicans to work in U.S. agriculture between 1942 and 1964 (*brazo* means "arm"). Getting a bracero contract would probably have brought Don Pedro and his relatives to the U.S. Southwest, and the history of Mexican migration in New York would have been quite different. Instead, Don Pedro and his brother hitched a ride with a New Yorker named Montesinos who vacationed in Mexico City every summer. Montesinos brought the two men to New York and put them up in a hotel for two days until they found work. Work was easy to get. "There was a war on, so they were happy to have us working," said Don Pedro. He worked in restaurants, in factories, and later as a mechanic. In the nearly sixty years since that first migration, the Mixteca region from which Don Pedro comes has been the origin of approximately two-thirds of New York's Mexican population (Valdes de Montano and Smith 1994; Smith 1995).

Don Pedro was not the first Mexican labor migrant to come to New York. In fact, during the 1920s migrants from the Mexican state of Yucatan came to New York in small numbers and established a social club at the Twenty-third Street YMCA. Why this migration from the Yucatan dried up is not known, though Yucatecos and their children still live in New York. More interesting is how the migration from the Mixteca region, and now other regions, has reflected larger trends. We can separate the migration from Mexico to New York into four phases, all of which implicate different processes pushing and pulling at each end of the migration route. The first two phases involve mainly migration from the Mixteca region, a cultural and ecological zone that includes the contiguous parts of three states: southern Puebla, northern Oaxaca, and eastern Guerrero. In 1992, the Mixteca accounted for two-thirds of Mexican migrants to New York, with 47 percent from Puebla alone (Valdes de Montano and Smith 1994; Smith 1995).

The first phase of migration, from the mid-1940s to the mid-1960s, involved small numbers of individuals from a few families and towns in southern Puebla who had relatives in New York. In the second phase, from the mid-1960s to the mid-1980s, this tightly networked dynamic was maintained, but increasing numbers of people, including the first appreciable number of women, began to come to the United States to seek their fortunes. The attraction of the United States in those days would have been obvious: much higher wages than in Puebla, and modern conveniences that most people could not even imagine. Indeed, most of the Mixteca did not get electricity until the mid-1960s, and this improvement was resisted by *caciques* (political bosses) who did not want outside influences, such as radio and electric lights, intruding on their control over their local populations. Flight from political violence also features prominently in the histories of many of the pioneer migrants from Puebla, including Don Pedro, who was living in Mexico City to escape his hometown's political violence when he met Montesinos.

The third stage of migration lasted from the late 1980s to the mid-1990s and can be characterized as an explosion. Three factors combined to create this explosion. First, by the late 1980s, Mexico had been in the grips of a profound economic crisis since 1981–1982, and conditions in many places were still dire. Indeed, poor states were especially hard hit, and Puebla experienced a net contraction of its economy between 1981 and 1985 (Cornelius 1986). Within Puebla, the Mixteca was one of the worst-off regions; in fact, it was one of the most marginalized areas in the entire country. Even worse, the "lost decade" of the 1980s stretched through the 1990s and into the new century for most Mixtecos and many *poblanos* (people from the state of Puebla). Severe economic conditions and the loss of faith in Mexico's future combined to create very serious pressures to migrate, or "push" pressures, in the Mixteca. These push pressures were matched by a second factor: U.S. demand, with Mexicans becoming identified in New York during the 1980s as a highly available and compliant labor force (Smith 1992, 1995; Kim 1999). Also, New York's Mexican population had reached a critical mass by the mid-1980s, such that the costs of migration for many people from the Mixteca region had been lowered a great deal by the presence of relatives and friends there (see Massey et al. 1987).

The key factor in catalyzing the explosion of migration in the late 1980s and early 1990s was the amnesty program of the 1986 Immigration Reform and Control Act, or IRCA. The amnesty provision enabled immigrants to apply for temporary, then permanent, residency if they had been continuously in the United States since 1981, or if they had worked in agriculture for ninety days during the past year. Mexicans surprised many by accounting for the second-highest number of amnesty applications in New York City, with about 9,000, behind Dominicans' roughly 12,000 (Kraly and Miyares, this volume). The amnesty program profoundly changed the nature of Mexicans' relationship to their hometowns. Migrants who had been caught in a holding pattern for years or even decades suddenly found that they could return home when they wanted. More importantly, they now had a legal right to reunite their families in the United States. Between the late 1980s and the mid-1990s, tens of thousands of wives and children left the Mixteca region and moved to New York to be with their families. The suddenness of this impact is reflected in an anecdote told by one school official in Puebla. On being investigated because his school reported only half as many students in 1993 than it did in 1992, he told officials that the explanation was simple: they had all gone to New York to be with their parents. Similar stories repeated themselves throughout the Mixteca region (Smith 1995). One corollary was the 232 percent increase in the Mexican birthrate in New York in the mid-1990s mentioned previously.

The last phase of migration, which began in the late 1990s and continues to the present, involves changes in the larger process of migration to the United States. The story has several parts. First, by now, many towns in the Mixteca region have reached an "asymptotic stability" (Smith 1995; see Massey et al. 1994; Durand et al. 1999), wherein most people there who want to leave have already done so, and those who remain behind are unlikely to migrate soon in large numbers (Massey et al. 1994; Durand et al. 1999; Massey and Espinosa 1997). At the same time, on the U.S. end, the number of settled Mexican migrants, both legal and undocumented, who plan to remain permanently in New York has increased. Hence, a first part of the story is that the internal process of migration from the Mixteca has reached a kind of consolidated stability, in which new migrants will continue to leave the Mixteca but the number will decrease from its former highs.

A second part of the story is that the process of migrating to and settling in the United States has changed (Cornelius 1994). Migrants crossing illegally are now less likely to engage in circular migration, in which the family stays at home and the migrant returns. An important factor in producing this change has been the tightened enforcement at the U.S.-Mexico border, which has had the ironic but predictable effect of causing increased settlement among migrants. The logic of family reunification fostered by IRCA has also reinforced this trend, even among the undocumented (see Durand et al. 1999; Sassen 1988). In effect, what Binford (1998) calls "accelerated migration" now is the pattern, in which new migrant towns pass through the stages of migration—from solo migrant to family reunification in the United States—much more quickly than before, or even skip stages and just go straight to settlement. Accelerated migration also includes a great increase in the medium-term to semipermanent migration of adolescents without their parents, as a by-product of the acceleration and subsequent disorganization of the migration process.

A third part of the story is that migration has returned to an earlier, pre–bracero program pattern of wider dispersal in the United States. The bracero program funneled nearly 5 million Mexicans to work, mainly in Southwestern agriculture, between 1942 and 1964, and this geographical pattern still largely persists. But in the 1990s, migration to varied U.S. destinations—including the Northeast and Southeast—boomed. Corresponding with this increased number of U.S. destinations is the increase in the variety of Mexican sending origins. During the 1990s, New York became an important site for migration from a variety of nontraditional origins, including the states of Tlaxcala; Tabasco; Morelos; and, perhaps most importantly, from Mexico City and its huge slum in the state of Mexico, Ciudad Nezahualcoyotl (or "Neza," as migrants call it). In 1992 about 15 percent of the immigrants in New York City were from Mexico City (Valdes de Montano and Smith 1994). Though no corresponding survey exists today, the number is likely to be closer to 25–30 percent. Indeed, migration from Neza has become so common that migrants now say that they live in "Neza York" (Vecino 1999). This change toward more urban origin and younger migrants is likely to have important implications for the future of Mexicans in New York.

Social, Economic, and Educational Futures of Mexicans in New York City

Mexican social, economic, and educational life in New York shows contradictory tendencies that are likely to persist. On the one hand, the Mexican-origin population showed alarming signs of social distress in the 1990 census as compared to the 1980 census, and my current ethnographic and interview work confirms that these trends continue. For example, Mexicans in New York went from having one of the highest incomes among Latinos in New York in 1980, nearly equivalent to that of Cubans, to among the lowest in 1990. The decline is particularly pronounced for those without a high school education, from $17,495 in 1980 to $13,537 in 1990, a net drop in nominal dollars of 22.6 percent, constituting a more than 50 percent drop in per capita income for this group. The only other Latino group to have a nominal drop was Colombians, whose per capita incomes dropped 3.4 percent; for Dominicans, group incomes increased 11.7 percent; Puerto Ricans, 6.4 percent; and Ecuadorans, 14.5 percent. A further sign of social distress is that Mexicans also had the highest rate of sixteen- to nineteen-year-olds who were not in high school and had not graduated—47 percent—as opposed to the next highest groups, Dominicans and Puerto Ricans, with 22 percent each.[4] My ethnographic work suggests that similar stories will be revealed by the 2000 census.

It is not just a tale of decline, however. In large part, these distressing trends are artifacts of the high levels of Mexican immigration, especially teen immigration, during the 1980s, which continued in the 1990s and into the new millennium. The influx of young Mexican immigrants with low levels of education masks the progress that a significant minority of Mexicans and Mexican Americans has been making in New York. A cohort analysis[5] of Mexican Americans between 1980 and 1990 shows that their levels of education were improving steadily, though not dramatically (and more so for women), and that 19 percent of men and 30 percent of women were upwardly mobile in terms of occupational prestige and associated pay and conditions.[6] An important path for mobility in the 1990s, especially for women, has been through semiprofessional, skilled secretarial niches and in retail. These jobs—such as legal or medical secretary, travel agent, or sales agent—require the completion of high school and either a short-term technical training program or an associate degree. Our informants and their immigrant parents understand these jobs as a significant advance; they are "clean" jobs "in an office," with health insurance, paid vacations, and other benefits. I discuss these developments more fully elsewhere (Smith 1998b, 2000, 2001; see also Myers and Cranford 1998). A fuller explication of these developments goes beyond the scope of this chapter, including a discussion of how this bifurcation is gendered (Moss and Tilly 1996; Smith 2001).

Still, it must be emphasized, the upwardly mobile are a minority—fully 81 percent of men and 70 percent of Mexican American women were not upwardly mobile in the 1980s. Moreover, the nature of Mexicans' insertion into the economy does not bode well. To simplify somewhat, a major thrust of research on immigrants and labor markets indicates that the more "niched"—concentrated in specific industries and jobs—an ethnic group is, the better for the group's collective futures because it gives members access to resources such as opportunities for jobs and for training. A growing niche allows the group to pull itself up; even a shrinking niche allows at least a part of the group to use ethnic ties to move up or maintain their position, especially if there is ethnic succession (see especially Waldinger 1996, but also much of the ethnicity and work literature, including Portes and Bach 1985; Portes and Zhou 1993; Nee et al. 1994; Sassen 1995).

Mexicans in New York—like those in California—are among the least niched of all immigrants (Waldinger and Bozorgmehr 1997). Indeed, while they were more niched in 1990 than in 1980, the highest concentration in job/industry category in 1990 was for 10 percent of Mexican men in restaurants. Most of the other niches each had only about 2 percent of the population. My current ethnographic research suggests that this has changed somewhat since 1990, especially for Mexican American women, who are more likely to finish school and get good service-sector jobs (see Smith 1998b; Smith and Lara 1999; Lara and Smith 2000).

The fact is that such dispersion across industries and jobs has negative long-term consequences for the group's collective advancement and development of both human and social capital. Immigrant parents of Mexican Americans have few resources to help their children move up within their own industries and in many cases cannot get them jobs in their own firms. In fact, many second-generation Mexicans we interviewed ended up getting their first work experience in the same industry or kind of industry as their parents, but often not in the same firm as their parents. When the parents can help their children get jobs, they are the kinds of entry-level jobs that undocumented immigrants occupy, illustrating the weakness of strong ties in bad niches (see Granovetter 1973).

The educational futures of Mexicans and Mexican Americans appear bright for some and grim for many. While increasing percentages of Mexicans Americans in New York finished high school and some college in the 1980s, most still had not done so by 1990. Moreover, the influx of younger migrants has made dropping out of school more common in part because it has dramatically increased the size of the population at risk to drop out. The problem can be put this way. The early to mid-1990s saw a significant increase in the number of preadolescent and teen immigrants being reunited with their families and entering school in New York. Before 1990, young people generally stayed in Mexico until they were seventeen or eighteen and then came to New York, where they entered the labor force directly and did not go to school. Under the old scenario, most entered low-wage labor markets and did not become involved in gang activity. Under the new scenario, Mexican young people enter the schools, the *sonidos* (dance parties), and other arenas as adolescents and undergo a secondary socialization that can have varied, and sometimes highly negative, impacts on their futures.

Moreover, the dramatic influx of Mexicans into New York City's schools in the last decade has suddenly made them a population with a public presence that, in many cases, has led to abuse from other groups. This abuse is especially experienced by young men, who report that they increasingly join gangs—or negotiate a looser association known as "hangin'" with gangs—for their own protection (see T. Waters 1999 for a fascinating analysis of the structural roots of immigrant gangs). The results have been marked increases in violence. Rising dropout rates for Mexicans and the Mexican Americans who hang with them are at least partly attributable to these dynamics.

The presence of a growing percentage of urban migrants, especially from Mexico City, is likely to exacerbate these problems. True, migrants from Mexico City tend to be more educated (with eight or nine years of education instead of five or six for rural immigrants) and more accustomed to an urban environment; these advantages may make it easier for them to adapt and do well in school. But other factors weigh in on the opposite side and put the youths at risk for a variety of problems. Large numbers of the urban migrants are teens who move to New York without their parents. Also—because they are from Mexico City and Neza, where immigration is much newer—they are coming into less tightly organized networks and communities in New York, with fewer resources and less adult supervision and social control. On top of this, some of the teen immigrants have prior experience in Mexico with drugs and gangs—some seem, in fact, to have imported their gangs with them—and this puts these youth at high risk for a variety of problems. The increase in gang activity among Mexican youth in New York also raises the possibility that the public perception of Mexicans in New York as diligent workers and conscientious students could change, thereby affecting the opportunities they are afforded in schools and labor markets there.

Obstacles to and Institutions for Political Mobilization of Mexicans in New York

A final issue is political mobilization. Despite the impressive growth in the Mexican population, its potential for political mobilization in New York City is limited in the short term for reasons that also pose long-term challenges. By political mobilization, I mean political activity broadly defined and focused on engagement with U.S. institutions, actors, and structures. Voting is one obvious form of mobilization, but participation in other forms of political action, such as community organizing or campaigning, are also included (see the interesting book by Jones-Correa [1998] on the larger topic of immigrant politics). This analysis applies mainly to Mexicans in New York City. Mexicans and Mexican Americans living elsewhere in the region and in the Northeast face some similar constraints, although, as I briefly discuss, in some locations they have decided advantages in the political arena.

One obvious limitation to the political mobilization of Mexicans in New York City is that a large percentage of the population is undocumented; many have no prospect of ever legalizing their status even as they live permanently in New York, and many receive extraordinarily low pay. Though estimating the percentage of a population that is undocumented is difficult, I would say that at least 50 percent of Mexican immigrants in New York are undocumented, and the percentage is likely to be significantly higher.[7]

Although the U.S.-born children of Mexican immigrants are citizens and can vote, they are quite young and politically unorganized and will not actively enter the electorate in any significant numbers for probably another ten years. As among other populations, the poverty of Mexicans exerts a negative influence on political participation.

A second major problem is that Mexicans in New York City are geographically dispersed and are largely remaining so. Census Bureau information for the 1990s shows that Mexicans were, not surprisingly, settling disproportionately in neighborhoods with other Latinos, where Spanish is presumably widely spoken and housing is relatively cheap (at least by New York City standards). During the 1990s, increasing numbers of "pioneers" also moved into non-Latino neighborhoods like Fort Greene, Bedford-Stuyvesant, and Brighton Beach in Brooklyn, or Flushing, Queens, where housing was cheap or close to the businesses of their Russian, Greek, and Korean employers. So although the emergence of "Little Mexicos" makes some political mobilization possible, the absence of one or two main concentrations—like Washington Heights for Dominicans, Chinatown for Chinese, or Flushing for Koreans—makes political mobilization more difficult. It should also be remembered that Dominicans' large and densely concentrated population converted relatively quickly into the election of Guillermo Linares in 1991 under propitious circumstances—the Redistricting Commission decided in effect to draw a "Dominican district"—unlikely to repeat themselves in the Mexican case.

A third factor that will make mobilization of the Mexican population problematic is its socioeconomic heterogeneity and uncertain relationship to New York City's established racial and ethnic hierarchies and to the related distribution of political space. A main issue is whether Mexicans will become "ethnics" or "racial minorities" in their public presentation in New York, an issue that can be usefully understood with reference to Kasinitz's (1992) instructive study of the history of West Indian political mobilization in New York. West Indians had long been disproportionately active as leaders of New York City's black community but had done so never as "ethnics" or "West Indian immigrants" but rather as "blacks"; race was the prime organizing principle. This changed, at least for a time (and in the absence of major racial issues like police shootings), during the Koch administration, when Democratic leaders reached out to West Indians as ethnic leaders, making appeals on immigrant and ethnic grounds in an effort to gain black support in the face of growing African American disapproval of Koch.

The racial/ethnic issue for Mexicans is more complicated. They are coming into a political system in which the ethnic and racial positions have already been largely set. New York is a "minority majority" city, in which nonwhites now outnumber whites. Moreover, there are important established political organizations led by blacks and Puerto Ricans (and to a lesser extent Dominicans and Asian Americans) who are often perceived as speaking for the entire "black community" or the entire "Latino community," respectively. Mexicans we have interviewed see Puerto Ricans as already occupying the political space for Latinos in New York; they often talk of the need to become, as one community leader put it, "powerful like the Puerto Ricans." Yet the issues that concern most Mexican immigrant leaders—especially relating to immigration and the rights of the undocumented—have not traditionally been the highest priorities of New York's "Latino" leaders; they have tended to be Puerto Rican, and Puerto Ricans have U.S. citizenship by birth (see Rodriguez et al. 1996; Jones-Correa 1998). Non-Puerto Rican Latino leaders have commented to me that even in organizing against the undercount of Latinos in the 2000 census, Puerto Rican leaders have paid insufficient attention to non-Puerto Rican concerns (Jones-Correa 1998:114–16 reports similar stories; see also Mary Waters 1994, 1999 for an insightful analysis of how race plays out in other arenas for black West Indians).

A key question is how Mexicans will fit into New York's ethnicized and racialized political system—as (immigrants turned) ethnics or as (native) racial minorities. The answer is not clear. On the one hand, first-generation Mexicans make clear that they see themselves as "not black" and "not Puerto Rican" (Smith 1996). Like other immigrants, Mexicans make a moral distinction between themselves and native minorities, whom they see as culpable for their own lack of success in New York's educational and economic institutions (see Roediger 1991; Omi and Winant 1986). Yet some of the second generation share the same views as their parents, as they assert superiority to native minorities in their attempts at upward mobility as ethnics. On the other hand, some members of the second generation see Mexican American lives and futures as closely linked to those of African Americans and Puerto Ricans. "I see us as the same," said one Mexican American in answer to how she perceives her African American classmates. Another even said that her African American and Asian classmates were her "role models" for doing well in school, and that she had to dissociate herself from other Mexicans in order to do well.

Variation within the Latino population, especially the potential division between those from the Caribbean (Puerto Rico, the Dominican Republic) and those from meso-America or Andean countries (Mexico, Ecuador, Peru, Colombia, and others), also complicates the race-ethnicity question. (John Mollenkopf, Philip Kasinitz, and Mary Waters use this distinction in their current project on the second generation [see Kasinitz et al. 1997].) Cultural differences exist between these regions in food, music, and kind of Spanish (idiomatic phrases and pronunciation) spoken. Also critical are racial differences. A large proportion of the Caribbean population has some African heritage, and they are more likely than other Latinos to be seen as black by most Americans. This fact crucially affects life chances (e.g., Massey and Denton 1993), which can have cumulative consequences for political organizing in the future. Racial issues may become more important to the Caribbean groups and thus undermine the potential for Latino political unity. It is also possible that "ethnic mobilization" might be used to incorporate the meso-American and Andean populations as immigrant ethnic groups rather than as racial minorities. This tendency may be reinforced by the different migration histories of the various groups in terms of when they entered the city. Puerto Ricans came to New York at a time when there were no other

Latinos; Dominicans were allotted political space through the chance happening of the Redistricting Commission. Later Latino arrivals are not likely to be afforded such an opportunity, and this could in itself become an important axis along which these Latinos organize.

Mexicans and Mexican Americans in the region living outside New York City face a very different set of obstacles and potentials than their counterparts in the city. Because they tend to be more geographically concentrated, they will form voting blocs more easily, be able to identify their own geographic and neighborhood interests, and will have others recognize these interests and voting potential, a key point in the social construction of community (Suttles 1968, 1972) and a help in transforming them from a loose ethnic community into an ethnic interest group that will be identifiable to other groups. Particularly in towns like those in the Hudson Valley and New Jersey with changing demographics—decreasing white populations; relatively new but rapidly growing nonwhite, Latino populations; and stable or shrinking black populations—Mexicans could become a pivotal group in local politics and then indirectly in state politics, as they have been, for example, in Chicago. Mexicans' educational and economic needs and problems are likely to be more important issues in local politics than in New York City. Also, the institutions of mobilization that I discuss later in this chapter—the Catholic Church, the governments of Mexico and the state of Puebla, local Mexican civic groups, and others—will no doubt play larger facilitating or assimilating roles than in New York City. If the political future seems brighter for Mexicans outside New York City, it should be noted that economic prospects may be bleaker. Mexican teens migrating to the most rusted places in the Rust Belt arrive in industrial cities like Newburgh that are in serious economic decline. Indeed, throughout the region, Mexicans are moving in large numbers into the most competitive and exploitative sectors of industries like garments and heavy manufacturing that have been in decline for at least fifty years.

Potential Institutions of Mobilization Among Mexicans in New York City

Despite difficulties of citizenship status, dispersal, and uncertain relationships to New York's ethnic and racial hierarchies, several developments point toward potential political mobilization for Mexicans in the city. Naturalization rates, for one thing, are on the rise among Mexicans in New York, especially among those who are potentially politically active. The combination of anti-immigrant politics of the mid-1990s (e.g., in 1994 by California governor Pete Wilson in the form of Proposition 187 and in the form of the U.S. Congress's harsh immigration law reforms) and the "no loss of nationality" change in the Mexican constitution in 1998 are largely responsible for the increase. Anti-immigrant politics made legal immigrants fear that they would be targeted and possibly lose access to benefits such as Social Security, to which they had contributed for years. The change in the Mexican constitution removed a significant emotional barrier to naturalization: one can now become a U.S. citizen and still hold a Mexican passport and Mexican "nationality" (not including the right to vote). Mexicans I know in New York, from retired garment workers to influential community and business leaders, have since become U.S. citizens.

The Mexican Consulate and the Mexican state of Puebla may also encourage political mobilization in New York. The Mexican government has an unofficial policy, often publicly stated in meetings with immigrant organizations, encouraging those who want to become U.S. citizens to do so (see Smith 1998a; Guarnizo,1998; Goldring forthcoming). The rationale was clearly stated to me by a senior official at the Program for Mexican Communities Abroad, a federal-level program in the Foreign Relations Ministry created in 1990 to attend to the needs of Mexicans abroad, mainly in the United States: "We want Mexicans in the United States and Mexican Americans to be Mexico's friends, and we want powerful, not weak, friends." The Mexican Consulate and the Communities Program have jointly organized several regional organizations in the Northeast (including the Federation of Mexican Sports Clubs in the Northeastern United States and the Chamber of Commerce for Small- and Medium-Sized Mexican Businesses) and have also begun reaching out to other, narrower civic or ethnic organizations dedicated to Mexican culture. After the election of Melquiades Morales Flores as governor of Puebla in 1998, the state created Casa Puebla, a nonprofit organization in the United States designed both to address certain needs in the poblano community and to help bolster political support for the dominant political party, the Partido Institucional Revolucionario (PRI), in an increasingly competitive electoral system. In this, it followed the federal government (Amparo Casar 1998, 2000; see also Sevi 1999).

Taken together, these Mexican organizations have the potential, even if largely latent, capacity to create a nucleus of organized leadership in New York City and the region. This is especially so given that many of the leaders, particularly those involved in Casa Puebla, are prosperous businesspeople in and around New York who have investments in Puebla, or will seek aid to pursue their interests in New York and involve themselves in New York politics, or both. This is a case where the manifest function of pursuing a political interest by Mexican politicians could result in the latent function of contributing to the potential political capacity of Mexicans in New York (see Merton 1968).

A more grassroots track for mobilization of Mexican New Yorkers could come from the Catholic church, in the particular form of Associacion Tepeyac (1997). Tepeyac was founded in 1997 by community leaders and a Jesuit brother, Joel Magállan Hernandez, who was sent to New York from Mexico at the request of church officials here. Tepeyac's main focus is the undocumented, which includes defending their labor rights and protesting against what they see as unfair INS enforcement; the association also works with youth, especially the burgeoning teen immigrant population and the growing number of gang members among them, and with other community and religious groups attempting to address youth problems (*www.tepeyac.org*). Tepeyac is thus focusing on a growing segment of the Mexican population that usually has little interaction with the consulate and the established Mexican leadership. Though the consulate continues to assist individual undocumented persons, Tepeyac is not constrained by a diplomatic position and has vigorously argued controversial stances, accusing the INS of racism in its implementation of immigration laws and helping to coordinate a nationwide demonstration for a general amnesty for undocumented immigrants. The question still remains as to how and to what extent these activities will have large-scale concrete effects in larger institutions or structures of power.

Much depends on Tepeyac's ability to mobilize the Catholic church to devote a full measure of its tremendous organizational and political capacity to the Mexican population. Although the New York archdiocese has shown commitment at the highest levels, giving Mexicans as a group more attention, priests in the parishes complain that the Catholic church's organizational hierarchy generally remains indifferent to this new population. In other dioceses, priests report that things are worse. The irony is that the Catholic church is singularly positioned to mobilize the Mexican population because of its strong, nationalistically informed Catholicism. Indeed, one of Tepeyac's most successful strategies has been to combine mobilizations for workers rights, for example, with religious holidays, such as the celebration honoring the Virgin of Guadalupe, thus linking workers' rights with closely held national and religious identities. For the church as an institution, there seems to be a kind of "institutional lag" at work here, as an overburdened organization attempts to come to grips with another new population presenting both new and old sets of challenges.

Tepeyac also has organizational and political potential beyond the institutional bounds of the Catholic church. Tepeyac's potential has been greatly increased by the fact that its leaders have been able "to negotiate a place for Tepeyac that transcends the realm of the New York archdiocese, building alliances with other movements that advocate workers rights" and related causes (Alejandra Leal, personal communication). Moreover, many immigrants view Tepeyac as an authentic representative of Mexicans in the United States, in a way that the consulate could not be, because of both its diplomatic position and its strong association with the PRI and its monopoly, through politics and "alchemy" (electoral fraud), on power for most of this century. Tepeyac can mobilize thousands of Mexican immigrants—and on Mexican national holidays, even tens of thousands—in support of its causes. And some Tepeyac volunteers are second-generation Mexican Americans who are thinking specifically about the future place in politics of Mexicans in New York.

Another institution that could mobilize Mexicans in New York are labor unions, especially the Union of Needle Trades, Industrial, and Textile Workers (UNITE). UNITE has placed more attention on the plight of the undocumented than other unions, for example, by defending its undocumented members in deportation hearings and advocating for them when wages are not paid. UNITE has even attempted an organizing campaign among the largely Mexican (but also Ecuadoran and Central American) greengrocery workers, who are among the most exploited workers in the city. This campaign was successful in many respects, including getting better pay and recognition for the workers (see McCoy 2000), but the challenge of organizing the Mexican population is daunting. UNITE's power as a mobilizer of Mexicans will largely be a function of its larger ability to improve the position of all undocumented workers.

As for the traditional structures in New York, the Democrats and the Republicans, too, could help mobilize Mexicans politically. They have made little effort in this direction so far, but it would behoove both parties to begin making links with this burgeoning population.

Conclusion

This chapter has presented an overview of some aspects of the Mexican population in and around New York City and analyzed some of the trends that will affect its future. In conclusion, I offer some additional reflections on the possible futures of Mexicans and Mexican Americans in New York and some theoretical implications of these outcomes. Mexicans, it is clear, are not following one path of integration and incorporation in New York. While most are not significantly upwardly mobile, significant minorities are, and current research suggests that this will continue to be the case.

In the economy and education, I fear that the tough start that so many new immigrants are experiencing will have cumulative negative consequences. The acceleration in migration processes toward more semipermanent or permanent immigration, including unaccompanied teen migration, could combine dangerously with the structural circumstances of incorporation in New York, including the lack of regular parental supervision and authority for many adolescents whose parents must work too many hours. Gangs have become very important social structures among Mexican youth, and their consequences are becoming increasingly serious. However, interventions can be made if we better understand the problems. For example, our current research shows that problems develop during the hours of 3:00 to 7:00 P.M. when no adults are around because they are all at work. After-school programs could be targeted at the large group of youth who must deal with the presence of gangs in their schools and neighborhoods. Efforts could be made, as Tepeyac has tried to do, to offer space for these youth and gang members to spend their time safely and capitalize on the leadership that many of them show (see Vigil 1988, 2000; Moore 1991; Venkatesh 1997, 2000; Brotherton 1998; Esteva 1999). Schools can also help and be helped by recognizing the special needs and problems of the growing number of young Mexican teens who arrive with little or no English and poor educational preparation in their home communities. This being said, our interviews show that many Mexican immigrant youth, as well as members of the 1.5 and second generation, are striding confidently into their futures, and I suspect that the 2000 census will have more good news than the 1990 census about these generations.

I offer one concrete reflection on the topic of intervention. In my meetings with Catholic priests concerned about the situation of Mexicans in New York, some priests said that they were closing their meeting halls and gyms to Mexican youth because it was too dangerous. The priests were not overreacting to news accounts but rather had taken these steps after serious violence had occurred in their halls and gyms during Mexican dances and weddings. Their move was a rational reaction to a difficult situation. Yet such a move makes the situation worse by moving the social encounters these youth have out of supervised areas and into the street. I offer an example to suggest an alternative. While I was writing this chapter, a dance was held in a church meeting hall to benefit a Mexican religious organization. Members of several gangs, including rivals, showed up, and some expected trouble to start. The dance ended at 2:00 A.M., without incident inside or outside the building. When I asked second-generation Mexicans attending why this happened, they answered quite sensibly: there was no alcohol served, so no one "got crazy," and adults were there, including the parents of some of the gang members. The sociological point is right from Durkheim: there was greater social control, and hence less danger to the youth, because adults provided guidance and authority and because the destabilizing effects of alcohol were largely avoided. These youth were imbricated within a structure that gave their interaction meaning and limited the extent to which they were willing to act out all of their impulses. The policy prescription: open up the halls and gyms of the churches every weekend so that Mexican youth have somewhere to go, forbid alcohol, and require that parents show up in force to help guide their children through these dangerous years. I am sure most parents would be glad to help.

Politically, an important question is how the various avenues and institutions of incorporation that I described will play out, in particular with regard to Mexicans' ethnic and racial social location in New York. On the one hand, the pan-immigrant, religious, and class-based concerns of the Catholic church and institutions like Tepeyac could help inform an immigrant and ethnic stance of incorporation that does not engage much with native minorities. On the other hand, the primacy of issues of discrimination and economic and social justice could lead to alliances with native minorities. UNITE, and its class- and immigrant-based efforts and approaches, might cut both ways, attempting to appeal to both immigrant and native-minority constituencies. Organizations linked to the consulate and Casa Puebla will continue to serve undocumented people in the United States, but it seems likely that their main significant contribution to political mobilization will come via helping to form ethnic, nationality-based organizations that have the potential for mobilizing Mexican Americans in the rising working class, middle class, or business class who are of strategic interest to home country political agendas. A potential conflict is between the growing number of

Mexican New Yorkers who are stuck in low-paying and low-status jobs and the upwardly mobile who seek to pursue their own interests through ethnic organizations.

My bet is that most Mexican organizations will emphasize ethnicity, although some, such as Tepeyac, will attempt to make common cause with other "people of color," especially through religious organizations, at the same time that they use the cultural idiom of Mexican-ness to fight problems in the Mexican community. The likely result is the simultaneous emergence of a set of Mexican organizations, dominated by the upwardly mobile middle class, that are affiliated with New York's political parties and emphasize issues of opportunity for business growth and cultural expression as well as a growing number of groups that emphasize traditional issues such as the rights of the undocumented. Which political party will Mexican New Yorkers support? They could end up as traditional ethnic constituents in the Democratic Party, as new "core Democrats," or as "Guliani Democrats" who vote Democratic in most cases but cross over for a candidate who has broader appeal and socially more conservative positions. Most likely, the least successful Mexicans will simply be inactive politically, like most poor people in the United States, even while they maintain a strong identification with the ethnic side of the immigrant analogy. Less likely, but still possible, is that these Mexicans will form part of a larger alternative coalition, who see their predicament as the result of racism and discrimination and who identify firmly with native minorities and other people of color.

Theoretically, what do these different possible outcomes mean? A first insight is that most of the theories mentioned in the introduction have some difficulty accommodating the apparently bifurcated assimilation that Mexicans seem to be experiencing. It is not so much that the theories cannot handle variation, but that the explanation proffered does not offer a consistent account, for example, for upward and downward mobility. One response to this problem is to concede that it is not necessary and probably not possible for any one theory to explain all aspects of a group's ethnic, racial, economic, and educational experience. While all the models mentioned in the introduction are theories about the relationship of race and/or ethnicity, and other important outcomes, such as education, work, or politics, different theories will work better or worse in explaining how ethnicity operates in different arenas. Even this short chapter considers at least three analytically different types of problems: migration, incorporation, and related processes among various segments of the first generation; socioeconomic and educational mobility among the first and especially subsequent generations; and obstacles to and potential agents for political mobilization among Mexicans and Mexican Americans as a group. Given this, it is still heuristically useful to see how well the theories explicate dimensions of the Mexican experience of incorporation.

The main point with regard to theories of migration and incorporation is that important factors in the causal story told here are not considered in the models sketched out in the introduction. None of the models that I mentioned there takes much notice of the role of changes in the nature of the processes of migration and settlement themselves, which seem to be very important for understanding the contingent outcomes among Mexicans. For example, the influx of teen and preteen migrants over the last ten years, especially those coming without their immediate families, has had a strong and in many ways negative impact on the youth subculture among Mexicans in New York. It thus raises questions about the effects of changes in migration policies and age composition and numbers on the social and economic futures of previous migrants and the second generation. In the context into which they come—overcrowded and understaffed schools, economic need, social disorientation, inverted parent-child relationships—these changes have had very negative effects that could influence subsequent generations. On a policy level, this means that interventions are needed that will affect the nature and course of these processes of incorporation. In particular, some sort of "immigrant policy" is desirable to ease the stresses associated with incorporation. Theoretically, it means that theories about immigrant incorporation need to consider how changes in the nature of the migration process itself can affect the kind of incorporation that particular groups, or particular cohorts within groups, experience. Even holding educational levels and other human capital factors constant, the same ethnic group may have different experiences depending on the size and concentration of the population, the maturity of the migration and local settlement processes, and other factors.

In terms of political incorporation, most of the story is still untold, because the majority of the Mexican population are still not citizens, and most of those who are either are not old enough to vote or do not vote. Still, there is some mobilization, and this suggests some degree of settlement and incorporation, even for the undocumented. If my earlier speculation is correct, and the upwardly mobile segments of citizens and other activists in the Mexican community emphasize their ethnic identity as they participate in politics through ethnic-civic and ethnic-business organizations, this would seem to reflect a kind of ethnic pluralism. It might also be considered a kind of segmented assimilation, where ethnicity helps frame and produce upward mobility, but not for the whole group, only the upwardly mobile parts of it. It might also suggest some version of assimilation in the sense that ethnicity comes less to determine their life chances, and could become less important in most other aspects of their lives—"symbolic," in Gans's (1979) language; that is, the upwardly mobile could have an ethnic Mexican organization in public life and politics while moving into mixed neighborhoods, schools, and marriage pools and into the mainstream economy. The downwardly mobile or not mobile would hold an ethnicity whose meaning could become more strongly politicized, and, indeed, more racialized and even oppositional as they come to understand their life's limits as the result of exclusion and discrimination. They could see American institutions as being against them, or at least as having nothing to offer. The ethnic frame for understanding such politics of the excluded could be strengthened by a close link with the Catholic church, through organizations such as Tepeyac noted previously. This might make their reality closer to that envisioned by the racialization perspective or the oppositional model. Segmented assimilation could also describe their situation if this opposition ceased to be understood as being Mexican and became instead racial, as something that resulted from their being minorities like African Americans or Puerto Ricans.

The socioeconomic and educational bifurcation noted earlier also seems to require different types of explanations. Among those who are upwardly mobile, there is a group who have a strong and positive meaning attached to their Mexican ethnicity; another group who are more pan-Latino, even neutrally or nonethnic; and still another who embrace a black upwardly mobile identity. The first of these suggests some soft form of segmented assimilation; the next some kind of soft assimilation; and the last, an adaptation to a minority culture of mobility. Those who are not upwardly mobile seem to be mainly adopting a very Mexican identity that is often posited to be higher in the ethnic hierarchy than blacks and Puerto Ricans, and sometimes, though rarely, in solidarity with them. These outcomes, as discussed previously with regard to politics, suggest a downwardly mobile segmented assimilation in the former case, or segmented assimilation to inner-city norms in the latter.

A final note that merits comment regards the perception of causality among the large majority of those who are not upwardly mobile in school or work (see Smith 2000). They are most likely to see their lack of upward mobility as the result of their own lack of initiative and, in their words, of the *"malas costumbres"* (bad habits) among them. They see their shortcomings and those of their compatriots as clearly the result of individual failures, or as the result of similar group traits, seldom perceiving larger structural forces as important, or when they do see them, seldom linking them to concrete outcomes in their own lives. Many seek refuge in the view held by their parents—we are failing due to our own lack of effort, but we are still better than blacks, we are still ethnics and not a racial minority (on this, see M. Waters 1999). Hence, it is a sort of ethnic "downward culture of mobility," segmented assimilation in the reverse direction. Others see themselves as failures because they had advantages their parents did not, such as citizenship and English-language fluency. Some see their lives as increasingly similar to those of marginalized blacks and Puerto Ricans, though they do not know how to reconcile this with their Mexican, immigrant past. While informants' own understanding or explanation of their situation is not usually a complete or theoretically satisfying analysis (Portes 1999), it is important because such beliefs can become part of the social causality that produces an outcome, as per W. I. Thomas's famous dictum. Hence the pessimistic conclusions that one reaches with these self-assessments should be taken seriously. The *"malas costumbres"* argument could lead to a belief among this sector in a kind of culture of poverty argument, that they as a group and individually are ultimately the cause of their poverty. The other various reactions do not augur well either. They could lead to racialization in the last instance, or a kind of apathetic resignation, doomed resistance, etc. In each case, these beliefs could become powerful intermediate variables mediating between individual and structural causality (Zhou 1999). These outcomes are not necessary. As suggested previously, feasible actions can be taken to change these perceptions and the contexts that nurture them, and the outcomes they can help produce.

Notes

1. By "Mexicans," I mean "Mexican-origin population," including both U.S.-born children of immigrants and immigrants themselves. Of those enumerated in the census, my guess is that about half are immigrants and half are native-born. These estimates derive from various sources: pooling Current Population Survey (CPS) estimates for 1998 and 1999. I thank John Mollenkopf for providing these data and Joseph Salvo of the New York City Planning Department for discussing these data issues and sources with me. The figure of 100,000 for 1990 is an estimate I derived based on the undercount estimate the Census Bureau did, modified for several factors not taken into account in their estimate; it agrees with New York City Department of City Planning estimates of the population in the early 1990s (Lobo et al. 1996; New York City Department of city Planning 1999). Alonso-Zaldivar (1999) cites Census expert Jorge del Pinal predicting that Mexicans will eventually be the largest Latino population on the east coast. That 50% of the total population is between fifteen and twenty-four comes from the survey of almost 400 Mexicans done by Valdes de Montano and Smith, 1994.

2. These estimates are from New York City Department of City Planning census expert Joseph Salvo; I thank him for his help. I have taken a somewhat higher estimate than his for the Mexican population to bring the current analysis in line with the averaged figure derived from the Current Population Surveys for 1998 and 1999, as are his estimates for Puerto Ricans and Dominicans.

3. This section on the history of Mexican migration to New York draws on a previous brief history in Smith 1996 and a longer history in Smith 1995. "Ticuani" is not the town's real name, which has been changed to protect confidentiality.

4. My thanks to Joseph Salvo and Peter Lobo of the New York City Department of City Planning for generating and generously sharing these statistics.

5. Cohort analysis considers the same category of people in two different census data sets, here 1980 and 1990. As developed by Dowell Myers, it also offers useful ways to disaggregate between Mexican American and Mexican populations. Though excessive mobility or morbidity among the population will affect the validity of the assumptions underlying cohort analysis, I agree with Myers (Myers and Cranford 1997; Myers 1999) that it offers a superior alternative to the static analysis of comparing the gross data included among the entire population labeled as Mexican in each census.

6. Social mobility is measured two ways here. First is through examination of the prestige and income of the occupations in which men and women work, using PUMS data. Second, a more qualitative measure is based on the perceptions of the informants in this project. For example, becoming a medical secretary or travel agent is considered significant upward mobility, more so than a job in a restaurant

making a similar income, because the latter is still immigrant work in important ways, and the former is an "office job" with work that is "clean" and has paid vacations, sick days, and the like. The comparison is both to what their parents did and to what some of their peers are doing.

7. Tepeyac (described in detail later in this chapter) and other advocacy organizations say that the percentage of Mexicans who are undocumented is 90 percent or more. I think this estimate is too high. Still, the numbers are staggering. In surveys I did in Mexico in the early 1990s, about 50 percent of migrants were undocumented in a town that had many migrants qualify for amnesty under the 1986 Immigration Reform and Control Act. This town was also experiencing a surge in undocumented immigration drawn by the legalization of relatives in the United States. Some undocumented immigrants have been able to legalize their status through relatives, but many more undocumented continue to come to New York.

References

Alba, Richard, and Victor Nee. 1999. "Rethinking Assimilation Theory for a New Era of Immigration." In Charles Hirshman, Josh DeWind, and Philip Kasinitz, eds., *Handbook of Immigration: The American Experience,* pp. 137–60. New York: Russell Sage Foundation.

Alonso-Zaldivar, Ricardo. 1999. "Big Apple Takes On a Flavor of Mexico." *Los Angeles Times,* February 19.

Amparo Casar, Maria, and Ricardo Rapheal de la Madrid. 1998. "Las elecciones y el Reparto del Poder" *NEXOS* 247 (July).

Amparo Casar, Maria. 2000. "Legislative Sin Mayoria: coma va el score" *NEXOS* 265 (Enero): 39–46.

Associacion Tepeyac. 1997. "Statement of Purpose and Goals." *www.tepeyac.org.*

Binford, Leigh. 1998. "Accelerated Migration from Puebla." Paper presented at the conference "Mexicans in New York and Mexico: New Analytical Perspectives on Migration, Transnationalization, and Immigrant Incorporation" at Barnard College and the New School University, October 14–16.

Brotherton, David. 1998. "The Evolution of New York City Street Gangs." In A. Karmen, ed., *Crime and Justice in New York City,* pp. 40–55. New York: McGraw Hill.

Cornelius, Wayne. 1986. *De la Madrid: The Crisis Continues.* La Jolla, Calif.: Center for U.S. Mexico Studies.

——. 1994. "Los Migrantes de la Crisis: The Changing Profile of Mexican Migration to the US." In M. Gonzalez de la Rocha and Agustin Escobar Lapati, eds., *Social Responses to Mexico's Economic Crisis of the 1980s.* La Jolla, Calif.: Center for U.S. Mexican Studies.

Durand, Jorge, Douglas S. Massey, and Emilio Parrado. 1999. "The New Era of Mexican Migration to the United Estates."*Journal of American History* 86:518–36.

Esteva, Juan Francisco. 1999, "Urban Street Activists: Gang and Community Efforts to Bring Peace and Justice to LA's Neighborhoods." Draft paper, Street Organization Project, John Jay College, City University of New York.

Gans, Herbert. 1979. "Symbolic Ethnicity: The Future of Ethnic Groups and Cultures in America." *Ethnic and Racial Studies* 2(1): 1–20.

Glazer, Nathan, and Daniel Patrick Moynihan. 1963. *Beyond the Melting Pot: The Negroes, Puerto Ricans, Jews, Italians, and Irish of New York City*. Cambridge: MIT Press.

Goldring, Luin. 2001. "From Market Membership to Transnational Citizenship: The Changing Politicization of Transnational Social Spaces." In Ludger Prie, ed., *Transnational Social Spaces*. New York: Routledge.

Gordon, Milton. 1964. *Assimilation in American Life: The Role of Race, Religion and National Origin*. New York: Oxford.

Granovetter, Mark. 1973. "The Strength of Weak Ties." *American Journal of Sociology* 78:1360–80.

Guarnizo, Luis. 1998. "The Rise of Transnational Social Formations: Mexican and Dominican State Responses to Transnational Migration." *Political Power and Social Theory* 12:45–94.

Jones-Correa, Michael. 1998. *Between Two Nations: The Political Predicament of Latino Immigrants*. Ithaca: Cornell University Press.

Kasinitz, Philip. 1992. *Caribbean New York*. Ithaca: Cornell University Press.

Kasinitz, Philip, M. Waters, J. Mollenkopf, and D. Y. Kim. 1997. "School to Work Transition in the Second Generation." Working paper, Bard College and circulated draft.

Kim, Dae Young. 1999. "Beyond Co-ethnic Solidarity: Mexican and Ecuadoran Employment in Korean Owned Businesses in New York City." *Ethnic and Racial Studies* 22:481–99.

Lara, S., and R. Smith. 2000 "Gendered Socialization: Concrete Talk and Gender Mobility and School Outcomes." Draft paper, in development.

Lobo, Aron Peter, Joseph Salvo, and Vicky Virgin. 1996. *The Newest New Yorkers, 1990–1994*. New York: Department of City Planning.

Massey, Douglas, Rafael Alarcon, Jorge Durand, and Humberto Gonzalez. 1987. *Return to Aztlan: The Social Process of International Migration from Western Mexico*. Berkeley: University of California Press.

Massey, Douglas, and Nancy Denton. 1993. *American Apartheid: Segregation and the Making of the Underclass*. Cambridge: Harvard University Press.

Massey, Douglas, and Kristin Espinosa. 1997. "What's Driving Mexico–U.S. Migration? A Theoretical, Empirical, and Policy Analysis." *American Journal of Sociology* 102(4): 939–99.

Massey, Douglas, Luin Goldring, and Jorge Durand. 1994. "Continuities in Transnational Migration: An Analysis of Nineteen Mexican Communities." *American Journal of Sociology* 99:1492–1533.

McCoy, Molly. 2000. "Fresh Fruit, Rotten Wages: Exploitation and Resistance Among Mexican Workers in Greengrocer Stores." Senior thesis, Sociology Department, Barnard College.

Mead, Lawrence. 1997. *The New Paternalism: Supervisory Approaches to Poverty*. Washington, D.C.: Brookings Institution.

Merton, Robert. 1968. *Social Theory and Social Structure*. New York: Free Press.

Moore, Joan. 1991. *Going Down the Barrio: Homeboys and Homegirls in Change.* Philadelphia: Temple University Press.

Moss, Philip, and Chris Tilly. 1996. " 'Soft' Skills and Race: An Investigation of Black Men's Employment Problems." *Work and Occupations* 23:252–76.

Myers, Dowell. 1999. "Dimensions of Economic Adaptation by Mexican-Origin Men." In M. Suarez Orozco, ed., *Crossings.* Cambridge: Harvard University Press.

Myers, Dowell, and Cynthia Cranford. 1998. "Temporal Differences in the Occupational Mobility of Immigrant and Native-Born Latina Workers." *American Sociological Review* 63:68–93.

Neckerman, Kathyrn, Prudence Carter, and Jennifer Lee. 1999. "Segmented Assimilation and Minority Cultures of Mobility." *Ethnic and Racial Studies* 22(6): 945–65.

Nee, Victor, Jimy Sanders, and Scott Sernau. 1994. "Job Transitions in an Immigrant Metropolis: Ethnic Boundaries and the Mixed Economy." *American Sociological Review* 59:849–72.

New York City Department of City Planning. 1999. *The Newest New Yorkers, 1995–1996.* New York: Department of City Planning.

Ogbu, John. 1974. *The Next Generation: An Ethnography of an Urban Neighborhood.* New York: Academic Press.

Ogbu, John. 1987. "Variability in Minority School Performance: Problem in Search of an Explanation." *Anthropology and Education Quarterly* 18:312–34.

Omi, Michael, and M. Winant. 1986. *Racial Formation in the United States: From the 1960s to the 1980s.* New York: Routledge and Kegan Paul.

Portes, Alejandro. 1999. "Conclusion." *Ethnic and Racial Studies* 22(2): 463–77.

Portes, Alejandro, and Robert Bach. 1985. *Latin Journey.* Berkeley: University of California Press.

Portes, Alejandro, and Min Zhou. 1993. "The New Second Generation: Segmented Assimilation and Its Variants." *Annals of the American Academy of Political and Social Science* 530:74–93.

Rodriguez, Orlando, R. M. Cooney, A. Falcon, G. Gilbertson, C. Hanson, A. P. Lobo, J. Salvo, V. Virgin, and K. Waltzer. 1996. *Nuestra America en Nueva York: The New Immigrant Hispanic Populations in New York City, 1980–1990.* Fordham University Hispanic Research Center Report Series. New York: Fordham University.

Roediger, David. 1991. *The Wages of Whiteness.* New York: Routledge.

Sassen, Saskia. 1988. *The Mobility of Capital and Labor.* New York: Oxford University Press.

——. 1995. "Immigration and Local Labor Markets." In A. Portes, ed., *The Economic Sociology of Immigration.* New York: Russell Sage Foundation.

Sevi, Rosa. 1999. "Casa Puebla and Transnationalism." Master's thesis proposal, oral history, University of British Columbia, Vancouver.

Smith, Robert C. 1992. "Mixteca in New York; New York in Mixteca." *NACLA (North American Congress on Latin America) Report on the Americas.*

——. 1995. *Los Ausentes Siempre Presentes: The Imagining, Making, and Politics of a Transnational Migrant Community Between Ticuani, Puebla, Mexico and New York City.* Ph.D. diss., political science department, Columbia University, New York.

——. 1996. "Mexicans in New York City: Membership and Incorporation of a New Immigrant Group." In S. Baver and G. Haslip Viera, eds., *Latinos in New York.* South Bend, Ind.: University of Notre Dame Press.

——. 1998a. "Transnational Localities: Community, Technology, and the Politics of Membership Within the Context of Mexico-US Migration." In Michael Peter Smith and Luis Guarnizo, eds., *Journal of Urban and Comparative Research.* New Brunswick: Transaction.

——. 1998b. "The Educational and Economic Mobility of Second Generation Mexican Americans in New York City: Some Preliminary Reflections." Paper presented at conference on "Mexican Migrants in New York and Mexico: New Analytical Perspectives on Migration, Transnationalization, and Immigrant Incorporation," at Barnard College and the New School for Social Research, October 14–16.

——. 1998c. "Reflections on the State, Migration, and the Durability and Newness of Transnational Life: Comparative Insights from the Mexican and Italian Cases." *Soziale Welt* 12:197–221.

——. 2000. "Contingent Fates: The Educational and Work Mobility of Mexicans and Mexican Americans in New York City." Paper presented at "Conference on Latinos in the Twenty-first Century," Harvard University, May.

——. 2001. "Gender, Ethnicity and Race in School and Work Outcomes of Second Generation Mexican Americans." In Marcelo Suarez-Orozco and Mariela Paez, eds., *Latinos in the Twenty-First Century.* Berkeley: University of California Press.

Smith, Robert, and Sandra Lara. 1999. "Concrete Talk, Acquired Knowledge and Gendered Pathways: Why and How Second Generation Mexican American Girls Are Doing Better Than Their Male Counterparts." Paper presented at American Sociological Association Meetings, Chicago, August.

Suttles, Gerald. 1968. *The Social Order of the Slum: Ethnicity and Territory in the Inner City.* Chicago: University of Chicago Press.

——. 1972. *The Social Construction of Communities.* Chicago: University of Chicago Press.

U.S. Bureau of the Census. Various years (a). *Current Population Survey.* Washington, D.C.: U.S. Department of Commerce.

——. Various years (b). *Census of Population Public Use Micro Data Sample.* Washington D.C.: U.S. Government Printing Office.

Valdes de Montano, Luz Maria, and Robert Smith. 1994. "Mexicans in New York: Final Report to the Tinker Foundation." Unpublished report.

Vecino, Agustin. 1999. "Gangs and Crews: Field Notes for NSF project." Unpublished manuscript.

Venkatesh, Sudhir A. 1997. "The Social Organization of Street Gang Activity in an Urban Ghetto." *American Journal of Sociology* 102:82–111.

——. 2000. *American Project: The Rise and Fall of a Modern Ghetto.* Cambridge: Harvard University Press.

Vigil, James Diego. 2000. "An Ecological Approach to Gangs in Los Angeles." Paper presented at conference "Latinos in the Twenty-first Century," Harvard University, May.

Vigil, James Diego. 1988. *Barrio Gangs: Street Life and Identity in Southern California.* Austin: University of Texas Press.

Waldinger, Roger. 1996. *Still the Promised City? African Americans and New Immigrants in Postindustrial New York.* Cambridge: Harvard University Press.

Waldinger, Roger, and Medhi Bozorgmehr. 1996. *Ethnic Los Angeles.* New York: Russell Sage Foundation.

Warner, W. Lloyd, and Leo Srole.1945. *The Social Systems of American Ethnic Groups.* New Haven: Yale University Press.

Waters, Mary C. 1994. "Ethnic and Racial Identities of Second Generation Black Immigrants in New York City." *International Migration Review* 27:795–820.

——. 1999. *Black Identities: West Indian Immigrant Dreams and American Realities.* Cambridge: Harvard University Press.

Waters, Tony. 1999. *Immigration and Crime.* Thousand Oaks, Calif.: Sage.

Willis, Paul. 1977. *Learning to Labor: How Working Class Kids Get Working Class Jobs.* New York: Columbia University Press.

Zhou, Min. 1999. "Segmented Assimilation: Issues, Controversies, and Recent Research on the New Second Generation." In Charles Hirschman, Josh DeWind, and Philip Kasinitz, eds., *Handbook of Immigration: The American Experience.* New York: Russell Sage Foundation.

Zhou, Min, and Carl Bankston III. 1998. *Growing Up American: How Vietnamese Children Adapt to Life in the United States.* New York: Russell Sage Foundation.

About the Contributors

MARK ELLIS is currently Associate Professor of Geography and a research affiliate of the Center for Studies in Demography and Ecology at the University of Washington, Seattle. He previously held faculty positions at Florida State University and the University of California, Los Angeles. He is interested in the racial and ethnic changes wrought by immigration in America's largest cities, especially the labor market effects of the arrival of new groups. His work has appeared in a number of journals, including *Economic Geography, International Journal of Urban and Regional Research, Annals of the Association of American Geographers,* and *International Migration Review.* He is writing a book entitled *Race, Region, and Nation: The Territorial Politics of Immigration* with Richard Wright.

NANCY FONER, Professor of Anthropology at the State University of New York at Purchase, has written extensively about immigration to New York and West Indian migration. She is the author or editor of nine books, the most recent being *From Ellis Island to JFK: New York's Two Great Waves of Immigration* (Yale University Press, 2000); *Immigration Research for a New Century: Multidis-*

ciplinary Perspectives, edited with Rubén Rumbaut and Steven Gold (Russell Sage Foundation, 2000); and *Islands in the City: West Indian Migration to New York* (University of California Press, 2001). She has been a visiting scholar at the Russell Sage Foundation and is a member of the Social Science Research Council Committee on International Migration.

PAMELA M. GRAHAM is the Latin American and Iberian Studies Librarian at Columbia University. She holds an M.A. and Ph.D. in political science from the University of North Carolina at Chapel Hill. Her dissertation on Dominican migration focused on dual nationality legislation and the creation of predominantly Dominican American political districts in New York. She has published research in the *Latino Studies Journal* and recently authored a chapter on Dominican political incorporation in *Migration, Transnationalism and the Political Economy of New* York (Temple University Press, 2001). Ongoing research interests include transnational political participation among Caribbean migrants and the use of new information technologies by immigrants and states to create forums for political communication.

ELLEN PERCY KRALY is Professor in the Department of Geography at Colgate University, where she is currently Director of the Division of Social Sciences. Kraly was a member of the National Academy of Sciences Panel on Immigration Statistics and has conducted research for the United Nations Statistical Commission, the U.S. Immigration and Naturalization Service, and the U.S. Commission on Immigration Reform. Her research interests include the relationship between immigration and population growth, environmental change and policy, and emigration, migration measurement, and status attainment among immigrant groups. She is currently collaborating with demographers at Fordham University on a study of economic integration of undocumented immigrants in the United States with funding from the National Institute of Child and Human Development.

PYONG GAP MIN is Professor of Sociology at Queens College and the Graduate Center of the City University of New York. His research has mainly focused on Asian Americans, particularly immigrant entrepreneurship, ethnic identity, gender roles, and immigrants' religion. Min is the author of *Changes and Conflicts: Korean Immigrant Families in New York* (1998), *Caught in the Middle: Korean Communities in New York and Los Angeles* (1996, the winner of two book awards), and *Ethnic Business Enterprise: Korean Small Business in Atlanta* (1988). He is a coeditor of *Struggle for Ethnic Identity: Narratives by Asian American Professionals* (1999) and the editor of *Asian Americans: Contemporary Trends and Issues* (1995). He is completing two book manuscripts, one focusing on Asian ethnic groups in New York and the other on Korean "comfort women," as well as three edited books.

INES M. MIYARES is Associate Professor of Geography at Hunter College, City University of New York, specializing in the geography of recent immigration, refugee resettlement, and Latin American transnationalism. She completed her Ph.D. in geography from Arizona State University in 1994, with a dissertation on the geography of Hmong refugee resettlement and the subsequent formation and function of Hmong enclaves in California. Her work has also focused on post-Soviet refugees, Cubans, Salvadorans on temporary protected status, and the social and political geography of Latin American immigrants in the United States. Since 1998, she has conducted a field school in Peru for undergraduate and graduate students interested in primary research on historical and contemporary Andean societies and on Andean natural environments.

ANNELISE ORLECK is Associate Professor of History and Women's Studies at Dartmouth College. She is the author of *Common Sense and a Little Fire: Women and Working-Class Politics in the U.S.* (University of North Carolina Press, 1995) and *Soviet Jewish Americans* (Greenwood Press, 1999). She is also coeditor of *The Politics of Motherhood: Activist Voices from Left to Right* (University Press of New England, 1997).

PATRICIA R. PESSAR is Associate Professor of American Studies and Anthropology at Yale University and director of Yale's Global Migration Project. Her publications on international migration in the Americas include: *When Borders Don't Divide: Labor Migration and Refugee Movements in the Americas* (1988); *Between Two Islands: Dominican International Migration* (1991, coauthored with Sherri Grasmuck); *A Visa for a Dream: Dominicans in the United States* (1995); and *Caribbean Circuits: New Directions in the Study of Caribbean Migration* (1997). She is the coeditor with Sarah Mahler of a special issue of *Identities: Global Studies in Culture and Power* (2000) on gender, transnational migration, and transnational contexts. Pessar's work in that volume includes her newest research on indigenous Guatemalan refugees and returnees.

ROBERT C. SMITH, Assistant Professor of Sociology at Barnard College, received his Ph.D. in political science from Columbia University in 1995 and has studied Mexican migration in the Northeast and in Mexico for more than a decade. He has received grants from the National Science Foundation, the Spencer Foundation, the Oral History Research Office at Columbia University, and the Social Science Research Council. He has published a number of book chapters and articles on Mexican migration and is currently completing two book manuscripts, *Migration, Settlement and Transnational Life* and, with Aristide Zolberg, *Migration Systems and Public Policy: Comparative Insights from the Inter-American and Maghrebi-European Experiences.* His current research focuses on educational and occupational mobility among second-generation Mexican Americans.

PAUL STOLLER is Professor of Anthropology at West Chester University. The recipient of numerous grants and fellowships, he has conducted ethnographic fieldwork among the Songhay people of the Republic of Niger (1976–1990) and among West African immigrants in New York City (1992–present). The author of numerous publications, his most recent books include *Sensuous Scholarship* (University of Pennsylvania Press, 1997), a book of essays, and *Jaguar: A Story of Africans in America* (University of Chicago Press, 1999), a novel. He is currently conducting research on West African art traders in America.

MILTON VICKERMAN, Associate Professor of Sociology at the University of Virginia, has conducted research on immigration and issues pertaining to race. He has carried out extensive fieldwork among West Indian immigrants in New York City and among blacks in Prince William County, Virginia. His publications include *Crosscurrents: West Indian Immigrants and Race* (Oxford University Press, 1999) and other chapters and articles dealing with West Indian immigrants in the United States.

RICHARD WRIGHT is Professor of Geography at Dartmouth College. His scholarship, with support from the NSF, SSRC, and the John Simon Guggenheim Foundation, concerns immigration—labor market operations, "assimilation" broadly conceived, nativism, the racialization of immigrants (and the native-born), transnationalism, and state sovereignty. Most of his work centers on the United States, but he has interests in the relationships between labor migration and capital mobility between all nations. He is the author of about three dozen journal articles and book chapters. The most recent papers have been published in the *International Journal of Urban and Regional Research, International Journal of Population Geography,* and *International Migration Review.* With Mark Ellis, he is writing a book entitled *Race, Region, and Nation: The Territorial Politics of Immigration.*

MIN ZHOU is Professor of Sociology and Asian American Studies at the University of California, Los Angeles. Her main areas of research are immigration and immigrant adaptation, race/ethnicity, ethnic economies, the community, and urban sociology. She has done extensive work on the educational experience of immigrant children and children of immigrant parentage, the employment and earnings patterns of immigrants and native-born minorities, immigrant communities, ethnic economies, and residential mobility. She is the author of *Chinatown: The Socioeconomic Potential of an Urban Enclave* (Temple University Press, 1992), coauthor (with Carl Bankston) of *Growing Up American: How Vietnamese Children Adapt to Life in the United States* (Russell Sage Foundation, 1998), and coeditor (with James Gatewood) of *Contemporary Asian America: a Multidisciplinary Reader* (New York University Press, 1999).

Index